D0745483

PARLIAMENT AND POLITICS IN LATE MEDIEVAL ENGLAND

PARLIAMENT AND POLITICS
IN LATE MEDIEVAL ENGLAND

VOLUME II

J. S. ROSKELL

THE HAMBLEDON PRESS

The Hambledon Press 1981
35 Gloucester Avenue
London N.W.1 7AX

History Series 8

ISBN 0 9506882 9 0
ISBN 0 9506882 7 4 (Volumes I and II cased)

British Library Cataloguing in Publication Data

Roskell J. S.
    Parliament and politics in late medieval England
    — (History series; 8)
    Vol. 2
    1. Legislative bodies — England — History — Addresses,
    essays, lectures
    I. Title II. Series
    328. 42' 09   JN515

Printed in Great Britain by
Biddles Ltd, Guildford, Surrey

CONTENTS

ACKNOWLEDGEMENTS

The articles reproduced here first appeared in the following places and are reprinted with permission.

1   *Nottingham Medieval Studies,*vol. II (1958)   24-37

2   *Wiltshire Archaeological and Natural History*
     Magazine vol. LVI (1956)   272-300

3   *Lincolnshire Architectural and Archaeological*
     Society, Reports and Papers, vol. 7, part I (1957)   27-45

4   *Transactions of the Bristol and Gloucestershire*
     Archaeological Society, vol. 75 (1956)   43-72

5   *Wiltshire Archaeological and Natural History*
     Magazine vol. LVI (1956)   301-41

6   *Northamptonshire Past and Present*, vol. II, no. 4 (1957)189-203

7   *East Herts Archaeological Society*, vol. XIV (1959)   20-41

8   *Nottingham Medieval Studies*, vol. V (1961)   87-112

9   *Nottingham Medieval Studies*, vol. VII (1963)   79-105

10   *The Publications of the Bedfordshire Historical*
     Record Society, vol. XXXVIII (1958)   12-48

11   *Northamptonshire Past and Present*, vol. II (1959)   313-23

12   *Yorkshire Archaeological Journal*, XXXIX (1958)   455-82

13   *Bulletin of the John Rylands Library* vol. 42 (1959)   145-74

PREFACE

It is hoped that it will be possible to publish a second collection of biographies of Speakers; in the meantime it may be useful to list those that have been published, but are omitted from the present collection. They are listed in order of their elections as Speaker.

1   Sir James de Pickering of Killington, *Transactions of the Cumberland and Westmorland Antiquarian and Archaeological Society*, new series LXI (1961), 79-103.

2   Sir Richard de Waldegrave of Bures St. Mary, *Proceedings of the Suffolk Institute of Archaeology*, XXVII (1957), part 3, 154-75.

3   John Doreward of Bocking: Speaker in 1399 and 1413, *Essex Archaeology and History*, VIII (1978 for 1976), 209-23.

4   Sir Arnald Savage of Bobbing, *Archaeologia Cantiana*, LXX (1956), 68-83.

5   Sir Henry de Retford, *Lincolnshire Architectural and Archaeological Society, Reports and Papers*, VII, part 2 (1957-8), 117-25.

6   Sir William Sturmy, *Transactions of the Devonshire Association for the Advancement of Science, Literature and Art*, LXXXIX (1957), 78-92.

7   William Stourton of Stourton, *Proceedings of the Dorset Natural History and Archaeological Society*, LXXXII (1960), 155-66.

8   Sir Richard Redmayne of Levens, *Transactions of the Cumberland and Westmorland Antiquarian and Archaeological Society*, new series, LXII (1962), 113-44.

9   Sir Walter Beauchamp (Speaker in March—May 1416), *The Wiltshire Archaeological and Natural History Magazine*, LVI (1956), 342-58.

10   Roger Flore of Oakham, *Transactions of the Leicestershire Archaeological and Historical Society*, XXXIII (1957), 36-44.

11   Sir Richard Vernon of Haddon, Speaker in the parliament of Leicester, 1426, *Derbyshire Archaeological Journal*, LXXXII (1962), 43-54.

12   William Allington of Horseheath, Speaker in the parliament of 1429—30, *Proceedings of the Cambridge Antiquarian Society*, LII (1959), 30-42.

13   John Bowes of Costock, Speaker in the parliament of 1435, *Transactions of the Thoroton Society of Nottinghamshire*, LX (1956), 8-19.

14   William Burley of Broncroft, Speaker for the Commons in 1437 and 1445-6, *Transactions of the Shropshire Archaeological Society*, LVI (1960), 263-72.

15   Sir John Popham, knight-banneret, of Charford, *Proceedings of the Hampshire Field Club and Archaeological Society*, XXI (1958), part I, 38-52.

16   William Allington of Bottisham, Speaker in the parliaments of 1472-5 and 1478, *Proceedings of the Cambridge Antiquarian Society*, LII (1959), 43-55.

17   Sir John Wood of Molesey, *The Surrey Archaeological Collections*, LVI (1959), 15-28.

J. S. ROSKELL

I

SIR PETER DE LA MARE, SPEAKER FOR THE COMMONS IN PARLIAMENT IN 1376 AND 1377

Although the Commons—the elected representatives of shires, cities, and boroughs—were coming to be summoned regularly to parliament by the beginning of Edward III's reign in 1327, it is not until much later that we have certain knowledge of the development of the machinery by which they dealt with their parliamentary business. By 1363, however, the King was allowing them to use a royal clerk to assist their work, the under-clerk of parliament as he was called; and before Edward III's death in 1377 they had a common speaker. But it was apparently only in the previous year, during the famous Good Parliament of 1376, the longest-sitting parliament thus far held, that the Commons employed for the first time a speaker who, elected from among the Commons, continued for parliament's duration to report their proposals to the King and Lords.[1] The man whom they chose, or who in a less precise sense chose himself, was Sir Peter de la Mare, then sitting in parliament as one of the two knights of the shire for the county of Hereford.

It should be pointed out that the enrolled official record of this last but one of Edward III's parliaments makes no reference to De la Mare at all. This need not astonish or trouble us. The parliament-rolls of this time generally give no more than brief and often jejune accounts of what transpired even among the Lords Spiritual and Temporal, much less details of the doings of the Commons. (The first Speaker to be named in the roll of a parliament is mentioned in that of the next parliament, the Bad Parliament of January 1377.) It is, therefore, upon the greater chronicle of the abbey of St. Albans and, more especially, upon the *Anonimalle Chronicle* of the abbey of St. Mary of York that we must rely for what we know of Sir Peter de la Mare's conduct as Speaker in the Good Parliament. That these chronicles, the one written in the south, the other in the north of the country, tell us quite a lot about him and the parliament is in itself significant of the great public interest aroused by what happened during the session.

In 1376 parliament had not met for two and a half years. In not convening it for so long a time as this, the royal government was running something of a risk. Pressure of criticism tended to mount if parliament was not used as a safety-valve for public feeling. So it was in 1376: in the Good Parliament there came to a head much of the discontent generated by the mis-management of

---

[1] The following abbreviations have been used in the footnotes:
CPR = *Calendar of Patent Rolls*;   CFR = *Calendar of Fine Rolls*;
CCR = *Calendar of Close Rolls*;   PRO = Public Record Office.

the war with France and, also, by the way in which (with Edward III becoming senile and out of touch with affairs of State) the royal administration was being subjected to a system of graft astutely operated, mainly to their private advantage, by a small clique of courtiers and London financiers. The most notorious of these ill-doers, after being impeached by the Commons, were not dealt with by the re-formed royal Council (as the Commons at first seem to have intended), but were eventually judged by the Lords. Among the peers there were clearly some who felt as the Commons did. These certainly included William of Wykeham, Bishop of Winchester, whose rôle in this business, as Mr. McFarlane has noted, was that of Satan rebuking sin, and Edmund Mortimer, Earl of March. Edward the Black Prince, although so ill that he died before the parliament ended, was sympathetic to the Commons' attitude, whereas his next younger surviving brother, John of Gaunt, Duke of Lancaster, cordially disapproved of it.

The Commons acted together in 1376, so contemporary chroniclers imply, with a remarkable sense of responsibility and with enterprise. Undoubtedly, however, Sir Peter de la Mare's leadership and eloquence were a source of strength. So much so that, since he was closely connected with one of the magnates who were dissatisfied at this time, the Earl of March, it has sometimes been urged that it was not the Commons at all who really set the pace in the Good Parliament but rather that they were prompted to take the initiative by the Lords. In other words, it has been argued that the capacity for independent action exercised (and seemingly decisively) in 1376 by the Lower House is illusory, and that a truer indication of the meagreness of its influence is supplied by the annulment of what the Good Parliament had done when parliament next met, early in the following year. (On that occasion Sir Thomas Hungerford, steward and counsellor to John of Gaunt, was the Commons' Speaker.) The question of the Commons' political independence is a large problem which cannot properly be discussed without an examination of a much wider range of evidence and related topics than would be in place here. Suffice it to say that enough is known of the proceedings of the Good Parliament to warrant the suggestion that the Commons were successful in 1376 in procuring the backing of the Lords for their plan to halt corruption in high places, rather than merely acting (subserviently) as the Lords' agents in this business, and that their political excitement was largely of their own generation.

Enough has perhaps been said to justify a detailed study of the career of the Commons' Speaker in the Good Parliament, in so far as it is possible to make one. De le Mare, moreover, was to be Speaker again in the first parliament of Richard II's reign which met in October 1377. Once more on that occasion he was knight of the shire for Herefordshire, and he subsequently represented this county of the Welsh border in five other parliaments: those of January and November 1380, of May and October 1382, and of February 1383.[2] After

---

[2] *Official Return of Members of Parliament*, i. 193, 198, 204, 206, 210, 212, 214.

1377 he was not again elected Speaker, unless it so happened (which is improbable) in one or other of the two parliaments of 1382, for neither of which is the Speaker's name known.

It is very doubtful whether the De la Mare family of Herefordshire, to which belonged Sir Peter de la Mare, was other than remotely connected with that family of the same name which had estates at Steeple Lavington and elsewhere in Wiltshire, at Baldon Marsh and Lower Heyford (Oxon), at Sparsholt and Aldermaston (Berks), at Cherrington and Minchinhampton (Glos), at Offley (Herts), and in Herefordshire itself at Caradoc-in-Sellack and Treezveryn.[3] These were the estates of a Sir Peter de la Mare who was steward, apparently in the south parts of the Duchy of Lancaster, to Henry of Grosmont (fourth Earl and first Duke of Lancaster). This Sir Peter had died in 1349.[4] His heir, Sir Robert de la Mare, was a feoffee and one of the executors of the will of Henry of Grosmont, and died in 1382, leaving a son and heir, Peter, who was then only thirteen years old.[5] It was this Peter who married Matilda, a daughter of Sir John Mautravers of Hook (Dorset), sometime before the latter's death in 1386; and it was also this Peter who was knighted when a member of the retinue of the Earl of Arundel in March 1387, and who died in 1396.[6] The earlier Sir Peter (who died in 1349) had had at least two other sons besides Sir Robert: Thomas, who was sheriff of Oxfordshire and Berkshire in 1369–71 and a retainer of John of Gaunt in the late 1370's, and Richard. Three brothers, a Thomas, a Richard, and a James de la Mare, in 1389 released to the Speaker's younger brother, Malcolm de la Mare, their rights in certain lands in Shropshire, which suggests kinship between the two families, if, as is possible, these three brothers were the sons of the Sir Peter who died in 1349.[7] This flimsy evidence is, however, all that connects these two De la Mare families. Even if they were related, there is nothing to show that the connection was of any significance. There is no demonstrable evidence to warrant the suggestion, which has sometimes been made, that Sir Peter de la Mare, the Speaker, and Thomas de la Mare, the great Abbot of St. Albans (1349–96), were related by family ties, and the very silence of the St. Albans chronicles on this question would seem to point to an absence of kinship, especially because their references to Sir Peter are uniformly encomiastic.

Sir Peter de la Mare the Speaker was seemingly the elder of the two sons of the Sir Reynold de la Mare who in 1349 and 1350 had been a collector of parliamentary tenths and fifteenths in Herefordshire, who in 1352 was pardoned for not having taken the order of knighthood before Ascensiontide 1335, but who had become a knight by November 1358 when, described as such, he complained

[3] R. Clutterbuck, *The History and Antiquities of the county of Hertford*, iii. 99, 100; T. D. Fosbroke, *Abstracts of records and manuscripts respecting the county of Gloucester*, i. 382.
[4] *Cal. Papal Registers, Petitions*, i. 133; R. Somerville, *History of the Duchy of Lancaster*, i. 88; *Cal. of Inqs. p.m.* IX. 309; ibid., XI. 3; *CPR, passim*.
[5] *CPR, 1358–61*, 575; ibid., *1361–4*, 495.
[6] R. Clutterbuck, *loc. cit.*; P.R.O., Exchequer, Foreign Accounts, E101/40/33; *Collectanea Topographica et Genealogica*, IV. 179; VI. 335.
[7] *Cal. of Inqs.p.m.* X. 98; *Catalogue of Ancient Deeds*, IV. A 8934.

of an assault upon himself at Greet in Shropshire.[8]   The Speaker's younger brother, Malcolm, was knight of the shire for Herefordshire in the Cambridge parliament of September 1388 and sheriff of the county in 1392–3; he had been appointed a collector of parliamentary subsidies in Herefordshire in December 1384, December 1385, and January 1392, and was to be so again, not long before he died, in May 1398.[9]   In 1384 Malcolm and his wife Alice were holding for her lifetime the manor of Kidderminster as tenants of the Sir John Beauchamp of Holt who was created baron by royal patent in 1387 but executed for "treason" in the Merciless Parliament of the following year.   Malcolm had also lands in Shropshire, but the main family estates in Herefordshire, such as they were, were in the possession of his elder brother, the Speaker.

Sir Peter de la Mare was holding the manor of Little Hereford in the north of the county and within easy reach of Ludlow, and the manor of Yatton in the south-east on 2 November 1382 when, by a final concord levied in the Court of Common Pleas at Westminster, between Malcolm and his wife (as claimants) and his own feoffees (as deforciants), it was arranged that the manors should pass to the former after the death of Sir Peter who held them for life.   Little Hereford, as two knights' fees, was held in mesne-tenancy of the Bohuns, as was also half a knight's fee in Morecote (near Evesham) in Gloucestershire. In December 1384, when Mary, one of the daughters and co-heirs of Humphrey de Bohun, Earl of Hereford and Essex, and wife of Henry of Bolingbroke, then Earl of Derby, proved her age, the overlordship of these estates formed part of her purparty.   Yatton was held in mesne-tenancy of the Mortimers, Earls of March, who themselves held it in chief of the Crown.[10]   It was this Mortimer connexion which proved of greater importance in Sir Peter de la Mare's career, but for other and more powerful reasons than those arising out of the tenurial relationship.   And well might it be so, for Roger, the son of his lord, Edmund, third Earl of March, and of Philippa, only daughter of Lionel, Duke of Clarence (the third son of Edward III), was to be, following the death of the Black Prince in June 1376, next heir to the English throne after Richard of Bordeaux by normal feudal rules of inheritance.

It is not possible to say when De la Mare entered Edmund Mortimer's service. When, however, he was first elected to parliament in 1376 he was already the earl's seneschal, as both the St. Albans chronicle and the *Anonimalle Chronicle* of St. Mary's abbey, York, tell us.[11]   But whether steward of household or steward of estates, is not made known.   As early as October 1371, and certainly for six years before that date if for no longer, De la Mare was appar-

---

[8] *The Genealogist*, N.S., XV. 152; *CFR, 1347–56*, 195, 270; *CPR, 1350–4*, 262; *ibid. 1358–61*, 160.

[9] *Official Return*, i. 234; PRO, *Lists and Indexes*, Vol. IX, *List of Sheriffs*, 60; *CFR, 1383–91*, 69, 115; *ibid., 1391–9*, 25, 263.

[10] *CPR, 1381–5*, 460; *ibid., 1388–92*, 80; *ibid., 1399–1401*, 349; *CCR, 1381–5*, 512–3; *Ancient Deeds, loc. cit.*; *DNB*, V. 751.

[11] *Chronicon Angliae* (Rolls Series), ed. E. M. Thompson, 108; *The Anonimalle Chronicle*, ed. V. H. Galbraith, 82 ("un chevaler de marche de Gales et seneschalle al count de la Marche").

ently responsible for the collection of the royal tolls from the iron mines of the royal forest of Dean, an office which he may very well have held by the appointment of Guy Lord Brian, who was keeper of this forest and had been since 1341.[12] The Mortimer connexion, however, was undoubtedly the dominant factor in De la Mare's career. To it may have been indirectly due his appointment as sheriff of Herefordshire, which office he held from 12 December 1372 to 17 July 1373, for this appointment roughly coincided with Earl Edmund's emergence.[13] Certainly, before the end of 1373 there is proof of the connexion.

In January 1373 Edward III had been approached with demands from Ireland that the Earl of March should take steps to protect in person his estates in Meath, Ulster, and Connaught, the idea being that, if the earl did this and other absentee lords did likewise, Irish taxation for defence against the rebels in the colony would be unnecessary. Mortimer was ordered to go. But the government of Ireland was not entrusted to him. It was, in fact, Sir William de Windsor, who had returned from Ireland under a cloud in March 1372, who went back in April 1374 as again the King's Lieutenant.[14] Possibly Mortimer was resentful of being passed over for the appointment. (This is not without interest in view of the attack that was to be made in the Good Parliament against Alice Perrers, Edward III's mistress, for by then Sir William de Windsor was her husband.) Late in 1373, however, there was apparently still some prospect of the earl taking a force to Ireland, because on 5 November 1373 royal commissions went out authorizing the impressment and arming of 140 picked mounted-archers from the Mortimer lordships in the English shires on the Welsh border and another sixty-four from the earl's fiefs in the home counties and East Anglia, who were to be made ready to go to Ireland (when summoned) in the earl's company and at his costs. Sir Peter de la Mare was one of the commission appointed for Herefordshire, Worcestershire, and Shropshire. It also contained the Abbot of Wigmore, a house of Augustinian canons of which the earl was hereditary patron, Sir John Talbot of Richard's Castle, who had been a member of the retinue of Lionel, Duke of Clarence (Mortimer's father-in-law), and Sir Ralph Lingen, who was to accompany the earl when (as King's Lieutenant) he did eventually go to Ireland in 1380 and who, at this moment, was representing Herefordshire in the 1373 parliament.

Little more than a year later—on 24 November 1374—the Earl of March was granted a royal licence under the Great Seal to make an enfeoffment of certain of his castles, lordships, and manors, mainly in the Welsh border counties and including his castles and property at Ludlow, Radnor, Cnwclas (Radnorshire),

[12] *CCR, 1369–74*, 258. (On 8 October 1371 the Upper Exchequer was ordered to cease to demand an account from Lord Brian and De la Mare and to discharge them of all distraints arising out of inquisitions held before William of Wykeham as late keeper of the royal forests south of Trent, provided that the tolls were regarded as part of the profits of the forest of Dean. Peter had been indicted of keeping the tolls for six years.)

[13] *List of Sheriffs*, 60.

[14] H. G. Richardson and G. O. Sayles, *The Irish Parliament in the Middle Ages*, 82. It was not until May 1380 that March went to Ireland, but then it was as the King's Lieutenant and "not primarily to enforce order in his own lands."

and Blaenllyfni and Dinas (Breconshire), all held in chief of the Crown. The feoffees were headed by a select group of Court and State officials—William Lord Latimer (the King's acting-Chamberlain), Richard Lord Scrope (the Treasurer), Nicholas de Carrew (the Keeper of the Privy Seal)—followed by a number of Mortimer administrators or retainers—Sir Peter de la Mare himself, John de Bishopston (a clerk who had been a feoffee and executor to the earl's father), Walter de Collumpton clerk, and Hugh de Boraston (one of the earl's attorneys in Ireland and sometime steward of the earl's lordship of Wigmore). The feoffees were to hold the estates in trust for life with remainder to a group of men in reserve—Bishop Sudbury of London, Bishop Wykeham of Winchester, Bishop Courtenay of Hereford (who, on 11 April 1374 at Usk, had baptized the earl's first son Roger), Sir Roger Beauchamp of Bletsoe (who was to follow Lord Latimer as acting-Chamberlain during the Good Parliament of 1376), and John de Birdwood (a clerk who was at this time another of the earl's attorneys in Ireland). The estate of all the original feoffees (save Lord Latimer, who died in 1381) was to be ratified after the earl's death by a royal patent of 14 March 1383, a few days after the dissolution of De la Mare's last parliament. In the meantime, on 20 January 1380, not long after Earl Edmund's appointment as Lieutenant of Ireland but before his departure from England, the estates in trust were leased to the earl for twenty years at a nominal rent of £100 a year.

When, on 1 May 1380 at Denbigh, immediately before he left for Ireland, the earl made his last will, he appointed Sir Peter de la Mare as one of the executors. Among the others were William Courtenay, now Bishop of London, Bishop John Gilbert of Hereford, Henry, Earl of Northumberland, whose son had married Mortimer's elder daughter, and Walter de Collumpton, one of the feoffees. The overseers of the will were Archbishop Sudbury of Canterbury, Philippa, Dowager Countess of March, the testator's mother, and Richard Lord Scrope of Bolton. The archbishop was murdered during the Peasants' Revolt in the following June, and the dowager countess survived her son by little more than a week, so that soon after Earl Edmund's death, on 27 December 1381, of the overseers only Lord Scrope survived. It was perhaps of some comfort to the executors and feoffees that at this time he was Chancellor of England.[15]

It is clear that throughout his parliamentary career—he represented Herefordshire in seven out of the eleven parliaments that sat in and between 1376 and 1383—Sir Peter de la Mare was intimately attached to the Mortimer interest. It was for the first time that he was elected as knight of the shire to the Good Parliament which met at Westminster on 28 April 1376 and lasted until 10 July following. In this unprecedentedly long session, as part of their programme of reform, a direct attack was made by the Commons on a number of royal ministers and agents. This was done in a series of impeachments, the most important of which were eventually entertained by the peers acting in their judicial capacity. Chief among the members of the court camarilla arraigned, especially on related

[15] CPR, 1370–4, 353; ibid., 1374–7, 34; ibid., 1381–5, 271; CCR, 1377–81, 365; CPR, 1385–9, 29; J. Nichols, Royal Wills, 104–16.

charges of financial corruption, was the acting-Chamberlain, Lord Latimer. He was one of the Mortimer feoffees: and yet, in these attacks, De la Mare, who, early but not quite at the beginning of the session, had been chosen by the Commons to speak for them before the King and Lords, played a commanding rôle. Although, as has been said, he is not mentioned at all on the actual roll of the parliament, the narratives of the St. Albans chronicler and the anonymous writer of St. Mary's abbey at York make this perfectly clear, as do also subsequent events.[16] De la Mare, in fact, became a popular hero, and verses were composed extolling his attitude and audacious eloquence.

It is highly probable that De la Mare's lord, the Earl of March, was sympathetic to the Commons' attack on the court party. Mortimer's attitude to John of Gaunt, who acted during Edward III's illness as his lieutenant in the parliament and who seems to have been inclined to regard the Commons' proceedings as an indirect attack on himself, was one of hostility. Perhaps this was because Lancaster was already, in view of the fatal illness of the Black Prince, taking steps to exclude the Mortimer claim to a place in the line of succession to the throne. However that may be, Mortimer was one of the four earls whom, along with four bishops and four other temporal lords, the Commons chose to help them to formulate their demands for reform. It is also worth pointing out that another of the earls on this liaison-committee was Hugh, Earl of Stafford, who had his connexions with Mortimer—on 21 November 1375 at Ludlow he had assisted as godfather at the baptism of the Earl of March's third child, his second daughter Philippa, and the Countess of Stafford had then held the child for its confirmation. Moreover, one of the four bishops of the committee, William Courtenay of London, when formerly Bishop of Hereford had baptized Mortimer's first two children, was one of his reserve-feoffees, and was to be one of his executors. Among the four barons of the committee was Henry Percy, whose son (Hotspur) was to marry Mortimer's elder daughter and who was himself to be made one of the Earl of March's executors; another was Guy Lord Brian, with whom De la Mare himself most probably had a connexion; and perhaps one more was Sir Roger Beauchamp of Bletsoe, who was another of Mortimer's reserve-feoffees. All of these five men and the earl himself were to be among the nine lords whom Edward III was advised (by a deputation from the Upper House) to accept as counsellors when De la Mare, on the Commons' behalf, demanded in parliament that the Council should be re-formed and "afforced" by three bishops, three earls, and three barons. Among the three others proposed to the King and accepted by him to make up the Council were two more reserve-feoffees of the Earl of March: Archbishop Sudbury (eventually an overseer of the earl's will) and Bishop Wykeham of Winchester. It would not be safe to say that this new Council was one dominated by the Earl of March, or even that it had a distinctly Mortimer complexion, but it was certainly made up of men with a majority of whom the earl was connected and whom, for the pursuance of his private affairs, he regarded

[16] *The Anonimalle Chronicle, ed. cit.,* 82–94; *Chronicon Angliae, ed. cit.,* 72–81, 392.

as useful and perhaps trustworthy. The same idea conceivably might be urged of Lord Latimer who remained one of the Mortimer feoffees under the original settlement of November 1374, but it is worth noting that no mention was to be made of Latimer in the Earl of March's will (drawn up in May 1380), not even as a beneficiary. The way in which Lancaster soon effected Latimer's pardon and restoration to royal favour after his impeachment in the Good Parliament and his condemnation there to loss of office, imprisonment, and exclusion from the Court, had inevitably bound the ex-Chamberlain to the ducal group.

Before the end of this parliament the Commons were deprived, by the death of the Black Prince on 8 June 1376, of the support of one whom they had good reason to believe to be in sympathy with their objects. (It is worth remarking that in his last moments the Prince was attended by the Bishop of Bangor, who, at Ludlow in the previous November, had confirmed Mortimer's second son Edmund.) Despite (or perhaps because of) the disheartening effect of this event, the parliament ended a month later (on 10 July 1376) in an atmosphere of apparent cordiality, the Speaker and the knights of the shire putting on a feast for certain of the Lords (who did not include Lancaster but did include his two surviving brothers and the Earl of March), the Mayor and some influential citizens of London, and other burgesses attending the parliament. But before Edward III's death most of what the Good Parliament did had been annulled. In next to no time, Latimer was back at Court. Quite soon even the newly-appointed Council was dismissed. This policy was followed up in a Great Council which met in the autumn of 1376, when a virulent attack was contrived against Bishop Wykeham, Mortimer's old guardian and an enemy of Lancaster. And its results were confirmed in the last parliament of the reign, which met in January 1377. Already, the Earl of March had been forced to resign the office of Marshal of England in favour of Henry Percy. In the meantime, none of the petitions of the Good Parliament resulted in statutes, and the Commons' Speaker, De la Mare, suffered imprisonment for his recent boldness.

Proceedings against Sir Peter de la Mare do not seem to have been initiated until the end of November 1376 when he was summoned to appear at Court. It was Alice Perrers (the King's mistress who had been successfully attacked in the Good Parliament), Lord Latimer, and Sir Richard Stury (a knight of the King's Chamber) who were responsible for this move, according to the St. Albans chronicle. Its story says that De la Mare was not allowed to answer but, without proper legal process, was imprisoned at Nottingham castle. One rumour had it that Lancaster ordered his execution and that such a course was only prevented by Lord Percy; another, that, at the instigation of Alice Perrers, Sir Peter was actually adjudged to death by the King, the execution of the sentence being prevented by Lancaster. Whatever may be the truth of this "judgment," De la Mare was certainly imprisoned: on 27 November 1376 orders by royal letters close were sent both to the constable of Nottingham castle and to the Earl of Cambridge as constable of Dover castle to receive and safe-keep him in prison until further notice; but it was to Nottingham that he went.[17]   He was not forgotten.

Even during the Bad Parliament of January 1377, when Lancaster had it nearly all his own way, a few of the knights of the shire, re-elected members of the Good Parliament, at great risk to themselves, so the St. Albans chronicle tells us, tried to get the Commons unanimously to demand De la Mare's liberation on the grounds that he was prepared to answer all charges in the presence of the Lords and submit himself to their judgment.   Sir Peter's friends did not succeed: but hostility to Lancaster was growing among the magnates, among the prelates who refused to do business in Convocation until Bishop Wykeham was allowed to take his place among them there, and especially, during February, in the City, where the Londoners rallied to the support of their bishop (William Courtenay) when Lancaster violently supported the heretic, John Wycliffe, at his examination before the bishops in St. Paul's. During the ensuing riot, from which Lancaster and his present short-term ally, Lord Percy, only with difficulty escaped, an unfortunate priest who spoke with contempt of De la Mare as a traitor who ought to have been hanged years ago was so badly mauled by the city mob, we are told, that he soon afterwards died. We are also informed that the Londoners were then demanding that the former Speaker be set free, and that, when arbiters were appointed by the Black Prince's widow to bring Lancaster and the citizens to see reason, the latter repeated their demand, requiring Lancaster to allow Bishop Wykeham and De la Mare a proper trial by process of law.   On 18 June 1377 Wykeham was restored to the temporalities of his see, of which he had been deprived.   The reign of Edward III was now all but over, but it was not until eight days after the old king's death that De la Mare's release was ordered on 30 June.

Sir Peter hastened to London to thank the new sovereign, Richard II, for clemency, receiving on his way, according to the St. Albans chronicle, a welcome recalling that given to Thomas Becket on his return from exile; the Londoners especially made much of him with presents and feasting.   According to this St. Albans source again, De la Mare was given a royal pardon of all that could be alleged against him, and this statement at least is confirmed by the terms of the royal order to release him: "the King, by the advice of the Council, fully remitted his contempt."   When, on 5 August 1378, with the assent of the Council, 50 marks were given him by assignment at the Lower Exchequer as a *donum* for past and future service to the present King and *in exoneracione anime Regis Edwardi*, he was stated in the record to have been detained at Nottingham for thirty-three weeks and more by the late King's precept, *certis de causis irracionabilibus*; on 11 February 1380 he was further paid £15 12s. 6d. at the Exchequer to discharge and acquit him towards Sir John Dabridgecourt, constable of Nottingham castle, to whom he was bound by letters of obligation,

[17] *Chronicon Angliae, ed. cit.*, 105, 392–3; *CCR, 1374–7*, 397; W. Dugdale, *Monasticon Anglicanum* (ed. Caley, Ellis, and Bandinel, 1817–30), Vol. VI, part 1, p. 354.

presumably for his upkeep when detained there. With this payment the incident of his imprisonment was doubtless considered closed.[18]

It is not very surprising that when Richard II's first parliament met, in October 1377, Sir Peter de la Mare, once more returned for Herefordshire, was again elected Speaker for the Commons. Two out of every three of his fellow knights of the shire had had previous parliamentary experience, nearly half of those (twenty-two out of the fifty-one) in the Good Parliament. Sir Peter's lord, the Earl of March, was one of those members of the royal Council, appointed at the very beginning of the reign, who continued to act when the Council was re-constituted during the parliament. This was in response to a petition of the Commons, and to that extent this new Council may be said to have been "fortified by parliamentary sanction" (Tout). The Commons reverted in other ways to the programme of the Good Parliament, for example, in their renewal of the demand for the nomination in parliament of certain of the major officials of State and of the royal Household, a requirement which (like so many demands made in this parliament) harked back to the substance, and even to the phraseology, of the Ordinances of 1311. With regard to the more important officials, the request was favourably met. The Commons' petition that those attendant on the person of the young King should also be nominated in parliament was virtually refused by the Lords. Another leading demand, that no law passed by parliament should be repealed without its consent, was, however, granted. Moreover, Lord Latimer was again removed from his membership of the Council (in which, restored by Edward III, he had been confirmed immediately after Richard II's coronation). The end of the parliamentary session, after the Commons had gone down on 28 November, saw the confirmation by the Lords of their judgment against Alice Perrers in the Good Parliament. Well satisfied by what had already been done before they departed, the Commons had voted a double subsidy (two tenths and two fifteenths), the proceeds being, however, ear-marked for the war with France and subjected to the control of special war-treasurers, two of their own number, the aldermen-members for the City of London. The results of the session, political and constitutional, were once more to prove short-lived.

Sir Peter de la Mare was not again, so far as we are aware, to be elected as Speaker for the Commons. Indeed, he did not even sit in either of the next two parliaments, although the first to meet did so (in October 1378) so near his home as Gloucester. He was not, in fact, again returned until January 1380. In the meantime, when the first parliament of the reign was only a week old, on 20 October 1377 he had stood surety for the English representative of the French Benedictine abbey of Lire, who (under the Exchequer) had farmed the English possessions of this monastery since the resumption of the war with France in 1369 and who was now confirmed in the custody. On 27 May 1379 De la Mare was appointed to the commission set up to assess in Herefordshire the recently

[18] *Chronicon Angliae, ed. cit.*, 112–3, 124, 126, 150–1; *CCR, 1377–81*, 7; Exchequer, Issue Rolls, E403/468, mem. 11; *ibid.*, E403/475, mem. 14.

granted, graduated poll-tax, and he was re-appointed on 8 August following to remedy defects in the assessment, especially errors of omission or under-assessment. In Easter term 1381, the Barons of the Exchequer were to take account of De la Mare's failure to act as a controller of a parliamentary subsidy in Herefordshire. It would appear that it was his neglect of this commission over the 1379 poll-tax which was in question. The royal writ issued on 3 May 1381 which excused De la Mare's neglect of the commission, did so on the grounds that he had been in Ireland at the time; describing him as retained for life by the Earl of March to serve him in war and peace, it stated that De la Mare *ad proficiscendum in dictam terram ad arraiandum pro adventu dicti comitis in terram illam ordinatus fuit.* . . . This preparation for the earl's arrival in Ireland De la Mare is most likely to have performed between the earl's appointment (for three years) as Lieutenant of Ireland in October 1379 and January 1380 when De la Mare was once more elected to parliament.[19]

The January parliament of 1380 had been in session only four days when the earl's feoffees, De la Mare among them, leased him back his estates for twenty years. Within a week of the end of the parliament (on 9 March), De la Mare was party with the Dean of Dublin to a mainprise in Chancery for John FitzRery, the King's Escheator in Ireland, who stood indicted for felony and trespass; the sureties undertook his appearance in Ireland. It looks as though Mortimer was already putting himself in close touch with Irish affairs. Although in no great hurry to leave England, the earl was soon clearly completing his preparations: on 19 April 1380 he appointed his attorneys in England for one year, De la Mare among them, and on 1 May, at Denbigh, he drew up his will, appointing De la Mare to be one of the executors. Within a fortnight Mortimer had crossed to Ireland. De la Mare obviously remained behind in England, and on 26 May 1380 he was for the first time made a justice of the peace in Herefordshire.[20]

In the autumn of 1380, De la Mare was re-elected knight of the shire to the parliament which sat at Northampton from 5 November to 6 December and which did so much to provoke the outbreak of the Peasants' Revolt of the following year by its grant of a poll-tax of three groats, that is, of a shilling a head. He was not this time even charged with any of the work of assessment or collection, but when the great rising had practically spent itself he was appointed to a number of local royal commissions set up to deal with the disorders created by it; he was made a member of the commission appointed on 7 July 1381 to make proclamation in Herefordshire that the rebels had murdered Archbishop Sudbury, the Chancellor, Sir Robert Hales, the Treasurer, and Chief Justice Cavendish, to forbid unlawful assemblies, and, under an authority to array loyal men, to organize resistance to any rebels in the county. Later in the same year, on 14 December, he was put on the Herefordshire commission to keep the peace,

[19] *CFR, 1377–83*, 24, 143, 163; Exchequer, Q.R. Memoranda Roll, PRO, E159/157 (I owe this reference to the kindness of Dr. G. A. Holmes of St. Catherine's Society, Oxford).
[20] *CCR, 1377–81*, 361; *CPR, 1377–81*, 459, 515.

its members being empowered to arrest those gathering unlawfully and to put down rebels, with force if necessary; on 8 March 1382 the commission was renewed, the commissioners being now authorized to call out the *posse comitatus* and to use powers of oyer and terminer.[21]   In the meantime, on 28 April 1381 De la Mare was appointed for two years by Henry de Cornewaile, a member of the Earl of March's household and retinue in Ireland, as one of his attorneys in England, his fellow-attorney being Roger Nash, a clerk in the Mortimer service and the holder of a living in the earl's patronage at Kingsland.   On 8 August 1381 De la Mare and one of his co-feoffees in the Mortimer estates were confirmed in their position of attorneys to the earl.   On 30 August Sir Peter was ordered at his peril to be before the Upper Exchequer on the morrow of Michaelmas prepared to account for such of the income of the chancellorship of the cathedral church of Hereford as had come into his hands during 1381.   This office, taken away by Pope Urban VI from the Cardinal of Glandèves, one of those schismatic members of the Sacred College who in 1378 had been responsible for electing the anti-pope, Clement VII, had been recently conferred on the Cardinal of Perugia, whose proctors in England had granted the fruits of the office to the King for this year.   It very much looks as if De la Mare was connected in some administrative capacity with the cathedral authorities of his own diocese, but unfortunately no other record has been found to throw light on the nature of this relationship.[22]

On 27 December 1381 De la Mare's lord, the Earl of March, died at Cork, and his body was brought back to England for burial in the abbey church at Wigmore, which he himself had done much to rebuild.   Earl Edmund's heir, Roger, was then only seven years old and so became a royal ward.   Those Mortimer lands originally enfeoffed in 1374 were excluded from the wardship and remained with the trustees, of whom De la Mare was still one; the earlier settlement was ratified under the great seal on 14 March 1383.   Within three months of the death of the earl (on 13 March 1382), in company with Bishop Gilbert of Hereford and Roger Nash, clerk, Sir Peter was granted by the royal Council the custody of the demesne lands under plough in some twenty-eight Mortimer manors in Monmouthshire and in other counties of eastern and southern England, on condition that at Michaelmas following they rendered at the Exchequer the value of the customary works of the tenants and 6d. per acre of land.   De la Mare was also, of course, doubtless active as one of the late earl's executors.[23]

In spite of the death of his lord, De la Mare remained influential in local circles for some little time yet to come.   He was elected to three parliaments on the run, to the May and October parliaments of 1382 and to the February

---

[21] *CPR, 1381–5*, 71, 73, 86, 138.

[22] *Ibid., 1377–81*, 618.   In March 1387 Nash was to be appointed the King's receiver in Cardiganshire and in July following as chamberlain and receiver in other parts of South Wales.   *Ibid., 1381–5*, 31; 16.   Henry de Cornewaile had been present at Denbigh when Edmund Mortimer made his will.   [*Royal Wills, loc. cit.*]

[23] *CPR, 1381–5*, 271; *CFR, 1377–83*, 288; *CPR, 1385–9*, 29.

parliament of 1383, but after this last occasion he never again acted as knight of the shire. He had not been included in the Herefordshire commission of the peace in December 1382, nor was he at any later time. In fact, although his younger brother Malcolm was to be knight of the shire in the autumn parliament of 1388 and sheriff in 1392–3, Sir Peter was to serve on no further royal commissions, locally or elsewhere, and he soon passes abruptly and almost completely out of view. At some time between June 1384 and May 1387, however, as feoffees of Sir Richard Burley, K.G., in the castles and lordships of Dorstone (Herefordshire) and Newland (Glos), he and some others settled these and other Burley estates on Sir Richard and his wife Beatrice, a daughter of Ralph, Earl of Stafford, and formerly widow successively of the Earl of Desmond and Thomas Lord Roos of Helmsley. Newland, Dorstone, and some other estates in Herefordshire were held in mesne-tenancy of the Earls of March, and this may account for De la Mare's inclusion among the feoffees. Sir Richard had died in May 1387 serving with John of Gaunt in Spain, but the estates had come into the King's hands in 1388 by reason of the forfeiture of Sir Richard's uncle, Sir Simon Burley, who was impeached and executed during the Merciless Parliament of that year. This is the last notice of De la Mare that we have.[24]

Precisely when Sir Peter died is not known, but it was almost surely before his brother Malcolm. Certainly, both were dead by 1400. The brothers died without issue, the family holding at Yatton eventually going to their cousin Margaret's son, Roger Seymour.[25]

It will have been realized that the little we know about Sir Peter de la Mare concerns the last twenty years of his life, and that in this period his career is really only very dimly illumined except in the closing stages of Edward III's reign and in the opening phase of that of his successor, Richard II. Our notice is inevitably drawn to the time when De la Mare was Speaker in 1376 and 1377, and for what knowledge is given us of this period when he briefly attracted the close attention of the government of the day and became the cynosure of his contemporaries we must be grateful. It certainly has the value of showing us how the Commons' Speaker began his institutional career as a leader of debate and political opposition and, our examination of De la Mare's career suggests, as something of a political partisan. Very soon the Speaker's potential capacity for managing the Commons was officially appreciated, and the government realized that it would be all to the good if he were able to represent the King in the Lower House of parliament as well as the Commons in the Upper House. Certainly, not long after De la Mare was Speaker, the Chancellor, when opening parliament on the King's behalf, actually began to instruct the Commons to proceed to the election of a Speaker, which then received the King's approval. The function had already become an office. Many of the mediaeval Speakers were royal servants, which in the strict sense Sir Peter de la Mare never was. Most of his successors in the office were men in the thick of affairs of State in

[24] *CPR, 1391–6*, 81; *CCR, 1385–9*, 502, 524–5, 543.
[25] *The Genealogist, loc. cit.* in n. 8.

an age when political life was often full of hazard to person and property, and some of them were to come by untimely ends.   But this was not because the Speakership was in itself a dangerous occupation.   Only one of the mediaeval Speakers suffered directly and expressly for his acts as Speaker: and he was the first of them, Sir Peter de la Mare.

2

SIR THOMAS HUNGERFORD

It was not until about the beginning of the reign of Edward III (in 1327) that elected knights of the shire, citizens and burgesses came to have an essential, if subordinate, place in parliaments. Before then, if only recently, they had been summoned with some frequency, but not regularly. At this time, too, perhaps because they were forming the habit of co-operating in the work of petitioning for redress of public grievance and voting taxes, it was possible for them first to be given a collective description as *communitates*, alias *communes*, alias commons. They represented the local communities of the shires of England (save two, the counties palatine of Durham and Chester) and of most of the towns that were of note. In the next half-century, during the course of Edward III's reign, the commons' claims to share in the work of parliament grew, more quickly, in fact, than did at first the machinery devised to assist their functions. Not until 1363, so far as we know, were they allowed by the king the services of a royal clerk specializing in their business, the under-clerk of the parliament. And seemingly not until 1376 did they feel the need to elect, from among their own number and for the duration of a parliament, one who, after his formal accept-ance by the king, would declare to him and the lords what the com-mons allowed him to say on their behalf: a common speaker. The speaker's potential importance as a controller or manager of the business and discussions of the lower house was soon realised, not least by the government, and in the course of Richard II's reign an order from the king to the commons to elect a speaker became a conventional part of the formal opening of a parliament. The function, as functions have a habit of doing, had turned into an office.

The first continuing speaker we know of was Sir Peter de la Mare, steward of the Earl of March, who led the commons in the Good Parlia-ment of 1376. It is clear from the accounts of some of the chronicles of the day that he was personally responsible for much of what the com-mons did in that important and significant session. But he is not men-tioned in the record of that parliament. The first speaker to be referred to in the roll of a parliament itself was Sir Thomas Hungerford, an official and supporter of John of Gaunt, Duke of Lancaster, who was speaker in the last of Edwards III's parliaments which met in January 1377, when he was knight of the shire for Wiltshire, his own county. Of his immediate successors in the office we know only a few, because the compiler of the rolls of the parliaments was not always at first careful to enter even their names. Not until 1397 does a consecutive list of them begin.

Down to the Reformation Parliament of 1529-36, the speakers seem to have been invariably drawn from among those who represented counties. The social standing of the knights of the shire was much higher than that of the rank and file of the parliamentary burgesses: they were members of the landed gentry, locally important for family and other reasons, and influential, too, because most of them and their kind saw that one of the best ways of working for themselves was to work in their ' country for the king and also, as a general rule, for one or more of the great lords, whose ' good lordship ' and fees they coveted in this time of ' bastard feudalism '; they frequently managed to combine these occupations with the furtherance of family aggrandisement by marriage and the accumulation of estates. The speakers were like their fellow knights of the shire, of course, in these respects. Most of them besides were constantly in the thick of affairs of state, usually connected, the courtiers, administrators, and lawyers among them alike, with the king or some dominant magnate or faction.

This is not to suggest that it may be implied that in the medieval period the speaker's election was a mock proceeding, in which a nomination was foisted upon the commons from above as a regular.thing. For one thing, the commons would have found it difficult to find for the speakership one of their most influential, knowledgeable and eloquent members who was not so occupied. The personal connections of a speaker with some branch of the royal administration or household, and his occasional payment by the royal exchequer for his prolocutorial services, sometimes suggest that he must have been as much the king's agent in the lower house as the commons' representative *vis-a-vis* the king. But the fact that now and then a particular speaker was an adherent of some strong aristocratic interest encourages the counter-suggestion that there were other than merely governmental influences operating in his election. It is perhaps safe to infer that even the election of an out-and-out partisan, whether the king's or some other magnate's, represented no more than the registration of a certain tilt of the balance of opinion in the lower house at the beginning of a parliament. There is other evidence to strengthen the view that the speaker's election was normally no ' put-up ' job. However he was elected, it was the speaker's duty to communicate the outcome of the commons' meetings to the king and lords in the way and form the commons themselves saw fit. The history of the careers of the early speakers clearly has some bearing on the question of the medieval commons' political independence, especially valuable because the inside workings of the lower house are largely hidden from us until the Commons' Journals, which did not begin until 1547, do something to remedy the defect.

As it happened, of the known seventeen knights of the shire who in the first forty years of the history of the speakership (1376-1416) occupied this office, no fewer than five were Wiltshire men. Sir William Sturmy of Wolfhall acted as speaker at Coventry in 1404, but he was then representing Devon, and William Stourton of Stourton, an apprentice-at-law, who was speaker for part of the single session of Henry V's first parliament in 1413, was then sitting as knight of the shire for Dorset. The other three, Sir Thomas Hungerford, speaker in the Bad Parliament of January 1377, his son Walter (later first Baron Hungerford), speaker in the Leicester parliament of 1414, and Sir Walter Beauchamp of Bromham, speaker in March 1416 in the first parliament which Henry V opened in person after his victory at Agincourt, were on these occasions, however, representing Wiltshire itself. Never afterwards was the speaker's chair filled by a knight of the shire for this county.

Sir Thomas Hungerford, speaker in Edward III's last parliament of January 1377. Knight of the shire for Wiltshire, in the parliaments of April 1357, May 1360, October 1362, January 1377; for Somerset, October 1378; for Wiltshire, April 1379, January 1380, November 1380; for Somerset May 1382; for Wiltshire, October 1383; for Wiltshire and Somerset, April 1384; for Wiltshire, October 1386; for Somerset, September 1388; for Wiltshire, January 1390; for Somerset, November 1390; and for Wiltshire, January 1393.[1]

The manor of Hungerford in the south-west corner of Berkshire, from which Sir Thomas Hungerford's family took its name, was one of those originally De Montfort estates which formed part of Henry III's endowment for Edmund, his second son, when he created him Earl of Lancaster; it was thus part of the complex of properties which, after their fourteenth century expansion and the promotion of the Lancastrian earl to the rank of duke, eventually became the duchy of Lancaster.

Almost from the first appearance of the house of Lancaster, the family of Hungerford, in one or more of its members, was connected with it, although the maintenance of their link with the town of Hungerford itself is not always demonstrable. Sir Thomas Hungerford himself, so far as can be ascertained, had no such link, although his heir, Walter first Lord Hungerford, was to receive the duchy manor and borough as a grant from the king before the end of his life. But certainly Sir Robert Hungerford, the elder brother of Sir Thomas's father, had a house in Hungerford, and here in the church of St. Laurence, where he founded one of his five chantries, he was buried[2]. And as a factor in promoting an early connection between the house of Lancaster and the Hungerford family, this domiciliary origin may have been of some significance.

Perhaps the Nicholas de Hungerford, who in 1300 was confirmed by Thomas Earl of Lancaster in the keepership of the forest of Duffield (Derbyshire), an office which he had first been granted by the earl's mother, was not a direct ancestor of Sir Thomas Hungerford[3]. There is no doubt, however, about the relationship between Sir Thomas and the Sir Robert Hungerford who was Earl Thomas of Lancaster's keeper of his lands in Wiltshire and wore robes of his livery (an office which for his alleged fidelity Edward II allowed him to retain after the great Lancastrian forfeiture of 1322), who continued in the Lancastrian service with Earl Thomas's brother and heir and successor in the title, Henry of Lancaster, and who was knight of the shire for Wiltshire nine times between 1324 and 1339[4]. Sir Robert, who was also (in 1332) steward of the bishopric of Bath and Wells, was Sir Thomas's uncle, and when he died (without issue) in 1352 Thomas acquired his lands in north Wiltshire and Berkshire and certain expectations, including a remainder in tail of the manor of Rushall (Wiltshire), which came to his heir Walter in 1404.[5] It is not known what estates came to Thomas from his father, Walter. A younger brother of Sir Robert, this Walter was by 1333 the Bishop of Salisbury's bailiff in the cathedral town, knight of the shire for Wiltshire in 1332, 1334, and 1336, royal escheator in Surrey, Sussex, and Kent from May to December 1335, coroner in Wiltshire in (and probably between) 1341 and 1346 (in both of which years his replacement was ordered), and in 1351 was included in the commission of the peace for this county.[6] Nor is it possible to say what were all the lands that came to Thomas Hungerford as a consequence of either of his two marriages.

His first wife was Eleanor daughter of John Strug and probably granddaughter of the Sir John Strug, one of the Contrariants of 1322 who compounded for their estates by making fine and ransom with Edward II, in possession of whose lands in Heytesbury (near Devizes) Thomas and Eleanor were confirmed in 1352 and again, by final concord, two years later.[7] Eleanor died sometime after 1366 but before April 1376, by which time Thomas had married a widow of no exceptional but quite solid prospects; Joan, daughter and coheir of Sir Edmund Hussey of Holbrook (Somerset) and formerly wife of John Whiton.[8] Joan certainly brought into her second husband's possession the manor and advowson of Teffont Evias, and property in Woolley in Wiltshire, and other Hussey lands in Holbrook and Bossington (near Minehead) in Somerset.[9]

But these were by no means all Thomas Hungerford's holdings, some of which surely came by purchase. In 1369 he secured the east Somerset manors of Wellow and Farleigh Montfort for 1100 marks,[10] from Bartholomew Lord Burghersh. The manor of South Court in Heytesbury near Devizes he had bought as early as 1352.[11] The manor of East Court in Heytesbury he had leased in 1355 from Margaret, widow of William Lord Ros of Helmsley, and after her death (in 1363) Thomas Hungerford and his first wife secured an extension of the lease from her son and heir, Thomas Lord Ros, for the term of their lives. This, in 1376, Lord Ros converted into a final sale and release, and in November 1383 Hungerford levied a fine settling (through feoffees) East Court on himself and his second wife and their issue in tail male. (On 28 November 1387 Hungerford received a royal pardon for his trespasses with regard to this estate by letter patent under the great seal.)[12] Not long before this settlement of East Court, Hungerford had rounded off his holdings in Heytesbury by securing the manor of West Court as well. This manor in the borough Edward III had granted to Henry Burghersh, Bishop of Lincoln, and it descended normally in his family until the death of Bartholomew Lord Burghersh in 1369. It passed as a dower estate first into the possession of his widow, Margaret (who now married Sir William Burcestre), and then, before November 1381, to Lord Burghersh's daughter and heir Elizabeth, widow of Edward Lord Despenser. This change of possession, resting on a dubious title, smoothed the way for Hungerford's conversion by dubious devices of a lease of the manor that he had enjoyed since 1370 into a tenure which eventually emerged in 1382 as one enjoyed by himself and his wife in fee tail male. The whole transaction was called into question by a petition which Sir William Burcestre and his wife laid before the King and Council in the parliament of November 1381, but without any very tangible result or effect on Hungerford's " bargaining " of the manor.[13] Other Wiltshire estates in Hungerford's occupation were the manor of Mildenhall (near Marlborough) which he acquired in 1371 and settled by a fine in November 1383 on himself and his second wife in tail male,[14] the manor of Horningsham (near Warminster) which he got in 1378-9,[15] the manor and advowson of Ashley, the manor of Codford (near Heytesbury), and lands in Woolley Green, La Slo (in Bradford-on-Avon), Knoyl Odyern, Ashridge, and Twyford. He had a fulling mill near Warminster[16], and the keepership of the royal forest of Selwood which he converted into an office held in fee tail male, an act for which both he (in February 1380) and his son Walter (in 1395) had to sue out royal letters of pardon from the Chancery.[17] In Somerset, apart from the manor and hundred of Wellow (near Bath), the manor of Farleigh Montfort, and the Hussey estates, Hungerford had the manors of Farrok and Charlton, and in Gloucestershire, just over the north Wiltshire border near Cricklade, he had the manor of Down Ampney and a toft and two carucates nearby in Wick by Maisey Hampton.[18] In the most important of his demesnes— Wellow, Farleigh Montfort, Heytesbury (East Court and West Court), Mildenhall, Teffont Evias, Ashley, Woolley, La Slo, and Down Ampney—he received on 13 May 1385 a royal grant, warranted by signet, of the right of free warren.[19]

Heytesbury, judging from the trouble taken in the acquisition of its component manors, was a key place in Hungerford's territorial scheme : it had the advantage of being no more than a day's riding from any one of his Wiltshire and East Somerset estates. But it was the manor-house at Farleigh Montfort that by November 1383 he fortified and received royal licence to hold ' come chastell ', and it was in the chapel of St. Anne in the church of Farleigh that he and his second wife were to be buried.[20] The licence to fortify Farleigh seems to have been part of a general tidying-up of his affairs. Only a week before its issue, he had levied on 18 November 1383 a series of fines settling his Mildenhall estates on himself with successive remainders in tail male to his four surviving sons by both his marriages (Robert and Thomas by his first wife, Walter and John by his second), but the fines relating to Heytesbury (East and West Court), Wellow, and Farleigh, and other smaller properties provided for their later descent in tail male to Hungerford's issue by his second wife only. Of all his sons, only Walter, later first Lord Hungerford, outlived him. On Sir Thomas's death in 1397, or rather on his widow's death in 1412, the estates descended to Walter without complication, none of his brothers having had issue.[21]

It is, perhaps, not without a certain interest that the first traceable reference to Thomas Hungerford should connect him with a high official in the Lancastrian administration, his own future connection with which had long been prepared for by the attachment of members of his family to each of the first three earls of Lancaster. On 4 November 1349 as the son of his father he acknowledged in the royal chancery a debt of £100 (leviable in Wiltshire) to Henry de Walton, archdeacon of Richmond, who was at this time attorney-general and treasurer of household to Henry of Grosmont, fourth Earl of Lancaster.[22] There is nothing to connect Thomas Hungerford again with the house of Lancaster until 1372, and it may well be that this solitary transaction of 1349 had simply to do with a duchy tenancy held by Hungerford's father, Walter, the details of which are unknown. (Walter, never conspicuous, fades out of view soon after this time, although I have not been able to fix the date of his death.)

It seems likely that Thomas Hungerford was already of age. Very soon he was receiving royal commissions in his own county of Wiltshire and sometimes outside it. On 20 March 1351 he was appointed one of a commission of three overseers of the administration of the statute of Westminster 1285, which had provided penalties for the taking of salmon at certain seasons, in the Wiltshire and Gloucestershire courses of the Thames and Severn. A patent of 27 May 1353 gave him membership of a commission of oyer and terminer regarding infringements in Wiltshire of the recent Statute of Labourers. He became sheriff and also escheator in Wiltshire on 24 November 1355, serving the former office for five years on end (until 21 November 1360) and the escheatorship for two of those five concurrently (until 16 October 1357).[23] Twice during this time he was able to return himself as knight of the shire, in April 1357 and May 1360.

In the meantime, his connections and interests were becoming more extensive and diversified. Robert Wyvill, Bishop of Salisbury since 1330 and destined to hold the see until 1375, on 27 June 1354 had appointed Thomas Hungerford as bailiff of the episcopal Wiltshire manors of Potterne and Ramsbury with right to appoint a deputy; the office carried with it an annual livery of an esquire's robe (or £1 in lieu) and customary fees estimated at 20 marks a year.[24] Hungerford retained the office until 4 April 1370, when he surrendered it to take up instead a grant for life of the office of bishop's bailiff or steward of the city of Salisbury and of the manors of Milford and Woodford at an annual fee of £10 and of his right to an esquire's livery. The preferment of Ralph Erghum, John of Gaunt's chancellor, to the See of Salisbury on Wyvill's death in 1375 can only have rendered his tenure more secure (Erghum was one of Hungerford's feoffees) and he certainly maintained his life estate in the appointment.[25] The office was clearly the product of a close and continuing attachment to the bishop; but this connexion was by no means exclusive of others.

Hungerford's relationship with the royal administration was never a directly close one after he relinquished the shrievalty in 1360 (his only occupation of that office), but his administrative experience was certainly enriched—and doubtless his coffers—by his connexions with members of the royal family and others of great estate, although he came at some of these perhaps indirectly. Many of his royal commissions were undoubtedly the outcome of some of these outside fidelities. Whether or not he was connected with the administration of the estates of Edward III's queen, Philippa of Hainault, as early as 10 February 1357, when along with her steward he was one of a commission of oyer and terminer charged with a judical investigation in her southern lordships and liberties, by 20 October 1359 he was constable of her castle of Marlborough, where she and the king had spent part of the previous summer but one.[26] Perhaps his occupation of the shrievalty at this time accounts for this office, as it would for a royal commission he had received in the previous July to demolish and sell the material of some houses at Norton Bavant (Wiltshire) given by the king to the Dominican nunnery of Dartford (Kent). But what lay behind his appointment in May 1360 to a commission to survey defects in the structure of Dover Castle it is difficult to say, unless his occupations at Marlborough had brought him into touch with William of Wykeham, who was another member of the party. (The constable at Dover, who died before the end of the year, was a brother of the Earl of Warwick and Hungerford had no connexion with either).[27]

Sometime between the end of June 1361 and May 1362 Hungerford became under-steward of the Black Prince's honours of Wallingford and St. Valery in the Thames Valley, which were parcels of his duchy of Cornwall, Hungerford's superior in office being Bartholomew Lord Burghersh.[28] Burghersh followed his father in closely identifying his interests with those of the royal heir-apparent. The father had been a member of the prince's council (as well as chamberlain of the king's household). The son had been a constant companion-in-arms of the prince, with whom he was much of an age, during the period of successful war against France, slipping comfortably into some of his father's offices in the prince's administration when the elder Bartholomew died in 1355. Since 1351 he had been steward of the honours of Wallingford and St. Valery and of the four and a half hundreds of Chiltern and also constable of Wallingford castle. On 10 February 1365, described in a letter under the prince's privy seal of Gascony as the prince's yeoman, Hungerford was confirmed in his appointment as under-steward during Burghersh's tenure of office and occupation of the farm of the honours, and within a matter of weeks short of Burghersh's death in April 1369 he was his under-constable of Wallingford castle. [29] Whether or not he continued in this branch of the prince's administration after Burghersh's death is not known, but it is very doubtful. In no other way was he directly connected with the Black Prince in the years covered by the latter's Registers (that is, down to 1365) or later, although his connexion with Burghersh brought him into touch with other members of the prince's retinue and circle, Burghersh's cousin, Sir Walter Paveley K.G., for example. [30]

It is probable that with Burghersh's demise Hungerford's association with the eldest of the king's sons came to an end. It may well have arisen in the first place solely through the younger Burghersh, with whom he was closely linked in other and more immediately personal ways. We may regard it as a bye-product of his association with Lord Burghersh which was a distinct and significant phase of his career. On 9 May 1365, before proceeding on royal service to Flanders, Burghersh took out letters under the great seal nominating Sir Walter Paveley and Hungerford as his attorneys in England for a year; a month later, when Burghersh made a settlement of his Sussex manor of Burwash, Hungerford was a feoffee with John Gildsborough; and another month later still, when Burghersh took out a royal licence to make a settlement of his castle and moiety of the lordship of Ewyas in the march of Herefordshire and of three Wiltshire manors (including West Court in Heytesbury, which Hungerford was himself eventually to acquire) Hungerford was with Paveley and again with John Gildsborough a member of the committee of feoffees. In the meantime, in the middle of May he was put on a royal judicial commission of oyer and terminer in the Devon stannaries, an appointment which he doubtless owed to Burghersh's occupation of the office of warden of the stannaries there (in which Burghersh had followed his father in 1355.) [31] In May of the following year (1366) when Burghersh was preparing to go on a royal embassy to Urban V at Avignon he again made Hungerford one of his attorneys. This appointment was to last until Christmas, but in all probability Burghersh was back home before then because the papal letter of credence to Edward III given to him and his fellow ambass-adors was dated 1 August 1366. Two days before this, Burghersh had taken the opportunity to petition in the Curia for the privilege of plenary remission at the hour of their death for nineteen English people who included Hungerford and Gildsborough and their wives. On 1 August the petition was re-presented but with only a partial success. [32] Burghersh died on 5 April 1369, Hungerford being then not only his feoffee but also one of his executors. [33]

Hungerford appears to have used this position to advantage, securing for himself first (in 1370) a lease of the manors of West Court in Heytesbury, Colerne, and Stert (of which he was a feoffee) from the widow as life-tenant, and then (before 1381) manipulating a purchase of the Heytesbury portion from the daughter and heir, Elizabeth Baroness Despenser. [34] In the spring of 1382 West Court was settled on him and his wife in fee tail male. This, after he had successfully withstood a petition of Burghersh's widow made in the parliament of November 1381, charging him with falsity in undoing her life-interest (to the creation of which he had been party as a feoffee), and with maintenance and embracery in an attempt to render secure an unlawful entry which he had advised the Baroness Despenser to make (on the ground that her step-mother's life estate had never been properly effected). The charges of the petition and Hungerford's replications furnish further evidence of the closeness of Hungerford's relations with Lord Burghersh, including (in the former) a statement that being ' del conseil Monsr. Bartholomeu de Burghersh . . . . et pur estre de son conseil ' Hungerford had been granted for life (as a retaining fee) land worth 40 marks a year. Hunger-ford himself stated that the lands were worth only £20 a year, but he added that the grant had been made four years before Lord Burghersh's espousals with his second wife, the petitioner, which takes Hunger-ford's retainer in this capacity back at least to 1362. Hungerford was able to state that he could not answer for the actions of Burghersh's attorneys when the formalities of the enfeoffments creating a life-interest for his wife were in train, because at the time he was out of the neighbourhood, being in Hampshire and elsewhere about the business of the late bishop of Winchester to whom he was 'seneschal de ses terres'.[35]

This is the only reference we have to the fact of Hungerford's occudation of this office of steward of the lands of the See of Winchester during perhaps only the very latest years of the episcopate of William of Edington. A native of the Wiltshire manor of that name which belonged to the bishops of Salisbury, first a protégé of Adam Orleton, and later from 1341 to 1344 treasurer of the royal Household, then treasurer of the Exchequer from 1345 to 1356, and finally in November 1356 promoted to the custody of the great seal which he held for a little more than six years (that is, until February 1363), Edington was one of the great professional administrators of the Crown of the old ecclesiastical type of important civil servant. He had been elevated to the See of Winchester in May 1346. Twenty years later, almost to the day (10 May 1366) he was elected at the king's instance to the archbishopric of Canterbury on the death of Islip, but he was not well enough to accept this translation and, in fact, died on 7 or 8 October later in the same year.[36] Whether Hungerford came into touch with Edington through his connexion with the administrative system of the Black Prince, to whom Edington was himself closely attached as a member (in 1347) of his council and then (certainly in the years 1355-60) as his general attorney in England, or through his connexion (as steward of Salisbury) with Bishop Wyvill, it is impossible to say. Perhaps it was simply because of his own intrinsic ability, or because of the share he already enjoyed in the regulation of a highly complicated network of different interests to which a flair and instinct for business as a land-agent and governor of franchises was already giving him the entrée: to him that hath shall be given.

Hungerford's office as steward of the episcopal estates of Winchester under Edington certainly makes it easier to understand certain other of his connexions with this bishop. He was one of Edington's feoffees in some estates which the bishop settled on members of his own family, for example, in the manor of Baddesley (Hampshire) and a moiety of Timsbury (Somerset), which were entailed on the bishop's brother (John, then warden of the hospital of St. Cross near Winchester) with certain remainders in tail to others of his kindred. (Hungerford himself was a joint lessee of these manors for a term of 17 years.) He was also the bishop's feoffee in the manor of Coleshill, in an estate at Buscot, and in certain reversions of other property in Berkshire when, on 8 October 1366 (probably the day after Edington's death), a

royal licence was issued authorising these lands to be granted in mortmain to the Austin priory of ' Bonhommes ' into which (at the desire
of the Black Prince) the bishop, in 1358, had converted the college he
had founded in 1345 at his native place of Edington. [37] On the same
day as this royal licence was issued Edington's executors, of whom
Hungerford was one, were given the custody of the bishopric of
Winchester and of all the temporalities of the see during the vacancy,
the executors undertaking to pay £200 each month to the Exchequer. [38]
Less than two months later, however, the custody was entrusted (on
1 December 1366) to William of Wykeham, who had already at the
king's instance been elected to the see. [39] There is no evidence to suggest that Hungerford's office as land-steward to Edington was
continued under his successor in the bishopric of Winchester.

Compensations for the setback which the death of Edington doubtless occasioned were not, however, wanting. Indeed, one such had
already come Hungerford's way sometime before the bishop's death.
Lord Burghersh's niece was Countess of Salisbury, [40] and it may well
have been through his Burghersh connexion that Hungerford came
into the service of her husband, William Montagu, second Earl of
Salisbury, another founder-knight of the order of the Garter, who had
made heavy personal investments in Edward III's French wars and was
also a member of the royal council. On 1 January 1365, by an indenture written at his Wiltshire manor of Winterbourne Bassett, the earl had
appointed Hungerford to the office of steward of his lands of the earldom an an annual fee of 20 marks (plus expenses), which was to be
made up by a grant of all the earl's rent from an estate at Ashridge
(Berkshire), including the issues of the courts and hundreds, and £1 a
year from the manor of Amesbury (Wiltshire). The fee was to be
forthcoming even if Hungerford were unable to act as steward, provided that he continued to be the earl's retainer and counsellor. [41] The
appointment and grant were for life, and the Montagu connexion
certainly seems to have been maintained. On 4 July 1367 the earl made
formal complaint that his free warren at Swainstone (Isle of Wight) had
been trespassed upon and Hungerford was put on the resulting royal commission of oyer and terminer. When, in the parliament of 1371, the earl's
younger brother, John Lord Montagu, petitioned the King and Council
regarding the withdrawal of the feudal services and rent of the Wiltshire manors of Norton Bavant and Fifield Bavant due to his late uncle,
Bishop Grandison of Exeter, following a royal grant in free alms to
the prioress of Dartford, Hungerford was one of the two official com-

missioners appointed to make an inquest. Sometime before November 1384 a case was successfully brought before the court of the Constable and Marshal by the Earl of Salisbury against his brother (for breach of faith in detaining an indenture and statute merchant, the covenants of which Lord Montagu had infringed). When Lord Montagu appealed against the decree, Hungerford was one of four witnesses who were, the earl submitted, vital to his case.[42]

Though important for Hungerford this Montagu appointment of 1365 doubtless was at the time, it was not by any means a connexion exclusive of others. Hungerford still remained connected with Bishop Edington and attended to his interests after his death. His Burghersh attachment was still a powerful and seemingly very personal tie until at any rate 1369, and in the following year Hungerford strengthened his old link with Bishop Wyvill of Salisbury by taking up the stewardship of the cathedral city. But the best was yet to be. It is possible that before 1372 Hungerford was known to some of those who, locally if not regionally, helped manage and organise the great accumulation of estates, franchises, and other rights, upon the income from which were based the English and continental policies of their lord, John, Duke of Lancaster, *jure uxoris* King of Castile and Leon. Something has already been said of the long-standing association of the Hungerford family, especially of Thomas Hungerford's uncle, Sir Robert Hungerford, with the house of Lancaster. But in 1372 when first, surviving records show, Thomas Hungerford appears as a retainer of John of Gaunt, twenty years had passed since Sir Robert's death. And, in the meantime, there is no anticipation of the important part that Hungerford was now to play in the Lancastrian administration. John of Gaunt's first extant register, however, only begins in the previous year, 1371, and it is possible that Hungerford was already attached to the duke's service. The Hungerford family tradition apart, opportunities for contact between Hungerford and Lancaster (or those who acted for him) are not likely to have been wanting: Hungerford, as we have seen, had had dealings with Thomas Lord Ros of Helmsley, an important member of John of Gaunt's military retinue, and Walter Heywode, one of Hungerford's fellow custodians of the temporalities of Winchester in 1366, was the duke's steward in Wiltshire. However this may be, he was by this time a known man. His membership of other administrative systems, the Earl of Salisbury's, for instance, is only likely to have increased his political usefulness to the most powerful of his masters; his inclusion and promotion in the Lancastrian executive meant that potentially the web of Lancastrian influence was spun the further. As far as we can see, Hungerford's Lancastrian connexion, whenever it originated, now became and henceforward remained the central, focal one of his career.

What seems to make it less probable that Thomas Hungerford came freshly into the Lancastrian administration with his appointment on 13 August 1372 as ' chief steward and surveyor of all lands and lordships ' in Wales and in Surrey, Sussex, Hampshire Wiltshire, Berkshire, Dorset, Somerset, Gloucestershire, Devon, Cornwall, and Kent, is the fact that this office ' in itself was an innovation.' ' This district or bailiwick may have been formed then for the first time.'[43] A newcomer to the Lancastrian service is not likely to have been given such an appointment. At the same time Hungerford was made duchy steward of Kidwelly, on which lordship was charged his annual fee of £10; he was to receive an additional allowance of 3s. 4d. for each day of actual duty. On 18 June 1374 the Lancastrian receiver in the south was authorised to increase this daily allowance to 4s. as from the original date of the appointment.[44] Early in the following year, on 18 February 1375, Hungerford was appointed chief steward of the duke's lands and lordships south of the Trent, except in Derbyshire and Staffordshire. His fee was to be 100 marks a year and his daily allowance, when acting as a member of the duke's council or when engaged on other ducal business away from London and out of the household, was to be 6s. 8d., these payments being put to the charge of the duke's receiver in Hungerford's own county of Wiltshire. The chief stewardship, which he held at the duke's pleasure, Hungerford was to retain until 1393. Not until nearly five years after Hungerford's appointment (November 1379) was there to be a similarly unitary system provided for the duke's estates north of Trent, from which even then Lancashire was excluded. On the same day that Hungerford was made chief steward he was formally made a member of John of Gaunt's council. In view of the duke's intention to knight him, he was at the same time granted for life the constableship of the castle of Monmouth and the stewardships of Monmouth and the Three Castles (Grosmont, Skenfrith, and Whitecastle). Hungerford was, in fact, knighted sometime between his appointment and 5 March 1375, when he was about to leave England for Flanders with Lancaster, who was at the head of the English mission sent to negotiate for a peace with France at Ghent and then at Bruges.[45]

From this time forward it was probably his place in the Lancastrian administration which monopolized most of Sir Thomas Hungerford's attention. Thomas Walsingham, the monk-historian of the abbey of St. Albans, who was at this period very hostile in his attitude to Lancaster, when referring to Hungerford's election as speaker for the commons by a majority of the knights in what proved to be Edward III's last parliament (27 January to 2 March 1377) was able to describe him as 'miles duci familiarissimus, utpote senescallus ejus; qui nil aliud voluit quod pronunciaret admittere, quam quod scivit oculis sui domini complacere.'[46] There is no reason to question the 'familiarity'; his eldest son, Thomas, was also a member of the Lancastrian retinue.[47] Hungerford's Lancastrian connexion can only have been a very influential factor in his election as speaker. For it came about in a parliament whose main political object (and result) was to put the seal on Lancaster's already contrived reversal of the impeachments and other acts of its predecessor (the 'Good Parliament' of 1376), whose sessions had been so disagreeable to the duke and the court 'camarilla' that he was prepared to champion.

It was for the first time for over fourteen years that Hungerford sat in the commons. He had now been elected for Wiltshire as on earlier occasions. He was, of course, a figure of some importance in his own county as well as outside it. He had so far served on comparatively few royal commissions that had not been evoked by those with whom he was specially connected or that were not merely concerned with routine chancery inquiries into property or local complaints of trespasses. In July and November 1370, however, he had been a royal commissioner of array in Wiltshire, in July 1375 had been appointed to an oyer and terminer commission on the subject of the repair of Midford Bridge near Bath, a year later to an oyer and terminer following a complaint by the Dean and Chapter of Wells of breach of their rights of free warren at North Curry (Somerset). Moreover, since March 1361 he had continuously been a member of the commission of the peace for Wiltshire and, for a short time in the late 'sixties, had served as a justice of the peace in Hampshire, and from July 1374 to December 1375 in the same capacity in Somerset as well.[48] Apart from certain intervals (May 1380—February 1381, July 1389—June 1390, July 1391—June 1396) Hungerford was to be a continuing member of the commission for the peace in Wiltshire, and also in Somerset, acting here from July 1377 to March 1378, from May 1380 to July 1389, and from June 1390 until his death in 1397.[49]

His greater importance as duchy of Lancaster chief steward and the interest of his lord, John of Gaunt, probably account for the way in which, from the time of his speakership in 1377 until 1393, Sir Thomas Hungerford came regularly to sit in the commons for either Wiltshire or Somerset (in one instance, in the Salisbury parliament of 1384, actually for both), almost rhythmically alternating from one to the other, with the result that of the twenty-one parliaments which sat in this period of sixteen years he was knight of the shire in thirteen, and that only three years went by, in which parliament was in session, when he was not elected. Not only did his Lancastrian chief stewardship apparently involve Hungerford in more or less continuous parliamentary activity: it involved him in a multitude of multifarious commissions emanating from the royal as well as the ducal chancery, some of them relating to parts of the country far distant from Heytesbury or Farleigh Montfort, but capable of being discharged in the course of his pursuit of his obligations to the duke. On 20 May 1375, along with the duchy feodary in Wiltshire (Robert Toly), the duchy receiver in Gloucestershire who was also in this year the king's escheator in that county (John Sargeant), and others, Hungerford was put on a royal commission of inquiry into the seizure by force of arms at Whittington (Gloucestershire) of cattle belonging to some tenants of the duke of Lancaster's manor of Aldbourne (Wiltshire). and the detention in the Dominican friary at Gloucester of some of the tenants who had brought an action for novel disseisin regarding a holding in Whittington. The scene of this inquiry was comparatively handy for Hungerford. The appointment of the Lancastrian chief stewards to membership of the royal commissions of the peace in the shires of their bailiwick, a position which was to be regularized by statute in 1416, seems to have been adumbrated in Hungerford's case before the end of Edward III's reign, although merely now and then and merely here and there.

It can only have been as duchy chief steward that on 5 March 1377 (three days after he relinquished his speaker's office) Hungerford was appointed justice of the peace throughout Lincolnshire, where John of Gaunt himself headed the commissions, and he was re-appointed at the beginning of Richard II's reign; he did not, however, figure on the next commission issued in May 1380. Similarly in Norfolk he was made a justice of the peace on 5 May 1377 and, although he was not re-appointed in the following November, he was appointed again in February 1378; as in the case of Lincolnshire he dropped out in May 1380. In neither case was he again included. He was even for a time, by the duke's own warrant of 8 August 1379, a justice in Lancashire which was not, of course, even in his jurisdiction as chief steward.[50] In the meantime, on 4 March 1377, the day before his appointment as justice of the peace in the Lincolnshire ridings, he was made a commissioner for sewers in the parts of Holland in south Lincolnshire. In February 1381 he was put on the same sort of royal commission in Lindsey (where he was again appointed in April 1383), a day or two later for the Sussex coast in the neighbourhood of the duchy lordship of Pevensey (where, and for further along the coast into Kent, he was again commissioned in July 1389 and February 1390), and by a patent of November 1382 at various places in the Isle of Ely in Cambridgeshire.[51] In these commissions he doubtless represented the duchy interest. How far he himself sought representation by deputies, it is not possible to say. To some of his commissions he can only have given a perfunctory attention.

As a member of the duke's council during these years as well as his chief administrative agent in southern England, Sir Thomas Hungerford must have spent some of his time at the palace of the Savoy between the City and Westminster. He was, for example, present in the chapel of the Savoy on 17 April 1377 when a royal chancery clerk, Thomas Thelwall, was there appointed chancellor ' in the duchy and county of Lancaster ' and solemnly, by the duke himself, given custody of the great seal ordained ' pro regimine regalitatis comitatus palatini '; this was seven weeks after the restoration by Edward III of the county's earlier palatine status (formerly enjoyed 1351-61) during the course of the recent parliament when Hungerford was speaker. The closeness of Sir Thomas's attachment to Lancaster is further evinced by the fact that when, on 26 July 1378, a royal letter patent was granted to the the duke allowing his executors the custody for a year of all his estates in the event of his death, Hungerford for the first time appeared among them, along with other important household and duchy officials, including the duke's chamberlain, his steward and controller of household, his chief of council, his receiver-general, and his chancellor.[52]

Among the increasing number of royal commissions on which in the next decade or so Hungerford was appointed to serve, several that were of peculiar Lancastrian interest can be detected, apart from the commissions of the peace and of sewers outside the region of his own landed interests. On 22 May 1382, for example, he was put on a royal commission of oyer and terminer, along with (among others) Justice Skipwith, following a complaint from the duke of breach of his free warren in four of his Norfolk manors where damage, loss of livestock (worth 200 marks), and burning of charters had occurred. What is referred to here is a series of incidents in the peasants' risings in western Norfolk during the great revolt of June 1381. The same commissioners were appointed by a patent of two days later to hold another oyer and terminer regarding a complaint by Corpus Christi College, Cambridge (of which John of Gaunt was patron), of a riotous entry into the college during the rising and of the spoiling of the college, which resulted in the destruction and removal of some of its muniments when its common chest and other coffers were broken open.[53] Hungerford seems to have been representing the duchy interest when he was appointed on 16 June 1384 to a general government inquiry into felonies and trespasses and concealments of feudal incidents in the rape of Pevensey and elsewhere in Sussex, and to a similar inquiry in Gloucestershire into felonies and trespasses in March 1387; his fellow commissioners in Gloucestershire included the duchy deputy-steward in the county (Thomas de Brugge). Within less than a week of the end of his service as shire-knight in the first parliament of 1390, Sir Thomas was appointed (by patent of 6 March 1390) to a royal commission of oyer and terminer after the Duke of Lancaster's complaint (by petition in parliament) that the exercise of the franchises arising out of his hereditary keepership of the castle and bailey of Lincoln had for the last five years been impeded by the mayor and bailiffs of the city; the duke had alleged that the infringement of his officers' right to entertain presentments arising out of the assize of bread had alone cost him £1,000. Sir Philip Tilney of Tydd (Lincolnshire), knight of the shire for Lincolnshire in the recent session and at this time chief steward of the duchy north of Trent, and Thomas Pinchbek, late chief baron of the royal exchequer and now duchy chief steward in Lancashire (and, three years later, Hungerford's successor as chief steward of the duchy south of Trent), were also members of the commission. In this same parliament the bishop, dean and chapter of Lincoln had complained of detrimental acts on the part of the civic authorities regarding the collection of their rents in the city, and the dean and chapter followed this up by objecting to interference by the mayor and bailiffs with their sole jurisdiction over cases arising out of contracts made by merchants within the cathedral close, which had involved them in an alleged loss of £1,000. The same commissioners, including Hungerford, were appointed for the oyer and terminer set up on 11 May 1390 to deal with this last complaint.[54]

Occasionally, Hungerford's Lancastrian connexion led to his standing surety in the royal Exchequer for members of the ducal retinue and administration when they were granted the right to farm estates that were under the Exchequer's control. When in May 1381, for example, Sir John Marmion secured a renewal of his custody of the Yorkshire and Wiltshire estates of a royal ward (at a reduced rent), Hungerford was one of his mainpernors; Marmion was a Lancastrian retainer and steward of Knaresborough at this time. When the alien priory of Deerhurst (Gloucestershire) and its estates were re-let (at an increased rent) in February 1383, Hungerford was a surety for the small syndicate that collectively replaced the prior as farmers; the re-letting was done by John of Gaunt's special advice, and of the three new farmers, one (Richard de Burley) was duchy steward in Gloucestershire and another (Hugh Vaughan) was a clerk in Lancastrian employment.[55]

Some of Hungerford's royal commissions came to him virtually because of his place in the Lancastrian administration, but in these years of his chief stewardship he was appointed to act on many more of a purely local character and unconnected with his office. And his inclusion probably arose simply and generally out of the fact that he was himself one of the foremost of the notables of Wiltshire and Somerset, and a justice of the peace in these counties. He was, for example, a commissioner of array in Wiltshire in April and July 1377 when there was a threat of French raids from the Channel. On 1 September 1377 he was one of a royal commission of inquiry into cases in Wiltshire of tenants banding together to refuse to perform the services and payments customarily due to their lords and to resist the lawful distraints of their lords' bailiffs (under colour of exemplifications of extracts from Domesday Book); the commissioners were empowered to demand surety or, alternatively, commit to gaol. Similar authority was being given to commissions in Surrey and Hampshire, and in Richard II's first parliament the commons made general complaint on this subject and an ordinance safeguarding seigneurial rights resulted. In the spring of 1378 Hungerford was one of a commission of oyer and terminer empowered to take indictments of those Wiltshire bond-tenants of the Abbess of Shaftesbury who were refusing their services and to imprison them. On 20 March 1380 Hungerford was again made a royal commissioner of array in Wiltshire.[56]   Nothing is known of his movements during the Peasant's Revolt which was characterised by a fervid hostility to John of Gaunt and resulted in much damage to his property (including the destruction of his palace of the Savoy along with most of the duchy muniments) and damage to the property of some of his household and administration. But on 14 December 1381, at a time when he was being attacked in parliament for his sharpness in acquiring the Burghersh estate in Heytesbury, Hungerford was included in the Somerset and Wiltshire commissions for keeping the peace which were given powers to arrest for incitement and unlawful assembly and to put down rebels with armed force. He was re-appointed to similar commissions in these areas in March and December 1382, now with powers of oyer and terminer. In March 1383 Sir Thomas was made one of a commission appointed to survey the Avon between Bath and Bristol with a view to removing weirs and other impediments to river traffic; a previous commission, appointed in the previous reign following a parliamentary petition by the commons of Somerset and Wiltshire, had been ineffectual. [57]

On 10 May 1385 Hungerford was made one of a commission to inquire how it had come about that sixteen of the bishop of Salisbury's tenants in the manor of Bishop's Cannings (Wiltshire) were assessed by the collectors of parliamentary subsidies with the men of Burton (where they lived) and Easton and not with the men of Cannings, as had been the case until sometime during Edward III's reign. In April 1386 Hungerford was put on a royal commission charged to investigate the alienation of an estate in his own place of Heytesbury which ought to have escheated to the Crown because of the tenant's idiocy, an inquiry which was still pending in July 1390 when Hungerford was again a commissioner. Presumably in the summer of 1386 he was a commissioner for the array of archers in Wiltshire when a French invasion from the Low Countries was a serious threat, and on 28 January 1387 he was put on the Wiltshire commission of oyer and terminer ordered to inquire into the embezzlement by local bailiffs and constables of the archers' wages that were levied on the townships although the archers had never reached their appointed rendezvous. On 18 March 1387 he was one of several commissioners ordered to report into Chancery on the threats offered at Salisbury to a king's clerk, John Chitterne, a prebendary there who had been thereby prevented from prosecuting the king's suit to recover the presentation to the church of St. Thomas the Martyr in the city, pending which suit the king had presented him. Some three months later, at the end of June, he was made a commissioner for sewers in Somerset. On 18 July he was authorised to assist in an inquiry into the complaint of Sir Peter de Courtenay of certain trespasses at his place at Newton St. Loe (Somerset), including the breaking of his seal of arms. Five days later he was commissioned by Chancery to inquire into wastes in the manor of Stower Provost (Dorset), an estate of the Norman nunnery of St. Leger at Préaux then in the king's hands. (In 1394 Hungerford successfully resisted the Exchequer's process against him as a commissioner on the grounds that the letter patent of 23 July 1387 never reached him.)[58]

These last few were the only commissions that Sir Thomas Hungerford was appointed to serve during the perilous eighteen months which followed the impeachment of the Earl of Suffolk in October 1386, a crisis which saw the government of the country put into the control of a parliamentary commission regarded as treasonable by Richard II, the coming to power of the Lords Appellant, and the bloody proscriptions of the Merciless Parliament of 1388. It had been, of course, John of Gaunt's departure from England for Spain in the summer of 1386 which had made possible this head-on collision between the King's curialist party and the pseudo-constitutional country party of magnates headed by Thomas of Woodstock and the Arundels. The Duke of Lancaster's domestic policies from the beginning of the reign until his three years absence from England had frequently been equivocal, but Richard's support of Lancaster's views on policy towards France would always have ensured the latter's loyalty, had there not been more normal reasons. But Lancaster's heir, Henry of Bolingbroke, became one of the Appellants and hostile to the court party, and Hungerford had his connexions with Henry: in the critical year, 1387-8, he was his receiver in the Wiltshire manor of Upavon. But in July 1387 he was still an active member of John of Gaunt's council in England, and doubtless his administrative preoccupations as well as his age enabled him to play an unobtrusive rôle so far as the political issues of the day were concerned.[59] He had sat in the parliament which impeached Suffolk in 1386; he did not secure election to the Merciless Parliament of February 1388. It is probable, however, that he sympathized with the aims of the Appellants. With a supporter of theirs, one of those bishops who in 1388 were complacently translated by Urban VI to more profitable dioceses, Ralph Erghum, who now left Salisbury for the See of Bath and Wells (and so remained Hungerford's diocesan), Hungerford had had a long-standing connexion. He had been, of course, episcopal bailiff of Salisbury for life from the time of Erghum's predecessor. Moreover, Erghum had been John of Gaunt's chancellor until his elevation to the episcopate in 1375 and a fellow ducal executor of Hungerford's, Hungerford's co-feoffee to William Lord Botreaux, and Hungerford's own feoffee in the most important of his Somerset manors.[60] On the day after the original three Appellants laid their accusations before the King at Westminster on 18 November 1387, Bishop Erghum and Sir Ivo Fitz Waryn were bound over in Chancery to keep the peace towards each other; Hungerford was one of four knights who found surety for the bishop under pain of 4,000 marks. There was probably some political animus in this vendetta; Fitz Waryn's sureties were members of the royal Household. Hungerford himself may well have been regarded by the King as politically unreliable. Since 1361 he had been a justice of the peace in Wiltshire and since 1374 in Somerset. Occasionally he had been dropped from the commissions of the peace in these counties, but his omissions had been short-lived and never from both commissions together. Now, after Richard II's own coup d'état of May 1389, Hungerford was excluded in the following July from the office of justice of the peace in both counties at once. His omission was as before, however, of short duration. He was put back on both commissions again within a year, at the end of June 1390, and stayed there.

By this time, of course, John of Gaunt had returned from Spain.[61] It was just before his re-instatement as justice of the peace that Hungerford served on the Lincoln commissions in which Lancaster's interests were among those at stake. After these he was appointed to no other royal commission of a special character, except one in October 1391 to hear and determine an appeal on the part of a citizen of Salisbury against the sentence of a maritime court.[62] He must now have been at least well turned sixty years of age. In January 1393 he sat for the last (and sixteenth time) as knight of the shire. In the same year he retired from his Lancastrian chief stewardship. He continued to act as episcopal bailiff of Salisbury, however, apparently until the end, having a life interest in the office. On 19 September 1397 he had a royal letter patent by which the King undertook to repay him a loan of 100 marks within a fortnight of Easter following.[63] It was, of course, only one among many loans that Richard II took up in this time of the beginning of the second tyranny. Hungerford's executors must have had the recovery of the loan as one of their duties. For Sir Thomas died on 3 December 1397. He was buried in the chapel of St. Anne in the parish church of St. Leonard at Farleigh Montfort, where some fourteen years later his widow, who survived him until 21 March 1412, was also to be buried.

A week after his death letters went out from the royal Chancery ordering the escheators in Somerset, Wiltshire, and Gloucestershire to take into the king's hands Hungerford's estates in their bailiwicks and to proceed with the usual formalities of inquest regarding them and the heir. Hungerford's heir was his elder son by his second wife: Walter, who had been born about midsummer 1378. He was the only one of Sir Thomas's sons to survive their father. Sir Thomas had already on 8 October 1396 covenanted for Walter's marriage to Katherine, daughter of Thomas Peverell by Margaret, a daughter of Sir Thomas Courtenay of Southpool and granddaughter of Hugh Courtenay, first Earl of Devon. Walter was still a minor at his father's death but sufficiently nearly of age to make the wardship an unprofitable one to farm, especially in view of the heir's marriage having already been contracted; there is no record that Hungerford's estates were farmed out by the Exchequer. That Walter was still not quite of full age at his father's death probably accounts for his not being one of Sir Thomas's executors. To administer his will the latter had appointed his wife, Joan, and John Snappe, doctor of decrees, an advocate of the court of Canterbury, rector of Pewsey in the diocese of Salisbury, and a kinsman. The will was proved in the Prerogative Court of Canterbury on 6 June 1403.[64]

Sir Thomas had himself as long ago as 1365 amortized lands to the house of Bonhommes at Edington (with which he had a connexion as feoffe and executor to Bishop Edington of Winchester, its founder) for the keeping of his obit, and the obits of his then wife, his father, mother and uncle. As late as May 1397 he and John Marreys (parliamentary burgess for Bath in 1395 and January 1397) had royal licence to alienate in mortmain the reversion of certain messuages and lands which he held for life in Farleigh, Farleigh Wick, and Allington by Chippenham to the Cluniac priory of Monkton Farleigh in aid of a chantry. But the chantry in the church of his burial at Farleigh Montfort his heir did not found until 1426[65], the year in which he, Sir Thomas Hungerford's only surviving son, entered the ranks of the parliamentary peerage. The first Lord Hungerford was to serve his family well, but its aggrandisement rested squarely on the foundation of the policies, acquisitions, and administrative connexions of his father, Sir Thomas Hungerford.

FOOTNOTES

These abbreviations will be used:

C.C.R.—Calendar of Close Rolls.
C.P.R.—Calendar of Patent Rolls.
C.F.R.—Calendar of Fine Rolls.
Cal. Inq. p.m.—Calendar of Inquisitions post mortem.
C.Ch.R.—Calendar of Charter Rolls.
Rot. Parl.—Rotuli Parliamentorum.
H.M.C.—Historical Manuscrips Commission.
D.K.R.—Reports of the Deputy Keeper of the Public Records.

1 *Official Return of Members of Parliament*, vol. I, 160, 165, 171, 197, 200, 203, 205, 207, 211, 219, 221, (for his service in the parliament of April 1384 which was held at Salisbury, Hungerford was paid as knight of the shire for Wiltshire; only his fellow-knight of the shire for Somerset, Sir William Bonville, received a writ *de expensis* for payment in that county, *C.C.R., 1381-5*, 454), 230, 235, 239 (although Hungerford was apparently at first returned for Somerset to the parliament of January 1390, he was not one of the two knights of the shire who sued out writs *de expensis*, and was paid only for his service as knight for Wiltshire, *C.C.R., 1389-92*, 179), 240, 246.

2 Hoare, *Wiltshire*, vol. 1, part, 2, 113; his other chantries were at Stanley abbey, Easton priory, the church of St. Mary, Salisbury, and the church of St. Mary, Calne; that Sir Robert lived at Hungerford is clear from *C.P.R., 1327-30*, 280.

3 *Catalogue of Ancient Deeds*, VI. C 6870; Nicholas does not find a place in the Hungerford pedigree compiled by Hoare (*op. cit.*, vol. 1, part 2, 117), but his pedigree is transparently not complete.

4 *C.C.R., 1318-23*, 472; ibid.,*1327-30*, 67; *C.P.R., 1327-30*, 106, 425. *Ancient Deeds*, VI. C 7449; it is the continuing Lancastrian connexion which accounts for Sir Robert's employment (in 1334) as a justice in eyre in the Lancastrian forest of Pickering (Yorkshire), for his association with the forest eyre in Lancashire(in 1336) and with the commission of inquiry there (in 1342) into frauds in the collection of the king's wool and into official abuses, and (in the next year) for his appointment as one of the overseers for the defence of the salmon of the four main Lancashire rivers of Lune, Wyre, Ribble, and Mersey (*C.P.R., 1334-,8*, 2, 261; ibid., *1338-40*, 246; ibid., *1340-43*, 25, 586-7; ibid., *1343-5*, 87, 172).

5 *C.P.R., 1354-8*, 308-9; *Cal. Inq. p.m.* (1821), iii, 217; for Sir Robert's stewardship of the bishopric of Bath and Wells, see *The Register of Ralph of Shrewsbury, Bishop of Bath and Wells, 1329-63*, ed. T. S. Holmes, 109, 136.

6 Hoare, *op. sit.*, ii. 698; *Official Return*, 97, 103, 112; P.R.O., *List of Escheators*, 159; *C.C.R., 1341-3 28*; ibid; *1346-9*, 102; *C.P.R., 1350-4*, 92.

7 Hoare, *op. cit.*, V. 2, 27; for Sir John Strug, see *C.F.R., 1319-27*, 168; *C.P.R., 1321-4*, 197; ibid., *1327-30*, 77; *C.C.R., 1323-7*, 27. The Contrariants were those who sided with Thomas, Earl of Lancaster, against Edward II. in 1322.

8 Hoare, *op. cit.*, IV. part 1, 110, 203; *Cal. of Papal Registers, Papal Petitions*, 1. 531; ibid., *Papal Letters*, IV. 220; *C.C.R., 1374-7, 362*.

9 *C.P.R.*, *1485-94*, 145-6; *C.C.R.*, *1377-81*, 137; *C.Ch.R.*, V. 297; *Cal. Inq. p.m.*, III. 217; Hoare, *op. cit.*, vol. IV, part 1, 110, 203.

10 Hoare, *op. cit.*, vol. I, part 2, 89; III. 217; *C.P.R.*, *1485-94*, 145-6; *C.C.R.*, *1381-5*, 420; *ibid.*, *1396-9*, 275; *C.Ch.R.*, V. 297; *Cal. Inq. p.m.* (1821); *Feudal Aids*, IV. 377.

11 Hoare, *op. cit.*, vol. I, part 2, 89.

12 *ibid.*, V. 29; *H.M.C.*, *Report on MSS. of R.R. Hastings*, I. 227; *Cals. of Inquisitions post mortem for the reign of Edward III* (H.M. Stationery Office), XI. 403; *C.C.R.*, *1374-7*, 362; *C.Ch.R.*, V. 297; *C.P.R.*, *1385-9*, 380; *Cal. Inq. p.m.* (1821), III. 217. Margaret, widow of William Lord Ros, acquired East Court, being the eldest of the four daughters of Bartholomew Lord Badlesmere and sister and coheir of Giles Lord Badlesmere, who died without issue in 1338.

13 Hoare, *op. cit.*, vol. I, part 2, 87-9; *ibid.*, V. 30 (Hungerford's lease of 1370 from Margaret, widow of Bartholomew Lord Burghersh, comprised the manors of Colerne and Stert as well as West Court Heytesbury at a rent of 200 marks a year); *C.P.R.*, *13811-5*, 121; *ibid.*, *1485-94*, 145-6; *C.Ch.R.*, V. 297; *Rot. Parl.*, III. 109. This last reference is to the petition presented in the parliament of 1381 in the king's own presence by Sir William Burcestre and his wife, Margaret, formerly wife of the Bartholomew Lord Burghersh who died on 5 April 1369. It alleged that Sir Thomas Hungerford as one of Lord Burghersh's feoffees in West Court Heytesbury, Colerne, and Stert, and other land had been charged by him to make a re-enfeoffment which would give his wife (Margaret) a life interest in these estates, that this had been done, that on Burghersh's death she had had livery out of the king's hand, and that Hungerford himself had received her fealty. Subsequently Hungerford had leased the estates and had undertaken to defend her interests if she discharged her other retained counsel, which he advised her to do. He was then alleged to have informed Burghersh's daughter and heir, Elizabeth Lady Despenser, that her father had died *sole* seised and that the estates were therefore hers to enter. Whereupon after these acts of ' procurement, covine et malice ' Hungerford ' bargained ' the manor of Heytesbury (West Court). The petitioners further complained of the ' grant maintenance ' of Hungerford and others of his 'affynyte' in Wiltshire and of his abuse of his office of J.P. to prevent the establishment of their right. Hungerford was required to answer to the bill in parliament. He pleaded that relating to the re-enfeoffments to secure Margaret a life interest he had only a common responsibility with his co-feoffees and that, in any case, he was absent when they were put in charge, that he did not undertake to act as retained counsel to Margaret, that he did not remember taking her fealty by royal command (according to a Close Roll memorandum of 15 June 1369 he did in fact do so), that he farmed the manors at Margaret's request and on terms favourable to her, that later he merely advised Lady Despenser to ascertain from the inhabitants of the manors the truth of her father's estate at his death before even she took steps to secure an entry, that he was himself no maintainer or embracer of quarrels, that he had no estate in fee or reversionary interest in Heytesbury (West Court), and that any declaration he had made on Lady Despenser's behalf at the Wiltshire sessions in support of her claim was in defence of his good name after he had been slandered in a county court at Wilton by Sir William Burcestre and his men. That Hungerford's influence over his fellow members of the Wiltshire

bench was, in fact, considerable is suggested by the issue on 21 May 1381 of a royal writ of *supersedeas* to the justices of the peace in Wiltshire in favour of Sir William Burcestre, who was in fear of imprisonment until he should find security to do no hurt or harm to Sir Thomas Hungerford (*C.C.R., 1377-81 523*).

14 *C.C.R., 1369-74*, 280-1; *C.P.R., 1485-94*, 145-6; *C.Ch.R.*, V. 297.

15 Hoare, *op. cit.*, V. 29.

16 *C.Ch.R.*, V. 297; *Cal. Inq. p.m.* (1821), III. 217.

17 *C.P.R., 1377-81*, 428; *ibid., 1391-6*, 636.

18 *Cal. Inq. p.m.* (1821) iii. 217.

19 *C.Ch.R.*, V. 297.

20 See *C.P.R., 1381-5*, 340, for the royal pardon of 26 November 1383 for crenellation without licence. But cf. P.R.O., Ancient Petitions, S.C. 8, file 226, no. 11256, for his request for a licence to enclose with wall of stone and lime, embattle, tower, and enfoss, without fine or fees to pay. Hoare (*op. cit.* vol. 1, part 2, p. 89) says that he was fined 1,000 marks for fortifying without licence.

21 *C.P.R., 1485-94*, 145-6.

22 *C.C.R., 1349-54*, 144; for Henry de Walton, see R. Somerville, *History of the Duchy of Lancaster*, 1, 358.

23 *C.P.R., 1350-54*, 59, 451; P.R.O., *Lists and Indexes*, IX, *List of Sheriffs*, 153; P.R.O., *List of Escheators*, 177.

24 *C.P.R., 1354-8*, 419; the dean's deputy and chapter of Salisbury confirmed the appointment, and on 14 July 1356 Hungerford secured a royal *inspeximus* and confirmation under the great seal.

25 *C.P.R., 1367-70*, 30; the deputy-dean and chapter's ratification was dated 28 November 1370 and a royal *inspeximus* and confirmation, 22 January 1371; Hoare, *op. cit.*, Salisbury; Benson and Hatcher, II. 698 (list of episcopal bailiffs of Salisbury). The office had been held by Thomas Hungerford's father, Walter. Thomas had other connexions with the city. He was not the same man as the Thomas Hungerford who was mayor of Salisbury in 1351-2, but this Thomas was doubtless a relative (*Ancient Deeds*, VI. C 5292; *C.P.R., 1350-54*, 216. cf *ibid., 1354-8*, 308-9). Thomas was still occupying the office of bailiff of the city in 1393 and 1397 (*Ancient Deeds*, 1. B 1465; V. A 12038). He had been executor to a former parliamentary burgess, Henry Russell, in 1357 (*C.P.R., 1354-8*, 630).

26 *C.P.R., 1354-8*, 613: *ibid., 1358-61*, 303.

27 *C.P.R., 1358-61*, 245, 419. Hungerford was made, in July 1361, a commissioner of inquiry regarding suit from Norton Bavant to the hundred court of Warminster (*ibid., 1361-4*, 73); on 18 June 1371 he was appointed to another royal commission relating to Norton Bavant (and, this time, Fifield Bavant) after John Lord Montague, nephew of Bishop Grandison of Exeter, had petitioned in the previous parliament for a rectification of the royal grant in free alms to the priory of Dartford, which had not included provision for the rendering of the proper feudal services and rent to the bishop and his heirs. But Hungerford was by this time connected with the Earl of Salisbury, Lord Montagu's elder brother (*ibid., 1370-4*, iii.)

28 *Register of Edward the Black Prince*, IV. 434, 529-30, in succession to John Alveton, 9 times knight of the shire for Oxfordshire 1332-52 (*ibid.*, 378, 387);

the primary duty of the under-steward was to hold the prince's courts and leets in the honours.

29 *ibid.*, IV. 546; *C.P.R, 1367-70,227*; in May 1375 Aubrey de Vere became-steward of the honours of Wallingford and St. Valery, and with him Hungerford had no known tie at all.

30 Sir Walter Paveley of Hilperton (Wiltshire), founder-knight of the order of the Garter like his cousin, Burghersh, was one of the knights bachelor of the Black Prince's retinue (see *Register*, IV. 380, 384; Beltz, *Order of the Garter,sub nomine*); on 30 April 1364 Paveley, going overseas, nominated his cousin, Burghersh, and Hungerford as two of his four attorneys in England for a year (*C.P.R., 1361-4, 489.*)

31 *C.P.R., 1364-7*, 111, 114, 160; *C.C.R., 1364-8*, 178-9; *C.P.R., 1364-7*, 148.

32 T. Rymer, *Foedera*, VI. 510; *Cal. of Papal Registers, Papal Petitions*, 1. 531. It is not stated in the *Calendar* whether Hungerford was successful in obtaining his indult ;on 30 March 1376 he was to obtain a papal privilege to choose his own confessor, and on 12 April he and his second wife (Joan) were given an indult to have a portable alter (*ibid., Papal Letters*, IV. 220).

33 Lambeth Palace Library, Whittlesey Register, fo. 98. The will, dated on 4 April 1369, was proved on 27 April in the Prerogative Court of Canterbury, letters of administration being issued to Hungerford and Gildsborough who were executors along with the widow, Sir Walter Paveley, and two clerks of standing, one of them William Steel, Burghersh's own clerk, who was archdeacon of Totnes.

34 See above p. 276 and note 13. The dowager Baroness Burghersh remained as life-tenant in the manors of Colerne and Stert, the reversion of which was granted in 1387 by the Baroness Despenser to William of Wykeham and his feoffees for his foundation of New College, Oxford (*C.P.R., 1385-9, 368*).

35 *Rot. Parl.*, iii. 109-11.

36 T. F. Tout, *Chapters*, III. *passim*.

37 *C.P.R., 1367-70*, 17. Master John Edington, in September 1368 when going overseas, made Hungerford one of his attorneys (*ibid.* 152). *Ibid., 1364-7*, 310; the only other foundation of 'Bonhommes' in England was the one founded by the Black Prince himself at Ashridge (Bucks.) Hungerford was still involved as late as September 1392 in the endowment of the Edington establishment (*ibid., 1391-6*, 156); in 1365 he had himself granted it lands for the celebration of the obits of some members of his family and his own (see note 65).

38 *C.F.R., 1356-68,339*; Hungerford was still acting as executor, along with the others who still survived, in June 1374 (*C.P.R., 1370-4, 439*). One of the group, John de Blewbury of Shellingford (Berkshire), who because of the vacancy was presented by the king on 6 December 1366 to the episcopal living of Witney (Oxfordshire, diocese of Lincoln), died early in 1372, when Hungerford was one of his executors and feoffees (*ibid.*, 187, 437). Hungerford's interest in the custody of the Winchester temporalities and the stewardship, which doubtless he was still retaining, would account for his inclusion in a royal commission of oyer and terminer appointed on 2 November 1366 to investigate breaches of the episcopal parks in Hampshire (*ibid., 1364-7, 364*).

39 *C.P.R.*, *1364-7*, 353; the custody was granted to Wykeham for a great sum paid into the Chamber. The see had already (on Edington's death) been reserved by Urban V who, on 11 December 1366, invested Wykeham with the administration of the see in spirituals and temporals. Not until 14 July 1367 did the pope provide Wykeham as bishop-elect, and not until 12 October did the king invest him with the temporalities as bishop by papal provision, two days after his consecration at St. Paul's. His enthronement at Winchester only took place on 9 July 1368. By this time Wykeham had been chancellor of England for the best part of a year.

40 Salisbury, after his divorce from Joan of Kent, married Elizabeth, eldest daughter of John Lord Mohun of Dunster (a member of the Black Prince's household) by Joan, sister of the Lord Burghersh who died in 1369 (see *Complete Peerage, sub nomine*).

41 *C.P.R.*, *1364-7*, 169; the appointment received the royal *inspeximus* and confirmation by letter patent, on 26 October 1365, following the payment of a fine of £10 into the hanaper of Chancery.

42 *ibid.*, 447; *ibid.*, *1370-4*, 111; *ibid.*, *1381-5*, 510. When this case was pending Lord Montagu was steward of the royal Household. On 29 November 1384 a commission of magnates was specially appointed to examine Hungerford and other witnesses of the earl, who were all old men and, so the earl feared, likely to be unable to appear at the hearing of the case. After a series of commissions to hear and determine Lord Montagu's appeal, the decree of the Court of Chivalry was eventually upheld (*ibid.*, 507, 509, 584, 587; *ibid.*, *1385-9*, 67, 375).

43 R. Somerville, *Duchy of Lancaster*, I. 113.

44 Royal Historical Society, Camden 3rd Series, vols. XX-XXI *John of Gaunt's Register*, ed. S. Armitage-Smith, vol. I, 114; he was also apparently joint-steward in Herefordshire by May 1373 (*ibid.*, vol. 2, 181; *ibid.*, 213).

45 *ibid.*, vol. I. 153-5 (Hungerford was already steward of Kidwelly); R. Somerville, *op. cit.*, 113-4, 117, 119, 367. For the first reference to Hungerford as a knight, see *The Register*, vol. 2. 325, confirmed by *C.C.R.* 1374-7, 241; *C.P.R.*, *1374-7*, 122.

46 *Chronicon Anglie*, ed. E. M. Thompson (Rolls Series). 112.

47 Royal Historical Society, Camden 3rd Series, vols. LVI-VII, *John of Gaunt's Register*, *1379-1383*, ed. E. C. Lodge and R. Somerville vol. I, 8; Monsire Thomas Hungerford le fitz (the Speaker's son by his first wife) soon died but not before November 1383. He was almost certainly the Sir Thomas Hungerford who as a young knight bachelor accompanied Sir William Windsor (the husband of Edward III's mistress, Alice Perrers) when the latter joined the expedition of Thomas of Woodstock into France and Brittany in 1380-1 (Exchequer, Accounts Various, P.R.O., E 101/39/7.)

48 *C.P.R.*, *1361-4*, 63, 528; *ibid.*, *1364-7*, 205, 429, 434; *ibid.*, *1367-70*, 192, 444; *ibid.*, *1370-4*, 34, 478; *ibid.*, *1374-7*, 139, 154, 157, 327.

49 *C.P.R., passim.*

50 *C.P.R.*, *1374-7*, 154, 157; 490; *ibid.*, *1377-81*, 46, 96; *D.K.R.*, XLIII. 363; On two occasions when he sat among the commons, in the successive parliaments of January and November 1380, his fellow executor and feoffee to Lord Burghersh, John Gildsborough, was speaker for the commons; Hungerford

was one of Gildsborough's feoffees at Wennington (Essex) as late as April 1388 and probably up to Gildsborough's death (*C.C.R.*, *1385-9*, 632).

A feodary was a local official whose duties were similar to those of a royal escheator, namely, to look after wardships and escheats.

51 *C.P.R.*, *1374-7*, 485; *ibid.*, *1377-81*, 576; *ibid.*, *1388-92.*, 132-3, 200-1.

52 *D.K.R.*, XXXII. 348; *C.P.R.*, *1377-81*, 262. Lancaster had first appointed a group of executors in February 1369 which had not undergone much change by May 1373 (*ibid.*, *1367-70*, 212-3; *ibid.*, *1370-4*, 279), but between then and July 1378 there had occurred some notable additions to the executorial body and withdrawals from it; Hungerford was one of the new members.

53 *C.P.R.*, *1381-5*, 143-4 (Skipwith, as well as being secondary in the Court of Common Pleas was also the duke's chief justice at Lancaster and a member of his council); the rebels clearly included Lancastrian tenantry for, in pursuance of their commission, Skipwith and Hungerford levied fines, some of which went to the duke (*Register*, *1379-83*, vol. 2, 273).

54 *C.P.R.*, *1381-5*, 429; *ibid.*, *1385- 9*, 322; *ibid.*, *1388-92*, 220, 270; Somerville, *op. cit.*, I. 367.

55 *C.F.R.*, *1377-83*, 248, 351; in February 1378 Hungerford had been a surety for two chaplains who became farmers of the alien priory of Avebury and its estates (*ibid.*, 83).

56 *C.P.R.*, *1374-7*, 498; *ibid.*, *1377-81*, 38; 50 (*Rot. Parl.*, III 21 b), 24, 251, 254 (similar commissions to those procured by the Abbess of Shaftesbury, who took out another commission for her recalcitrant Dorset tenantry, were sued out by the Abbot of Chertsey (Surrey) and by the Prior of Bath); 473.

57 *ibid.*, *1381-5*, 85, 140-1, 248, 259.

58 *C.P.R.*, *1381-5*, 598; *ibid.*, *1385-89*, 177, 315; 320, 283, 384, 386-7; *ibid.*, *1388-92*, 346; *C.C.R.*, *1392-6*, 375.

59 Duchy of Lancaster, Accounts Various, P.R.O., D.L. 28/1/2/; Hungerford by 1391 was farming this manor of the Earl of Derby at 40 marks a year (*ibid.*, 3/3); *John of Gaunt's Register*, *1379-83*, *op cit.*, ii. 407 where, in the duke's letters from Castile, he is among those addressed as members of the ducal council in England.

60 *C.P.R.*, *1381-5*, 542; *C.C.R.*, *1369-9*, 275. On 26 February 1384 Hungerford had stood surety in the Exchequer for Lord Botreaux when the latter acquired a royal wardship (*C.F.R.*, *1383-91*, 40). The great-niece of Botreaux's wife was to marry Hungerford's son and heir, Walter.

61 *C.C.R.*, *1385-9*, 450-1; *C.P.R.*, *passim.*

62 *C.P.R.*, *1388-92* 491.

63 *ibid.*, *1396-9*, 180.

64 Hoare, *op. cit.*, vol. I, part 2, 113; *Bulletin of the Institute of Historical Research*, XVIII. 38; Lambeth Palace Library, Arundel Register, pars. II, fo. 152a; *C.F.R.*, *1391-9*, 268; *H.M.C.*, *Report on MSS. of R. R. Hastings*, I. 299; Oxford Hist. Soc., vol. LXXX, *Snappe's Formulary*, ed. H. E. Salter, 2; of the four sons of Sir Thomas Hungerford surviving in 1383, only Walter and John, the sons of his second wife, were alive in 1395.

65 W. Dugdale, *Baronage o England*, II. 203; *C.P.R.* *1396-9*, 121; *ibid.*, *1422-9*, 347.

3

SIR JOHN BUSSY OF HOUGHAM

It was rather more than half a century from the time when elected representatives of the local communities of shires and towns were first summoned (in 1265) to attend a general parliament together to the time when their presence came to be regarded as essential. About the beginning of Edward III's reign (in 1327), knights of the shire, citizens, and burgesses—the Commons—were being not merely frequently but regularly summoned. Roughly half a century later still (in 1376), for the first time (so far as we know) they began to elect a spokesman or speaker from among their own number and for the duration of a parliament. Down to 1533 he was invariably chosen from the knights of the shire, who, mainly for social reasons, carried most weight in the Commons.

Once his election was accepted by the King, it was the Speaker's business to declare to King and Lords what the Commons directed or allowed him to say on their behalf. How soon he came to manage, and in what manner, the proceedings of the Lower House, we cannot say precisely. (The parliament rolls mostly record the formal transactions of parliament, and there are no Commons' Journals until 1547.) But the Speaker's potential importance as a controller of the Commons' doings certainly was early realized, not least by the King and his administration. Even so, it is difficult to say when the Speaker became in some sense the King's agent in the Commons as well as their representative *vis-à-vis* the King and Lords. For this and other reasons, it is important to discover the careers of the individual Speakers. It is an enquiry that has at least some bearing on the vexed problem of the political significance of the Lower House in the pre-modern phases of its development.

The fact that now and then in this period of ' bastard feudalism ' a particular Speaker was a retainer of some very influential magnate or a supporter of some strong aristocratic interest, whatever its bearing on the question of the Commons' political independence, suggests that there were likely to be other than merely royal influences operating in his election. Their choice of such a man as Speaker might mean that the Commons thought it advisable to influence in their favour some dominant magnate or section of aristocratic opinion. The election of an out-and-out royal retainer and partizan need not perhaps mean more than that the Commons wished to emphasize their proper loyalty to the Crown, or recognized that their recommendations, and maybe criticisms, would be all the more telling if offered to the King by one of their number who was acceptable to him on personal grounds.

The exercise of direct pressure on the Commons to elect a royal nominee as Speaker, whose business it would then be to manage them in the King's interest, cannot of course be ruled out. Sir John Bussy of Hougham, Speaker in 1394 and in both parliaments of 1397–8, was a royal retainer and (as we shall see) was to acquire an evil reputation as one of the most sinister members of Richard II's Council in the period of his autocratic rule, so that his execution in the rebellion which ended in Richard II's deposition in 1399 was almost a foregone conclusion. But it would be an over-simplification of a complex and bigger problem to pretend that one like Bussy was *throughout* his career as Speaker foisted on the Commons to be no more than a royal mouth-piece. When he first (so far as we know) became their Speaker in 1394, Bussy had sat in each of the previous five parliaments. Possessing eloquence as well, his experience was a weighty qualification. He was also, and for long had been, a retainer of John of Gaunt, Duke of Lancaster, the eldest and by far the most important of Richard II's uncles, and was soon to be the Duke's steward for his lands north of Trent. The Commons may very well have regarded Bussy as a symbol of that desirable alliance between the King and Lancaster which profitably secured some semblance of internal peace in the period between the frontal attack on Richard II's party and prerogative in the years 1386–8 and the King's revengeful measures of the years 1397–9. We need hardly hesitate to say, however, that Bussy's Speakerships were characterized by what was at times a remarkable servility on the part of the Commons and his own.

Whatever we may think of these aspects of his larger career, there is no doubt that Bussy was a power in his day in Lincolnshire. He was one of its two knights of the shire in each of the parliaments of 1383, September 1388, January and November 1390, November 1391 (when he was also elected for Rutland), January 1393, January 1394, January 1395, January 1397, and September 1397–January 1398.[1] In the last eleven years of his life, therefore, Bussy quite monopolized one of the two county seats in parliament. He was, moreover, three times sheriff in the middle years of Richard II's reign, in 1383–4, in 1385–6, and in 1390–1.

In the fourteenth and fifteenth centuries the interest and authority of the House of Lancaster in Lincolnshire were very strong. One of John of Gaunt's hereditary titles was that of earl of Lincoln. He had property and rights at Lincoln ; he held considerable lands in the county. Bolingbroke had been the birthplace of his son and heir, the later Henry IV. Even his mistress was a Lincolnshire lady.

The following abbreviations have been used in the footnotes :—

CPR	— Calendar of Patent Rolls.	PPC —	Proceedings and Ordinances of
CCR	— Calendar of Close Rolls.		the Privy Council, ed. N. H.
CFR	— Calendar of Fine Rolls.		Nicolas.
DKR	— Deputy Keeper's Reports.	PRO —	Public Record Office.
Rot. Parl.	— Rotuli Parliamentorum.	RS —	Rolls Series.

(1) *The Official Return of Members of Parliament* (1) 218, 235, 238, 240, 242, 245, 247, 250, 253, 256.

Bussy was a Lancastrian before and after he became a royal retainer.   So also had been Sir Henry de Retford, who represented
Lincolnshire in those parliaments of Henry IV which met in January
1401, September 1402, and October 1404.[1a]   His being chosen as a
member of an Anglo-French embassy to the rival papal courts of
Avignon and Rome in 1397 suggests that Retford was regarded by
Richard II as having diplomatic ability.   So, too, does his election
by the Commons as their Speaker in Henry IV's fourth parliament
of September—November 1402.   Retford was retained by Henry
IV, as he had been by Richard II, and served him under arms on
more than one occasion in the unquiet time of his reign.   But it is
very doubtful whether he should be regarded simply as a " King's
friend " when he served the Commons as their Speaker.   He
seemingly got no royal reward.   He, too, was possessed of considerable influence in Lincolnshire.   He was sheriff in 1392–3,
1397–8, and 1406–7.   But he cut nothing like so important a figure
in the county as Bussy had done.   Both men share a claim on the
interest of the local historian, however, in that one from Kesteven,
the other from Lindsey, they were the county's only parliamentary
representatives in pre-Tudor times to occupy the office of Commons'
Speaker.

Sir John Bussy came of a family which by the end of the fourteenth century had certainly been settled at Hougham in the parts
of Kesteven in Lincolnshire for a hundred years and probably for
much longer.   In a pedigree to be found in a cartulary of the family
and compiled in the fifteenth century for Sir John Bussy, son of the
Speaker, the claim is made that the family had come over with
William I.   Be that as it may, one of their ancestors, Sir Hugh de
Bussy had been sheriff of Lincolnshire in 1300–02 and, more recently,
Sir William Bussy, father of the Speaker, had been sheriff of the
county in 1372–3, its royal escheator in 1376–7, and knight of the
shire in the parliaments of 1368, 1376, 1378, and January 1380.
These facts tell their own tale of the family's significance in fourteenth century Lincolnshire society.   So do such of its marriage
alliances as we have knowledge of.   Sir John's mother was Isabel,
daughter of John Paynell of Boothby near Grantham.   He himself married in 1382, as his first wife, Maud, daughter and heir of
Sir Philip Neville of Scotton in north Lincolnshire.   This lady had
already been married twice.   Her first husband was Sir William de
Cantilupe (grandson and heir of William Lord Cantilupe, peer of
parliament from 1336 to 1354), who was murdered at Scotton in
1375 by members of his own household, Maud herself being indicted
before the King's Bench at Lincoln both as a principal and as an
accessory to the crime.   The sheriff at the time, Sir Thomas de
Kydale of South Ferriby, became her second husband shortly afterwards.   He died not long before the end of November 1381, and

(1a)   *ibid.* 261, 263, 267.

then, before 27th October, 1382, she married John Bussy. Maud died sometime before April 1398, when Sir John Bussy's wife (presumably his second) was called Mary. (It was Mary who with Sir John procured in that month a papal indult allowing them the use of a portable altar.) Of Mary's family origins, nothing has been discovered. She was dead by July, 1398[2].

What landed estates these marriages of Bussy's brought him is not precisely known, but his own family holdings in the East Midlands were certainly of considerable local importance. By the end of his life he had either an hereditary or a purchased interest in a score of townships in Nottinghamshire, the parts of Kesteven and Holland in Lincolnshire, and Rutland. In east Nottinghamshire, he held lands in Wigsley, Spalford, Balderton, Farndon, Syerston, and Elston, being in the manors of Balderton and Elston and their scattered members a tenant of the bishop of Lincoln. All these vills of the Trent valley were within the hundred of Newark. His residential manor of Hougham was the westernmost of a group of estates in central Kesteven which included lands at Willoughby, Great Hale, Haceby, Ingoldsby (these being held of the Lords Beaumont as 1½ knights' fees of the Gaunt fief), Silkeby and Dembleby. Further eastwards in Lincolnshire, in the parts of Holland and in the immediate hinterland of the Wash, he eventually came to have another collection of lands in the townships of Spalding, Surfleet, Pinchbeck, Gosberton, and Quadring, and (not far south of Boston) the manor of Dowdike, all of which he purchased in the last year of his life from the feoffees or executors of John Lord De la Warr. Just over the Lincolnshire border with Rutland, he held the manor of Cottesmore and half a knight's fee in Thistleton[3].

The estates in central Kesteven were all situated immediately close to or actually upon Lincoln Edge, good sheep-rearing land, and it seems likely that Bussy's interest in wool-growing was a source of considerable income to him. This is strongly suggested by the fact that at his death and forfeiture a contract, which had been arranged sometime in the years 1395–7 between him and two Lincoln merchants and which in 1399 came to the notice of the Exchequer, provided for their buying wool from him worth as much as 400 marks. By the time of his death they had repaid roughly three-quarters of this sum, part in cash at his London inn in St. Benet's parish in Castle Baynard ward, at Hougham, and at Lincoln, and the rest in goods purchased to his order at Bruges and elsewhere.[4]

John Bussy's father, Sir William, was appointed to serve his last royal commission in Lincolnshire (one of array) in March, 1380. It

(2) British Museum, Harley Ms. 1756, p. 4 ; R. Thoroton, *Antiquities of Nottinghamshire* (1677), 183-4 ; *The Genealogist*, iii. 361 ; *Lincoln Record Society, Publications*, vol. XXX (' Some Sessions of the Peace in Lincolnshire, 1360-1375,' ed. R. Sillem) ; *CPR*, 1381-5, 185 ; *Cal. of Papal Registers, Papal Letters*, V. 141 ; *CFR*, 1391-9, 271.
(3) *Calendar of Feudal Aids, IV.* 118-9 ; R. Thoroton, *op. cit.*, 173, 183-4 ; *Cal. of Inquisitions Post Mortem, Edward III*, XII. 293-4 ; *CPR*, 1399-1401, 99, 143 ; *ibid.*, 15 ; *Feudal Aids* iv. 213.
(4) Q.R. Memoranda Rolls, Exchequer, PRO., E. 159/176, Communia, Recorda, Trinity term 1400, mem. 11.

is probable that he died shortly afterwards. John was almost certainly of age by this time, and he had not long to wait for his own first local commission by royal letter patent. The Peasants' Revolt had passed its crisis in the south when, on 24th June, 1381, Bussy was included among the Lincolnshire commissioners ordered to prevent unlawful assemblies and punish insurgents. A week later he was one of those appointed to proclaim in the county that all tenants should perform their customary services, and to imprison all contrariants. On 10th July a further commission was issued ordering the commissioners to raise forces to resist any rebels.[5]

Probably between then and the autumn of 1382 he married his first wife, Maud, successively the widow of Sir William de Cantilupe and Sir Thomas de Kydale; on 27th October, 1382, for a fine of 10 marks, he secured a royal pardon for the marriage which had not been sanctioned by the Crown. (Sir Thomas de Kydale was the tenant of the heir of Henry Lord Beaumont, then a minor in royal wardship.) Bussy and his wife had recently had difficulty in securing the Chancellor's assignment of certain of her dower lands from the estates of Sir William de Cantilupe in Yorkshire, and they accordingly petitioned the King on this score, apparently through the mediation of Sir Michael de la Pole, who in the next year was himself to become Chancellor. For a reasonable fine the petition was granted, and on the same day as the marriage was pardoned the King's escheator in Yorkshire was instructed to assign to Bussy and his wife, in the presence of representatives of De Cantilupe's heirs (John Hastings, Earl of Pembroke, and William Lord Zouche of Haringworth), dower of the manor of Farnham and lands in Lofthouse Hill, Staveley, and Beechill (in York).[6] Both Lofthouse Hill and Staveley were in Knaresborough, one of the great duchy of Lancaster strongholds of the north country, and it may very well be that it was just about the time of his acquisition of these dower estates of his wife (or within the next twelve months) that Bussy first entered the retinue of John of Gaunt, Duke of Lancaster, as a knight bachelor, just as his wife's first husband, Cantilupe, had done some ten years before. Bussy was not a knight when pardoned his marriage in October 1382, but he had been knighted by November, 1383. He was later to rise high in the Lancastrian administration.[7]

Bussy's career now began to take shape. His royal commissions certainly multiplied apace: on 15th November, 1382 he was appointed a member of a commission of overseers of the rivers Witham and Brant (his own ancestral manor of Hougham being on the banks of the Witham) ; five weeks later (on 20th December) for the first time he was included on the commission of the peace for Kesteven,

(5) CPR, 1381-5, 70, 74 ; CCR, 1381-5, 74.

(6) CPR, 1381-5, 185 ; Ancient Petitions, PRO, SC. 8, file 222, no. 11086 (the petition is subscribed ' Pole ') ; CCR, 1381-5, 171.

(7) John of Gaunt's Register (Camden Series, Royal Historical Society, LVI), ed. E. C. Lodge and R. Somerville, vol. 1, p. 9.

and on the next day he was made keeper of the peace, one of a very large Lincolnshire commission endowed with wide powers to arrest and imprison rebels and do justice; and by a series of royal letters patent issued in 1383 he was made a commissioner for sewers on the Trent, mainly in its Lincolnshire courses. In October 1383 he served the county for the first time as knight of the shire, and during the parliament, on 1st November, he was for the first time appointed sheriff of Lincolnshire. (He served as sheriff until 11th November, 1384.[8]) The session was noteworthy for the impeachment by Sir Michael de la Pole (who was now Chancellor) of Bishop Despenser of Norwich, the conception of whose recent disastrous crusade in Flanders had run counter to the Spanish schemes of Bussy's lord, the duke of Lancaster.

During Bussy's shrievalty in 1383-4 quite a number of special royal commissions not unnaturally came his way. On 23rd November, 1383, three days before the autumn parliament ended, he was one of those ordered to investigate the unlawful ejection of a royal chaplain from a messuage in Fillingham (Lincs.) belonging to the alien priory of Cammeringham, whose estates the chaplain was farming by the authority of the Exchequer. In January following, Bussy was being ordered as sheriff to gaol accused felons in Lincoln castle. On 18th February, 1384 he was appointed one of a small committee to take temporary charge of the house of Austin canons at Thornholm, pending the settlement of an appeal over a contested election there. Sir Michael de la Pole was patron of the house, but was too busy as Chancellor (the writ states) to act for himself. During the summer of this year, Bussy was authorized to act as a surveyor and auditor of accounts in the priory. It seems possible that he was *persona grata* with De la Pole at this time. For it was following a complaint by the Chancellor of a trespass in a close of his at Blyborough (N. Lincs.) that on 18th July in the same year Bussy was made a commissioner of oyer and terminer.

Within a few days of his ceasing to act as sheriff in November, 1384, Bussy was confirmed in his commission of the peace in Kesteven, where he also acted in the following spring as a commissioner of array during a French invasion scare. In the meantime, on 20th March, 1385, he had been made a commissioner of oyer and terminer when Bishop Buckingham of Lincoln complained of interference with his franchise of frankpledge-view at Dunsby, which he exercised as lord of the soke of Sleaford. Less than a year after the expiry of his first term of office as sheriff (and so contrary to Edward III's statutes requiring three years to pass before a sheriff was reappointed), Bussy was once again made sheriff of Lincolnshire on 20th October, 1385 and served until 18th November, 1386. During the year, late in September, 1386 when there was a repetition of the

(8)   *CPR*, 1381-5, 200-2, 245, 254 ; *PRO, Lists and Indexes*, IX, *List of Sheriffs*, 79.
(9)   *CPR*, 1381-5, 357, 418, 378, 495, 496.

French threat to invade of the previous year, Bussy was one of a Lincolnshire commission appointed to take steps to prevent local dealers in armour and horses from raising their prices.[10] Whatever we may think of the threat, the scare was evidently real enough. Less than a month later, during the autumn parliament of 1386, the aristocratic opposition of the duke of Gloucester, the earls of Arundel and Warwick, and Bishop Arundel of Ely, had swept Richard II's court party out of control of the administration, the late Chancellor (now earl of Suffolk) underwent a successful impeachment, and before the parliament ended the authority of the Crown had been virtually handed over to a parliamentary commission.

With Lancaster out of the country in Spain, there was little to bridge the gap between the King and the new, aristocratically composed junto, and the situation came to a head in the proceedings of the Lords Appellant and their attacks on the King's friends, Suffolk among them, in 1387 and subsequently during the Merciless Parliament of 1388. In precisely what ways Sir John Bussy showed himself unfaithful to his antecedent connexions and disposed to support the parliamentary commission, is not known. He was required to serve on only one official commission between October 1386 and March 1389, soon after which Richard II resumed his royal authority. But, after Richard had taken his revenge on the principal Appellants in 1397, Bussy was to see fit to sue out a royal pardon on 1st May, 1398 expressly for having adhered to Gloucester and Arundel during the time when the parliamentary commission of 1386 was in operation and particularly when these lords rose in arms at Haringhay Park in November, 1387. Certainly, when, at the end of the first session of the Merciless Parliament, writs were issued to the sheriffs on 20th March, 1388 ordering them to take oaths from local gentry and notables (similar to those taken in parliament by the Lords and Commons) to keep the peace and to stand with the Lords Appellant to the end of the Parliament, Bussy was among those knights in Lincolnshire who took the oath.[11] Lancaster's heir, Henry of Bolingbroke, was one of the Lords Appellant, and it may have been that which moved Bussy to support them. In the second parliament of 1388 which met at Cambridge in September he sat for the second time as knight of the shire for Lincolnshire, his fellow-knight (Sir Philip de Tilney) having been re-elected. On 29th March, 1389, while the Appellants were still in control, he was put on a commission to extend (that is, value) three former De la Pole manors in Notts. and Lincolnshire forfeited by the Earl of Suffolk ; the income from these estates, Sir Michael (the Earl's eldest son) had complained, did not amount to the sum of £100 a year which, with the assent of the Merciless Parliament, the King had granted him and his wife for their maintenance. It may well be that on

---

(10)   *ibid.*, 502, 589, 594 ; *ibid*, 1385-9, 86, 261 ; *List of Sheriffs, loc.cit.*
(11)   *CPR*, 1396-9, 331 ; *Rot. Parl.*, iii. 401a.

this commission Bussy was acting for the young De la Pole. Some sort of connexion between Bussy and this family certainly persisted, for in August 1391 he was a witness to one of Sir Michael's charters.[12]

Sir John Bussy's election as knight of the shire to the Cambridge parliament of 1388 was the beginning of what proved to be his virtual monopoly of one of the Lincolnshire seats in the Commons for the rest of Richard II's reign, for he was re-elected to each of the eight parliaments of the 1390's. Just before the first of these parliaments, in December 1389, he was a mainpernor for three men imprisoned in the Tower for a short time, undertaking to produce them before King and Council during the parliament.[13] Between the two parliaments of 1390, he was (in July) put on an Exchequer enquiry into wastes in Crown lands in Lincolnshire and into cases of concealment of sources of royal revenue ; and just before the second parliament of the year he was once more appointed sheriff of Lincolnshire. (He was sheriff from 7th November, .1390 to 21st October, 1391.) On 6th December, 1390, three days after the end of the session, the custody of the royal castle and manor of Somerton in north Kesteven and of a mpiety of the nearby manor of Carlton-le-Moorland was granted him for life at an annual farm of 50 marks. The grant was, however, in February, 1393 made conditional upon the death of the then farmer, but Bussy got the custody in a conclusive form on 22nd February, 1394 (during his first recorded Speakership) and enjoyed it until his death and forfeiture in 1399. Moreover, he was eventually enabled to deduct from the 50 marks farm-rent the 40 marks annuity which, as a King's knight retained by Richard II for life, he had been granted on 4th December, 1391, and was authorized to expend the residue of the rent on repairs to the castle. (The 40 marks annuity had been at first charged on the issues of the county.)[14]

In the meantime, confirmed in his justiceship of the peace in Kesteven and in February, 1392 for the first time appointed J.P. in Lindsey too, Bussy had been much occupied in 1393 on a number of local commissions, the most important of which were concerned with the civic and cathedral authorities of Lincoln itself. On 5th March, 1393 he was put by the then Chancellor of England (Archbishop Arundel of York) on a commission authorized to compose the differences which had arisen between the dean and chapter of the cathedral and the commonalty of the city on the one hand and some of the wealthier citizens on the other, over the election of the mayor and bailiffs. This commission was the object of a Chancery writ of *supersedeas* on 23rd March following. Then, on 10th June, Bussy was appointed to act on a royal enquiry after information had been laid that pavage dues in the city had been embezzled by the recipients and the funds misapplied to the re-building of the civic

(12) *CPR*, 1388-92, 58 ; *CCR*, 1389-92, 501.
(13) *CCR*, 1389-92, 38, 512.
(14) *CPR*, 1388-92, 347 ; *List of Sheriffs, loc.cit.* ; *CFR*, 1383-91, 346 ; *CPR*, 1391-6, 2, 219, 291, 380 ; *ibid*, 1399-1401, 42.

guildhall. Next, on 6th September, he was ordered (in a writ addressed to him alone) to take securities from four Lincoln citizens of the middling party not to whip up feeling in the town ; John of Gaunt had arranged a truce between the parties in the city, and Bussy was instructed to order the mayor and bailiffs to admit these men who on the mayor's report had first been imprisoned in the Fleet Prison in London and then only released on the understanding that they kept away from Lincoln. No more than a week had passed before Bussy (again alone commissioned) was ordered to be present in person at the election of the mayor and bailiffs, and to ensure that it was carried out in customary form ; he was to have power to imprison contrariants. It would seem that he was intended to support the wealthier party, and, judging from the outcome of the election, that he managed to do so. The city had clearly not settled down even by the end of the year, because on 8th January, 1394 Bussy was put on yet another Lincoln commission, this time to enquire into assaults on the clergy resulting in the pollution of the cathedral and its precincts before Christmas (when there were no services in the minster), and to produce those responsible for the outrages before King and Council.[15]

Bussy's first recorded Speakership followed in the first parliament summoned to meet after all these upsets at Lincoln, in January 1394. It was the sixth parliament running to which he was elected for Lincolnshire. Politically, it was marked by a strengthening of the carefully fostered friendship between the King and the eldest of his royal uncles, the Duke of Lancaster. The Earl of Arundel's violent attack during the parliament on John of Gaunt, when opposed by the King, petered out in a shame-faced apology. Bussy's election as Speaker suggests that the Commons had appreciated the realities of the situation and exercised their choice in a way bound to be agreeable to both the King and the most powerful magnate in the Upper House. Bussy was a retainer of each. He was in receipt of fees and emoluments from Richard II as a King's knight, and his early membership of the Lancastrian retinue had by this time developed into a closer connexion, which perhaps already had brought him into the higher officialdom of the Lancastrian duchy. John of Gaunt's son and heir, Henry of Bolingbroke, at this time Earl of Derby, made Bussy the recipient of one of his new year gifts early in 1394—a broach of gold with an emerald, worth 15 shillings. Two years later Derby's new year gift to him was worth 46s.8d.: an ouch of gold fashioned as an ' ursus amailatus.' Bussy's stocks were evidently rising. Certainly by (if not before) the summer of 1394, he had succeeded Sir Philip de Tilney of Tydd (Lincs.), who had been his fellow-knight of the shire in the parliaments of September 1388 and January 1390, as chief steward of the parts of the duchy of

(15) *CPR*, 1388-92, 345, 526 ; *ibid.*, 1391-6, 90, 240, 296, 355, 429 ; *CCR*, 1392-6, 133, 162. The troubles at Lincoln are discussed (in greater detail than I have been able to afford) in J. W. F. Hill, *Medieval Lincoln* (Cambridge, 1948), pp. 259 ff.

Lancaster north of Trent ; in 1395 he was acting as a member of the duchy council, and later events suggest that he was still occupying these offices in 1397 ; he was replaced by John Cockayne in the stewardship by the spring of 1398.[16] With other Lancastrian retainers, on 7th August, 1394, he went surety in Chancery for their fellow, Sir Hugh Shirley, knight of the shire for Leicestershire in 1393, undertaking that he would not do harm to Sir Thomas de Erdington ; it was on 20th September following that a family connexion of the house of Lancaster, John Lord Beaumont, nominated Bussy as one of his attorneys when he was preparing to accompany the King in his first expedition to Ireland.

While Richard II was in Ireland, and John of Gaunt away in his newly granted duchy of Aquitaine, parliament sat from 27th January to 15th February, 1395. Bussy was once more re-elected for Lincolnshire, but whether he again acted as Speaker is not known. (The parliament-roll records no Speaker's name.) It is, however, quite possible that he was re-elected to the Chair. Certainly, Richard ' even in his absence . . . . still had a real hold over parliament ' (Tout). Lollard activity and fears of Scottish and French attacks caused the cry to be raised for Richard's early return. Letters sealed by the Lords were dispatched to the King on behalf of the estates before the parliament came to an end. The Chancellor and the bishop of London crossed to Ireland, and Thomas of Woodstock and the King's half-brother, who had returned to England, went back. There is reason to believe that it was as members of a Commons' deputation that Sir John Bussy and Sir William Bagot (lately knight of the shire for Warwickshire) moved up in late February, 1395 to Denwall on the Dee estuary near Chester (in the company of Guy Mone, the receiver of the King's Chamber) to await passage to Ireland to join the King.[17] Payment of £20 each was made in the Lower Exchequer on 25th February to Bussy, Bagot, William Willicotes, Robert Cholmeley, William Askham, and Thomas Beaupeny, expressly as being about to proceed to the King in Ireland regarding certain articles moved and proposed in the late parliament ' ex parte communitatis regni.' In all probability Bussy returned to England with Richard II on 1st May, 1395.

Little is known of Bussy's doings in 1395 and 1396. He was certainly active as duchy of Lancaster chief steward in the north and as a member of John of Gaunt's council during the duke's absence in Gascony throughout the first of these years. With the King, it is likely that Bussy was moving forward into the position of a supporter of the royal prerogative in its extremest forms, in such a way as to cause his name to be a by-word among the political pamphleteers of the time. The last two years and more of his

(16) Duchy of Lancaster, Accounts Various, PRO, D.L. 28/1/4 (account-books of William Loveney, clerk of the Earl of Derby's Wardrobe) ; ibid, D.L. 28/1/5 ; R. Somerville, *The Duchy of Lancaster*, i. 125n, 135n, 367.

(17) *CCR*, 1392-6, 367 ; *CPR*, 1391-6, 576 ; *DKR*, XXXVI, App. II, 361 ; Exchequer, Issue Roll, PRO, E. 403/549, mem. 12.

career were crowded with incident : one of Richard's ablest and
probably most ruthless partizans, he was at the vortex of the
whirlpool of the Ricardian absolutism. Any reaction would have
imperilled him ; from the consequences of Henry of Bolingbroke's
return from an exile to which Bussy was party, and in the circumstances of rebellion in which this return was made, it was to prove
impossible for him to seek extrication.   But this was not yet awhile.
Early in 1397 he was still moving up.

When Bussy was once more re-elected knight of the shire to the
parliament summoned (after the conclusion of a long truce with
France) to meet on 22nd January, 1397, the Commons were com-
plaisantly prepared to choose him once more as their Speaker.
There was at first apparently some doubt as to his ability to handle
them over the King's proposed Milanese expedition. But, after
the scandal of Haxey's bill of complaint had upset the King, Bussy's
capacity for adroit management seemingly re-asserted itself. The
Commons' show of independence collapsed, but Richard did not
press his foreign policy to the point of demanding more than a renewal of the subsidies on trade.   The short session of three weeks
witnessed, of course, the royal legitimation of the duke of Lancaster's
children by Katherine Swynford, whom he had married in the previous year.

During this parliament, which ended on 12th February 1397,
Bussy was party to some important semi-private business.   On
4th January, along with the duke of Lancaster and Lord de la
Warr, he was one of a small committee given charge of the Gilber-
tine priory of Sempringham, following disputes between the prior
and the master of the Order.   He was much involved about this
time in the affairs of the family of Beaumont, patrons of this priory,
whose representative was now a minor in royal wardship.   On 15th
February he was associated with the widow of the late Lord Beaumont (and others) in receiving the right to farm all but the dower
estates until the full age of the heir, Henry, now aged 16 years (the
Exchequer charge being £120 a year net).   Over a year later, in
June 1398, the farmers' interest was to be augmented by a grant of
the custody of the heir's grandmother's dower estates, but in May
1399 the wardship passed to Edward, Duke of Aumâle, son of the
Duke of York.[18]   Again, three days before the end of the parliament
of January 1397, that is, on 9th February 1397, along with Archbishop Arundel, Henry of Bolingbroke (John of Gaunt's son and heir),
and the ex-receiver-general of the duchy of Lancaster, Bussy
(presumably in his capacity as steward of the duchy north of Trent)
was one of the feoffees party to a settlement (in the form of a final
concord) arranging for the entailing of certain of the duchy estates,
granted originally to the Duke by Edward III in exchange for the
earldom of Richmond, on John of Gaunt and his third Duchess,

(18) *CPR*, 1396-9, 51 ; *CFR*, 1391-9, 205, 258.

Katherine, and the heirs of his body, with reversion to the Crown.[19]

Between the January and September parliaments of 1397, Richard II determined to nullify all the opposition policy and acts of the years 1386–88, including the statutes and judgments of the Merciless Parliament, and to have his revenge on such of the Lords Appellant of 1387–8 as were still hostile to him, and on other important members of the parliamentary commission set up in 1386 who were still alive and of whose loyalty he was in doubt. Re-elected knight of the shire for Lincolnshire as usual, Bussy was re-elected Speaker for the Commons in the second parliament of the year. He was clearly designed to be as much the King's agent in the Lower House as the Commons' agent with the King. The St. Albans chronicler is insistent on the prominent part played by Bussy, whom he describes as *vir crudelissimus, ambitiosus supra modum atque rei alienae cupidus*. Of Bussy, he goes on to say that *pro terrena substantia vel consequendis honoribus, fidem et conscientiam desere parvipendit*. Powerful in eloquence, Walsingham says he was, *unde Rex constituit eum Prolocutorem presentis parliamenti*.

The proceedings in parliament against the Duke of Gloucester and the Earls of Arundel and Warwick were initiated by bill of appeal as used in 1388 against *their* enemies. From a proper place in such a procedure the Commons were excluded. But Bussy, already a member of the royal Council at the time of the arrest of these three great lords in July, had advised Richard to take this step (according to the Evesham chronicler), and now he moved the Commons to petition for the repeal of the royal pardons which these lords had formerly been able to procure, and during the trial of the Earl of Arundel he clamoured with his supporters for judgement on him as a traitor. The Earl rounded on Bussy and called him a traitor himself (perhaps with some justification, as Bussy's later pardon for his support of the Earl and Gloucester in 1387–8 suggests) : ' *Non fideles communes hoc petunt, sed tu quis sis, novi satis bene,*' the Earl is made to say in Walsingham's account ; according to the Evesham version of the trial, ' *Et fideles plebei regni non sunt hic . . . , Et scio, quia tu semper falsus fuisti.*' Bussy was, moreover, largely instrumental in getting the Commons to insist on the appointment of a proctor by the clergy, authorized to give their assent to any judgement of blood. Further, he was successful in moving the Commons to impeach the Earl's brother, Archbishop Arundel on a charge of treason for his share in the happenings of 1386–88. This attack was, of course, successful and the primate was condemned to forfeiture and exile. In all this, Walsingham says, Bussy showed to the King *non humanos honores, sed divinos, adinveniens verba adulatoria et insueta mortalibus minime congruentia*, in which Richard, nonetheless, took great satisfaction.[20] The

(19) *CPR*, 1396-9, 76, 516 ; *CCR*, 1396-9, 365 ; R. Somerville, *op.cit.*, i. 135ⁿ.
(20) *Annales Johannis de Trokelowe*, etc., ed. H. T. Riley (R.S.), p. 209 *et seq ; Historia Vite et Regni Ricardi II a monacho quodam de Evesham consignata*, ed. T. Hearne (Oxford, 1727), pp. 129, 137.

Commons had already petitioned for the annulment of the parliamentary commission of 1386, and they went on to be party to a wider definition of the law of treason than was comprised in the Statute of Treasons of 1352.

All went well for the royalist party : Lords and Commons proved servile ; the Earl of Arundel was executed ; Warwick was sentenced to forfeiture and exile ; Gloucester was posthumously condemned (having been already murdered at Calais) ; Archbishop Arundel was banished ; the absent Sir Thomas Mortimer was to stand convicted by default if within three months he failed to appear to stand trial ; John Lord Cobham also incurred forfeiture. Richard II ' emerged a despot in fact as well as in theory ' (Tout), after no more than a fortnight's session. Richard rewarded his aristocratic supporters with new titles, and parliament, after the Lords and the knights of the shire had sworn oaths to maintain the acts of the session, disbanded on 30th September, after being adjourned to meet at Shrewsbury on 27th January, 1398.

Bussy's management of the Commons, supported by Sir William Bagot and Sir Henry Green, had been exemplary from the King's point of view. And his services did not go unrecognised or unrewarded. Already, after the first parliament of the year, on 1st March, 1397 his annuity of 40 marks as a King's knight (enjoyed by him since December, 1391) had been raised by a further grant for life of 20 marks a year. Before the parliamentary session of September following was over, Bussy had (on 27th September) commuted his enlarged annuity for at first a life tenancy free of rent, and then a day later for a grant in tail male, of three Suffolk manors (Cavendish, Wratting, and Stansfield) forfeited by Sir Thomas Mortimer, a much more profitable arrangement. On 26th September, he and Sir Henry Green had jointly secured a grant of the household equipment of the Earl of Arundel's London inn (minus the silver plate) and the Earl of Warwick's barge. On 28th September Bussy secured in tail male the Earl of Warwick's Cambridgeshire manor of Kirtling. On 3rd October he and Green shared a further grant for life in survivorship of Lord Cobham's London inn with all its paraphernalia. (This grant was to be confirmed at Shrewsbury on 30th January, 1398.) Three weeks later, Green was one of Bussy's mainpernors when he was associated on 24th October with its prior in the custody of the alien priory of Hough-on-the-Hill near Grantham (at an Exchequer rent of £20 a year).[21]

The parliamentary recess was a busy time for the Speaker. Since certainly the beginning of August to the end of September he had been in constant daily attendance as a member of the royal Council (his fee as a councillor having been established on a *pro rata* basis at £100 a year on 1st August). There was much for the Council to do. At the beginning of the September parliament, the

(21) *CPR*, 1396-9, 84, 198, 217, 289 ; 253, 277 ; *CFR*, 1391-9, 235.

Chancellor had drawn attention to the general pardon which the King proposed to allow, except to fifty persons whom it would please him to name later and except to all those who were to stand trial during the parliament. It was probably immediately after the close of the session that the Council decided that writs under the great seal should be sent to those exempted from this " crooked pardon " ordering their appearance before it, their failure to come to terms on the question of their fines to be met with imprisonment. It was further decided, probably by the King, that none should be present at the assessment (taxacion) of these fines except the Chancellor, the Treasurer, the Keeper of the Privy Seal, and those three royalist knights in the Council, Bussy, Green and Bagot.[22]

After this business, it is doubtful whether Bussy moved off from Westminster for what remained of the period of the parliamentary adjournment. There is evidence to suggest that he was at his own London inn in Castle Baynard ward on 10th November; and it is likely that the transaction on 26th November, whereby he received from Thomas More, clerk, a grant for life of the office of underseneschal of the liberty of the abbey of Bury St. Edmunds, took place in London. (The confirmation by the prior took place at Bury three days later.) The King was to sanction this appointment at Coventry on 1st January following and again at Shrewsbury (during the parliament) on 29th January.[23] In the meantime, during the previous autumn, Bussy had been made commissioner for sewers in Kesteven and Holland (Lincs.) and justice of the peace throughout Lincolnshire and also in Cambridgeshire. On 14th December he had been put on a commission set up to investigate armed disturbances directed against Bishop Buckingham of Lincoln's men at Stowe and Upton in north Lincolnshire.[24]

Adjourned to meet at Shrewsbury on 28th January, 1398 the parliament re-assembled there, and Bussy continued to act as the Commons' Speaker. At the outset of the session all the proceedings of the Merciless Parliament of 1388 were annulled at the request of the new Appellants, the Commons affirming that they had intended to petition in this strain themselves. This decision was followed by an acceptance by all the estates of the conclusions of the judges made at Nottingham in August 1387 on the subject of the royal prerogative regarding the conduct and competence of parliaments. Meanwhile, the Commons moved for the conclusion of the trial of Lord Cobham who was then exiled, and Sir Thomas Mortimer was condemned in his absence. Four days were apparently sufficient for the Commons, under Bussy's guidance, to reach agreement on their financial grant : a whole and a half tenth and fifteenth were granted, and then the wool subsidies and tunnage and poundage

(22) CPR, 1396-9, 360 ; Exchequer, Issue Roll, PRO, E.403/561, mem. 14 ; PPC, i. 76.
(23) Exchequer, LTR Memoranda Roll, PRO, E. 368/171, Communia, Recorda, mem. 12 ; CPR, 1396-9, 278.
(24) CPR, 1396-9, 307, 309, 310 ; 231, 234.

were renewed for Richard II's lifetime, an act of parliamentary generosity quite without precedence. After fresh oaths had been taken to maintain all the acts of the parliament, the session come to an end on 31st January with the appointment, at the Commons' request, of a commission entrusted with powers to deal with certain petitions left unanswered during the parliament, and also to terminate the recent quarrel between Henry of Bolingbroke, now Duke of Hereford, and the Duke of Norfolk, the only two Lords Appellant of 1388 who were still unpunished.

This dispute was of crucial importance : as Bolingbroke's submission of its details to parliament had disclosed, Norfolk had laid himself open to a charge of treason for slandering the King. The parliamentary commission included from among the Commons six knights of the shire, at the head of whom was Bussy. He seems to have constantly acted as one of the *quorum* of the knights, for he was certainly party to some of the commission's most important decisions. He was at this time, of course, one of the ordinary royal Council as well. If the French author of the *Chronicque de la Traison et Mort de Richart Deux d'Engleterre* is to be believed, it was Bussy who himself opened the proceedings of the suit between Hereford and Norfolk on 29th April, 1398 at Windsor, and who announced the commission's decision that trial by battle should take place at Coventry on 16th September following ; it was he, too, who declared the commission's judgements of banishment against the two contestants, made on that occasion.[25]

In the meantime, on 1st May, 1398, in spite of his well established position, Bussy had seen fit to procure a pardon under the great seal for having " adhered " to the late Duke of Gloucester and the Earl of Arundel during the events of 1386–88 ; so did Sir Henry Green and on the very same day.[26] Between this time and the meeting in the lists at Coventry in mid-September, Bussy was engaged in presenting to a Convocation of the clergy of the province of York the King's point of view regarding his prerogative in the matter of certain episcopal translations : in one of these the northern province was immediately concerned, because of the vacancy of the archiepiscopal see of York itself by the death of Archbishop Waldby in the previous January. It was actually from Lichfield (the see of Bishop Richard Scrope who, on 2nd June 1398, was translated to York by Pope Boniface IX) that Richard II communicated with his Council about this business. The King desired to be legally advised on the whole subject of translations in a Council which was to meet at Nottingham at midsummer, and especially now over the situation at Lincoln where the see had been left vacant by the death of Bishop Buckingham in the previous March.[27]

(25) *Rot. Parl.*, iii. 360, 368, 373, 383 ; *Chronicque de la Traison et Mort de Richart Deux d' Engleterre*, ed. Benjamin Williams (London, 1846), pp. 13, 19.
(26) *CPR*, 1396-9, 331.
(27) *PPC*, i. 81.

After the Coventry business was over and Bolingbroke and Mowbray banished, Bussy again went north. Along with two other colleagues on the Council, Sir Henry Green and Laurence Drewe, and with Master William Ferriby, he was away from the King's side from 5th October to 20th November, 1398 ; their main business was on the Scottish border, where they were to hold a ' march-day ' with a deputation from King Robert III. On 5th March, 1399 Bussy again was about to set out for another ' march-day,' this time in the company of the Duke of Aumâle and with Green again.[28] Whether the group fulfilled this mission is doubtful, because on 18th March Aumâle, Bussy and Green were party to an act which did more than any other single event to precipitate the overthrow of the régime in the following summer and the deposition of Richard II at the end of September.

Thus far the parliamentary commission had not exceeded its authority ; but now the King falsified the roll of the parliament of 1397-8 in order to give colour to the enlargement of the commission's powers which he deemed necessary for the completion of his policy. The commission met on 18th March, 1399 to revoke the concession made to the dukes of Hereford and Norfolk at the time of their banishment, that their attorneys-general at home should be allowed to take possession of any inheritances to which they might succeed during their exile. The Duke of Lancaster's death on 3rd February, 1399 and the tempting prospect of the Lancastrian inheritance falling into royal control if his heir were disqualified from possession, were clearly the dominant factors behind this *démarche*. Richard II followed this up by having the commission then proceed to the posthumous condemnation of the former spokesman of the Appellants in the Merciless Parliament, Robert Pleasington, and, on 23rd April following, to the condemnation for treason of Henry Bowet (for his assistance to Hereford when the latter petitioned to receive his inheritance by attorney). This turned out to be the last meeting of the parliamentary commission, of which Bussy had been the foremost commoner-member. In the following month Richard II crossed to Ireland. When he returned his rule was over, and the end of his reign was being prepared.

Bussy had personally profited from the effects of the activity of the parliamentary commission on 18th March, 1399. For, only two days after that meeting, he and three other close supporters of Richard's autocracy—Bishop Richard Metford of Salisbury, Bishop Guy Mone of St. David's and Sir Henry Green—were granted the custody (under the Exchequer) of all the inheritance of the Duke of Norfolk as from the time of his banishment at Coventry on 16th September, 1398.[29]

The second royal expedition to Ireland of 1399 was ostensibly to

(28) Exchequer, Foreign Accounts, PRO, E. 364, no. 35. mem. A ; Exchequer, Issue Roll, PRO, E. 403/561, mem. 1. ; *ibid.*, mem. 16.

(29) *CPR*, 1399-1401, 164 ; *CFR*, 1391-9, 296.

take the opportunity of suppressing the rebellious barons and clans there, afforded by the killing (in battle at Kells in July 1398) of the King's Lieutenant, Roger Mortimer, Earl of March. At the time of his own death, later in the summer, Bussy was holding the office of steward of the Mortimer honour of Clare during the minority of the young heir, and it is probable that he came into it not long after Earl Roger's death.[30] Before the Irish expedition left S. Wales Bussy was appointed to act as attorney to two of the many lords who accompanied the King : the Duke of Aumâle and Lord Lovell of Titchmarsh. He was also at this time feoffee and councillor to William Lord Clinton of Maxstoke who also crossed to Ireland.

In Richard II's absence, along with Sir Henry Green and Sir William Bagot, Bussy stayed behind in England as a member of the Council to assist the ' custos ' (the Duke of York) and the other chief members of the administration, the virtual acting head of which was the Treasurer, William Scrope, Earl of Wiltshire. At first they were in London, and then, early in July, they counselled York to move out to St. Albans. It was here that on 7th July Scrope, Bussy, and Green were granted the keeping of the castles of Rochester and Leeds in Kent. This was probably in anticipation of a landing being made in these parts by Henry of Bolingbroke who was by this time known to be intending to break his exile and return from France. Already, however, Bolingbroke had landed in York- shire. On 12th July, at St. Albans again, the custody of Walling- ford castle, where the young Queen Isabel and her household were stationed, was given over to Scrope, Bussy, Green and Bagot (or to any two or three of them). Meanwhile, York had been gathering those whom he could muster of the royal retainers, and on this same day (12th July) Bussy was paid at the Exchequer £130 odd for a following of unstated size.[31]

News of Bolingbroke's march south with rapidly accumulating numbers soon prompted the foremost members of Richard's ad- ministration to move to Oxford. From here they soon fled further westwards to Bristol, presumably hoping that Richard would leave Ireland in time to join them before Bolingbroke's army came up. They took refuge in the castle, but when it was surrendered to Bolingbroke on 28th July, Scrope, Bussy, and Green were excluded from the amnesty granted to the garrison. Taken into custody, they were brought to Bolingbroke outside the castle, and then, on the next day (29th July), were produced before the Constable and Marshal of the rebel army, condemned for treason, and immediately beheaded, their heads being sent to London.[32] Two months later Richard II abdicated and was deposed, being succeeded by Boling- broke on 30th September.

(30) *CPR*, 1399-1401, 50.
(31) *ibid.*, 1396-9, 519, 541 ; 588, 591 ; *Rot. Parl.*, iv 152 ; *Annales Johannis de Trokelowe, etc.*, *op. cit.*, pp. 223, 243 ; Exchequer, Issue Roll, PRO, E. 403/562, mem. 14.
(32) *Annales .... de Trokelowe, op. cit.*, 246 ; *Historia Vite et Regni Ricardi II*, ed. T. Hearne, *op.cit*, 153 ; *Chronicque de la Traison et Mort, op.cit.*, 40.

There had been no more hope for Bussy than for the other two. He was regarded in the popular estimation as responsible for the downfall of the Appellants of 1388. References to the 'busch' in political songs of the time suggest that he was generally detested : for example,

> ' Ther is a busch that is forgrowe ;
> Crop hit welle and hold hit lowe,
> Or elles hit wolle be wilde,' and
> ' The busch is bare and waxeis sere,
> Hit may no lengur leves bere ;
>
> . . . .
>
> But hewe hit downe crop and rote
> And to the town hit lede.'

The disinherited Duke of Lancaster was especially regarded as owing him grudge :

> ' Upon the busch the eron [Henry] wolle reste ;
> Of alle places it liketh hym beste,
> To loke aftur his pray.'[33]

Even locally Bussy seems to have used his considerable authority in the last years of his career in a high-handed way. In Suffolk he had taken it upon himself to order the sheriff not to pay the priory of Eye a levy it had long received from the fee-farm of the borough of Dunwich. And on the very day of his execution at Bristol he made a confession, formally attested on 27th September, 1399 by Lord Roos of Helmsley, Lord Willoughby of Eresby, and Sir Thomas Rempston (steward of Bolingbroke's household), to the effect that he had long held a moiety of the manor of Marston, on the opposite bank of the Witham from his own place at Hougham, which right-fully belonged (*jure uxoris*) to John Ker esquire. When, in accordance with this confession, Henry IV granted the moiety to Ker and his wife on 22nd November, 1399, it was stated in the patent that Bussy had forced them to make him an estate in the property.[34]

By his condemnation for treason Bussy, of course, forfeited his estates. The judgements at Bristol against Scrope, Bussy and Green were confirmed in Henry IV's first parliament on 19th November, 1399. The new King, answering the plea of Scrope's father that his son's forfeiture should not disinherit him and his other children, said that by way of conquest he would disinherit none but these three, who had been guilty of all the evil that had befallen the realm : *their* lands he would have 'par Conquest.' They were deemed to have been 'juggez et conquiz en lour vies,' so that their condemnation should not be regarded as posthumous. For this 'droiturel jugge-ment' upon their late Speaker, the Commons thanked the King, and thanked God, too, that he had sent them ' tiel Roy et Governour.'[35] Enquiries had been already set afoot on 16th September as to the

---

(33) *Political Poems and Songs*, ed. T. Wright (R.S.), i. 363, 365.
(34) *CPR*, 1399-1401, 172 ; 174-5 ; Chancery Miscellanea, PRO, C. 47/14/7, no. 9.
(35) *Rot. Parl.*, iii, 453b.

whereabouts of Bussy's plate and other *personalia* ; in November 1400 proclamations were ordered to be made against their conceal- ment ; and as late as June 1402 a commission was appointed to discover and seize all his goods and chattels in Lincolnshire and Nottinghamshire.[36] Bussy's son, John, who acted as a J.P. in Kesteven from March 1437 to November 1439, had recovered some at any rate of his father's forfeited estates in Lincolnshire and Rutland, including Hougham itself. A Bussy family psalter rightly enough described him as the son and heir of the John Bussy ' qui obiit apud Bristow pro Ricardo secundo.'[37] It is unlikely that, out- side his own family, there had been many who regarded Sir John Bussy as a martyr to any cause but that of his own self-aggrandise- ment.

---

(36) *CPR*, 1396-9, 596 ; *ibid*, 1401-5, 134 ; *CCR*, 1399-1402, 293.
(37) *CPR*, 1436-41, 585 ; *Feudal Aids*, iii. 363, 365 ; IV 213 ; *Lincolnshire Notes and Queries*, vol. 2.

4

SIR JOHN CHEYNE OF BECKFORD, KNIGHT OF THE SHIRE FOR GLOUCESTERSHIRE IN 1390, 1393, 1394 AND IN 1399, WHEN ELECTED SPEAKER[1]

AMONG the Commons in Parliament in the medieval period the knights of the shire, those who were elected to represent the communities of the several counties, were generally much more important, socially and politically, than those who sat for the towns, although the latter outnumbered them. And from 1376, when first we meet with the Commons' Speaker, it was exclusively from among the knights of the shire that he was

The following abbreviations have been used in the footnotes :—

Rot. Parl. = Rotuli Parliamentorum.
V.C.H.   = Victoria County History.
C.C.R.   = Calendar of Close Rolls.
C.F.R.   = Calendar of Fine Rolls.
C.P.R.   = Calendar of Patent Rolls.
P.R.O.   = Public Record Office.
R.S.   = Rolls Series.
P.P.C.   = Proceedings and Ordinances of the Privy Council, ed. N. H. Nicolas.

[1] Official Return of the Members of Parliament, I, 237, 244, 247, 258; Rot. Parl., III, 424.

Sir John Cheyne of Beckford must not be confused with the John Cheyne of Long Stanton (Cambs), knight of the shire for Cambs. on seven occasions between 1355 and 1373; nor with the Sir John Cheyne, knight of the shire for Bedfordshire in 1372 and for Bucks. in 1373 and 1381 and sheriff in these counties in 1371–2, who was almost certainly of Isenhamstead Chenies (Bucks.) (V.C.H. Bucks. [III, 200] hopelessly confuses Cheyne of Isenhampstead and Cheyne of Beckford, especially regarding the latter's condemnation for treason in 1397 and the nature of the treason, because of a mistaken identification of John Lord Cobham with Sir John Oldcastle the Lollard). Neither should Sir John Cheyne of Beckford be mixed up with the John Cheyne who was treasurer of household to John of Gaunt from 1374 to c. 1379 and the duke's receiver for the honour of Tutbury from 1380 to 1383, for he was a canon of Lincoln and then of Salisbury, and in 1379 archdeacon of Exeter, and was clearly an ecclesiastic and remained one (R. Somerville, History of the Duchy of Lancaster, I, 365, 381). Another namesake of the Speaker was the Sir John Cheyne who married

[continued

elected. This was so until 1533, when the first parliamentary burgess to become Speaker was chosen.

The only knight of the shire for Gloucestershire ever to be elected by the Commons as their Speaker in Parliament was Sir John Cheyne of Beckford. Chosen and presented as Speaker at the virtual beginning of Henry IV's first parliament on the morrow of his coronation, Cheyne was, however, superseded on the very next day. The official account in the roll of the parliament relates simply that he successfully applied to be excused on the grounds of ill-health, but there is chronicle evidence to suggest that it was pressure from behind the scenes which resulted in his exoneration. To a historian of the medieval parliament, this is what makes Cheyne chiefly memorable: that, at the beginning of a period when the Commons were to show themselves of some considerable political significance, here was an instance of their own free choice of a Speaker being virtually over-ruled because of his personal unacceptability in certain influential circles. But, apart from this, Cheyne's career is of great intrinsic interest: one of the knights of the King's Chamber in the latter half of Richard II's reign, he became a member of the royal Council in the reign of his supplanter, Henry IV; under both these Kings he was engaged in important diplomatic enterprises, especially at the Roman Curia in some of the most

continued

Margery, daughter and heir of Sir John Devereux of Holme Lacy and Bullingham (Herefordshire) and Lower Hayton (Shropshire). For the heir of this Sir John Cheyne was his daughter, Joan. (The Speaker left sons to succeed him.) Moreover, Joan had entered into her inheritance sometime before January 1409 when the Speaker had still over five years to live. This other Sir John Cheyne is almost certainly he of that name who died in the summer of 1398 when his lands in Herefordshire and Shropshire, held by him (by the courtesy) as tenant of Roger Mortimer, late earl of March, were seized into the King's hands. It must have been this John Cheyne who as still an esquire went to Ireland in the Earl of March's retinue in August 1394 and who (having been in the meantime knighted) was still there in 1395 and 1397. To distinguish between the two Sir Johns is made difficult by the fact that their wives' names were the same (Margaret) and that the Speaker also went to Ireland in the royal expedition of 1394. It was, however, as a member of the King's own retinue that Sir John of Beckford went. There is no doubt of their different identity (*C.C.R.*, *1405–9*, 481; *ibid.*, *1422–9*, 448; *ibid.*, *1441–7*, 81; *C.F.R.*, *1391–9*, 271–2; *C.P.R.*, *1391–6*, 481, 562, 638; *ibid.*, *1396–9*, 146).

important phases of this period of schism in the Papacy; and by some of his contemporaries he evidently was suspected of sympathy with at least part of the programme of John Wyclif and the Lollards that was so disturbing to English churchmen in their day.

It has not been found possible to trace with any confidence the particular family of Cheyne to which this Sir John Cheyne belonged: his parentage remains undiscovered. The lands which he eventually came to hold were seemingly those he secured either in right of his wives or by royal grant at fee-farm; and it was, in fact, the estate of the alien priory of Beckford in Gloucestershire which, from the time of his being granted by the Crown in 1379 the right to occupy it, he made his usual home. If he is to be identified with the John Cheyne of Sussex who in November 1373 shared the custody of the temporalities of the see of Worcester (and I think that he may), he perhaps belonged to the same family which had produced Sir William de Cheyne, knight of the shire for Sussex in 1334 and 1348, and Roger and William Cheyne who sat in parliament for Chichester several times between 1358 and 1380. However this may be, it is probable that he was a younger son and that as such he was destined at first for a career in the Church and took minor orders. There is no reason to doubt the evidence of the chroniclers, Thomas Walsingham and John Capgrave, that (to use the latter's words) 'he had befor take the ordir of subdiacone and withoute dispensacioune aspired to the ordir of wedlak, and eke the degree of knythod,' and that even after the turn of the fourteenth century he was regarded in certain ecclesiastical circles as a renegade and apostate.[1]

However obscure his origins, it is fairly certain that John Cheyne was of good birth. His first marriage at least suggests it. For the first of his two wives was Margaret, daughter of William Deincourt, lord of Thurgarton (Notts.) and other estates in the east midlands, probably the same who (as a knight banneret) had been summoned to parliament from 1332

[1] *Thome Walsingham Historia Anglicana*, ed. H. T. Riley (Rolls Series), II, 266; John Capgrave, *The Chronicle of England*, ed. F. C. Hingeston (R.S.), 287.

until his death in 1364. When Cheyne married her in 1372–3, Margaret was the widow of Sir Robert de Tiptoft who had died on 13 April 1372. He, too, had been in receipt of an individual writ of summons to parliament in 1368 and 1371. In July 1372 Margaret had been granted as her dower and as estates held in jointure with Sir Robert de Tiptoft the manors of Langar (Notts), Easton (Lincs), Edmundthorpe (Leics), and Oxenton (Glos), and the advowson of Barrow (Norfolk). In 1374 the wardships and marriages of Sir Robert de Tiptoft's three daughters and coheirs were granted to the then Treasurer of England, Sir Richard Scrope of Bolton, who married two of them into his own family, Margaret to his eldest son (Roger) and Milicent to his third son (Stephen). When their mother died shortly before 7 April 1380, Scrope was granted the custody of her dower estates, which according to the extents made at Sir Robert de Tiptoft's death eight years before had been worth 230 marks (£153 6s 8d) a year. Her marriage with John Cheyne had clearly been contracted without formal royal approval: on 14 November 1373, the escheator in Nottinghamshire (Langar in that county was the Tiptofts' chief seat) and the like official in Gloucestershire were ordered to seize into the King's hand all the lands Cheyne and his wife held in these counties, the reason being that Margaret, as the widow of a tenant-in-chief, had married without royal licence against her oath; not until 26 June 1374 were they pardoned the trespass by the royal Council in return for a fine of £100. Cheyne was allowed to pay the fine into the Exchequer in half-yearly instalments of £10. He must have fallen behind in his payments, because on 4 March 1378, by which time £70 ought to have been paid over, he was pardoned £50 of the fine. The marriage had certainly caused him to run into some trouble elsewhere: shortly before 4 August 1374, as an esquire in the royal service, Cheyne complained of assault and mayhem suffered at the hands of Nicholas Deincourt (presumably a kinsman of his wife's), who had conspired his death and ambushed him at Langar when, so he alleged, he was on his way to Court, and on 10 January 1375 he secured the appointment of a commission of oyer and terminer; a few weeks later

an order for Deincourt's arrest and arraignment in the King's
Bench, first commanded on 6 January, was repeated. What was
the cause or outcome of this *fracas* is not known. The incident is
chiefly of interest as showing that Cheyne had already been retained as an esquire in the royal service, an entry which he had
perhaps owed to the connection his marriage brought about with
the Treasurer, Lord Scrope of Bolton.[1] The same connection may
also have eased his participation as John Cheyne of Sussex in
November 1373 in the custody of the temporalities of the
bishopric of Worcester, which he shared with a canon of
Chichester and two other clerks[2]. His own chief territorial
interests were very soon to lie in the diocese of Worcester, but
already in right of his first wife he had land there.

Probably soon after the death of his first wife, certainly before
October 1389, Cheyne married again, his second wife being
Margaret, daughter of Edward Lovetoft of Southoe (Beds).
How much land this marriage brought him immediately is not
clear, but when Lovetoft's widow died in 1405 Cheyne and his
second wife came into estates at Southoe and Orton Waterville
(Beds), the manors of Skillington, Bulby, and Aunby (S.W.
Lincolnshire), and the manor of Boughton (S. Huntingdonshire).
This second wife was the mother of Cheyne's two sons, John and
Edward. She survived him.[3]

By February 1378 John Cheyne had been knighted, being at
that time in command of a military retinue about to proceed to

[1] Dugdale, *Baronage*, II, 40; Thomas Blore, *Rutland*, 44; R. Clutterbuck,
Hertfordshire, III, 103; *C.C.R., 1369–74*, 396–7; *ibid, 1374–7*, 178; *C.F.R.,
1369–77*, 219, 251; *ibid., 1377–83*, 205; *C.P.R., 1370–4*, 413; 492; *ibid., 1374–7*,
63, 142; *ibid., 1377–81*, 132.

When Cheyne came to make his will on 1 November 1413 he left to the church
of Beckford (Glos.) a coverlet of gold, embroidered with the arms of Tiptoft, to
cover the Easter sepulchre. The recognisance for 40 marks into which he entered
on 9 May 1380 with Sir Gervase de Clifton of Clifton (Notts.) was in connexion
with some transaction arising out of his interests in Nottinghamshire; the sum
was leviable in Gloucestershire (*C.C.R., 1377–81*, 374).

[2] *C.F.R., 1369–77*, 223.

[3] *C.C.R., 1402–5*, 424, 427; *C.F.R., 1399–1405*, 298; the manor of Bulby
(S. Lincs.) Sir John Cheyne and his wife conveyed by a fine levied on 25 June
1406 to their elder son, John, and his wife, Elizabeth.

sea.[1] Quite clearly he had continued under Richard II to be a royal retainer. He was, moreover, closely connected with some of those former members of the Black Prince's household who were now becoming so important in the conduct of the household of the young King, partly through their influence with his mother, Joan of Kent. Cheyne's almost certain sympathy with at any rate some parts of the programme of the Lollards—he was after all an apostate clerk, having abandoned his orders without dispensation—probably predisposed him to friendship with a small circle in the Princess of Wales's household who were similarly inclined to adopt or favour heretical views, men like Sir Thomas Latimer and Sir Lewis Clifford. The language of the wills of these men was to have a common element of abject self-contempt and contrition cast in almost identically strong terms, and though Clifford's and Cheyne's heresy is (as Mr McFarlane has said) 'much less well authenticated' than, say, Latimer's, the evidence for it (as he submits) cannot be rejected out of hand.[2] Perhaps what most appealed to Cheyne in the Lollard aims was the demand for the disendowment of the regular clergy, the 'possessioners.' He was certainly not above profiting (but then neither were so many who can have had no truck with heresy) from the discomfiture that the war with France and the Papal Schism were occasioning the alien priories in England, to the extent of being ready to take his fees as a royal retainer in the form of custodies of the sequestrated estates of the dependencies of certain French abbeys and priories. And he may have hoped for the adoption of more revolutionary policies.

The first but not the most important of these royal grants to Sir John Cheyne was that which he received on 4 October 1379: the right to farm, for 100 marks a year (payable at the Exchequer), the estates of the non-conventual priory of Beckford in Gloucestershire, a dependency of the Augustinian priory of Sainte Barbe-en-Auge in the diocese of Lisieux in Normandy. Among his sureties were Sir Lewis Clifford and Sir Philip de la Vache. It is true that the fee-farm rent which Cheyne was to

---

[1] T. Carte, *Catalogue des Rolles Gascons, etc.*, tom. II, 124.
[2] K. B. McFarlane, *John Wyclif*, 146.

pay was slightly more (by 11 marks) than the latest of his
predecessors had paid earlier in this year. Later, on 6 February
1381, a yeoman of the King's Chamber and an esquire of John
of Gaunt were together prepared to pay an increment of £20 and
to contribute to clerical tenths, from which Cheyne had been
exempted; but on 18 February following Cheyne recovered his
farm at the old rate and, what was more, under an agreement
that he should enjoy the arrangement for life; the patent of his
competitors was accordingly revoked two days later. On 6 May
1380, as retained to stay with the King, Cheyne had already
been granted for life an annuity of 50 marks charged on the
farm of the priory, which meant, of course, that the rent he paid
for Beckford was halved; and the rent was virtually cancelled
altogether on 1 October 1383 when this life annuity was raised
to 100 marks. (If Beckford reverted to its rightful owners when
peace was made with France, the Exchequer was to become
chargeable.) Cheyne consolidated his holding at Beckford
further by securing on 15 October 1389 a royal patent enabling
him to acquire from the mother-house of St. Barbe a demise of
the priory for the term of his own life, the life of Margaret his
(second) wife, and the life of their elder son John, a rent being
due to the Exchequer when Sir John himself should die and his
annuity expire. Of this arrangement he successfully petitioned
for a papal confirmation when on an embassy to Boniface IX in
the autumn of 1390; the papal letter, which describes Sir John
as being of the diocese of Worcester, discloses that the alien
priory of Beckford had dependent estates at Barford (Warwickshire) and Colsterworth (Lincs) as well as in Gloucestershire. In
September 1395 Cheyne had to agree to find £8 a year to maintain a monk of St. Barbe who was to be sent over to look to the
priory's possessions in England (it had once had two monks
at Beckford), but this was probably only the result of an agreement which Cheyne had earlier arrived at with the mother-
house in Normandy prior to 1390, regarding the life interests of
himself, his wife, and elder son. He was confirmed in his royal
grant of the priory by Henry IV soon after his accession in 1399,
and the alien priory of Beckford remained with the family until

it reverted to the Crown (under the act of 1414) following the death of his widow in 1437, soon after which it passed into the endowment of Eton College.[1]

Sir John Cheyne's concern with Beckford was not his only interest in the estates of French religious houses which found themselves embarrassed by the double inconvenience of the Anglo-French war and their own adherence to the schismatic papal line of Avignon. On 2 February 1387 he was given a royal licence to acquire for life the farm of all the Gloucestershire estates of the Norman abbey of Beaubec, undertaking to pay the Exchequer a rent of 16 marks; this farm, too, was confirmed on 1 December 1399 by Henry IV who, moreover, conceded the rent to Cheyne's elder son, John. Only three days before this concession (on 28 November) Cheyne had procured for himself and Thomas Horston *alias* Shapwyke (canon of St. Paul's) a royal grant of the right to farm for £140 the rectory of the church of Frampton (Dorset) which was annexed to the alien priory of Frampton (a non-conventual cell of the Benedictine abbey of St. Stephen of Caen), together with the rectories of Newent, Beckford, and Dymock, which were annexed to the non-conventual alien priory of Newent (a dependency of the Norman abbey of St. Mary of Cormeilles). He and Horston shortly afterwards (in May 1400) surrendered the £40 a year profits of Frampton, but they held on to the three Gloucestershire rectories annexed to Newent priory at a farm of £100. Two-thirds of this rent (100 marks) Cheyne was from 26 May 1400 to receive as a life annuity at which he was already retained by Henry IV. A new patent of 11 February 1401, ratifying this arrangement, provided that they were not to be expelled from the custody, even if anyone were prepared to offer a bigger farm for it. In addition to sharing the rectories appropriated to the alien priory of Newent, Cheyne secured for himself alone in

[1] *C.F.R.*, *1377–83*, 167, 239–40; *C.P.R.*, *1377–81*, 490; *ibid.*, *1381–5*, 312; *ibid.*, *1388–92*, 118; *ibid.*, *1391–6*, 632; *ibid.*, *1399–1401*, 111; *Cal. of Papal Registers, Papal Letters*, IV, 328; T. D. Fosbroke, *Abstracts of Records and MSS. respecting the county of Gloucester*, II, 285–6; *Bristol and Glos. Arch. Soc. Trans.*, XIX, 64.

February 1400 the keeping of its temporalities for an annual
farm of £54 to the Exchequer (increased, by an annuity of 20
marks payable to the prior, to a charge of £67 6s 8d), namely,
the manors of Newent (Glos) and Kingstone (Herefordshire).
What he and Horston still owed for the rectories annexed to
Newent after his own annuity of 100 marks had been allowed
him, namely 50 marks a year, *plus* the £54 a year at which he
himself farmed the Newent temporalities, a total of £87 6s 8d,
was released to him on 14 December 1402, in full satisfaction of
his wages and rewards as long as he remained a member of the
King's Council. In December 1411, by which time he had ceased
to be one of the royal Council, he was still in possession of the
Newent temporalities, the reversion of which was then included
in the endowment of the Duke of York's collegiate foundation
at Fotheringhay in which Henry IV was taking a close interest.

What all this rigmarole means is that from 1383 Cheyne
enjoyed the Beckford alien priory estates rent-free, the Beaubec
abbey lands (first granted him in 1387) for a rent of 16 marks
(which from 1399 he paid to his elder son), the spiritualities
(shared with Horston) and the temporalities of the alien priory
of Newent rent-free (except for a charge of 20 marks for the
prior) while he was a member of Henry IV's Council, and for
just over £100 a year when he was not: in the time of his
counsellorship under Henry IV—and he was certainly counsellor
between June 1400 and April 1407 and perhaps until January
1410—the income which he and his family were credited at
the Exchequer as receiving in remissions of alien priory fee-
farms (granted in lieu of annuities) stood at £231 6s 8d a year.[1]
Alien priory extents were no less notoriously low than those of
other Crown lands, and Cheyne's occupation of his monastic
lands must have stood him at a much higher cash figure than
that. It was, moreover, sure and constant income and not
susceptible to the vagaries and inadequacies of the usual sources

[1] C.F.R., *1383–91*, 175; *ibid.*, *1399–1405*, 12, 41, 61, 105; C.P.R., *1399–1401*,
130, 200, 205, 288, 412, 431; *ibid.*, *1401–5*, 183, 237; *ibid.*, *1408–13*, 358; *Rot.
Parl.*, III, 653a.

of revenue on which Crown annuities were so often charged, Exchequer funds and customs dues.

The revolution of 1399, the deposition of Richard II and the accession of Henry IV, it will have been realized, proved nothing of a setback to Sir John Cheyne's career. By that time he had been, however, long and well established in political circles. His capacities for service in the diplomatic field were to be much exploited by Henry IV, but they had already and much earlier been exercised by Richard II's government. On 5 May 1380, the day before he was granted by Richard II an annual retaining fee for life of 50 marks (charged on his fee-farm for Beckford priory), he was allowed at the Lower Exchequer £40 for his wages for a recent embassy to Brittany to Duke John de Montfort 'causa allegiancie inter dominum Regem et predictum Ducem et Barones Brittanie'; he was still receiving payments in settlement of the £110 due to him in the following October and December.[1] Roughly a year later, in November 1381, he was being sent, accompanied by Lancaster Herald, 'in secretis negociis regis' to Wenzel, King of the Romans, Richard II's marriage with whose sister, Anne of Bohemia, had been already settled and was by this time impending.[2] On 1 October 1383 his royal annuity of 50 marks was doubled. He got the 100 marks charged again on his farm-rent for Beckford priory which, in fact, stood precisely at that same amount; the rise meant (as we have seen) his holding Beckford rent-free.[3]

The increasing 'spread' of Cheyne's interests at this time is suggested by the fact that in this year (sometime shortly before his death in September) William Street, Chief Butler of England to Edward III from 1361 to 1376 and from September 1376 to the end of Edward's reign his Controller of Household, when making his will in Rome gave instructions that Cheyne and Sir Richard Burley should be 'mingled' with his executors 'to levy his money in whatsoever Lumbardes or others hand in Rome.'

[1] Exchequer, Issue Rolls, P.R.O., E 403/478, mem. 19; ibid., 481, mems. 4, 12.
[2] ibid., E403/487, mem. 7.
[3] See above, p. 49.

Street was up at the Curia arranging for the payment into the
Papal Camera of the first-fruits (amounting to 10,000 florins)
due for the see of Canterbury from the new archbishop, William
Courtenay, Street's own expenses amounting to 3,000 florins.
He was clearly doing some financial business of his own 'on the
side.' His will, however, suggests that he needed to sell his lands
to provide for its administration; among other arrangements he
was prepared to let Cheyne have his manor of Mereworth (Kent)
for £2,000, 'on c^l (£100) better cheape then eny man.' There is
nothing to suggest that Cheyne ever bought the place.[1] Nor is
there any reason to believe that Cheyne was himself up at the
Curia at this time. Certainly he was in England early in October
1383 when (as Sir John Cheyne of Notts) he stood surety for
Sir Philip de la Vache, K.G., when the latter was granted the
farm of the manor of Chiltern Langley.[2]

In the next ensuing years, not a great deal is known of
Cheyne's activities, but on 18 October 1384 the custody of the
castle of Marck in the march of Calais was entrusted to him (as
from Michaelmas) instead of William, the younger son of Guy
Lord Brian, who had occupied the office certainly for the two
previous years. There were certain difficulties between the two
knights over delays in the handing-over of the castle: Brian
alleged that Cheyne was responsible; the matter came up before
the Council as late as 24 July 1389 when Brian offered proof
'par son corps come chivaler,' which might have taken the case
into the Court of the Constable and Marshal, but on 8 March
1390 the Council decided in Cheyne's favour. He had quite
clearly been no absentee captain and he held the post at a
difficult time, especially in 1385 when there was serious prospect of a French invasion of England. But shortly before the end
of January 1386 he was superseded by a Cambridgeshire squire,
Simon de Burgh, who was then treasurer of Calais.[3]

It is possible that Cheyne, despite his close association with

[1] *Collectanea Topographica et Genealogica*, vol. 3, 100.
[2] *C.F.R., 1383–91*, 8.
[3] T. Carte, *op. cit.*, II, 147–8; *C.P.R., 1381–5*, 481, 532; *ibid., 1385–9*, 58;
Parliament and Council Proceedings, Exchequer, P.R.O., E 175, file 3, no. 6.

Richard II's court and the considerable emoluments he already
enjoyed at his hands, swung over for a time to the aristocratic
party of opposition which seized control of the royal government in the autumn parliament of 1386. At Candlemas 1387 he
was confirmed by the new administration (the parliamentary
commission) in a recent grant for life of the right to farm the
Gloucestershire estates of the Norman abbey of Beaubec. This
is nothing very much to go by, of course, as evidence of a change
of political front on Cheyne's part. Nor is the record in the
account-book of the receiver of Henry of Bolingbroke, earl of
Derby, one of the Lords Appellant of 1387–8 who brought down
Richard II's first court party during the Merciless Parliament
of February–June 1388, that sometime during the critical year
September 1387–8, Cheyne made the earl a gift of a 'paltok.'[1]
Perhaps rather more important evidence of Cheyne's personal
policy at this time is his arrest and condemnation for treason in
1397, when Richard II was achieving his revenge on some of
these domestic enemies of ten years before, although it may be
that certain aspects of his career in the meantime had rendered
him 'suspect' rather than any action in 1387–8.

During the critical years 1386–8 Sir John Cheyne served on
no royal commissions whatsoever. Within little more than a
fortnight of Richard II's re-establishment of his royal authority,
Cheyne was given (on 20 May 1389) a commission to investigate
felonies, oppressions, false alliances, etc., in Gloucestershire.
Whatever his activities in 1387–8, it is clear that he was now
persona grata with the King. For it was as a knight of the King's
Chamber that he was paid at the Lower Exchequer £7 expenses,
when early in July 1389 he was despatched by the Council from
London to Sandwich, in order to meet the Comte de St. Pol and
other French ambassadors coming to England to take the King's
oath regarding the recently concluded Anglo-French truce.
Cheyne acted as their host on the way up to London. A few days
later the Council turned its attention to Cheyne's dispute with
Brian over the handing over of Marck castle five years before

[1] *C.F.R., 1383–91*, 175; Duchy of Lancaster, Accounts Various, P.R.O.,
D.L. 28/1/2.
A paltock was a sleeved doublet.

and eventually decided in his favour. On 10 November 1389 he was made a justice of the peace in Gloucestershire for the first time, and to the parliament of the following January (1390) he was for the first time elected as knight of the shire, for that county. On 15 October 1389 he had secured a royal licence enabling the mother-house of St. Barbe-en-Auge to demise the Beckford priory properties in Gloucestershire and Lincolnshire to him, his second wife Margaret, and their son John, for the term of their lives, the fee-farm rent due to the Exchequer to be in abeyance for Sir John's own life. Exactly a year later to the day (15 October 1390), this arrangement was ratified by Boniface IX in return for an appropriate fee, expressly in spite of the fact that the priory of St. Barbe was in the obedience of the anti-pope, Clement VII.[1] Cheyne was almost certainly at this time himself up at the Curia.

The January 1390 parliament had produced a second and more stringent version of the Act of Provisors of 1351, and by the middle of May following Cheyne had already left England for Rome in order to present to the Pope royal letters explaining the statute. He had received an advance of £160 (from the Treasurers for the War with the agreement of the overseers of the parliamentary subsidies) in aid of his wages and expenses, and there is no certain knowledge that he was home again before 9 February 1391, when the Lower Exchequer paid into his own hands a 'donum' of 100 marks, over and above his wages, for the embassy.[2] Re-appointed J.P. in Gloucestershire in June 1390, his continued absence might explain his omission from the bench in the patents which issued on Christmas Eve following.

There is no further reference to Cheyne's being re-included in the commission of the peace in Richard II's time nor to his continued membership of the royal Chamber. But he was certainly busy with certain aspects of administration at the centre for the rest of the reign. From a writ issued at Nottingham on 23 June 1392 ordering the sheriff of Gloucestershire to elect a

---

[1] C.P.R., 1388-92, 61, 118, 139, 342, 344; Exchequer, Issue Rolls, P.R.O., E403/524, mem. 14; Papal Letters, IV, 328.

[2] Exchequer, Issue Rolls, P.R.O., E 403/530, mem. 19; ibid., 532, mem. 16.

knight as coroner in the county instead of Sir John Cheyne, it appears that he was too occupied with divers business to exercise that office. How long Sir John had held it is not known. Three weeks later, still at Nottingham, where the administration had been shifted as a reprisal for London's current dispute with the King, Cheyne stood surety in Chancery for Lady Elizabeth Despenser whose son was still a royal ward, when she was given the wardship of the Glamorganshire estates of one of his tenants who was himself under age. In the Winchester parliament of January 1393 Cheyne was once again knight of the shire for Gloucestershire.[1] On 20 February following he was one of a group of suspect Lollard knights to whom (as feoffees to fulfil his will) Sir Lewis Clifford, a Chamber knight and very probably himself another of the sect, was then licensed by royal patent to convey the castle, manor and lordship of Ewyas Harald (Herefordshire); Cheyne's co-feoffees were Sir Philip de la Vache (Clifford's son-in-law), Sir Thomas Latimer, and Sir' John de Montague. The last named became Earl of Salisbury in 1397 and, still faithful to Richard of Bordeaux after the revolution of 1399, incurred forfeiture for his share in the rising of January 1400 during which he met his death. The forfeiture apparently caused Clifford and his remaining feoffees such trouble that, on 12 January 1400, they 'bargained' their estate to William de Beauchamp, Lord Abergavenny, a transaction which was licensed by royal patent on 20 February. In the autumn of 1404, by which time Walsingham (the St. Albans chronicler) says that he had deserted the Lollards, Clifford made an abjectly penitent end; on 17 September 1404 he had appointed La Vache and Cheyne overseers of his will.[2]

In January 1394 Cheyne was re-elected as knight of the shire for Gloucestershire, and in the following autumn he accompanied Richard II on his first expedition to Ireland, taking out royal letters of protection for half a year as a member of the

[1] *C.C.R.*, 1392–6, 3; *C.F.R.*, 1391–9, 51.
[2] *C.P.R.*, *1391–6*, 227; *ibid.*, *1399–1401*, 204, 220; *C.C.R.*, *1399–1402*, 116; N. H. Nicolas, *Testamenta Vetusta*, 165.

King's retinue.[1] There is no reason to believe that he did not return with the King in May 1395. In these years of comparative political quiet in the 1390's, Cheyne began to form (or perhaps develop) a connection with Richard's foremost enemy, whose threats to depose him in 1386 and 1387 and whose part in the destruction or proscription of his friends in the Merciless Parliament the King was never to forget or forgive: Thomas of Woodstock, duke of Gloucester, Constable of England, the youngest of his uncles. It is not possible to say when first Cheyne began to officiate in the Court of the Constable and Marshal as the Constable's deputy and president of the court, but the first appointment of a royal commission of oyer and terminer to be prompted by an appeal against a sentence pronounced by Cheyne in a cause of arms brought before him in this Court is dated 18 November 1393. There were a number of such commissions, following appeals against Cheyne's sentences, between 1394 and 1397. One commission to re-open such a case was appointed as late as November 1406, but that describes him as *late* lieutenant-constable. There can be little doubt that the period of Cheyne's occupation of the deputy-constableship began no later than 1393 and ended in 1397. In August 1396 he was himself a commissioner to hear an appeal from Bordeaux exhibited in Chancery against proceedings in the Court of Admiralty.[2] It is not improbable that Cheyne, perhaps before he abandoned his ecclesiastical orders, had had some legal training as a civilian and maybe as a canonist; such an education would go far to explain his employment in the Court of Chivalry, where civilian processes were used, and his earlier and later ambassadorial work, especially at the Papal Curia.

Sir John Cheyne's name does not appear in the formal record of the proceedings of Richard II's last parliament of 1397–8. But there is ample chronicle evidence that the King had come to regard him as 'unsafe.' It is impossible to say whether this was because he had been implicated in the events of 1387–8, because

[1] *C.P.R., 1391–6*, 472.
[2] *ibid.*, 332, 340, 380, 410, 531, 550, 576, 668; *ibid., 1396–9*, 23, 28, 42, 58, 83, 165; *ibid., 1405–8*, 269.

of his later connection with Gloucester, or because of other grounds. A London chronicle says that he was arrested on 21 July 1397 at the same time as Gloucester, Arundel, Warwick, and Lord Cobham, all of whom were certainly proceeded against and suffered forfeiture during the 1397–8 parliament. Another anonymous chronicle says that after their arrest Cobham and Cheyne were brought before parliament on 24 September 1397 and condemned to be drawn and hanged for treason, but sentenced merely to perpetual imprisonment 'prece ac magna instancia dominorum.' The chronicle known as the *Continuatio Eulogii* assigns their judgment to perpetual prison to 28 January 1398, that is, to the second session of this parliament which was at Shrewsbury.[1] That is the date on which (according to the *Placita Corone coram Domino Rege in parliamento suo* enrolled on the parliament roll) the Commons at Shrewsbury recalled their impeachment of Lord Cobham during the first session at Westminster, and on which he was then adjudged to imprisonment for life. That Cheyne, whose name does not appear among the *Placita*, was in fact proceeded against seems clear from the nature of the formal excuse he made in Henry IV's first parliament when he sought exoneration from the office of Speaker (according to the version of the incident supplied by the St. Alban's chronicler, Thomas Walsingham). The roll of the October 1399 parliament itself, after noting his presentation by the Commons, his acceptance by the King, and the King's agreement to his Speaker's 'protestation,' says no more than that the Commons on the following day asked for his excusation because of his present 'infirmitee et maladie.' But Walsingham says that Cheyne asked to be exonerated 'ratione debilitatis et infirmitatis *quas contraxerat dum in carcere detentus fuerat, suorum adversariorum procuratione*,' and further demanded that the cause of his imprisonment should be publicly made known and that he should be able to declare his innocence. Whether he had been

---

[1] *Chronicles of London*, ed. C. L. Kingsford, p. 18; *Anonymi Chronicon Godstowianum*, ed. T. Hearne, (Oxford, 1716), p. 235; *Continuatio Eulogii* in *Eulogium*, ed. F. S. Haydon (R.S.), vol. III, 376.

actually in custody until the liberations that followed Bolingbroke's return from exile is not known, but his inclusion in a
commission appointed to survey weirs on Gloucestershire rivers
on 20 June 1398 (as Sir John Cheyne of Beckford) can only have
been a piece of Chancery inadvertence, unless he had been set at
liberty as early as that date.[1]

The Lords and Commons of this first parliament of Henry IV
had been summoned to witness (as a gathering of estates) the
deposition of Richard II and the new King's accession. Sir John
Cheyne had been elected for the fourth time for Gloucestershire.
After the acceptance of Richard's resignation of the Crown and
of Bolingbroke's claim to it on 30 September, parliament,
formally re-summoned, met on 6 October and was then adjourned until the morrow of Henry IV's coronation, 14 October.
On that day the Commons presented Cheyne as their 'parlour et
procuratour en parlement.' He was accepted by the King and
his 'protestation' agreed to. On the very next day, however, he
sought and secured exoneration on the formal grounds of
physical weakness and illness, the Commons having already
chosen one John Doreward, knight of the shire for Essex, to
replace him. The roll of the parliament evidently gives nothing
away. Fortunately, Walsingham of St. Albans felt moved to say
more. He tells us that when parliament had met on 6 October
Archbishop Arundel instructed the Commons to proceed to
elect a Speaker, and (his narrative implies) that right-away they
chose Cheyne. On the following day the convocation of the
southern province had met in St. Paul's. In the course of its
proceedings Arundel alluded to the anti-clericalism of many of
the parliamentary knights; especially dangerous, he said, were
the 'sensus et opiniones' of Sir John Cheyne, already the
Speaker-elect, who had long been an enemy of the Church (*qui
perante fuit infestus Ecclesie*). If, Arundel is reported to have
gone on, Cheyne knew anything derogatory to the clergy he
would speak out 'in dedecus clericorum.' And the Archbishop

[1] *Rot. Parl.*, III, 424b; *Johannis de Trokelowe et Henrici de Blaneforde
Chronica et Annales (Annales Henrici Quarti)*, ed. H. T. Riley (R.S.), 302;
C.P.R., 1396–9, 371.

advised the adoption of certain measures to anticipate anti-
clerical criticism on the part of laymen, especially on the score
of pluralism and non-residence of beneficed clerks.[1] It looks very
much as though Cheyne's abandonment of his office as Speaker
a week later was due to pressure on the Commons from the
restored Archbishop, either directly or indirectly through the
King.

However much Arundel disapproved of him, Cheyne's own
relations with the new King were soon, in spite of this *contretemps*, established on a basis that was certainly satisfactory
from Cheyne's point of view. Within half a year of Henry IV's
accession he had strengthened his hold, by patents of confirmation, on the alien priory of Beckford and on the Beaubec
abbey lands, virtually rent-free in each case; had got a share of
the custody of the spiritualities—the profits of three rectories—
of the alien priory of Newent and a grant on his own sole account
of the custody of its temporalities; and, partially offsetting the
financial obligations to the Crown involved in these last two
grants, he had secured from Henry IV as a King's Knight a life
annuity of 100 marks at the Exchequer, granted him on 23
February 1400[2]. This latter grant was a fresh annuity additional
to the one of like value granted him for life by Richard II in 1383
and confirmed on 20 November 1399.

How closely attached to Bolingbroke Cheyne was, even at this
early period of the reign, is clear not only from these concessions of sources of income and grants of royal annuities but
from other evidence as well. When, according to Froissart's
circumstantial account of the matter, one of the two French
ambassadors who left Paris for England on 1 October 1399 (to
negotiate for the return of Isabel of Valois, Richard II's young
queen) died in London not long after their arrival, Henry IV's
Council sent Sir John Cheyne (Sir Jehan Chesnay) to ask about
the other ambassador's plans for the disposal of his companion's
body, and to proffer the attendance of members of the Council,

[1] *Annales Henrici Quarti, op. cit.,* 290.
[2] See above, pp. 50–1.

the mayor of London and others at the funeral service.[1] Considerably more important than this incident was Cheyne's appointment very early in the reign as a member of an embassy, also including Bishop Trevenant of Hereford and a John Cheyne esquire (probably Sir John's elder son), to go to the Roman Curia to show by what title Henry IV had assumed the Crown, other embassies being also sent to France, Spain and Germany.[2] This is what the St. Albans chronicler says. There is, however, no record of any Exchequer payment made to Cheyne in this connection, and it is therefore improbable that he went.

By the middle of June 1400 Sir John Cheyne had become a member of the King's Council; he was to remain a royal counsellor certainly until April 1407 (when the last reference to him in this capacity occurs),[3] receiving as his fee from Michaelmas 1402 a remission of what from the farms of the spiritualities and temporalities of Newent priory he had been hitherto still required to pay to the Exchequer, £87 6s 8d a year. In these years he began to be more actively employed on royal commissions, some of them local. For the first time since 1390, he was appointed on 28 May 1400 as justice of the peace in Gloucestershire, where he had recently acted on an inquiry into alleged wastes (by its custodians) in the property of the alien priory of Deerhurst and into the removal of its muniments. He remained a justice of the peace in Gloucestershire until his death in the winter of 1413–14. For a short time, in 1405, he was a justice of the peace in Huntingdonshire also.[4] In August 1401 he was put on investigations of a case of asportation of goods belonging to the abbot of Evesham at Morton Abbots (Worcs.), and of cases of homicide and wounding at Bromyard (Hereford-shire), and of breaches of the bishop of Hereford's park at Prestbury (Glos.). In May 1402 he was included in the Gloucestershire

---

[1] *Oeuvres de Froissart, Chroniques,* ed. Baron Kervyn de Lettenhowe (Brussels, 1872), tom. XVI, 371.

[2] *Annales Henrici Quarti,* 320.

[3] *P.P.C.,* I, 122, 127, 146, 191, 222, 223, 238, 295; II, 99; T. Rymer, *Foedera,* VIII, 446 452, 479.

[4] *C.P.R., 1399–1401,* 218, 559; *ibid., 1401–5,* 517; *ibid., 1405–8,* 492; *ibid., 1413–16,* 419.

commission of inquiry into cases of malicious rumour concerning the King's political and constitutional intentions; in the following August he was appointed to try the fencibles of Worcestershire before they joined the royal forces at Hereford for service in the war against Owen Glendower in Wales. A year or so later, in September 1403, he was told to get busy down in Gloucestershire and co-operate with the town authorities at Bristol in buying up stores (there and locally) for the replenishing of the castles of Cardiff and Newport, and a week later to assist with the rapid raising of a royal loan of 2,000 marks to keep the King going in Carmarthenshire. In August 1405 he was a member of a commission set up to arrange for the submission of Welsh rebels in the lordships of Usk, Caerleon, Edlogon, and Dingestowe.[1] On the 18 November 1400 he had taken out a royal patent of exemption for life from jury service, from being appointed sheriff, escheator, or other local officer, justice of oyer and terminer, collector of Crown revenues (including parliamentary taxation), leader of men-at-arms and archers, etc.[2] It is not perhap surprising, then, that he never became sheriff in Gloucestershire. But, in any case, the commitments and obligations arising out of his membership of the royal Council were probably very absorbing in this first half of Henry IV's reign. His membership from time to time between 1400 and 1406 of many committees set up with powers of oyer and terminer to deal with appeals of one sort or another from judgments given in the Court of the Constable and Marshal and the Court of Admiralty, was doubtless a consequence partly of his own earlier experience as deputy-constable and partly of his membership of the Royal Council, of which these jurisdictions were, in a sense, branches.[3]

Sir John Cheyne's most important work as a royal counsellor was in the diplomatic field, for which his earlier embassies to Germany in 1381, his mission to Boniface IX in 1390, and

[1] C.P.R., 1399–1401, 552–3; ibid., 1401–5, 128, 138, 293, 296; ibid., 1405–8, 64.
[2] ibid., 1399–1401, 381.
[3] ibid., 231, 416–17, 429, 502, 519, 524, 548; ibid., 1401–5, 211, 213, 315, 469; ibid., 1405–8, 95, 113.

perhaps his earlier clerical background in some degree prepared him. His appointment in February 1401 (following the arrival of envoys in London from the anti-Kaiser Rupert III) to help promote the marriage of Henry IV's elder daughter to the newly crowned Emperor's son and heir, Lewis of Bavaria, was followed (a year later) by his being chosen one of the knights to accompany this royal lady to Germany for the wedding. Granted letters of protection on 19 February 1402, Cheyne presumably crossed with the princess's retinue, which left for Cologne in June. Blanche was married at Heidelberg on 6 July, her escort returning on the 25th of that month. On 15 July Blanche's treasurer had made Cheyne a grant of £4.[1]

Two years later, in the spring and summer of 1404, Cheyne was busy over efforts then being intensified to prevent Anglo-French relations from deteriorating into open hostilities and further taxing a government which, in the past four years, had been increasingly harassed by the need for campaigns against Scotland and Wales and by internal rebellions and commotions. The English pinned their hopes to the continuation of parallel internal divisions in France between the Burgundian and Orleanist factions, but were doing their best to protract the state of uneasy truce. In March 1404 Sir John Cheyne was appointed to go to Paris to confer with Charles VI and Duke Philip of Burgundy, with special instructions to object to the recent hostile attitude adopted by the Duke of Orleans and the Comte de St. Pol and to protest against the blockade of Bordeaux. He was advanced £100 at the Lower Exchequer on 6 March. On 18 March a letter from the deputy-captain of Calais to Burgundy, referring to breaches of the truce, alluded to the absence of information on the English side about Cheyne's safe-conduct. On 25 April the English Council discussed the draft of Cheyne's instructions. Four days later he left London for Calais. The situation, as events were to prove, had been (from a long-term point of view) already further complicated by the death of Burgundy on 27 April. But the news can only have met Cheyne on his landing at Calais. The widowed duchess was prepared to come to terms with the

[1] T. Carte, *op. cit.*, 183; Exchequer, Issue Roll, E 403/573, mem. 20.

English representatives in order to open up the channels of trade between England and the Flemish ports. As regards his projected embassy to the French King about the truce, Cheyne could make little headway, although some communication was achieved between him and the Sire de Hugueville and Maître Guillaume Boisratier sometime between 6 June and 20 July, when he handed over certain formal correspondence from Henry IV and the English Lords and Commons and made some arrangement for a later and more formal meeting. He returned to England on 23 July. (For this embassy he was given 100 marks in addition to daily wages.) On 5 August, after he had apparently reported to Henry IV at Leicester, he was sent out again to the other English commissioners with further instructions. On 1 September 1404 the English embassy, still at Calais, wrote to the French Council, deploring Cheyne's inability to treat directly with them and referring to his having forwarded to the French negotiators the articles of his embassy. A fresh English embassy was ready to treat while the autumn parliament at Coventry was still in session, but Cheyne's direct participation in the negotiations seems to have been by that time concluded.[1] If we are to believe the St. Albans chronicler, he was busy during the parliament about other matters and had a heavy dispute with Archbishop Arundel on his hands.

It is, in a sense, rather odd that though the most active phase of Sir John Cheyne's political life fell in the first part of Henry IV's reign when he was a member of the Royal Council, his career as a knight of the shire ended with the parliament of 1399. He did, however, most probably attend Henry IV's parliaments during the period of his membership of the Royal Council: in the parliament of September 1402 he was put on a committee specially appointed to investigate charges of oppression brought against the aldermen of London in a petition presented by John Cavendish, a citizen; in the parliament of January 1404 he had

[1] Exchequer, Issue Roll, E 403/578, mem. 23; *ibid.*, 580, mem. 8; Privy seal warrants for issue, P.R.O., E 404/19/334; 20/149; *Royal and Historical Letters of Henry IV*, ed. F. C. Hingeston (R.S.), I, 224, 306; *P.P.C.*, I, 223, 241; Exchequer, Enrolled Foreign Accounts, P.R.O., E 364/38, mem. Aᵛ; T. Carte, *op. cit.*, tom. II, 187; J. H. Wylie, *Henry IV*, I, 439 *et seq.*

been one of those seven commoners whom, with the rest of the
Council, the King was prevailed upon to nominate in parliament
'a les grantes instances et especiales requestes a luy faitz
diverses foitz en cest parlement par les Communes de son
Roialme'.[1] And he surely must have attended the parliament
which sat at Coventry from 6 October to 14 November 1404, the
parliament which, owing to the King's exclusion of lawyers from
election to it, was given the title of 'parliamentum illiteratum'.

According to Walsingham, the parliamentary knights in the
session at Coventry, obliged to find some means of aiding the
King in the dangerous state of financial embarrassment in which
he was placed by the internal and foreign situation, pressed for
the confiscation of the temporalities of the Church, for one year
at any rate, in addition to a general resumption of Crown lands.
(The parliament-roll states that a resumption for a year was
agreed.) Archbishop Arundel, taking strength from the glories of
St. Thomas and St. Edmund Rich, forcibly resisted this attack,
supported by his colleague of York, the bishop of Rochester, and
certain of the Lords Temporal, foremost among them Edward
of Norwich, Duke of York. He rebutted the knights' assertion
that, whereas they fought for and with the King, expending
their wealth and hazarding their persons, the clergy sat idle at
home and offered no other assistance, by stating that the clergy
made frequent grants, sent their tenants to fight, and prayed for
the King's success. When, according to Walsingham, as 'prolocutor militum' Cheyne suggested that their prayers were of
little avail, the archbishop rounded on him in a personal attack,
telling him that though he held the religion of the clergy in
contempt he must not think, so long as he (Canterbury) lived,
that he could with impunity seize the possessions of the Church
because he evilly took them for himself. Arundel went on to
remind Henry IV of his oath to maintain the Church and her
liberties. After drawing a favourable answer from the King, the
archbishop then attacked the knights again, stating that their
support for the royal sequestration of the property of alien
priories had not profited the King, but only themselves, and

[1] *Rot. Parl.*, III, 519b, 530a.

that their motive in their present proposal with regard to the possessions of the Church at large was just as selfish, so that the King would not be a farthing the richer a year later. The Lords Spiritual and Temporal drew together, came to an agreement to resist the proposals of the knights both for a resumption of Crown lands and grants and for the confiscation of clerical temporalities, and (states Walsingham) the parliamentary knights in the end begged the primate's pardon. Cheyne who, Walsingham says, had deserted the 'militia Christi' as an apostate for the 'sors Martis', having without dispensation abandoned his order as a deacon, is stated by the chronicler to have been the knights' speaker in these attacks: 'prolocutor militum.'[1] He was certainly, nevertheless, not even a knight of the shire, and if Walsingham was using the word 'prolocutor' in its technical, official sense, he was in error for that reason. According to the record of the parliament-roll itself, the Commons' Speaker in this session was Sir William Sturmy, knight of the shire for Devon. It was, however, by no means unusual for the Commons to have recourse for the promotion of their views to one outside their own body. Such an auxiliary was normally one of the Lords, but on this occasion they may very well have used Cheyne as a member of the royal Council to be their 'prolocutor' in the untechnical sense of occasional spokesman. The incident is instructive on other grounds: it suggests something of a cleavage within the ranks of the Council itself.

There is no doubt that in spite of the Coventry incident, Cheyne retained his place in the royal Council and in the next parliament was confirmed in office. This was the long parliament whose three sessions extended over the period, March–December 1406. During the first session, on 22 May 1406, when the King was asked by the Commons for a token of his intention to provide 'governance habundante', he again nominated his Council in the parliament and agreed that it should virtually control the administration. Cheyne was one of its three

---

[1] *Annales Henrici Quarti, op. cit.*, 391–4; *Historia Anglicana, op. cit.*, II, 265–7 (I have conflated the two accounts).

commoner members, each of whom was a survivor from the Council nominated over two years before, in January 1404.[1]

It was during the second recess of the 1406 parliament that on 18 July Cheyne and Dr Henry Chichele, the future primate, were commissioned as the King's proctors to the Roman Curia. Already, on 18 May, £200 had been advanced to Cheyne for his passage and return as being sent by order of the King and Council to Rome with certain letters from Henry IV to Innocent VII 'pro certis materiis statum ipsius domini Regis intime moventibus'. For Chichele, then chancellor of the cathedral church of Salisbury and vicar-general to the bishop, this was his baptism into Anglo-papal diplomacy and 'his introduction to the politics of the Great Schism' (Jacob). Cheyne must have counted himself as something of an old-hand in such work. The embassy to the Pope and Cardinals in Rome was probably intended to help supply a basis for the arrangement of a compromise between, and perhaps the eventual resignation of, both Innocent VII and his Avignonese rival, Benedict XIII, and so to bring the Schism to an end. But the achievement of such a *démarche* was inextricably involved with Anglo-French diplomacy. And, before they were ready to start for Rome, Chichele and Cheyne were associated on 6 October 1406 with Sir Hugh Mortimer, chamberlain to Prince Henry of Monmouth, in an embassy to the French court with instructions to treat for peace on the basis of a marriage between Prince Henry and a daughter of Charles VI or, at least, a reformation of the existing truces. Cheyne got a grant in aid in the form of a remission of 100 marks from his farm of the alien priory of Newent. He and Chichele did not get away from England until 20 November 1406. Their mission was to prove a long one: they did not return home until the middle of August 1408. By this time Cheyne's expenses alone, at the rate of £1 a day, amounted to some £642. Both ambassadors had been advanced in the meantime £100 each on 25 April 1408 by the hands of the English agent of the Apostolic Camera, Philip de Albertis, a member of a Florentine firm of wool exporters and bankers with a large English connection.

[1] *Rot. Parl.*, III, 572b.

While they were away from England the papal situation underwent some important transformations. Not until late in January 1407 did Cheyne and Chichele reach Venice. Innocent VII, however, had died on 6 November 1406, a fortnight before they had even left England. The Lancastrian government, when eventually the news of this event came through, perhaps hoped that in the interests of union Innocent's cardinals would abstain from electing his successor. But on 8 January 1407 letters were written individually to a number of the cardinals expressing polite hopes that if a new Pope were elected he would be some cardinal friendly to England, and drawing attention to the fact that Cheyne and Chichele were already half-way to Rome. On 18 January a letter was written to the two ambassadors informing them that the government was now aware of Innocent VII's death and instructing them to proceed to the Curia and ascertain whether the Sacred College intended to hold or suspend the election of his successor. Henry IV's own views were, the letter went on, in favour of a suspension, and the ambassadors were to let this be known to the cardinals. And, should an election be made, they were to consider carefully how they acted, taking steps to find out political reactions beforehand—whether other princes readily or tardily recognised the new pope. For, the King's letter warned, 'nous ne vouldrions pas estre le primer ne le darreiner en si grand besoigne.' All this solicitude was vain: the Venetian, Angelo Corraro, had been elected as Gregory XII as far back as 30 November 1406, and certainly Cheyne and Chichele must have known it when they reached the new pontiff's native city of Venice at the end of January 1407, if no earlier. When reaching Rome they must have acted according to further instructions in the letter of 18 January and submitted their subsidiary business to the new pope; whatever they did in this respect was later covered by a renewal of their commission on 26 April 1407. As regards the larger issue of the termination of the Schism, they can have done no more than lend their help to such efforts as were still being made to secure the double resignation of the contending popes. Both ambassadors were, of course, still at the Curia when, on 4 October 1407, Gregory XII, probably falling in with the desires of the English government, provided Chichele to the vacant Welsh see of St. David's. In the spring of 1408 they moved up with the Curia to Lucca, performing routine work for the English Council, Chichele being consecrated by Gregory XII at Siena in March. At Lucca occurred the great defection of Gregory's cardinals, and at Pisa on 13 May 1408 the major part of the Sacred College took the first steps that terminated (following their collaboration with Benedict XIII's dissident cardinals) in the summoning on 24 June of a General Council to meet there on Lady Day 1409 in order to arrange for the repudiation of both popes and the election of one Vicar of Christ. By this time other English representatives were in Italy, whose actions suggest Henry IV's inclination to support Gregory's faithless cardinals, or at any rate re-insure himself with both sides: the Keeper of the Privy Seal himself, John Prophet, met the cardinals at Pisa; Richard Dereham, Chancellor of the University of Cambridge, had already left Lucca in their company. The latter was in England in time for an interview with Henry IV on 11 July 1408. A month later, on 15 August, Cheyne and Chichele were back, too, after an absence of nearly two years. Only reluctantly and under pressure from Archbishop Arundel and Convocation did Henry IV finally abandon Gregory XII. Not until the visit to England of the advocate of Gregory's cardinals, Cardinal Uguccione, Archbishop of Bordeaux, in November 1408, did the English official attitude become clear: in a resolve to support the impending General Council. In the face of Uguccione's urgent arguments for union by the 'via concilii,' Sir John Cheyne and Bishop Chichele, who are said to have held a brief for Gregory XII, can have done no more than hold their peace. Cheyne was first and foremost 'consiliarius regis,' and Chichele was soon chosen to represent the southern Convocation at the Pisan assembly.[1]

[1] *Foedera*, VIII, 446; 452–3, 479; T. Carte, *op. cit.*, tom. II, 192–4; Exchequer, Enrolled Foreign Accounts, L.T.R:, P.R.O., E 364, no. 42, mem. C; Exchequer, Issue Roll, E 403/595, mem. 1; *P.P.C.*, II, 140 *et seq.*; E. F. Jacob, *Chichele Register*, I, XXVI–XXVIII; J. H. Wylie, *Henry IV*, III, 1–37, 337–71.

At this time Sir John Cheyne was almost certainly still a member of the Royal Council. Quite certain it is that he did not retain this position after the domestic political crisis of the winter of 1409–10: the parliament of January 1410 saw the appointment of a new Council (with the Prince of Wales at its head) from which Cheyne and, in fact, all commoners were excluded. Bishop Chichele was eventually included in the small aristocratic body that emerged. The new administration continued, however, to make use of Cheyne's diplomatic *expertise*, perhaps at the instance of Chichele himself. On 20 May 1410 the prelate and his former colleague during the long stay in Italy were both appointed to another ambassadorial mission to France: to treat at Leulinghen in Picardy regarding violation of the truces and for redress of injuries, and, as usual, for a firm peace. The embassy, which took six weeks, achieved no more than a renewal of the still-existent if precarious truce, for four months from 1 July.[1] In the following year, when Prince Henry's administration eventually moved forward into a policy of active military intervention in France on the side of the Burgundian faction, the embassy of 1410, Cheyne among them, were again engaged in France in the tedious work of prolonging truces and keeping the prospect of a final peace alive as a formal diplomatic possibility: their commissions were dated 18 February, 27 March (Flanders being included in the conspectus of this one's agenda), and 1 July 1411.[2]

These embassies constituted Sir John Cheyne's last official employment and little else is known of the closing stages of his life. No longer in receipt of his counsellor's fees, his tenure of the temporalities of the alien priory of Newent in Gloucestershire was now conditioned by his payment of the formerly stipulated charge of £67 6s 8d which, according to a provision of the parliament of November 1411, was appropriated to the endowment of the Duke of York's collegiate foundation at Fotheringhay (Northants), to which the estates were to remain after

[1] *Foedera*, VIII, 636–7; T. Carte, *op. cit.*, tom. II, 200; Privy Seal warrants for issue, P.R.O., E 404/25/366; 25/391; Exchequer, Issue Roll, E 403/605, mem. 7.
[2] *Foedera*, VIII, 678, 694; Carte, *op. cit.*, tom. II, 201–3.

Cheyne's death. By York's feoffees the manor of Barton-by-Bristol was granted to Cheyne for life under a royal licence of 22 November 1412, perhaps in consideration of some arrangement connected with the Fotheringhay foundation.[1] Cheyne did not live long enough to enjoy his occupation of this estate for more than a year or so. He was still holding the lands of the alien priory of Beckford, of which he had been in continuous possession since 1379, and from 1383 free of fee-farm rent. Here had been his main residence. And it was as Sir John Cheyne of Beckford that on 1 November 1413 he drew up his will, in which he arranged for his burial there. He died sometime between that date and 28 April 1414 when probate was granted in the Prerogative Court of Canterbury.

The phraseology of Sir John Cheyne's will at times recalls that of the wills of some of those former members of Richard II's household who were stigmatized as favourers of the Lollards in the St. Albans chronicles of the time. There is the same expression of sentiments of contrition and self-abasement: in much the same terms as are used in the wills of Sir Thomas Latimer (1401) and Sir Lewis Clifford (1404), Cheyne described himself as 'fals and traitour to my lord god and to his blessid moder our lady seynt marie and to all the holy compagne of hevene'; his 'wretched stinking carrion' was to be buried outside the new chapel established in the church-yard of Beckford, his head to the wall under its east window; no cloth of gold or silk but only russet cloth at 1s 3d a yard was to lie on his body. The doles among his funeral expenses were to be kept down to £7 in groats and pennies for poor men attending. He left certain heirlooms to his elder son John, including a Bible in French in two books and also a psalter (glossed) of Richard Hampool (Richard Rolle of Hampole), very probably an English translation by this Yorkshire hermit, mystic, and popular author of devotional books. Cheyne's executors were his cousin, Richard Clifford (parson of Stepney), John Sudbury (parson of Langstone, S. Herefordshire), Edward Cheyne (his younger son), and Richard Vaus. The overseers of the will were Bishop Chichele, Master

[1] *Rot. Parl.*, III, 653; *C.P.R.*, *1408–13*, 358, 406, 451.

John Prophet, dean of York and keeper of the King's privy seal (since 1406), and Sir Thomas Picworth (lieutenant-governor of Calais). Henry Chichele, Cheyne's old diplomatic colleague who may very well have become his friend and perhaps played some part in purging him of heretical tendencies during the two years of their companionship in Italy, was still bishop of St. David's when Cheyne's will was made; when probate was granted on 28 April 1414 he had already been postulated as Arundel's successor at Canterbury and, in fact, on the day before the probate (27 April), the bull of translation had issued from the Chancery of John XXIII. As primate, Chichele did more than was perhaps formally required of him to promote the administration of Cheyne's will. On 3 January 1416, for example, he issued letters exhortatory regarding Sir John Cheyne's provision in his chapel at Beckford of a loan chest for helping his necessitous tenants; out of a sum of £20 then in the keeping of Sir John's son and heir (John) and John Buckland, master of the college of Fotheringhay, loans up to £2 might be advanced for as long as a year.[1]

Cheyne's son and heir, John, and his younger son, Edward, survived him. So did his second wife, Margaret Lovetoft. She went on to survive her two sons by Cheyne as well. The younger son died in 1415 and was buried with his father at Beckford. The heir, John, who was eventually knighted, was dead by November 1421. By this time his mother, Sir John Cheyne's widow, had married William Herle, a Gloucestershire squire. She lived on until 1437.[2]

[1] *Bedfordshire Historical Record Society*, vol. 2 (1914) (*Bedfordshire Wills and Administrations*), p. 16; E. F. Jacob, *Chichele Register*, II, 45; *ibid.*, IV, 144. In the Beds. Record Society volume the place-name Beckford is transcribed as 'Bedford'. The same error is made in *Chichele Register*, II, 45 in the will of Edward, Sir John Cheyne's son, but rectified at vol. IV, 144. There is no doubt of the error: among the places mentioned in Edward Cheyne's will where poor men were to receive doles are Beckford Ashton, Beyngrove and Grafton, all hamlets in the parish of Beckford (Glos.), and Aston upon Carrant near Tewkesbury. Sir John Cheyne's will is to be compared with Sir Thomas Latimer's (1401) (Nicolas, *Testamenta Vetusta*, 158–9), of which Sir Lewis Clifford was an overseer, and with the latter's own will (1404), of which Cheyne himself had been an overseer (*op. cit.*, 164–5).

[2] *C.C.R.*, *1419–22*, 178; *C.F.R.*, *1437–45*, 3.

5

SIR WALTER HUNGERFORD

Sir Walter Hungerford, first Baron Hungerford. Speaker in Henry V's second Parliament (at Leicester in April 1414). Knight of the Shire for Wiltshire in the Parliaments of January 1401, October 1404 (at Coventry), October 1407 (at Gloucester) ; for Somerset, January 1410 ; for Wiltshire, May 1413, and April 1414 (at Leicester). [1]

Born about 1378, Walter Hungerford was the first son of Sir Thomas Hungerford by his second wife, Joan, daughter of Sir Edmund Hussey. He already, therefore, had the prospect of eventually coming into the estates to which his mother was coheir. At the time of his birth he had two surviving elder brothers (Robert and Thomas), the sons of Sir Thomas by his first marriage. These two, however, died before their father, as did Walter's own younger, uterine brother, John, and at Sir Thomas's death in December 1397 Walter was his father's sole surviving son and, as such, heir to all his proper estates, none of his elder brothers having apparently married, certainly none having produced a still surviving heir.

On coming of age in 1399 Walter can at first have succeeded to little more than the manors of Mildenhall, Ashley, Codford St. Mary (Wiltshire), and Down Ampney (Gloucestershire). For in the manors of Heytesbury (Wiltshire), Farleigh, and Wellow, and other lesser estates, which were all entailed on Sir Thomas's second wife's male issue, the widow (Walter's mother) had a life interest, and she was to survive her husband for over fourteen years. Not until 1412 did Walter, therefore, come into the whole of his patrimony. His estates were then further augmented by those to which he succeeded as his mother's heir, these including the manors of Teffont Evias (Wiltshire), Holbrook and Bossington (Somerset). [3] Already in October 1396, he had been contracted in marriage exceedingly well, especially as events were to befall : to Katherine, one of the two daughters and coheirs of Thomas Peverell, a Cornish squire who had been knight of the shire in 1379 and sheriff in 1389—90. Katherine's mother was Margaret, one of the two daughters and coheirs of Sir Thomas Courtenay of Southpool and his wife, Muriel, herself a coheir (being the elder daughter of John Lord Moels). The covenant between Sir Thomas Hungerford and Peverell provided for estates in Wiltshire or Gloucestershire worth £40 a year to be settled by Sir Thomas on the married pair with the final prospect of entailed estates worth 300 or 400 marks annually. In return for this Peverell was to pay £140 for the marriage and entail, and settle the manor of Stoke Bassett (Oxfordshire), worth £20 a year. The marriage had taken place

before the end of May 1399. Margaret Courtenay, Sir Walter Hungerford's wife's mother, a niece of the Earl of Devon (Hugh) who died in
1377 and cousin of Archbishop Courtenay of Canterbury (1381—96),
surviving her husband, died in 1422, and it was not until then that her
own and her dower estates were parcelled out between Hungerford and
his wife on the one hand and Katherine's sister, Eleanor, and her husband, Sir William Talbot, on the other. Hungerford took the Somerset parts of the inheritance, including the manors of Clapton, Halton,
Maperton, South Cadbury, Wootton Courtenay, Pymtree, and Sutton
Lucy, and he shared the Devon lands; in 1439 the Cornish and the
other Devon lands of Peverell and Courtenay (comprising thirteen
manors) also fell to Walter Hungerford under the terms of a settlement
when his first wife's sister died without issue. [4]

At first, as a result of Margaret Courtenay's death in 1422 and of
Eleanor Talbot's death in 1439 only a moiety of the whole of the Moels
inheritance and barony came to the Hungerfords, but the other moiety
was eventually to come into the possession of the family (although not
during Walter's lifetime), through the marriage between Robert,
Walter's eldest son, and Margaret, daughter and heir of William Lord
Botreaux. This Hungerford-Botreaux alliance, which was eventually
to bring into the family's possession over fifty manors (mainly in the
West Country) was probably contracted early in 1421, when Hungerford had returned after an absence of nearly four years in France, and
just about when a previous marriage contract, effected by him, was
yielding dividends. [5]

On 8 November 1416 Henry V had granted to Sir Walter Hungerford the marriage of Margery, one of the three daughters and coheirs
of Edward, the only son of Hugh Lord Burnell, who (in September
1415) had died before his father, together with the custody of her
person and lands during her minority. (Margery was then about
seven years old.) The royal letter patent embodying this grant
sanctioned Sir Walter's bargain with Lord Burnell arranging for his
granddaughter's marriage with Edmund, Sir Walter's third son, at a
stated cost to Hungerford of £1,000. Sir Walter had feared a disturbance of the marriage and of the settlements which depended on it.
For, by midsummer 1416, Margery's sister, Katherine, had been
affianced to John, son and heir of John Talbot, Lord Furnival (the later
first Earl of Shrewsbury), and a settlement had been contrived to give
the couple the main *bloc* of Burnell estates in Staffordshire and Shropshire. This marriage had not, however, taken place when Lord

Burnell died in November 1420 and, in fact, the Talbot settlement never did mature, this sister marrying Sir John Radcliffe, K.G., of Attleborough (Norfolk). Even had it done so, the terms of the Burnell-Hungerford settlement would have been favourable enough to Sir Walter. Drawn up on 12 July 1416 (some three weeks after the Talbot arrangement), they had provided for the manors of Rotherhithe and Hatcham (Surrey), Rollright (Oxfordshire), Little Rissington (Gloucestershire), Suckley (Worcestershire), Compton Dando (Somerset), Great Cheverell (and a fee-farm of 20 marks from Biddestone) (Wiltshire), Stanstede Montfichet, Waltham Powers, Walkfare and Latchingdon (Essex), and certain burghal properties and rents in Bristol, to remain at Lord Burnell's death to Sir Walter, Edmund his son, and the latter's wife, Margery Burnell. The expiry of a life-interest, secured to Margery's mother, would further release the Essex manors of East and West Ham and Borham. By May 1421, the estates concerned, held by Lord Burnell at his death, had passed into Sir Walter's hands. The latter did, of course, settle certain of his own estates on his son; the manors of Jenkingescourt, Burton, Stratton St. Margaret, Stoke by Bedwin (Wiltshire), and Down Ampney (Gloucestershire); perhaps these were comprised in the £1,000 costs he had undertaken, perhaps additional to them.[6]

Apart from the trusts and royal wardships with which Hungerford temporarily augmented the stock of land upon which he could count for ready income (for example, the wardships of Philip Courtenay of Powderham, nephew and heir of Bishop Courtenay of Norwich, and Walter Rodney, both of whom married daughters of his), his estates were considerably increased by purchase. It was probably by this direct method of acquisition that over the years there came into his possession some thirty additional manors, mainly in Wiltshire and Somerset,[7] together with his London inn in Charing. Some of the most important of these purchases were in his hands before his occupation of the Treasurership of England from 1426 to 1432, and many of the rest before the end of his term of office; it was while he was Treasurer that in the autumn of 1429 and the first half of 1430 he engineered a whole series of enfeoffments covering a considerable number of these purchased estates.[8] The whole estate was a large enough complex to demand a proper system for its administration and a hierarchy of administrative and financial officials. By 1413 there was a receiver who took the rents from the manorial bailiffs and collectors, and there was a steward. When, in 1420-21, the Burnell and Rodney lands were attached to the core of Hungerford's own estates, the receiver became receiver-general and there were separate receivers for the different manors or groups of manors. The stewardship eventually had also to be divided; this was done on a county basis, one steward being appointed for Wiltshire, one for Somerset and Devon, and one for Dorset. In Berkshire and Wiltshire there was an under-steward. The Hungerfords did not themselves ever hold any very notable estate in Dorset, but during the later stages of Sir Walter's life a steward was needed to administer the lands there brought into his control by his second marriage, which took place sometime between June 1429 and May 1439.

Sir Walter's second wife was Eleanor, Countess of Arundel, daughter and heir of Sir John Berkeley of Beverstone (Gloucestershire), successively wife and widow of John Arundel, Lord Mautravers, who had died in 1421, and of Sir Richard, the son and heir-apparent of Robert Lord Poynings, who was killed on active service near Orleans in June 1429. Eleanor had no issue by Hungerford. Her children by her two earlier unions had married well. John, Eleanor's elder son by her first marriage who was admitted in 1433 to be Earl of Arundel, had married the daughter of Lord Fanhope (a granddaughter of John of Gaunt) and later a daughter of Robert Lovell, a Dorset notable, but he was probably dead before Sir Walter's marriage to the countess took place. Her second son, William, his brother's heir and summoned to parliament as Earl of Arundel in 1422, was to marry the first daughter of Richard Neville, Earl of Salisbury. Her daughter by her second marriage, Eleanor Poynings, before midsummer 1435 was already married to the son and heir of the Earl of Northumberland.

The countess's lands were, however, doubtless her chief attraction for Hungerford, and in her right he came to hold thirteen manors in Dorset, six in Wiltshire, five in Gloucestershire, and two in Somerset.[9] As Hungerford's will explains, he met the countess's debts to the Crown and in London which far exceeded the 700 marks she gave him after their marriage. But he could well afford to do so. These estates held by Hungerford *jure uxoris* were bringing him in during the 1440's almost £700 a year: more, that is, than his own estates and those under his control had been yielding in (say) 1420-21, when the total sums handled by his receiver-general had amounted to close on £650 a year. By 1429-30 his annual receipts from landed estate had risen to £1,047. By 1444 they were averaging over £1,700, and in the year before his death were as high as £1,800.[10] What were the revenues of his French lordships, secured to him by royal grant, there is no knowing.

By the latest possible date for Hungerford's marriage with the Countess of Arundel (May 1439) the family's territorial interests and prospects had been further extended by the marriage of his grandson, Robert (the eldest son of Sir Walter's own eldest son, Robert), who by March 1439 had been contracted with Eleanor, the daughter and heir of William Lord Moleyns who had been killed ten years before at the siege of Orleans: a match which was to bring into the Hungerford family's possession between twenty and thirty manors in Buckinghamshire, Oxfordshire, Wiltshire, and Cornwall, and to the young heiress's husband besides an individual summons to Parliament in 1445 as Lord Moleyns.[11]

All this remarkable accumulation of landed interests and proliferation of family connexions and associations, which it fell to Sir Walter during his life time largely to control and use to his profit, was developing all through a political career of considerable diversity and complexity, upon the progress of which it can only have favourably reacted.

From the presence of his heraldic arms among the embellishments of Mickle Hall in Oxford it would be rash even to conjecture that Sir Walter was ever on its books in his youth. But that he had some schooling in the University is possible. He was certainly literate: judging from a bequest in his will to one of his Courtenay grandsons, who was a clerk, of a two-volume great bible 'eciam cum omnibus libris meis de facultate theologie' (which were already in the beneficiary's hands), it is tolerably certain that he had Latin; and we know for sure that he read English with facility. In later life certainly he had his connexions with the University of Oxford. When, in February 1435, the University wrote to Archbishop Chichele commending one of its proctors, Master John King, a scholar in theology, another similar letter went to Lord Hungerford (as he then was). Not long before his death Hungerford was interesting himself in the work then going forward on the bell-tower of Merton College chapel, and when he came to make his will he had already advanced some two-thirds of a promised bequest of £100 towards the fund.[12] These links with Oxford may well have been formed, however, much later than his youth, and if ever a career for Hungerford in the Church had ever been thought feasible (a tenuous conjecture), that prospect had evaporated by his eighteenth year when (on 10 November 1395) he received a royal letter patent pardoning and confirming his acquisition in fee-tail of the bailiwick of the forest of Selwood from his father who held the custody in chief.[13] Less than a year later his marriage with Katherine Peverell was arranged for, and before the end of Richard II's reign the contract had been fulfilled. Walter's father had died in the meantime (December 1397), leaving him, as his only surviving son and heir, with solid prospects which would only mature, however, when his mother's death ended her life-interest in so many of the Hungerford entailed estates.

Young Hungerford quite clearly reacted to the political crisis which ended in the accession of Henry IV, with whom his father had had connexions. It may have been the long-standing Lancastrian attachments of his family, intensified by his father's strong ties with John of Gaunt, which influenced him to give Henry of Bolingbroke his corporal service. And so far as he was concerned, the Lancastrian usurpation paid immediate dividends: Walter Hungerford was one of the forty-six esquires knighted on the eve of Henry's coronation on 13 October 1399. Only three weeks later, by letters patent dated 2 November, he was granted for life the manor and barton, and the custody of the castle, of Marlborough with their appendant franchises, together with the mills and hundred of Selkly, and 'housbote' and 'heybote' and pasture rights in the forest of Savernake, for an annual rent of £120 payable in the Exchequer; and, after another fortnight had passed, on 16 November Hungerford shared (with Sir Thomas Beauchamp) a royal grant of £200 from the estates of the late Duchess of Norfolk expressly 'to recompense them for their great expenses in the king's service after his last coming to England'.[14] The following year, however, was apparently one in which at times Sir Walter's position can only have been a source of acute discomfort to him.

Early in January 1400 occurred a plot of a group of Richard II's closest supporters among the nobility who had been degraded in Henry IV's first Parliament from the new dignities they had won in the late king's coup d'état of 1397. Their plan was to seize Henry IV at Windsor and restore Richard II. Henry acted with decision, raised London, and compelled the conspirators to retire with their forces westwards to Cirencester. Here the townsfolk rose against them and executed out of hand the Earls of Salisbury and Kent. A similar fate soon met Lord Despenser at Bristol and the Earl of Huntingdon at Pleshey. Sir Walter Hungerford found himself awkwardly involved. An inquest held at Cirencester on 25 January 1400 found that he had been with the rebels there and had actively adhered to and supported them against the king's lieges in the town. His name was specially linked in the indictment with the Earl of Kent, but it is perhaps worth pointing out that Lord Despenser was his superior lord in his holdings at Farleigh and Wellow, and that elsewhere he was a tenant of the Earl of Salisbury. Judicial proceedings at a higher level had not ended even as late as 25 November following, when a further inquest was ordered to be taken regarding Hungerford's actions at Cirencester, its findings to be submitted to one or more royal justices of either of the two Benches or before the justices of assize in Gloucestershire. These later proceedings, however, may well have been only formal, because at a trial on 27 January 1400 at Newgate, where a London jury had indicted those privy to the plot of conspiring in the City, it had been found that Sir Walter Hungerford, king's knight, had been forced (with others) by the rebels to go with them, and had been robbed of a collar of the king's livery (worth £20) which he was wearing at the time of his capture. Perhaps he had been taken prisoner when the rebels made their first move and broke into Windsor Castle to search for the king and his sons on the night of 4 January. This particular act, the offence of accroaching the royal power, was one of the treasons of which Thomas Merk, late Bishop of Carlisle, was pardoned on 28 November 1400.[15] It is possible that during and immediately after the riot at Cirencester Hungerford was under arrest. If this were so, he can only have been in custody a matter of a few weeks at most, for on 18 February 1400 he had been able to stand surety for two Somerset magnates, Sir Hugh and Sir John Luttrell, in their royal grant of all the English estates of the alien abbey of St. Nicholas-lez-Angers.[16]

By the end of 1400 the clouds had lifted clear, and in January 1401 Sir Walter was returned for the first time as knight of the shire, being elected for Wiltshire, and on 16 May 1401 he was appointed a J.P. for the county, a commission to which he continued to be re-appointed until January 1406. In the summer of 1401 by privy seal writ he was summoned as a Wiltshire knight to a Great Council convened at Westminster to discuss the emergency arising out of French and Scottish hostility, Irish turbulence, and the rebellion in Wales. Between this and his summons as one of four Wiltshire knights to another Great Council sometime in 1404, there is little to record of his activities.[17] On 15 August 1402 he and his wife and mother procured a papal indult to have a portable altar, and it is not improbable that at this time Hungerford was himself in Rome as a pilgrim on his way to or from the Holy Land. His own will says that his father had made an enfeoffment to uses of the manor of Tidworth for the Austin priory of Longleat, which manor the priory sold for 160 marks to John Chitterne, a master in chancery, the purchase price being lent to Sir Walter for his voyage to the Holy Land, he in turn (to fulfil his father's will) appropriating the church of Rushall to the priory. It is true that it was not until November 1407, when he was knight of the shire for Somerset in the Gloucester Parliament, that Hungerford secured a royal licence enabling the priory to appropriate the church, but he was certainly in touch with John Chitterne as soon after the conjectural date of his pilgrimage as January 1403 when he was his mainpernor in a grant of the custody of the alien priory of Hayling. It is very doubtful whether in any year but 1402, the intervals between his royal commissions would have allowed him to take a long tour. He received no royal commission at all during 1402.[18]

In the early years generally of Henry IV's reign Hungerford was by no means busily employed on royal local commissions. Possibly this was because he was still a young man, but more probably because much of his time was being spent with the king, at court or in the field, especially during the unquieter period of the reign. But on 20 April 1403 he was put on a commission of oyer and terminer regarding an appeal against a judgement given by a deputy of the admiral for the West in a case over broken contracts. In September following he was a commissioner of array in Wiltshire for the defence of Southampton against a threatened attack.[19] He attended a Great Council in the summer of 1404, and in the autumn sat for Wiltshire in the Unlearned Parliament of Coventry. When next Parliament was summoned to meet in March 1406 he was not elected, being by then sheriff of Wiltshire. He held this office from 27 November 1405 to 5 November 1406. For the greater part of this year, however, he was acting as chamberlain to the king's younger daughter, Philippa, who (nearly four years after the contract was made) was married by proxy at Westminster on 26 November 1405 to Eric, King of Denmark, Norway, and Sweden, and on 8 December proclaimed as his queen. Hungerford was a member of the Anglo-Danish retinue of over 200 persons who accompanied the young queen to Denmark, and he received a grant of livery for the voyage and on 26 July 1406 an advance of 100 marks at the Exchequer. The flotilla sailed from Lynn in the second half of August. The marriage was celebrated in Lund cathedral on 26 October and by Christmas most of the escort of Englishmen were back home.[20] Earlier in the year, on Lady Day, Hungerford had already been granted a gift of 100 marks, one payment of an annuity for that amount (charged on the castle and town of Marlborough). This annuity had been surrendered by its former recipient following an act of resumption passed in the Coventry Parliament of 1404; the fresh grant to Hungerford was made in view of the great charges he had previously incurred in the royal service and especially lately at Calais where he had upheld his king and country's honour in arms against a knight of France. [21]

Hungerford was certainly back in England by the end of 1406, for on 30 December he was on a panel of knights and esquires from which a jury was to be chosen for the settling of a law-suit between the heirs of Sir John de Mohun, whose widow had sold the reversion of his West Somerset estates, and Sir Hugh Luttrell, whose mother had been the purchaser. [22] On 16 February 1407 his continuing interest as Exchequer lessee at Marlborough presumably procured Sir Walter's inclusion in a royal commission of inquiry into reported breaches of the assizes of wines and victuals by recent mayors of the town.

In October 1407 Wiltshire once again elected Hungerford as knight of the shire to the Parliament summoned to Gloucester, and it was during the session that (on 19 November) he procured a royal licence to amortize and appropriate the advowson of Rushall (Wiltshire) to Longleat priory, and that (three days later) he and five other knights of the shire, including the Speaker, witnessed a quitclaim in favour of Sir Thomas Brook, M.P. for Somerset, a deed to which the common seal of Gloucester was affixed. [23] It was for Somerset that Hungerford himself was to be returned to the next Parliament of January 1410. In the meantime, in May 1408 he had been re-included in the commission of the peace for Wiltshire, and in November of the same year for the first time had been put on the commission for Somerset; he was to be excluded from the Wiltshire commission in February 1410, but only for two years, and thenceforward he was J.P. in both counties until his death nearly forty years later. On 6 July 1409, the feast of the translation of St. Thomas the Martyr, he had been on pilgrimage to Canterbury, where he was then received into the confraternity of the priory of Christchurch. [23a]

It was in the course of the 1410 parliament that Hungerford and William Stourton, a lawyer, then M.P. for Dorset, were ordered ' for particular causes moving the king and council ' to meddle no further with the temporalities of the Cluniac priory at Farleigh in Somerset (where Hungerford had his chief residence). He and Stourton, who was also one of his feoffees, had received on 18 May 1409 a royal grant of the custody of the priory's estates to the use of the convent. This was pending the settlement of a dispute between Henry IV and the prior of Lewes over the nomination of a new prior at Farleigh. (The king claimed patron's rights through his first wife, Mary de Bohun, while the prior of Lewes claimed on the grounds that Farleigh was a dependency of his house.) On 3 September 1409 the king had compromised by nominating (in letters under the seal of the duchy of Lancaster) the candidate of the prior of Lewes. On 1 February 1410 Hungerford and Stourton received the order not to meddle further with the Farleigh temporalities, and on 12 February they secured letters of pardon, protesting that they had received none of the priory's revenues and should therefore be free of all Exchequer process to compel them to render account. Two days before this concession was formally made, however, an inquiry into allegations of waste and asportation of goods by Hungerford and Stourton had been made the subject of a royal commission. This investigation was conducted with sufficient despatch to allow of Hungerford's laying a petition before the Commons on 2 May 1410, just a week before the Parliament ended. In this petition he declared his intention of traversing the inquest, which had evidently been damaging, and asked the Commons to request the king to ordain by parliamentary authority that the traversing jury should include no man with less than £20 landed income in the county, that the sheriff should ensure this on pain of a £200 fine, and that the return should be null if this arrangement miscarried. The Commons promoted the bill and the king granted it.[24] Not long after the dissolution of the 1410 Parliament, by the new royal Council, of which Prince Henry of Monmouth was head, Hungerford was made (by patent of 14 June 1410) one of a commission to raise speedy loans amounting to 500 marks in Somerset and elsewhere in the diocese of Bath and Wells, on the security of the recent parliamentary subsidy; this sum the commissioners apparently put up themselves within a matter of days in return for a preferential tally drawn on the subsidy collectors in the county.[25] Hungerford's local territorial standing in Somerset and Wiltshire was soon to be considerably improved when at Teffont Evias his mother died on 1 March 1412. Sir Walter was one of her executors. Her death released such entailed estates as had been settled on her for life in 1383. The royal escheators involved were given their orders on 11 April 1412 to deliver seisin to Sir Walter at Heytesbury, Teffont Evias, Wellow, Farleigh, and Holbrook.[26]

The struggle for control of the royal Council that was going on in the last years of Henry IV between the Arundel *bloc* (supported by the decrepit king) and the Prince of Wales and the Beaufort group which lined up behind him, was virtually settled for nearly two years during the 1410 Parliament in favour of the latter party. In the last proper Parliament of the reign, during the winter of 1411, there was a reaction towards the party of which the king's second son, Thomas, and Archbishop Arundel together now shared the leadership. In this competition there is no way of knowing for sure which side Hungerford favoured. But his diocesan and near neighbour, Bishop Bubwith of Bath and Wells, was a member of the Council of which the future Henry V was chief; he had himself a slight connexion with Robert Lovell at whose London inn this Council occasionally met;[27] and the accession of Prince Henry in March 1413 was soon followed by Sir Walter's employment at important administrative, diplomatic, and then military levels, in close touch with the new king. It is likely that he had been in Henry V's confidence for some time.

Right at the beginning of his reign Henry V made some important changes in the higher administrative staff of his duchy of Lancaster, including the appointment of a new chamberlain, a new chancellor, and new chief stewards north and south of Trent. It was to the last of these offices, the chief stewardship of the duchy south of Trent and in Wales, which his father Sir Thomas Hungerford had relinquished just twenty years before, that Sir Walter was appointed on 5 April 1413. It was an office which carried with it membership of the duchy council and, after an act of the Parliament of March 1416, a commission of the peace in each of the counties of his bailiwick. He continued to hold it until May 1437, even after his appointment as chamberlain of the duchy in February 1425, although after Henry V's death his jurisdiction seems to have been limited to the estates under the control of Henry's feoffees in the duchy.[28]

Soon after his appointment as duchy chief steward Hungerford was elected for Wiltshire to the first of Henry V's Parliaments, which met in May 1413 and in which his friend, William Stourton, was for a time the Commons' Speaker. He himself was Speaker in the next Parliament which met in April 1414 at Leicester, having been re-elected for Wiltshire. So far as is known, it was the last Parliament which he attended as knight of the shire. Had the statutory prohibition on the return of sheriffs been strictly enforced, however, he would not have been elected on this occasion, because he was sheriff of Somerset and Dorset in this year (November 1413-14).[29]

As in 1406, Sir Walter can only have been very much of an absentee from his bailiwick. Apart from his duchy interests, not only was he away in the midlands for the month's duration of the Parliament in April and May, but from 16 July to 20 September 1414 he was out of the country on an embassy to the Emperor Sigismund at Coblenz ' pro certis materiis specialibus dominum Regem intime moventibus' (actually to treat for an alliance), and he was only back in England for a matter of five weeks or so when, on 27 October, he left for the General Council of the Church then being held at Constance. He went in the company of, among others, his own diocesans of Bath and Wells (Bubwith) and Salisbury (Hallum), and the Earl of Warwick and Lord FitzHugh. The object of the embassy was to act ' pro salute animarum christianorum ibidem congregatorum necnon pro aliis certis de causis dictum dominum nostrum Regem erga dictum Imperatorem moventibus'. More prosaically, this second embassy was to treat for the Anglo-Imperial alliance with greater urgency now that Henry V had decided to prosecute his rights in France. From it Hungerford did not return until May 1415. His allowances were £1 a day for himself and *pro rata* payments for his men and servants. (He took 28 horses.) The Exchequer audit of his expense claims disclosed that on 13 May 1415 £79 out of a total of £279 owing to him were still outstanding. (A tally for that amount, drawn on the collectors of tunnage and poundage at Bristol, was given him at the Lower Exchequer on 21 June.)[30] Hungerford took advantage of his stay at Constance to secure on 10 February 1415 a papal dispensation for his son Walter, who is described in the bull as a scholar and in his eighth year, enabling him, when he should have made up his thirteenth year and been tonsured, to hold any benefice with cure (including a parish church or perpetual vicarage) or an elective dignity in a cathedral or collegiate church, to hold there and then any benefices without cure, including prebends, and to resign such, by way of exchange, as often as he wished. And on 18 March, two days before John XXIII's flight from Constance to Schaffhausen, a bull issued, at Sir Walter's impetration, ordering the prior of Bath to transfer the disused Hungerford chantry in Heytesbury parish church to a chapel in his manor-house there, it being understood that Hungerford would augment the revenues of the chantry and appoint a resident chaplain and clerk, who were later to be joined by others when further resources had been found.[31]

When Hungerford returned to England early in May 1415, preparations for resuming the war with France had been going ahead since the previous autumn with increasing urgency. Recruitment of retinues by indenture had already been proceeding for a month. By 9 June Hungerford's own retinue was at least in course of formation, and he finally contracted to serve with 19 men-at-arms and 60 archers. [32] Presumably he was with the king at Winchester when, on 28 June, he appointed a deputy in his office of duchy chief steward, as did his fellow steward for the north. This his first deputy, Roger Hunt, may not have been his own choice, but, a year later, William Westbury and, two years later again (in 1418), William Alisaundre were his deputies and both these men were to be among his own feoffees and were Wiltshire men. This appointment of chief stewards' deputies was a new departure in duchy history, necessitated by the impending absence of their principals in France. [33] On 22 July at Southampton Henry V made a series of enfeoffments (comprising most of the original Lacy and Ferrers estates and his mother's share of the Bohun inheritance, and worth about £6,000 a year clear) for the fulfilment of his will, which was sealed two days later. Hungerford was both one of the feoffees and one of the executors nominated in these instruments; in fact, with one exception, all the executors now appointed were also members of the committee of feoffees and, moreover, were a majority of it. Both bodies included the chancellor and receiver-general of the Duchy of Lancaster as well as Hungerford. The feoffees included additional members of the higher administrative staff of the duchy in the persons of the duchy chamberlain and the chief steward for the northern parts. Time was to bring changes in the ranks of both feoffees and executors, and when, on 10 June 1421, Henry V drew up his last will Hungerford was to be appointed one of the eight executors charged with the actual administration of the will, a position in the scheme he had not previously held. [34]

On 5 August 1415, the very day of the condemnation and execution of the conspirators of the Southampton plot, chief of whom was Richard, Earl of Cambridge, the latter's elder brother, Edward, Duke of York, received the royal licence to mortgage certain of his estates, mainly in Wiltshire and Yorkshire, in order to raise loans to help meet his costs in the first of Henry V's expeditions to France and also his outlay on the endowment and building of the great collegiate church at Fotheringhay, where within a few months, after his death at Agincourt, he was to be buried. Among the feoffees, who included Bishop Beaufort, was Sir Walter Hungerford; another was his future colleague, Roger Flore of Oakham, a lawyer who was to be Speaker in 1416,

1417, 1419, and 1422, and chief steward of the Duchy of Lancaster for the north parts. [35]

Hungerford crossed with the expeditionary force and, after the taking of Harfleur, fought at Agincourt. On the eve of the battle it was he (according to the author of the *Gesta Henrici Quinti*) who expressed a wish for another 10,000 archers, a remark which drew from the king, who heard it, a rebuke and an assertion of his royal faith in God to win them triumph over superior numbers. [36] Within a month of the great victory some of Hungerford's prisoners (eight or more in number) were returning home from England under safe-conduct in quest of their ransoms. For his own and his retinue's services in the compaign Hungerford had by June 1416 received at the hands of the treasurer of the Household some £295, payment being made by assignment on a recently voted parliamentary tenth and fifteenth. [37]

By this time Henry V was bent on seeking to be successful in France by diplomatic methods which might also serve his interests in the General Council at Constance where papal union and church reform were still outstanding problems. He meant to do his best with the Council's imperial protector, Sigismund, whose purpose was to off-set the threat to its usefulness and even existence contained in Henry's claim to the French throne and his recent triumph of arms. Lack of success in Paris moved the Emperor to visit England, and on 1 May 1416 he landed at Dover. In the previous month the royal council had discussed the visit and had decided to suggest to the king that Hungerford should be attached to Sigismund while in England and have the oversight of his household here. Sir Walter's embassy of 1414-15 was sufficient qualification. Three days after Sigismund's arrival (4 May 1416) Hungerford was appointed to treat with an embassy from the Archbishop of Cologne for the latter's alliance and homage. [38]

Well before the conclusion of the imperial visit, Hungerford was directly engaged, however, in the naval measures being taken to relieve the English garrison at Harfleur, then hard-pressed by a Franco-Genoese fleet, and on 26 July 1416 he was commissioned as one of the two admirals of the fleet which was to serve under the Duke of Bedford. This appointment was made without prejudice to Thomas Beaufort, Earl of Dorset (made Admiral for life of England, Ireland and Aquitaine in March 1412), who as Lieutenant of Normandy was in Harfleur itself at this time. Hungerford was presumably in part-command as admiral in the great English naval victory of the Seine of 15 August. A fortnight later he was on sick-leave, the Duke of Bedford's licence being dated on 28 August aboard the *Holy Ghost*, then in the river off Harfleur. Hungerford probably returned to London where, on 14 September, the civic sheriffs had orders by royal letters close to liberate four of his retinue who had apparently been seized as deserters. [39]

On the very day of the sea-battle the Treaty of Canterbury had been signed between Henry V and Sigismund; it involved an offensive and defensive alliance and, after a further diplomatic understanding had been arrived at with Burgundy, the winter was spent on preparations in England for a renewal of the war. Hungerford himself used the brief lull to further his private scheme for marrying his younger son, Edmund, to one of the coheirs of Lord Burnell; the contract already had the king's approval. [40] By the middle of February 1417, if no earlier, Hungerford was a member of the royal Council, [41] and was frequent in his attendance. Certainly this was so during the early months of the year, when those advising the king were a peculiarly small and select group, mainly of officials. All was in train for the expedition which sailed on 30 July 1417 for the conquest of Normandy. Meanwhile, on 18 July at Titchfield Sir Walter was made an additional feoffee in certain of the Hampshire and Wiltshire estates of Thomas Montagu, Earl of Salisbury, who was forced to mortgage them as security for loans which he was raising to equip himself for the expedition and to ensure support for his mother, sisters, and daughter. [42] On 21 July Hungerford was presumably at the drawing up of Henry V's ' second will ', a series of instructions to the Lancastrian duchy feoffees of whom he was one, for two days later he was with the king at Southwick priory when the great seal was transferred from Bishop Beaufort to Bishop Langley of Durham, who thereby began a seven years period of office as Chancellor. It was expressly as steward of the royal Household that Hungerford was present at this transaction. How long he had occupied this superior position in the Household is not known, but it is possible that he owed his membership of the royal Council earlier in the year to it. He was to retain the office until the end of the reign and was separated but seldom from the king's side in the intervening five years. [43]

When he sailed to Lower Normandy with the expedition of 1417 Hungerford's retinue was just three times what it had been in 1415, namely 60 men-at-arms and 180 archers. [44] The next three-and-a-half years were for him a time of continuous military service, only interrupted by his part in negotiations for the surrender of fortresses and in diplomatic exchanges with the French. He helped arrange the surrender of the castle of Caen on 9 September 1417 and there, three weeks later, was made one of an embassy to treat for a truce. It was a week or so after the fall of Alençon that here on 1 November he was granted for life the constableship of Windsor castle with the custody of its forest and parks (Windsor, Guildford, South Henley, Easthampstead, and Folly John), and he was not to be deprived of this office until 1438 (when it was given to Edmund Beaufort, then Earl of Dorset).[45] It was doubtless Henry V's desire to give his youngest brother, Humphrey Duke of Gloucester, the benefit of an experienced staff which moved him to include his steward of the Household in the task-force which (after the fall of Falaise) Gloucester was to lead into the Cotentin in February 1418, Cherbourg being its chief objective. This town endured a five months' siege and not until Michaelmas 1418 were its investing forces free to take part in the greater siege of the Norman capital itself. Before the town and castle of Cherbourg actually fell, Hungerford had been made captain of both on 11 August 1418; he was to hold this office continually until certainly as late as 1431.[46]

The siege of Rouen had begun on 30 July 1418, but diplomatic exchanges with Armagnacs and Burgundians alike were still proceeding. The Dauphin's offer of a treaty and alliance drew from Henry V the appointment of an embassy on 26 October 1418 of which Hungerford was one; he and his fellows were to treat for a marriage between the king and Charles VI's daughter, Katherine, but there was to be no question of Henry's disgorging any of his military gains. The abortive negotiations took place at Alençon between 10 and 22 November. At the beginning of December Hungerford was one of an embassy appointed to treat with a mission from Burgundy, which at Arras resulted in Burgundy's acceptance of the English terms and in an armistice which created a neutral zone round Paris. Again, after the surrender of Rouen on 19 January 1419, which he had helped to negotiate, in late January, in March, and in May following, Hungerford was one of those who met the Dauphin's envoys to try to effect a personal interview between Charles of Valois and Henry V.[47]

Already captain of the town and castle of Cherbourg, Hungerford continued to do well for himself out of the conquest of Normandy. During the long siege of Rouen he had been granted (on 20 December 1418) the castle and barony of Homet in tail male on condition of a yearly rent of a lance with a fox's brush attached and the provision of 10 spearsmen and 20 archers for service in France. On 16 March 1420 he was given the lordship of Warenquebec and the fortalice of Beuseville; on 12 January 1421 lands in Tourny in the *bailliage* of Gisors, and on 19 May following the lands of Breautè and the château of Neville, lands in Coulombe Tenneville, and Villequier, and the fortalice of Hibouville, these being the forfeitures of three Norman ' traitors '. By May 1422 he had followed John Lord Clifford, recently killed in the siege of Meaux, as captain of Château Gaillard. And then, of course, apart from the unrecorded profits of war, there were wages and rewards as an indentured royal retainer: the treasurer of the Household paid him some £974 for the last eighteen months of Henry V's reign. [48] The grants of 1420 and 1421 are almost all we know of the French side of Hungerford's life in these years. As steward of the Household he was most probably with Henry V continually. After the conclusion of the Treaty of Troyes in May 1420 the war went on and Hungerford was with the king at the protracted siege of Melun from 13 July to 18 November 1420; he was one of the negotiators for its surrender. [49]

Almost certainly in company with Henry V, Hungerford returned to England when the king visited it for the last time in the first half of 1421 for the coronation of his new Queen (Katherine of Valois), the ratification of the Treaty of Troyes in the Parliament of May 1421, and for the harnessing of further support for the conquest of Dauphinist France. Loans were to be an important feature of this support, and on 21 April Hungerford was put on loan-raising commissions in Wiltshire, Somerset, and Dorset. On 3 May, in a chapter at Windsor, he was elected and installed as a Knight of the Garter. He took the chance given by his stay in England to arrange for the conveyance into his hands of those estates which would come eventually to his son Edmund, through the latter's marriage with one of the coheirs of Hugh Lord Burnell who had died in November 1420. And this was perhaps the time when his eldest son, Robert, was contracted with the eldest daughter of Lord Botreaux. When the king made his last will at Dover on 10 June, the eve of his departure for France, Hungerford's previous appointment as an executor (in 1415) was confirmed, only now he was to be one of the ' working ' executors. Already, he had renewed his royal letters of protection on 28 May and he presumably sailed with the king. [50] After a demonstration near Orleans which did much to offset the moral effect of the defeat of Baugé, Henry V in October 1421 took on the siege of Meaux, the most important Dauphinist centre near Paris. Here Hungerford was in command on the west side of the town, the Duke of Exeter and the Earls of Warwick and March being in charge of the other sectors. Not until 2 May 1422 did the place surrender, Hungerford being one of the English commissioners to make

terms.[51] Meanwhile, in the conditions of a winter siege, the king's
health had given way. His case was soon hopeless, and he died at
Bois de Vincennes on 31 August.

Hungerford, his steward of Household, already appointed by Henry
V in his written will to attend on the person of his infant heir (Henry
VI), was confirmed in this position of guardian when the king made
his final death-bed dispositions. Hungerford himself was there. For
four-and-a-half years later he was required, along with Henry's erstwhile secretary, the Earl of Stafford, and Lord Bourchier, to testify to
the dying king's intentions regarding the Duke of Bedford's future
position in Normandy and France, and in a parliamentary petition of
1427 was mentioned as being present when Henry V at the last pardoned his Household officers their debts.[52] Almost certainly Hungerford came back to England with the funeral cortège of the dead king via
Paris, Rouen, Boulogne, and Calais, London not being reached until
5 November. Two days later Henry V was buried. Two days later
again, on 9 November, his successor's first Parliament met.

Of first-rate importance on the agenda of this parliament were certain matters in which Hungerford had an immediate interest: the
arrangements to be made for the fulfilment of the late king's will, of
which he was one of the ' working ' executors and for which he was a
feoffee in parcels of the Duchy of Lancaster, and the constitutional
provisions to be made for government during the minority of the new
king, in which he was also concerned as one of the latter's guardians.
The result of the session regarding the second and more important of
these issues was the establishment of a Protectorship and the recon-
struction of a royal Council charged with the exercise of the royal
authority when Parliaments or Great Councils were not sitting. The
new Council, as presently composed, was to consist of the Dukes of
Gloucester and Exeter, five prelates, five earls, and five others. Of the
last five all were knights, two barons and three commoners; Hungerford
was one of these three. He did not retain his stewardship of the royal
Household, an office now somewhat deflated, but he remained as one
of the two chief stewards of the Duchy of Lancaster. His membership
of the royal Council—as steward of Household to Henry V he had
almost certainly been a member of his Council continuously from
1417—was a foregone conclusion. He was among the magnates named
as present in the great chamber at Windsor on 17 November 1422 when
the great seal of silver, brought back from overseas by Henry V's
Chancellor of Normandy, was entrusted to the old Chancellor of

England, Bishop Langley. Apparently on 9 December the Council took office. Hungerford took the oath on 26 January 1423 at a meeting in the Dominican friary in London.[53] Salaries were not seemingly fixed, in a scheme of payments graduated according to rank, until 10 July 1424 when, after an inspection of records for the previous half century or so, Hungerford's own stipend as a knight banneret was decided as being £100 a year (minus 10s. a day for absence in term-time). As things turned out he was to remain a member of the Council certainly until after the end of Henry VI's minority, and perhaps for longer. In fact, in November 1437, when his councillor's annual salary was reduced to 100 marks he was to have this fee for life even if unable to attend, and he was paid £50 for Michaelmas term 1438. Until then, since 1422, not a year had passed in which, in the imperfect records of the Council, his attendance is not noticed, and certainly until 1432 his attendance was frequent except from spring to spring 1423-4, when he was overseas.[54] This preoccupation explains Hungerford's almost complete absence from local commissions of royal appointment in these years, although his inclusion in the commissions of the peace continued.

As early as 18 February 1423 Hungerford was given permission by the Council to go to France with the Duke of Exeter. He had asked to be temporarily discharged of his obligation (under the terms of Henry V's will) to attend continually on the king and from his functions as one of Henry V's executors, and that after his service in France he might perform certain religious vows. These requests were granted by the Council 'libenti animo', and a Council minute of the same day allowing the wardship of the heirs of tenants-in-chief dying overseas to go to their wives or executors was expressly extended to Hungerford. At a Council meeting on 26 April at which he was himself present, it was decided that he should have his letters of protection without further demand, and on the same day he took out letters appointing his general attorneys. On the next day it was agreed that the Treasurer should take from him certain pledges he held as creditor to the late king until the administration of the royal will should be properly begun. From now until May 1424 there is no record of Hungerford's appearing at council meetings. But, although his indenture of *service de guerre* specified that he was to begin it on 28 June, he did not take out letters of protection until 8 July 1423, and although an order to take his muster issued on 18 June, he was still in England a month later when he personally received at the Lower Exchequer an advance of some £294. His contract to serve for a year with a retinue of 2 knights, 17 esquires, and 60 archers, had certainly been drawn up as early as 14 March. [55]

What was the purpose of Hungerford's visit to France it is not easy to see: it may have been intended to supply Bedford with a welcome source of counsel in this year of diplomatic difficulty, although the triple alliance of Bedford, Burgundy and Brittany had already been achieved when Hungerford eventually crossed the Channel. One of his objects may have been to see to his own French estates and to put Cherbourg in order. In the meantime, his private affairs in England had almost certainly benefited from his membership of the royal Council. During the Parliament of 1422 he had been given (on 24 November) the custody of the estates of his recently deceased mother-in-law while they were in the king's hands, and on 27 January 1423, the day after he took his councillor's oath, orders were sent out to the escheators in Somerset, Cornwall and Devon to give livery of seisin of all the estates of which Margaret Peverell had died possessed to Hungerford and his wife and to her sister and *her* husband. Whether Hungerford was back in England or not by 18 November 1423 he then secured from the Council the guardianship and marriage of Philip Courtenay, nephew and heir of Richard Courtenay, the Bishop of Norwich and friend of Henry V who had died at Harfleur in 1415, paying 800 marks for the marriage alone (his sureties being Lords Scrope and Cromwell). Before the end of 1424 Sir Walter had married young Courtenay to his own daughter, Elizabeth; a dispensation for their marriage, which was within the prohibited degrees of kinship, already granted by Bishop Beaufort of Winchester, was confirmed by Pope Martin V on 28 December 1424. [56]

By May 1424 Hungerford was certainly back in England and he then resumed his attendance at the meetings of the royal Council. On 15 July the Council appointed him to his old office of steward of the Household, and on the next day he was present with other councillors at Hertford castle when the great seal was surrendered by Bishop Langley and delivered to Bishop Beaufort who so returned to the Chancery after an absence of seven years. On 31 October, four days after the death of Nicholas Bubwith, Hungerford's own diocesan of Bath and Wells, the Council gave to Hungerford, who was overseer of the late bishop's will along with Bishop Beaufort, and to four of Bubwith's executors the keeping of the temporalities of the see during the vacancy. In the course of their custody they made a loan to the crown of £400 and met other drafts on the revenues made by the Exchequer, but these payments were taken into consideration when the final account was rendered in February 1427 and the total payment due was assessed at £872 odd. Elected to the see in December 1424, Dr. John Stafford, Treasurer of England since the beginning of the reign and as already Dean of Wells favourably placed for this promotion, got livery of the temporalities on 12 May 1425.[57]

Not long before this, on 12 February 1425, Hungerford had been made chamberlain of the Duchy of Lancaster, in addition to his office as duchy chief steward south of Trent. The office of chamberlain was coming to carry little more than dignity but it still involved the presidency of the duchy Council, and it made Hungerford the formal chief of those members of the committee of Henry V's feoffees in the duchy who were actually duchy administrators. Hungerford was to retain this office of duchy chamberlain until February 1444, when his younger son, Edmund, after securing the reversion of the office on 10 November 1441, followed him in possession of it.[58] Hungerford's membership of the royal Council continued to pay him dividends. Any tendencies for his councillor's salary to fall into arrears in these early years of Henry VI's reign and any calls on his goodwill for government loans—on 3 March 1425 he made a loan of 250 marks— were offset by grants within the control of the Council. By this very loan he bought his way into a syndicate of councillors (altogether £1,000 was subscribed) granted the marriage of John, the son and heir of the late Earl of Oxford, then a royal ward. (If this grant came to nothing the group were to recoup themselves from the estates of Thomas, son and heir of John Lord Ros of Helmsley, whose minority had still two-and-a-half-years to run.) And on 20 May 1425, he and his young son-in-law, Philip Courtenay, acquired for seven years (as from midsummer 1425) the custody of the borough, manor, mill and courts of Lydford, the manor of Teigncombe, and all the royal lands called Dartmoor, including the coal-pits and turbaries, for an annual rent of £105.[59]

On 13 June 1425, when an advance of 500 marks was furnished him at the Lower Exchequer, Hungerford was about to go to France again to join Bedford's council of regency for half a year, a decision of the English Council. By the beginning of August he had seemingly crossed with Bishop Kemp of London. Again, as in 1423, it may have been diplomatic business that was responsible, especially perhaps the difficulties arising out of the Duke of Gloucester's invasion of Hainault (in support of his wife, Jacqueline) between October 1424 and April 1425, which were still disturbing the Anglo-Burgundian alliance. Certainly

Hungerford was in Bedford's council when a papal bull of 24 April 1425 prohibiting a duel between Gloucester (the challenger) and Burgundy was delivered to the Regent by the Archbishop of Rouen on 24 September following, and then read before those present.[60]   At the end of October Bedford was asked by the Council in England to return home to settle the quarrel between Gloucester and their uncle, Henry Beaufort, the Chancellor, which had reached the point of open conflict between their retinues. Bedford did return in December 1425, Hungerford in all probability with him.

As a member of the English Council since 1422 Hungerford is likely in this period of tension to have been in sympathy with Bishop Beaufort, or at any rate to have belonged to a moderate group in the Council holding the balance between the Protector and the Chancellor but offering resistance to Gloucester's recurrent bids for a bigger share of authority vis-à-vis the Council than had been allowed him as Protector at the beginning of the reign. It is probable that he was inclined to support Beaufort, but his first summons to Parliament as a baron on 7 January 1426—his fellow councillor Tiptoft was also now first summoned—was more probably due to a movement in the Council to strengthen its hands than to the Chancellor himself alone. The appeasement of the quarrel between Gloucester and Beaufort took up much of the time of the first session of the Parliament which met on 15 February 1426, far away from the scene of the recent disturbances, at Leicester, where twelve years before Hungerford had acted as Speaker. Part of the price Beaufort paid for the reconciliation of 12 March was his resignation of the great seal on the following day. But Bishop Stafford of Bath and Wells who resigned the Treasurership three days later (16 March) was almost certainly a friend of Gloucester, and his retirement was, therefore, perhaps part of a compromise.   It was Lord Hungerford who was immediately appointed to follow his diocesan at the Exchequer, the first lay Treasurer since 1417, and it was as Treasurer of England that he was present in Leicester Abbey at the delivery of the great seal to Beaufort's successor, Bishop Kemp of London. Bishop Kemp, soon to be promoted Archbishop of York, had in his youth studied at Merton College, Oxford, and had later become a fellow there. If, as is possible, Hungerford had an earlier as he most certainly had a later connexion with this college, the new Chancellor and Treasurer had interests in common there. In any case, the two officials had had more recent contacts: Kemp had been Hungerford's companion on his trips to France in 1423 and 1425.[61] Both men can only have taken office as acceptable to the acting Protector, Bedford. Hungerford retained his Duchy of Lancaster offices but now resigned his stewardship of the royal Household. This office went to his fellow councillor, Tiptoft. In sum, the re-shuffle of offices at Leicester meant a consolidation of strength on the part of the moderate elements in the Council rather than any success for Gloucester, whose quarrel with Beaufort was not, from the Council's point of view, the first (or last) consequence of his ambitions.

On Whit-Sunday 1426, during the second session of the Leicester Parliament, the Duke of Bedford knighted the four years old Henry VI who then dubbed thirty-six young men, lords and lords' sons, including the new Treasurer's younger son Edmund.[62] After this parliamentary session Hungerford was put on a Crown loan commission of 23 July 1426 that was to operate in Wiltshire, Somerset, Dorset, and at Bristol, and he again served on a like commission for the same area in 1428.[63] But these were almost the only local commissions, apart from his commissions of the peace, on which Hungerford served in these years of his Treasurership, when in term-time at any rate he was more or less continuously at Westminster in attendance on the Council.

On 24 October 1426 it was decided by the Council that, instead of the £100 a year which Hungerford had been receiving as a councillor of the rank of knight-banneret, he should from the time of his appointment as Treasurer take a fee of 200 marks a year as a member of the Council. In addition to this he now enjoyed 100 marks a year plus an established increment of £300 a year simply as Treasurer. Apart from his duchy of Lancaster fees, his official stipends now amounted to £500 a year. Moreover, as head of the Exchequer, he was able to ensure that their payment did not fall into heavy arrears, and while he was Treasurer his lowest annual receipts were £380 and his highest, £580. Although his payments as a councillor were always behindhand—he had been paid little during the first two years of the reign—his payments as Treasurer were usually actually in advance, so that, when he came to resign from the Exchequer in 1432, all his treasurer's fees had been paid up (save £12). From the beginning of the reign until then the total sum due to him was in the region of £3,600: of this by 1432 he had his hands on over £3,400. Averaging it all out, he was receiving in the first nine years of Henry VI's reign something like £400 a year, compared with an income from his estates at the beginning of this period of about £650 a year and at the end of it of about £1,050 a year.[64]

What his incidental fees and perquisites of office were there is no means of knowing. But their total can hardly have been negligible.

His importance at the centre of things was clearly growing, and one result of this was to bring Hungerford into prominent membership of committees of feoffees to uses. The list of those who sought his good offices in this way is a long one. Even in Henry V's reign, to name only the most important, he had been feoffee to Edward Duke of York, Thomas Earl of Salisbury, Chief Justice Sir William Hankford, and Sir John Tiptoft, and in Henry VI's reign he became feoffee to Richard Duke of York, Humphrey Earl of Stafford, Ralph Lord Cromwell, Reginald West Lord de la Warre, William Lord Lovell, and also to Richard Melbourne, knight of the shire for Wiltshire in 1421, 1423, and 1425, who was one of Hungerford's estates-stewards in Wiltshire[65]. Hungerford's membership of the little group of four overseers of the will of Thomas Beaufort, Duke of Exeter, which was drawn up on 29 December 1426, may have been due partly to friendship, partly to Hungerford's then occupying the Treasurership. His being chosen on 12 May 1429 as overseer of the will of John, Duke of Norfolk, was almost certainly due to his being Treasurer, because his co-overseer was the Chancellor, and Norfolk suggested that either of them would do. On 15 January 1431 one of the two chamberlains of the Exchequer, John Wodehouse, made 'his lord' the Treasurer one of the overseers of his will. Their association at the Exchequer had been by no means the beginning of this connexion; Wodehouse had been made chancellor of the Duchy of Lancaster when Hungerford was made one of the duchy chief stewards (in 1413) and they had been fellow-members of the duchy council for the next eleven years; moreover, both men had been feoffees and executors to Henry V.[66]

For nearly six years, from March 1426 until February 1432, Lord Hungerford was to remain Treasurer of England. During this period he was one of the mainstays of the Council, was party to all the most important of its acts, and generally took up an attitude designed to continue its control of affairs without any undue subservience to the Protector. On 3 March 1428 in Parliament, for example, he subscribed the Lords' declaration of Gloucester's limited authority, confirming the settlement of 1422. As Treasurer and councillor, chamberlain and chief steward of the duchy of Lancaster, executor and feoffee of Henry V, he was the administrator pure and simple, the foremost single agent in the manipulation of the finances of the Crown. There was no question of his taking up again any military duties, and his request on 25 January

1427 to be allowed to cross to Cherbourg, where he was still captain of castle and town, to see to its strengthening against attack from Brittany, can only have been meant to guarantee him against any charge of negligence if the place were lost.[67]

At this time Hungerford's two elder sons, Robert and Walter, were both serving in France with Bedford. The former was at the siege of Orleans in 1429 and the latter was a prisoner of war when the autumn Parliament of this year was in session, having been taken at Patay on 18 June by Lord Beaumanoir, a Breton noble, who held him to ransom at 12,000 ' saluz '. The Lords in the Parliament, in fact, undertook to write to Bedford recommending some arrangement whereby Lord Talbot and Sir Walter Hungerford junior could be exchanged for a French prisoner of note, Sir William Barbazan, if this was not likely to upset the Duke of Burgandy. (Barbazan had evidently been involved in the murder of John the Fearless at Montereau ten years before.) Over this son's ransom Lord Hungerford was to have much trouble, in spite of his being favourably placed to effect his liberation. On 8 May 1431 he was given a formal licence to send £2,000 out of the country to pay the ransom. He himself subscribed a quarter of the total sum due (3,000 ' saluz '), and Lords Scales, Cromwell and Tiptoft put up the rest, and an acquittance had been received. An additional 6,000 ' saluz ' had been promised, unknown to Lord Hungerford, by his son. The father had paid off 5,000 ' saluz ' of this sum, being assisted by a subscription of 1,000 ' saluz ' from the Duke of Brittany and a loan of 4,000 from merchants. All was therefore paid up except 1,000 ' saluz ' which the receiver of Queen Joan (Henry IV's dowager) in Brittany was in February 1433 willing to pay off. Although liberated, the younger Walter had died by this time, but Lord Beaumanoir refused to conclude the transaction, so that the royal Council on Lord Hungerford's behalf ordered a complaint to the Duke of Brittany.[68]

As early as 1429 English affairs in France were going ill, and there was no improvement in the years that followed. Finance was clearly one of the main difficulties, and it may have been Hungerford's realization of the dangers of his own very responsible position as Treasurer that prompted him to ask in Parliament on 16 March 1431 for it to be recorded that he had frequently demanded that the late Earl of Salisbury (killed at Orleans in 1429) should be better supplied with funds. And it may have been a sense of the need for financial circumspection at home which prompted him on 28 November following to state in a specially well-attended Council that, though he was agreeable to Duke

Humphrey taking as ' custos ' 2000 marks a year in addition to the 4000 marks he already had been granted, while Henry VI was out of the country for his coronation in France, Gloucester should revert to his previous salary (plus a ' reward ') when the King came back. Gloucester's supporter, Lord Scrope, concurred that Gloucester's stipend should be raised to 6000 marks a year but recommended that on the King's return it should drop by merely 1000 marks to 5000. Those who stood out against this were outnumbered by three to one, and the minority finally acquiesced, the Chancellor and the Bishop of Carlisle last of all. [69] His opposition to Gloucester was to cost Hungerford dear not long afterwards when the Duke on Henry VI's home-coming in February 1432 took the opportunity to secure extensive changes in the administration. The Treasurer had only recently tried to ensure his control of the national finances, but his attempts had fallen short of success. At Canterbury on 28 January 1432 he was party to certain stipulations agreed to by the Council regarding its procedure. It had been established as one of its rules of conduct that at least four councillors and an official member should approve any measure, but that if so many agreed it should pass provided that they were a majority of those present. It was now decided that if no official member assented a matter might still pass, provided that over half of the Council were present. The special knowledge of both Chancellor and Treasurer was acknowledged to be an important consideration, and their advice and reasons must be heard, but it was nevertheless decided that whatever one of the Kings' uncles and a majority of the Council deemed advisable should pass, and that the Keeper of the Privy Seal should make out all necessary writs even if no official subscribed the warrant. Four weeks later Hungerford was present at Westminster at the tradition of the two great seals to Bishop Stafford of Bath and Wells when Archbishop Kemp of York was required to give up the Chancery. It was his last official act as Treasurer: on the following day, 26 February 1432, he was himself superseded as Treasurer by Gloucester's supporter, Lord Scrope. [70] At the same time Lord Cromwell gave up the Chamberlainship and Lord Tiptoft the Stewardship of the royal Household.

The Parliament which came together in May 1432 saw Cardinal Beaufort's attempt to justify himself against allegations of treason fizzle out in a denial of any such rumours, and Cromwell's complaint to the Lords that he had been dismissed contrary to the Council ordinances of 1429 fell through. Probably thanks to Bedford, the next

Parliament, meeting in the summer of 1433, was to witness the restoration to power of the Beaufort group, including the appointment of Cromwell to the Treasurer's office which he was then to retain for almost ten years. Hungerford was not called upon for high office, but he remained a member of the royal Council, and was influential there if only because of his experience and his position as a feoffee and executor of Henry V and as a member of the Duchy of Lancaster council and administration. He attended the Parliament of May 1432 and was a trier of English petitions. By this time his younger son, Sir Edmund, was close to the person of the young King, being one of the four royal carvers or sewers.[71] In the middle of July 1432 Lord Hungerford was about to go to France with a large retinue of 300 men (50 men-at-arms and 250 archers) at a wage rate of over £1,100 a quarter, and he was to carry £2,500 to the Duke of Bedford. But he was back in England in October when he was present at an assay of coinage at the Tower mint. In April 1433 he and his old colleague in diplomacy, John Kemp, Archbishop of York, were commissioned to go to the General Council of the Church at Basel where, Pope Eugenius IV was making efforts to bring about peace between England and France. What were their instructions in this mission are not known, but Hungerford at any rate was to confer with Bedford on the way out.[72] It is very doubtful whether Hungerford went to Basel (there being no Exchequer record of any payment), but if he did so he was back in England again in time for the Parliament of July—December 1433 in which Bedford began the first session with a defence of his policy in France and ended the second with an undertaking to remain in England as head of the Council. Hungerford was once more a trier of petitions, and before the Parliament ended was one of the Lords who, in answer to a Commons' petition, took an oath to observe the King's peace and not to maintain those who broke it. In the following May (1434) he was a commissioner to administer the oath to the notables of Wiltshire, the list of whom is headed by his two sons, Sir Robert and Sir Edmund. Meanwhile, on 22 November 1433 he had attended a meeting of the Council during the Parliament, and from 24 April to 8 May 1434 was present at a Great Council which met to consider proposals from the Duke of Gloucester that he should be given charge of the war in France.[73] The latter's views resulted in a quarrel with his brother Bedford but naught else, and in June the senior duke returned to France. Before his departure, on 13 June, he had laid some important suggestions before the Council regarding the future conduct of the war, including certain financial stipulations which affected Hungerford as one of Henry V's Duchy of Lancaster feoffees.

'The administration of Henry V's will had proceeded slowly. Indeed, Henry IV's will had only been settled in December 1429, and in May 1432 Henry V's executors had pointed out in Parliament that their liabilities under his will still amounted to £8000. The feoffees had then virtually taken over its administration. Now, in June 1434, Bedford proposed that the enfeoffed portions of the Duchy should be resumed by the present King and that the revenues of the whole Duchy should then be appropriated to the war and to the maintenance of a a permanent force of 200 spears and bows. On 14 June Cardinal Beaufort and Hungerford, the two politically most important feoffees still alive, promised an answer on the following day when, in fact, they partially consented to Bedford's plan. The Lords agreed that the feoffees might honourably release their estate in the enfeoffment if assignments were made by the Exchequer to meet the loans made by the feoffees to the Crown, the expenses for Henry V's chantry and tomb, and his outstanding debts. After demanding an inspection of their books by a committee of the Council so that the soundness of their administration could be attested in the next Parliament, the feoffees agreed that if the current year's revenues from their estates and the income from the proposed assignments proved more than enough to meet all their obligations under Henry V's will, they would not only direct the surplus to meet the costs of the war as from Michaelmas following but also then settle the estates in their trust on Henry VI.[74] Their undertaking to bring the enfeoffment to an end was conditional. Not for a long time yet were Hungerford and his cofeoffees to feel able to honour it, but in the next year, 1435, they made further considerable advances to the Crown out of their income. Again, on 3 February 1436 Beaufort, Chichele and Hungerford in their own names and in the name of Bishop Langley of Durham granted £4000 from the enfeoffment, on condition that they were given security on the Southampton customs and that for a year from June following they should be free from need to make loans to the government. In May 1438 the feoffees made another assignment of 2000 marks. In Parliament, on 14 January 1440, it was again left to Beaufort and Hungerford to obstruct the conclusion of their estate under Henry V's arrangement of 1415. By this time the only feoffees left alive were Archbishop Chichele and themselves. Both the Cardinal and Hungerford objected to the proposed employment of their income from the trust to meet the expenses of the royal Household. They did so on the grounds that the administration of Henry V's will had not even yet been fully completed because of loans to the Crown amounting to 'many thousands'. They were prepared, however, to acquiesce in the appropriation to the Treasurer of the Household of what was left out of their revenues after the payment of Beaufort's and Chichele's debts and after the reservation of £2000 for the continuing administration of the will, provided that they should each have royal letters patent declaring the cause of the delay in the fulfilment of the will and indemnifying them, that each should be free from impeachment or claims, and that any conveyances or releases of any of the enfeoffed estates, made by them at the instance of Henry V or Henry VI, should not be held against them. The three surviving feoffees were clearly touchy on the subject of their administration and conduct as feoffees. But not until another two years had elapsed could they be prevailed upon to surrender their trust. And then in the Parliament of 1442 the Commons requested that there should be set up a parliamentary commission to hear the feoffees' declaration regarding the will, failing which the King was to enter the enfeoffed estates and they stand discharged. Beaufort's and Chichele's debts, it was said, had long (but since 1439) been paid up, and the Commons expressed themselves as concerned about the danger of Henry VI being disinherited if possession, now enjoyed by only three feoffees, should happen to fall upon one of them and descend to his heirs, especially, as the Commons noted in their petition, if 'it fortune upon a Temporall man'. The Commons evidently had their doubts about Hungerford who was the only layman left alive of the original feoffees. This attempt of 1442 to recover the enfeoffed duchy estates for the King was eventually successful, and by February 1444 Henry VI was in possession so that the way was left clear for him to begin a series of duchy enfeoffments to ensure the fulfilment of his own will.[75]

In 1434 the attempt to terminate the estate of the Duchy of Lancaster feoffees of Henry V was part of a programme to supply the sinews of war to safeguard the English conquests in France. But in the following year, Bedford, himself in failing health and now somewhat estranged from his ally of Burgundy, agreed to the making of an attempt to save the game by diplomacy. The result was the great congress of Arras, which met in August 1435. On 20 June Hungerford, still a member of the royal Council, had already been chosen as a member of the English embassy and given a licence to take 2000 marks out of the country for his upkeep; his personal wages were to be £2 a day. He left London for Arras on 11 July and returned on 18 September,[76] The proceedings began on 3 August and the English withdrew on 6 September, in spite of the French being prepared to make large concessions. Within little more than a week Bedford was dead. Burgundy's adherence to Charles VII of France followed almost automatically. This desertion made the English position in France precarious and the preservation of the English hold on Calais and the march of Picardy of especially urgent importance. Hungerford was one of the Lords present in Parliament when on 29 October 1435 the Duke of Gloucester, now heir-presumptive to the throne, indentured with the King for the custody of Calais for the next nine years as from July 1436. The Duke of York was appointed as Bedford's successor as Regent of France and, in February 1436, Hungerford was one of the recipients of privy seal writs asking for loans for the equipment of the army which York was to take over to France. Paris had already been lost and Calais was under siege. At the end of January with his eldest son Hungerford had been made a commissioner to assess both baronial and other incomes in Wiltshire for the new graduated income tax (on land and offices) voted in the recent Parliament; he himself also served in Somerset. His other son, Edmund, one of the King's carvers, was sheriff of Wiltshire in this year (November 1435-6).[77] Whether Hungerford's force of 2 knights banneret, 30 men-at-arms, and 378 archers, which by the end of August 1436 he had raised for service in France (being advanced some £320 at the Exchequer), was actually employed by York or for the relief of Calais is not clear. But that Hungerford fully approved at this juncture of an active anti-Burgundian policy in Flanders is suggested by his apparently warm approval of the tract composed in these latter months of 1436, entitled ' The Libelle of Englyshe Polycye '. Advocating the maintenance of naval supremacy in the narrow seas and a blockade of Flanders to enforce a diplomatic accommodation and secure a resumption of commercial intercourse, the book was given to Hungerford to approve of, which he did ' whanne he thee redde alle over in a nyghte ': ' trewe . . . . nexte the Gospell ' was his alleged comment.[78] On 9 April 1437, he was appointed one of a group of commissioners ' pro materia pacis ', just about when York was giving up his lieutenancy of France in favour eventually of Warwick. A week later he had agreed to make a loan to the King of £100 ' si non ibit in servicium regis '.

Hungerford at this time was still in constant attendance at the royal Council, and in November 1437 was among the existing members who were re-appointed with four additions; his fee of £100 was now reduced from £100 to 100 marks but granted him for life, even if he were unable to attend, and on 20 March 1438 a suitable Exchequer assignment for his payment was made on the issues of the alnage of cloth in his own county of Wiltshire. On 28 March a privy seal warrant was issued authorizing the repayment by the Exchequer of a loan of £40 which he made towards the cost of raising the siege of Guînes and sending an army to Normandy under the Earl of Dorset. Quite recently, in January 1438, to Hungerford had come a reminder of earlier and more spacious days with a bequest of a drinking cup given in the first place by the Emperor Sigismund to Simon Sidenham, Bishop of Chichester, who now gave it to Hungerford, the sole overseer of his will.[79]

In February 1439 Hungerford was present at a Great Council. The war was going unsatisfactorily, but the peace party had to go slow in its approaches to Charles VII, and parallel negotiations to win back Burgundy to an English alliance went on as well. Hungerford was away from Westminster from 11 June to 8 August and again between 28 August and 7 October 1439 on an embassy to Calais engaged in negotiations for a peace with France (*alias* matters touching the King and the ' res publica ' of his two realms), which resulted in a truce for three years with Burgundy. Between the two visits (with Archbishop Kemp and the Earl of Stafford) he was back in England for instructions. From the second visit he returned to this country on 1 October, rode up from Sandwich to London via Canterbury with the Bishop of Norwich and Thomas Beckington, the King's secretary, and on 10 October reported to Henry VI at Kennington. His advances at the Exchequer in cash and assignments came to £290, £54 of which were outstanding until midsummer 1440.[80] This diplomatic mission of 1439 was to prove Hungerford's last. He was well out of it.

In 1440, after the retaking of Harfleur by the English, the Duke of York was given the management of the war as lieutenant-general in France; his commission was to last from 2 July 1440 to Michaelmas 1445. The instructions advised by the duke's chief council suggested Hungerford's inclusion in the council of nine that was to operate with York in France and Normandy.[81] Nothing, however, seems to have come of this proposal, and Hungerford, now turned sixty years of age, drops out of the diplomatic picture. His stock of diplomatic knowledge had largely been gained when it was a fair wind all the way in France; the diplomacy of defeat and withdrawal was perhaps not congenial. He had ceased to be a chief steward of the Duchy of Lancaster in 1437, in 1438 to be Constable of Windsor; his duchy feoffeeship was become an embarrassment. But his territorial and family position was very healthy, and he was still a member of the King's Council and chief of the Duchy of Lancaster council. And he was far from lacking influence. He was still powerful enough to get the reversion of his duchy chamberlainship granted in 1441 to his younger son, Edmund, who was still a sewer to Henry VI. His own future royal commissions, however, were to be mainly local. In August 1440 he was one of the lords ordered to guard against unlawful assemblies and to join the King if need be. In October 1441 he was included in a commission of oyer and terminer regarding treasons and other offences in London and in the counties north and south of the Thames nearby, which suggests his attendance on the Council still. He attended Parliament in January 1442 and was a trier of petitions. In March 1442 he was put on a Crown loan raising commission in Wiltshire, in August on another down at Bristol. A few days before this last commission he subscribed a personal loan of £100 for an expedition to Guienne, and so that he might have a good assignment for repayment he loaned 100 quarters of wheat as well. [82] On 15 March 1443 he was stated in the royal Council to have quelled riots at Salisbury, and it was decided that he should be specially thanked and asked to keep his eye on the situation there. [83] By February 1444 Henry VI was in possession of his inheritance of the Lancastrian duchy, and Hungerford, then (since Archbishop Chichele's death) the only sharer of Cardinal Beaufort's trust from Henry V, gave up at the same time his office of chamberlain of the duchy in favour of his son, Edmund. The two of them had recently (on 29 November 1443) been appointed by Henry VI as feoffees in certain parcels of the duchy to ensure the performance of his will, especially regarding his colleges at Eton and Cambridge. On 10 November 1444, Hungerford loaned another £100 to the government. He remained a J.P. in Wiltshire, Somerset, Devon, Cornwall, Oxfordshire and Bucks until his death, but he was appointed to his last casual royal commission on 1 June 1446, —a loan raising commission in Dorset and Somerset. [84]

It was in this same year, 1446, that Lord Hungerford was enabled to round off a property that he had long been developing in Hungerford (Berks). During the years of his Treasurership he had acquired the manors of Hungerford, Engleford and Charlton-in-Hungerford and he had fishery rights in the township. Now, in 1446, the Duchy of Lancaster manor, town and borough of Hungerford, granted nine years before to the Duke of Gloucester, came his way to be held by fealty and for a rent of 20 marks. In July 1447 the duchy manor, park and hundred of Mere (Wilts), which he had held by a grant for life since 1416, were given to him and his son Edmund in survivorship.[85]   The family was still doing well enough. Robert, the heir, was no politician and by this time something of a stay-at-home, but Sir Edmund was at the centre of things as a member of the royal Household. In August 1447 this younger son shared (with a squire of the body to the King) a grant in survivorship of the keeping of the castle and honour of Berk-hamstead. In February 1449 he was made for life controller of all royal mines in England, Wales and Ireland, outside Devon and Cornwall, at a fee of £40 a year. All these mines had been granted three days before to the Duke of Suffolk, which suggests that here was his principal connexion at Court. And Edmund shared on 2 August 1449, just be-fore his father's death, a royal grant of the offices of constable of Cardiff castle, and chancellor, master forester, and receiver of the Beauchamp lordships of Glamorgan and Morgannok.[86] Lord Hungerford's grand-son, Robert (the son of his heir Robert), had been summoned to Parlia-ment as Lord Moleyns since 1445 in right of his wife, Eleanor de Moleyns, the marriage being another sign of the way in which the Hungerford family fortunes were connected with Suffolk's at this time.[87] Lord Hungerford himself, of course, continued to be sum-moned to Parliament until his death, but it is doubtful whether he attended after his grandson's first Parliament of 1445. In 1444 he had been excused by the sovereign's letters from being present at the annual chapter of the Order of the Garter, having since his election in 1421 attended every single chapter of which there is a record (that is, all ex-cept those from 1439 to 1443); and from 1444 onwards he always ex-cused himself. Neither of his two surviving sons, Robert and Edmund, became a member of the Order, although each was nominated on three occasions between 1445 and 1453.[88]

It was to his two sons and his grandson, Lord Moleyns, that on 31 July 1449 Lord Hungerford received a royal licence under the great seal to grant all his possessions. This was clearly in preparation for the end, for he died at Farleigh on 9 August. On 15 August were issued from the royal Chancery the writs of *diem clausit extremum*. Livery of seisin to his heir, Robert, was ordered on 26 October. His will, drawn up on 1 July, had already been proved at Croydon on 21 August by Archbishop Stafford, and on the following day order had been given to commit the administration of the will to the executors, provided they were willing to act; the Prerogative Court of Canterbury was to be certified by Michaelmas whether this was so. The executors were Hungerford's son and heir (Sir Robert), his younger son (Sir Edmund), his grandson (Lord Moleyns), Sir John Fortescue (Chief Justice of the King's Bench), Master John Chedworth, Walter Bailly, William Stirrop (recently M.P. for the seventh time since 1432 for Chippenham), and John Mervyn (Hungerford's receiver-general). The will's supervisors were ' carissimus dominus meus ', John Viscount Beaumont (husband to a niece of Cardinal Beaufort and a kinsman of the wife of the heir), Sir Philip Courtenay (Hungerford's son-in-law), Master Gilbert Kymer (Dean of Salisbury and also Chancellor of the University of Oxford), and Master Andrew Hulse (a canon of Salisbury). [89]

It was no light burden that these committees undertook. The religious provisions of the will alone were formidably multiple, in spite of the fact that Hungerford had already founded and endowed (during his period of office as Treasurer of England) a chantry at Farleigh Hungerford (by royal licence of 14 June 1426) and another in the chapel of St. Stephen in the palace of Westminster, and later on other chantries in the cathedral church of Salisbury, where he intended to be buried with his first wife, and at Heytesbury and Chippenham. There were bequests of varying amounts to the canons residentiary at Salisbury, to the priory at Bath, to the Augustinian canons at Bruton (Somerset) and Maiden Bradley (Wilts), and to the only two Carthusian houses in south-west England, at Witham and Hinton (Somerset), a sign perhaps of a devotion inspired by the interest taken in this Order by Henry V, to whose own foundation at Sheen (between Windsor and Westminster) Hungerford bequeathed 10 marks. The Bonhommes at Edington (Wilts) were remembered, and so were the two Wiltshire nunneries of Amesbury and Lacock. The great gift to Merton College, Oxford, of £100 ' ad fabricam campanilis ' had already been two parts paid up. Houses of the Mendicants all over the south came in for more modest allowances, something of a preference for the Dominicans creeping in here and there: at London, Oxford, Salisbury, Marlborough, Bristol, Bridgwater, Ilchester, and Exeter. 175 marks were to be distributed by the testator's chantry chaplains at Salisbury to priest-vicars and old priests-perpetual in the cathedral; 100 marks among poor men, especially poor husbandmen (*iconomi*), poor labourers with many children, and so on, in his own estates; one mark each to fifty poor men, especially bed-ridden ones, and further to the poor a mark for every year of his own life. The bequests to the family and to retainers of one sort or another were of the same order of generosity. To Hungerford's second wife, the Countess of Arundel, who was to survive him till 1455, were to go his silver and gold, plate and other chattels, but not the 700 marks which she had made over to him at their marriage—he had met her debts at the Exchequer and in the City, which exceeded that sum. And she was to get the stock at Pynkeden (Sussex), the sheep at Heytesbury (of which his heir was to have the use), and £100 for her expenses for the year after his death, provided that she sued out her dower and made the proper releases to his heir in recompense for it. The heir, Robert, the second Lord Hungerford, came by various bequests including all unsown corn, all the sheep and other stock except at Heytesbury and Fenny Sutton. The artillery and contents of the armouries in his castles overseas, which by the custom of that ' patria ' ought to be shared between sons and daughters, were to remain there for their defence. There were the usual gifts of goblets, basins and cups, but especially to Viscount Beaumont as descended lineally from the house of Lancaster went the silver cup from which John of Gaunt had often used to drink until the end of his life. One son-in-law, Sir Philip Courtenay, got £40 for a good courser. The other, Sir Walter Rodney, of whom the testator perhaps disapproved, was to pay up to the executors within a year a debt of 500 marks, which sum was then to go in furnishing marriage-portions for the Rodney grandchildren. 700 marks were to be devoted to the marriages of Hungerford's heir's younger children, another £100 to the marriage of the surviving eldest Courtenay grandson. Bequests of plate and moneys amounting to £90 went to members of his household staff, to which as a whole were to go a full year's wages. The executors were to get £10 each, over and above legacies. £100 were to stand for funeral expenses, not including over £12 for bell-ringing. Hungerford was to be buried next his first wife in the chantry founded by him on the north side of the nave in the cathedral church of Salisbury.[91]

(I am indebted to Mr. J. L. Kirby and to the University of London for permission to read his M.A. thesis entitled ' The Hungerford Family in the later Middle Ages.' I am especially grateful to Mr. Kirby for his willingness to let me use his data relating to the management of Lord Hungerford's estates and the income which he derived from these and other sources.)

130

1 *Official Return of Members of Parliament*, i. 261, 267, 273, 275, 280, 282.

2 *Bulletin of the Institute of Historical Research*, XVIII. 38.

3 *Ante.*

4 *Historical MSS. Commission Report, MSS. of R. R. Hastings*, i. 299; *The Complete Peerage*, VI. 615; Dugdale, *Baronage*, i. 635; ii. 204 *et seq.*; *The Genealogist* (N.S.), XVI. 166; *The Archaeological Journal*, X (Courtenay pedigree); Somerset Record Society, vol. XXII (*Feet of Fines, Henry IV–Henry VIII*, ed. E. Green), 157; *Calendar of Close Rolls (C.C.R.)*, *1422-9*, 29; *ibid.*, *1435-41*, 217, 227; *Calendar of Fine Rolls (C.F.R.)*, *1422-30*, 31; *Calendar of Patent Rolls.* (*C.P.R.*), *1422-9*, 70.

5 *H.M.C. Report, Hastings MSS*, i. 287. Margaret Botreaux's great great grandmother, Isabel, was the younger daughter and coheir of Sir John de Moels and sister of Muriel, Margaret Courtenay's mother. The Botreaux marriage was eventually to bring into Hungerford possession no fewer than 52 manors (18 in Cornwall, 6 in Devon, 10 in Somerset, 8 in Hants, the rest in other counties, including Maiden Winterbourne in Wilts). But Walter Hungerford did not live to see this happen. Nor did even his son and heir, Robert, the husband of Margaret Botreaux, because her father outlived both Walter and Robert, dying in 1462, three years after his son-in-law. (Hoare, *Wiltshire*, vol. I, part II. p. 92).

6 *C.P.R.*, *1416-22*, 49, 362; *The Ancestor*, no. 8. The Burnell-Hungerford settlement was later to be somewhat disturbed by the prosecution of a claim by William Lord Lovell to certain of the estates involved, on the ground of his descent from Hugh Lord Burnell's grandmother by an earlier marriage of hers. But not all the settlement was upset (cf. Manning and Bray, *Surrey*, iii. 421).

7 In Wiltshire: Bramshaw, Britford, Chippenham (*C.P.R.*, *1422-9*, 269; *ibid.*, *1485-94*, 145), Corston, Great Durnford, East Harnham (*C.C.R.*, *1447-54*, 147), Horningsham, Imber, Louden, Shieldon, Rowley *alias* Wittenham (*C.P.R.*, *1485-94*, 145 (7); *C.C.R.*, *1429-35*, 54), Little Somerford, Stanton, Titherington, Upton Scudamore (*C.P.R.*, *1485-94*, 145 (17); Hoare, *Wiltshire*, iii, i. 50), Winterbourne Honington (*C.C.R.*, *1447-54*, 147), Winterbourne Stoke (*C.P.R.*, *1485-94*, 145 (9, 16); *C.C.R.*, *1429-35*, 55), Biddenham, Biddestone, Martin Bradley, Pombury, Fenny Sutton. In Somerset: Flintford, High Church, Tellisford (*C.C.R.*, *1413-9*, 194), Hardwick, Pouthley, Feltham. In Oxfordshire: Stoke Moyles. In Dorset: Folke (*C.C.R.*, *1447-54*, 147; Hoare, *op. cit.*, vol. I., part II. 161). For the Charing property, see *C.P.R.*, *1485-94*, 145 (10, 14), and *C.C.R.*, *1429-35*, 53.

8 *C.P.R.*, *1485-94*, 145 *et seq.*

9 Hoare, *op. cit.*, vol. I, part II, 117; *C.P.R.*, *1436-41*, 300; *C.C.R.*, *1454-61*, 87. The manors held by Hungerford in the right of his Countess were Durlston, Frome Whitfield, Hymeford, Langton, Loders, Lytchett, East Morden, Okeford Fitzpaine, Philipston (in Wimborne St. Giles), Bere Regis, Upper Wimborne, Woolcombe, Wootton Fitzpaine, in Dorset; Boyton, Coate, Elston, Knighton, Sherrington, Stapleford, in Wiltshire; Achards, King's Stanley, Shurdington, Winterborne Hill, Woodchester, in Gloucestershire; Stoke Tuister, Spargrove, in Somerset.

10 Ex inf. Mr. J. L. Kirby.

11 *Complete Peerage*, IX. 43. At the request of Sir Walter when Treasurer, it

was Cardinal Beaufort's cousin, Thomas Chaucer of Ewelme (Oxon), who had arranged for the infant Eleanor to be brought home from the Loire, perhaps in the company of his own daughter, Alice Countess of Salisbury, who had been widowed during the blockade of Orleans; in 1431 Chaucer secured (for 500 marks) Eleanor's wardship and marriage. (She was his wife's greatniece.) Eleanor's marriage with Robert Hungerford, who came of age in November 1440 (*C.P.R., 1441-6*, 35), must have been arranged in good time between Sir Walter and Chaucer, if this was the way of it, for Chaucer died in 1434. In the meantime, on 30 March 1439, Sir Walter and his son, Robert, had been granted by the Crown the keeping of the estates of the young heiress's paternal grandmother pending Eleanor's majority (*C.F.R., 1437-45*, 82).

12 Oxford Historical Society, *Proceedings*, XXXV (*Epistolae Academiae Oxoniensis*), 112; *ibid.*, XVIII (*Oxford City Documents, 1268-1665*), 314, 326, 328-30; Lambeth Palace Library, Stafford Register, fo. 114.

13 *C.P.R., 1391-6*, 636.

14 *The Great Chronicle of London*, ed. A. H. Thomas and I. D. Thornley, 73; *C.P.R., 1399-1401*, 62. (On 1 December 1403 the rent was diverted from the Exchequer to Henry IV's youngest son, Humphrey, later Duke of Gloucester, together with the reversion of the premises after Sir Walter's death (*ibid., 1401-5*, 320); *ibid.*, 154. (Margaret, daughter of Thomas of Brotherton, Countess of Norfolk in her own right, had been created a duchess by Richard II in 1397; she had died on 24 March 1399.)

15 *C.P.R., 1399-1401*, 385; *C.C.R., 1399-1401*, 228; R. R. Sharpe, *Letter Books of the City of London*, I, 3; *Bristol and Gloucestershire Archaeological Society Transactions*, vol. 50, 148.

16 *C.F.R., 1399-1405*, 54.

17 *C.P.R., 1401-5*, 520; *Proceedings and Ordinances of the Privy Council*, ed. N. H. Nicolas (*P.P.C.*), i. 161; ii. 87.

18 *Calendar of Papal Registers, Papal Letters*, IV. 351; Stafford Register, *loc. cit.*,; *C.P.R., 1405-8*, 384; *C.F.R., 1399-1405*, 192.

19 *C.P.R., 1401-5*, 221, 289.

20 Public Record Office, *Lists and Indexes*, IX (*List of Sheriffs*), 153; P.R.O., E 101/406/10, but cf. transcript in *Archaeologia*, LXVII. 176-7, 186; J. H. Wylie, *The Reign of Henry IV*, ii. 434-51.

21 *C.P.R., 1405-8*, 161.

22 *Somerset and Dorset Notes and Queries*, XVI. 162; the dispute had attracted special notice during the parliament of 1406 (in which Sir Hugh Luttrell sat for Somerset) and the Commons had requested that if there were a normal trial by the 'patria' nobody should be a juryman who had not £40 a year in land (*Rotuli Parliamentorum*, IV. 597).

23 *C.P.R., 1405-8*, 308, 384; *C.C.R., 1405-9*, 350.

23ᵃ British Museum, Arundel MS., no. 68, fo. 57.

24 *C.F.R., 1405-13*, 149; *C.P.R., 1408-13*, 143, 163, 181; *C.C.R., 1409-13*, 28; *Rot. Parl.*, iii, 632b.

25 *P.P.C.*, i. 343; *C.P.R., 1408-13*, 204, 208.

26 *C.F.R., 1405-13*, 216, 236-7; Joan Hungerford's will, made on 25 February 1412, was proved in the Prerogative Court of Canterbury, letters of administration issuing on 23 March 1412 (Arundel Register, fo. 152).

27 *C.C.R.*, *1413-9*, 62.

28 R. Somerville, *The Duchy of Lancaster*, i. 428. The office of chief steward very soon involved Hungerford (on 12 June 1413 by patent under the great seal of England) in a commission of oyer and terminer regarding treasons and rebellions in some of the duchy lordships in S. Wales and the March, and on 20 June he again was appointed to act with duchy officials, inquiring into concealments and maladministration on the part of duchy foresters, parkers and warreners in the south parts of the duchy and making all necessary dismissals and re-appointments, certifying the King and Council in Chancery, a similar commission being appointed for the north parts (*C.P.R.*, *1413-6*, 112-3).

29 *Lists of Sheriffs*, 123.

30 *Deputy Keeper's Reports (D.K.R.)* XLIV (French Rolls), 554; T. Carte, *Catalogue des Rolles Gascons etc.*, ii. 216-7; Exchequer, Issue Rolls, P.R.O., 403/617, mem. 8; *ibid.*, 619., mem. 2; Exchequer, Accounts Various, E101/321, no. 28; *C.C.R.*, *1413-9*, 214.

31 *Papal Letters*, VI. 461. This may or may not be the Walter Hungerford, the younger son of Sir Walter, who was to take up a military career, undergo capture at Patay in 1429, and be freed only to die sometime not long before February 1433. Sir Walter may have had two sons of the name of Walter: certainly there was a Walter Hungerford who was granted for life by the King in February 1449 the hospital of St. Lawrence by Bristol (*C.P.R.*, *1446-52*, 223), but there is no Walter Hungerford among the beneficiaries of Lord Hungerford's will, drawn up and proved later in that same year. *Ibid.*, 490.

32 *D.K.R.*, XLIV. 563; Privy seal warrants for issue, P.R.O., E404/31/165; N. H. Nicolas, *The Battle of Agincourt*, 381; *Transactions of the Royal Historical Society*, 3rd Series, V. 138.

33 R. Somerville, *op. cit.*, i. 183, 430; *C.P.R.*, *1485-94*, 145 et seq.

34 *C.P.R.*, *1413-6*, 356-7; *ibid.*, *1422-9*, 64, 136, 176, 181, 188, 313, 337; *Rot. Parl.*, IV. 172-3, 393.

35 *C.P.R.*, *1413-6*, 350.

36 *Incerti Scriptores, Chronicon Angliae*, ed. J. A. Giles; *Gesta Henrici Quinti*, 47.

37 *D.K.R.*, XLIV. 575-7; Issue Rolls, P.R.O., E 403/624, mem. 4.

38 *D.K.R.*, XLIV. 579; T. Carte, *op. cit.*, ii. 228.

39 *C.P.R.*, *1416-22*, 39; *H.M.C.*, *15th Report*, 161; *C.C.R.*, *1413-9*, 321.

40 See above, pp. 302-3.

41 *P.P.C.*, ii. 208, 213-4, 220, 227, 229, 231, 233.

42 *C.P.R.*, *1416-22*, 108; *ibid.*, *1422-9*, 474. Hungerford was still a feoffee of the earl at the time of his death in 1429, and in Salisbury's will was to be referred to by him as ' amicus noster ' (*The Register of Archbishop Chichele*, ed. E. F. Jacob, ii. 394).

43 *C.C.R.*, *1413-9*, 435; *Rot. Parl.*, IV. 129.

44 *Ex inf.* Mr. J. L. Kirby.

45 T. D. Hardy, *Rotuli Normanniae*, 153, 169, 195; *C.P.R.*, *1416-22*, 236; *ibid.*, *1436-41*, 181; *C.C.R.*, *1429-35*, 261.

46 Camden Society, *The Historical Collections of a citizen of London in the Fifteenth Century*, ed. J. Gairdner, *William Gregory's Chronicle of London*, 121; *The Great Chronicle of London*, *op. cit.*, 103; *D.K.R.*, XLI. 696, 803; *ibid.*, XLII. 378, 424; Exchequer, Accounts Various, P.R.O., E101/187/14; 188/7;

D.K.R., XLVIII. 222, 261, 280. According to British Museum, Harley MS. no. 782, fo. 49v, the captaincy of Cherbourg had first been given to Richard Lord Grey of Codnor who died, however, on 1 August 1418, and then to Hungerford ' apres son decez '.

47 *D.K.R.*, XLI. 705, 733, 741, 745, 776, 783; J. H. Wylie and W. T. Waugh, *The Reign of Henry V*, iii. 191.

48 *D.K.R.*, XLI. 706; Dugdale, *Baronage*, ii. 204; *D.K.R.*, XLII. 387, 413, 452; Exchequer, Foreign Accounts, E 364/61, mem. C; E 101/404/7.

49 C. L. Kingsford, *English Historical Literature in the Fifteenth Century*, App. 319.

50 *C.P.R.*, *1416-22*, 385, 362; *C.C.R.*, *1419-22*, 150,156, 201; J. Anstis, *The Register of the Most Noble Order of the Garter* (London, 1724), 73. (The payment of £92 17s. 10d. to Hungerford at the Exchequer on 3 May 1423 (a part payment of £146 4s. 6d. still due to him for his service in France in 1415) was made ' per manus Willelmi Bruges ', Garter King of Arms, and may have been connected with the fees Hungerford would be called upon to pay on his installation (Issue Rolls, E 403/660)). *Rot. Parl.*, IV. 172-3, 393; *D.K.R.*, XLIV. 627 (a laggard member of his retinue from Driffield, Glos., was still in England in mid-July 1421, *C.C.R.*, *1419-22*, 206).

51 *Receuil des Chroniques, etc., par Jehan de Waurin*, ed. W. Hardy (Rolls Series), 404; Wylie and Waugh, *op. cit.*, iii 348-9.

52 *Vita et Gesta Henrici Quinti*, ed. T. Hearne (Oxford, 1727), p. 337. Only this chronicle alludes to Hungerford in this way. He was a patron of its author and encouraged him to write the work, but the appointment is undisputably confirmed by record evidence (*P.P.C.*, iii. 37, 248; *Rot. Parl.*, IV. 324.

53 *Rot. Parl.*, IV. 175; *C.C.R.*, *1422-9*, 49; *P.P.C.*, iii. 22.

54 *Rot. Parl.*, V. 404; *P.P.C.*, V. 71; *ibid.*, 111-V, *passim*; P.R.O., E404/52/160.

55 *P.P.C.*, iii. 37-8, 67; T. Carte, *op. cit.*, ii. 249-50; *C.P.R.*, *1422-9*, 124; P.R.O., E403/658, mem. 14, /660, mem. 13; E404/39/166.

56 *C.F.R.*, *1422-30*, 25, 31, 76; *Papal Letters*, VII. 379. In 1436 Hungerford was one of Courtenay's feoffees (*Catalogue of Ancient Deeds*, VI. C6409.).

57 *C.P.R.*, *1422-9*, 211; *C.C.R.* ., *1422-9*, 154; *C.F.R.*, *1422-30*, 96; *C.P.R.*, *1422-9*, 298, 397; *Chichele Register*, *op. cit.*, ii. 300. (Bubwith left to Hungerford his best horse and £20).

58 Duchy of Lancaster, Accounts Various, P.R.O., D.L. 28/5/3, 5; R. Somerville, *op. cit.*, i. 417.

59 *P.P.C.*, iii. 167; *C.P.R.*, *1422-9*, 271; *C.F.R.*, *1422-30*, 100.

60 P.R.O., E 403/671, mems. 8, 17; *Letters and Papers, The Wars of the English in France, Henry VI.* (R.S.), ed. J. Stevenson, vol. ii, part ii. 414.

61 *C.C.R.*, *1422-9*, 269; *P.P.C.*, iii. 197.

62 *William Gregory's Chronicle of London*, *op. cit.*, 160; *The Great Chronicle of London*, *op. cit.*, 149.

63 *C.P.R.*, *1422-9*, 354, 481, 403.

64 *P.P.C.*, iii. 212; P.R.O., E403/675, mem. 10; 700, mem. 14. For Hungerford's total and average payments between 1422 and 1432 I am indebted to information supplied by Mr. J. L. Kirby.

65 *Feudal Aids*, V. 269, 277, 279; *C.C.R.*, *1429-35*, 134, 214, 260, 264 (Edward, Duke of York). *C.P.R.*, *1422-9*, 474; *Chichele Register*, *op. cit.*, ii. 394 (Thomas

Earl of Salisbury). *C.C.R., 1422-9*, 110 (Chief Justice Hankford). *Ibid., 1413-9*, 194 (Sir John Tiptoft). *C.P.R., 1429-36,* 514; *Feet of Fines for Somerset, op. cit.,* 193, 201 (Richard, Duke of York). *C.C.R., 1422-9,* 318 (Humphrey, Earl of Stafford). *C.P.R., 1422-9,* 212; *ibid., 1436-41,* 292; *H.M.C. Report, MSS. of Lord de l'Isle and Dudley,* i. 172 (Ralph Lord Cromwell). Somerset Record Society, *The Register of Bishop Stafford,* ii. 248 (Reginald Lord de la Warre). Manning and Bray, *Surrey,* iii. 421 (William Lord Lovell). *Ibid.,* ii. 744 (Richard Melbourne).

66 *Chichele Register, op. cit.,* ii. 361, 474, 439.

67 *Rot. Parl.,* IV. 327; *P.P.C.,* iii. 230.

68 *Rot. Parl.,* IV 338; *D.K.R.,* XLVIII. 282, *P.P.C.,* IV. 149.

69 *P.P.C.,* IV. 104.

70 *Rot. Parl.,* V. 433; *C.C.R., 1429-35,* 181; *P.R.O.,* E403/700, mem. 14.

71 *Rot. Parl.,* IV. 388; *C.P.R., 1429-36,* 267.

72 *P.R.O.,* E404/48/319, 340, 365; *C.P.R., 1429-36,* 218, 259; *P.P.C.,* IV. 158. In 1433-4 negotiations were in train for the ransom of Hungerford's prisoner, Jean de Vendosme, Vicomte of Chartres, who received a safe-conduct to France in April 1434 to enable him to get his ransom (*D.K.R.,* XLVIII. 294-6; *H.M.C., 15th Report,* part X. 162).

73 *Rot. Parl.,* IV. 419, 422; *C.P.R., 1429-36,* 370; *P.P.C..,* IV. 184, 212.

74 *Rot. Parl.,* V. 435; *P.P.C.,* IV. 229-32. (The only other feoffees of Henry V still alive in June 1434 were Archbishop Chichele, Bishop Langley of Durham, and John Leventhorpe esquire).

75 *Rot. Parl.,* V. 8-9, 56-9; *P.R.O.,* E404/52/199 and 54/291; R. Somerville, *op. cit.,* i. 205-6. By 1439 Cardinal Beaufort had acquired a peculiarly personal interest in certain of the Norfolk and Cambridgeshire manors enfeoffed, and Hungerford refused to ratify this estate and release his own and Chichele's interest, because the will of Henry V had not yet been executed; when he later gave way he took good care to have an indemnity under the great seal and the duchy seals (Somerville, *op. cit.,* i. 205).

76 *P.P.C.,* IV 289, 302; *P.R.O.,* E403/719, mem. 12; E101/322/36; *Wars of the English in France ,op. cit.,* vol. ii, part ii. 431. For the purposes and results of the Congress, see J. G. Dickinson, *The Congress of Arras 1435* (Oxford, 1955).

77 *Rot. Parl.,* IV. 484; *P.P.C.,* IV. 317; *C.F.R., 1430-7,* 259-60, 268; *List of Sheriffs,* 153. On 8 February 1436 Hungerford and his son-in-law, Sir Philip Courtenay, shared a royal grant of the custody of the Cornish manor of Tywardreath (*C.F.R., loc. cit.,* 264), and in 1439 the keeping of the dower lands of the late widow of Sir John Luttrell.

78 *P.R.O.,* E403/724; *The Libelle of Englyshe Polycye,* ed. Sir Geo. Warner, p. 57.

79 *P.P.C.,* V. 6, 13, 71; *Rot. Parl.,* V. 438; *C.P.R., 1436-41,* 144, 240; *P.R.O.,* E404/54/181; *Chichele Register, op. cit.,* ii 559.

80 *P.P.C.,* V. 108, 336; *P.R.O.,* E364/73; E403/735, mem. 7; *ibid.,* 739, mem. 8.

81 *Wars of the English in France, op. cit.,* vol. ii, part ii. 586.

82 *C.C.R., 1435-41,* 387; *C.P.R., 1441-6,* 109, 62, 93; *P.P.C.,* V. 202; *Rot. Parl.,* V. 36.

83 *P.P.C.,* V. 247,

84 *Rot. Parl.,* V. 70; P.R.O., E403/755, mem. 4; *C.P.R., 1441-6,* 430.

85 *V. C. H., Berkshire,* IV. 185, 191, 194; *C.P.R., 1446-52,* 79.

86 *C.P.R., 1446-52,* 84, 213, 274.

87 *The Complete Peerage,* IX. 42-3. The Duke of Suffolk had married Alice, daughter and heir of Thomas Chaucer of Ewelme (Oxon), cousin of Cardinal Beaufort. It had been at Ewelme that Eleanor's parents had been married; Alice Chaucer (then Countess of Salisbury) had been one of her godmothers at her baptism in June 1426; to Thomas Chaucer had been granted her marriage in 1431.

88 J. Anstis, *op. cit.,* 73 *et seq.*

89 *C.P.R., 1446-52,* 268; *C.F.R., 1445-52,* 97, 142-4; Lambeth Palace Library, Register of Archbishop Stafford, fo. 114 *et seq.* . The date of Hungerford's death is both confirmed and contradicted in a missal which in 1870 was in the municipal library at Tours. Given on 24 July 1449, during his last illness, by Lord Hungerford to his grandson, Lord Moleyns, an entry in it says that he died at Farleigh at half past one on the vigil of St. Lawrence (16 October), but in a note on a later folio, 9 August, the correct date as it appears, is given. Lord Moleyns was to be taken prisoner in Guienne in 1453 and to remain for some seven years in France; it was probably during that time that the missal came into the possession of Jean de Beuil, Comte de Sancerre, who fought in Normandy and Maine and was at the siege of Cherbourg in 1450. The missal remained in the keeping of his family (*Notes and Queries,* 4th series, vol. V (1870), p. 112).

90 *C.P.R., 1422-9,* 347; *ibid., 1441-6,* 36, 94, 151, 327; Hoare, *Wiltshire, op. cit.,* vol. I, part 2, p. 92; Dugdale, *Baronage,* ii. 204 *et seq.* . In 1427-8 Hungerford gave to the dean and canons of St. Stephen's, Westminster, houses and shops in the parish of St. Anthony in the City, so becoming a sharer of all their masses and prayers for life, and on condition that his obit was celebrated each year after his death. In 1428-9 he received a licence to amortize and appropriate the advowson of the parish church of Olveston (Glos) to Bath Priory, which was to maintain a chantry priest at Farleigh. In aid of his chantry of two priests and two chaplains in Salisbury Cathedral he appropriated the parish church of St. Samson at Cricklade and the reversion of the manor of Cricklade (called Abingdon's Court) to the dean and chapter; this fund was also to help maintain in repair the tall spire-steeple of the cathedral. The royal licence to found a chantry at Farleigh, first granted in 1426, was renewed in November 1441, and then this repetition of the grant was superseded in March 1445 by a further licence allowing for the fact that the Farleigh chapel was now part of the castle there, the site of the parish church having been moved to another place in the town.

91 Stafford Register, *loc. cit.*

6

WILLIAM TRESHAM OF SYWELL
SPEAKER FOR THE COMMONS UNDER HENRY VI

I

Not until 1376, seemingly, did the medieval Commons proceed to elect a common Speaker from among their own number and for the duration of a Parliament. The list of the Speakers is complete after 1397. As before, so from then onwards down to 1533, they were chosen from among those of the Commons who represented counties. The main single reason for this was that the medieval knights of the shire were in rank and social standing generally superior to the parliamentary burgesses: they were members of the landed gentry, important in their locality, useful to the King in his provincial administration, and frequently well connected with one or more members of the titular nobility, sometimes even by family ties. The medieval Speakers were, of course, like their fellow knights of the shire in these respects, and most of them, besides, were constantly in the thick of affairs of state, the courtiers, professional administrators, and lawyers among them alike, tied up with the King, some branch of his government or household, or associated with some dominant magnate or faction.

In the medieval period many knights of the shire were often elected for their own counties, and some of them sat at times for other counties. A few of them secured re-election to successive Parliaments, occasionally over many years. Election to the Speakership was then, however, a very chancy business. A Speaker was by no means bound to be re-elected as knight of the shire, and, even if he were, it was not very likely that he would be re-elected as Speaker. During the course of the fifteenth century nearly sixty Parliaments met, but there occur in this period only seven instances of a Speaker in one Parliament being re-elected in the next. One Speaker of Henry IV's time, Thomas Chaucer of Ewelme (Oxon.), son of Geoffrey Chaucer, and cousin of Cardinal Beaufort, was Speaker in three Parliaments running, and under Henry V so was Roger Flore of Oakham, Chief Steward of the Duchy of Lancaster north of Trent. In general, however, the speakership went the rounds. Only nine normally elected fifteenth century Speakers acted more than once.

William Tresham, a Northamptonshire lawyer in Crown service, was Speaker under Henry VI as many as four times, namely in the parliaments of 1439-40, 1442, 1447 and 1449-50, his first two speakerships being in successive Parliaments. Of all previous Speakers, only Thomas Chaucer had served in more Parliaments (five) than he, and Roger Flore in as many. Tresham's Speakerships fell in a period when the Lancastrian régime was becoming discredited and un-

In this article the following abbreviations have been used in the footnotes:—

C.Ch.R. = *Calendar of Charter Rolls.*
C.C.R. = *Calendar of Close Rolls.*
C.F.R. = *Calendar of Fine Rolls.*
C.P.R. = *Calendar of Patent Rolls.*

P.R.O. = Public Record Office.
P.P.C. = *Proceedings and Ordinances of the Privy Council,* ed. N. H. Nicolas.
Rot. Parl. = *Rotuli Parliamentorum.*
V.C.H. = *The Victoria County History.*

popular, partly because its military policy and its diplomacy (directed to salvaging as much as possible of Henry V's conquest in France) were proving expensive but futile, partly because its administration at home was becoming similarly bankrupt, and profitable only to a narrowing circle of its supporters among the nobility and their partizans.

Between 1423 and his death in 1450, William Tresham represented Northamptonshire in no fewer than twelve out of the sixteen parliaments which met in that time. In fact, in the last ten years of his life he quite monopolized one of the two Northamptonshire seats. This fact alone is sufficient indication of Tresham's power in the county. His constant employment by the Crown as an apprentice-at-law (culminating in his appointment as Chancellor of the Duchy of Lancaster in the year before his death), his nearness at Court to the fount of royal grace and favour, his acquisition of local offices, his membership of so many local royal commissions, and his control of patronage as an agent for royal estates in the region of his own considerable landed property, gave him great influence in Northamptonshire and neighbouring shires. Tresham's career is an example of how it was possible for a thriving administrative official to take advantage of the very weakness of the government he served for the furtherance of his own ends, provided he did not over-reach himself and seek to be all things to all men, as perhaps at the end Tresham was trying to do.

The facts of William Tresham's career leave no doubt of his ability and reputation as a manager of other men's business besides his own. That all was not well with his general reputation, however, the manner of his death suggests. The "engrossing" or accumulation of many offices and occupations in the hands of one man might have its administrative conveniences, especially if the beneficiary were one whose heart and mind a weak royal administration felt itself able to trust. But it raised resentments, including local resentments, which were apt to be dangerous in this period of "bastard feudalism," and at a time when the royal authority was coming to afford little protection. This was especially likely to be the case if the profiteer from royal favour, by his conduct raised doubts of his fidelity. There was no wide hiatus, either in time or in circumstances, between Tresham's death in 1450 and the open armed conflict of the Wars of the Roses, the early phases of which virtually completed the political bankruptcy of the House of Lancaster and brought Henry VI's reign to an end in 1461.

II

WILLIAM TRESHAM, apprentice-at-law, was knight of the shire for Northamptonshire in the Parliaments of October, 1423; October, 1427; September, 1429; May, 1432; July, 1433; October, 1435; November, 1439; January, 1442; February, 1445; February, 1447; February, 1449; November, 1449; and Speaker for the Commons in those of 1439, 1442, 1447 and November, 1449.[1]

The estates held by Tresham at Sywell, Hannington, Rushton, and elsewhere in Northamptonshire,[2] in which by royal charter of 10 November, 1441, he was granted rights of free warren, would appear not to have been very long in the possession of his family. The manor of Sywell had been held as recently as 1394-5 by the Dallingridges and only passed into

---

[1] *Official Return of the Members of Parliament*, i., 306, 313, 316, 322, 327, 333, 336, 339, 342; App. xxiii; J. C. Wedgwood, *History of Parliament, 1439-1509, Biographies*, 871. All the Parliaments between 1423 and 1449 referred to above were summoned to Westminster except that of 1447, which met at Bury St. Edmunds.

[2] For William Tresham's estates, see Miss M. E. Finch, *Five Northamptonshire Families*, (N.R.S. vol. xix), p. 67.

possession of the Tresham family at some time between then and 1441, but whether to William, or first to his father, Thomas, is not known. And not until 1445, when Brown's manor was conveyed to him by Richard Waldegrave, did William Tresham possess himself of the whole vill of Hannington, in a quarter part of a knight's fee in which he had had an interest since 1428 (at latest). His tenure of the manor of West Hall in Rushton and of the advowson of the church there was released to him in 1437-8. An early reference to Tresham (in 1415) describes him as being of Gloucestershire. It is unlikely, however, that this important Lancastrian administrative lawyer was himself responsible for the first establishment of his family in Northamptonshire. His marriage with Isabel, daughter of William Vaux, lawyer of Northampton, and sister of William Vaux of Harrowden, need not suggest that his family was already settled in the county.[3] But the first of the many references to William Tresham in the records of the royal Chancery connect him with Northamptonshire, and at as early a date in his career as 1411-12, when he can have been little more than of age: on 23 February, 1411, described as of Northants, he was a surety for the grantees of the custody of a meadow in Northampton fields forfeited to the Crown for felony[4]; and, exactly a year later (23 February, 1412), he himself shared a royal grant of a messuage in the town at an annual rent of 5s. payable in the Exchequer.[5] Already presumably a trained lawyer, Tresham may have depended for his income mainly on private practice in the courts in the earlier stages of his career.

In a later royal grant of an annuity to Tresham of May 1440, the patent refers to his good service to Henry V as well as to Henry VI. There is no suggestion in the Chancery enrolments of any official employment coming his way in Henry V's reign, except that on 15 March 1415 he was appointed by bill of the Treasurer to be one of the auditors of all the accounts of royal officials in South Wales, at a daily wage of 5s. while he was away from London on this business. It is quite probable, too, that he was the William Tresseham "clerk" commissioned, on 11 April following, to pay the masters and owners of ships seized along the length of the south coast from the Thames estuary to Bristol for use in Henry V's first French expedition, and to arrange for the concentration of the commandeered English vessels at Southampton and of the foreign shipping at London, Sandwich, and Winchelsea.[6] He served during Henry V's reign on no other royal commissions requiring the authority of the Great Seal. On 17 October, 1415, however, he shared with two other Northamptonshire gentlemen,[7] a royal grant of the wardship and marriage of the heir to the Tyndale estates in the county. Five years later (by patent of 28 October 1420) he shared with William Thirlwall, probably the same who was the Duke of Clarence's receiver-general, a temporary grant at a farm of £5 a year of the keeping of the estates of the late chief bailiff of the honour of Wallingford, Thomas Beston, in the Northamptonshire vills of Sywell and Hannington (where were some of Tresham's own properties), and at Earls Barton as well; these were in the King's hands because of the late owner's debts to the Crown. Again, less than three weeks after this concession (on 16 November 1420), Tresham entered into a shared grant of another royal wardship and marriage (for £100 payable into the Exchequer), namely, of the heir of Ralph Parles esquire. In 1428 Tresham was farming the

[3] C.Ch.R., vi.30; Feudal Aids, iv. 33; G. Baker, The History and Antiquities of the County of Northampton, ii. 68, 147; V.C.H., Northants, iv. 133, 172-3; C.F.R. 1413-22, 126.

[4] C.F.R., 1405-13, 206.

[5] ibid., 236.

[6] C.P.R., 1413-6, 385, 342.

[7] Ralph Grene, who had been knight of the shire at Coventry in 1404 and at Westminster in 1410, and William Aldwincle, who was to represent the county in 1432 with Tresham himself.

Parles lands in Watford, Silsworth, and Murcot, on his own account.[8] His local roots were clearly striking deeper at this time. In January 1421, for example, he and William Babington, Justice of Common Pleas, were presenting to the living of St. Andrew's, Broughton, presumably as feoffees on behalf of the abbey of St. Mary (Delapré Abbey) outside Northampton, which held the patronage. And in April, 1421, he became a feoffee of John Waldegrave in lands in Warwickshire and Leicestershire. In the following year he was party with William Lord Lovell and other gentry in a bond for 700 marks payable to Archbishop Chichele at Christmas following.[9]

To the second Parliament of Henry VI's reign, which met in October 1423, William Tresham esquire was for the first time elected as knight of the shire for Northants. It was during this session that he acted (on 30 November, 1423) as a mainpernor for Thomas Chamberlain that the latter should keep the peace, especially towards the widow of the Sir John Pilkington who had been sheriff of the county in 1419-20.[10] In the following summer, by patent of 20 July, 1424, he was for the first time included in the Northants commission of the peace; and he continued to serve as justice of the peace, and as a member of the quorum of the commission, until his death in 1450.[11] Little is known of his activities in the 1420's, beyond the fact that in 1423-4 he was involved as a feoffee in a final concord relating to the Huntingdonshire manor of Waresley; that in the spring of 1425 he attested the Northants indenture of election to the third Parliament of Henry VI's reign; that in July following a lady friend of his, Margery Maureward of Brampton (presumably Church Brampton, Northants) bequeathed him in her will £1 and 'a book called Brute,' no doubt one of the cycle of chronicles that went under that name; that in June, 1428, he was appointed to act as the umpire in an action arising out of a petition to the Chancellor relating to a small estate in Peterborough; and that on 8 December 1429 he shared with Thomas Woodville a grant of the right to farm for £20 a year the royal wardship of the Buckinghamshire manors of Gayhurst and Stoke Goldington, together with (for 80 marks) the marriage of the heir, John, son of Sir Robert Neville. (Tresham was later to be the ward's feoffee at Gayhurst).[12]

This wardship grant was made when Tresham was acting as knight of the shire for Northants, and his co-grantee as sheriff of the county. On this occasion Tresham had been *re-elected*, having been returned as knight of the shire in 1427. His election in 1427 was to prove the beginning of Tresham's virtual monopoly of one of the Northamptonshire seats in Parliament for more than two decades. For he was to be elected to all the thirteen Parliaments which sat from 1427 to 1449, except those of 1431 and 1437. He served, moreover, as parliamentary proxy to the abbot of Croyland in the parliaments of 1429, 1431, 1432, 1435, 1439, 1442, and 1447. He acted in this way for the abbot of Peterborough in those of 1431, 1432, 1435, and 1445, and also for the abbot of Cirencester in the parliament of 1442.[13]

It is a rather curious fact that throughout this time Tresham was never once appointed

[8] *C.F.R.*, *1413-22*, 125, 356; *C.P.R.*, *1416-22*, 308; *Feudal Aids*, iv. 35; Ralph Parles had been sheriff of Northants in 1388-9, 1408-9, and 1412-3. Tresham's partners in the farm of the wardship were Thomas Billing, a lawyer, and Thomas Compworth, who was to represent the borough of Northampton in the Parliament of 1427.

[9] G. Baker, *Northants*, ii. 86; *C.C.R.*, *1422-9*, 272, 72.

[10] *C.C.R.*, *1422-9*, 131.

[11] *C.P.R.*, *1422-9*, 567; ibid., *1429-36*, 622; ibid.,

1436-41, 587; ibid., *1441-6*, 475; ibid., *1446-52*, 592.

[12] *The Register of Archbishop Chichele*, ed. E. F. Jacob, ii. 320; *C.C.R.*, *1422-9*, 407; *Cambridge Antiquarian Soc. Procs.* xxxvii, G. J. Turner, *Cal. of Feet of Fines relating to Huntingdonshire*, 103; *C.F.R.*, *1422-30*, 289; *C.C.R.*, *1435-41*, 198; *C.P.R.*, *1436-41*, 227.

[13] P.R.O., S.C. 10/48-50 (nos. 2390(7), 2401, 2411, 2422, 2439, 2452, 2472; 2403, 2409, 2423, 2466; 2458).

either as sheriff or escheator for the county in which he obviously commanded a considerable influence. He continued throughout the period, right down to his death, in fact, to be a member of the quorum of the Northants commission of the peace, he was a justice of the peace in Huntingdonshire also from April 1446 to his death, and he fairly frequently served on other royal commissions of a more casual character. He was, for instance, of the quorum of a commission of gaol delivery at Northampton in the spring of 1436.

Tresham acted as a commissioner for the raising of Crown loans in the county on a number of occasions between 1430 and 1449,[14] and occasionally himself made loans to the Exchequer. In February, 1436, for example, when the Council proposed to issue privy seal writs asking for subscriptions for the equipment of an army to be led into France by the Duke of York, he was put down for as much as 100 marks. In May 1443 he made a loan of £20; in August 1444 two of 20 marks each (for one of which he received a tally which had to be returned to the Exchequer and re-issued in November following); in October 1446 he was one of a syndicate which raised a loan of £231 odd; and in October 1449 he advanced 100 marks to the Exchequer, for which, as for all his other loans, he received Exchequer tallies of assignment.[15]

Other local commissions of royal appointment that he undertook were to inquire into liability in Northants to contribute to a special parliamentary aid early in 1431 which proved too complicated to admit of collection, and as knight of the shire he served on the commissions charged with apportioning the county's share of the general national rebate of £4,000 (later increased to £6,000) on every subsidy of a tenth and fifteenth granted in the Parliaments of 1433, 1435, 1439, 1442, 1445, and 1449.[16] After the Parliament of 1433 he and his fellow knight of the shire were required to submit to the Chancellor a list of the local gentry who ought to be sworn to maintain the peace, and later to help to take the oaths already sworn in Parliament by the Lords and Commons. In July, 1434, and February, 1448, he was appointed to act on commissions of general inquiry into cases of concealment of royal feudal incidents, wastes on Crown lands, unlicensed alienations, failure to pay customs, and royal reversions, etc.[17] Other commissions of his of a like nature, and whose outcome was of special interest to the Exchequer, were an inquiry authorised in May 1439 into the value of the Crown lands in the shire, with special reference to the state of the manors there held in dower since 1403 by Henry IV's queen, Joan of Navarre, until her death in July 1437; an inquiry necessitated by a writ of 27 February, 1442 (issued during Tresham's second speakership), following a complaint by the burgesses of Huntingdon that Henry V's duchy of Lancaster feoffees were exacting an unwarranted increase of the fee-farm of the borough (for tolls at the St. Ives fair which had long fallen into disuse); and an investigation ordered in May 1443 into the wasted condition of the estates of the alien priory of Everdon (Northants).[18] Tresham was a commissioner for sewers in the shires of Cambridge, Huntingdon, Northampton, and Lincoln by several patents of 12 February 1438, 22 August 1439, and 21 January 1441. In February 1445 he was a commissioner of oyer and terminer following complaint of a trespass by the Cluniac prior of St. Andrew's, Northampton.[19]

The years of Tresham's almost continuous membership of the Commons in Parliament

---

[14] By virtue of royal patents of 6 March, 1430 (for Rutland also), 26 March, 1431, 26 February, 1434, 19 March, 1439, 28 November, 1440, 30 March and 28 August 1442, 1 June, 1446 and 25 September, 1449. *C.P.R. 1429-36*, 50, 125, 354, 607; *1436-41*, 250, 505; *1441-46*, 62, 431; *1446-52*, 298.

[15] *P.P.C.*, iv.323; Exchequer, Issue Roll, E 403/749, mem.4; E403/753, mem.11; E403/755, mem.3;

E403/765, mem.3; E403/777, mem.2.

[16] *C.P.R.*, *1429-36*, 136; *C.F.R.*, *1430-7*, 187, 289; *1437-45*, 140, 214, 325; *1445-54*, 32, 121.

[17] *C.C.R.*, *1429-35*, 271; *C.P.R.*, *1429-36*, 425; *ibid.*, *1446-52*, 140.

[18] *C.P.R.*, *1436-41*, 313; *1441-6*, 79, 204.

[19] *ibid.*, *1436-41*, 148, 266, 535; *1441-6*, 340.

had been a time of his increasing involvement in royal administration at the centre. It is possible that as early as February, 1434—when an assignment of £12 to the Treasurer of the royal Household was made 'per manus Willelmi Tressam'—he was on the check-roll of the Household staff. Certainly long before September 1441, from when until his death he was in receipt of a livery of cloth as one of the 'scutiferi' of the Household,[20] he was in direct governmental employment in his capacity as an apprentice-at-law. On 14 June 1434, he and another lawyer, John Hody, were paid each £1 at the Lower Exchequer as a special reward for work which they had been ordered to do expressly by the new Treasurer, Lord Cromwell. This unspecified business may well have been part of a general overhauling of the Exchequer finances undertaken by Cromwell. Again, three weeks before the 1435 Parliament came to its end, namely, on 2 December, Tresham (described as apprentice-at-law) was paid at the Lower Exchequer 10 marks (£6.13s.4d.), as appears in the record, for labouring in the present Parliament about the furtherance there for the King's profit of divers business and necessary matters of the lord King himself, and on 16 December he was paid an additional £3 as a special award for laborious writings and the engrossment of divers grants made to the King for his profit by the Lords and Commons of the realm of England in this present Parliament.

Tresham was then knight of the shire. Eight other lawyers receiving varying grants for their services in expediting the work of the Parliament were almost to a man members of the Lower House: John Bowes for Notts. (the Speaker); John Hody for Somerset; William Burley for Shropshire; Nicholas Metley for Warwickshire; Nicholas Ayssheton for Helston; and Robert Rodes for Newcastle-on-Tyne. The other two were John Vampage, the King's Attorney-General, who had his individual summons to Parliament, and another apprentice-at-law, John Chamberlain. This 1435 session, faced with the need to provide the sinews of war, especially for a campaign against the Duke of Burgundy, had seen the grant of a tenth and fifteenth (reduced as in 1433 by £4,000 and with its collection spread over the next two years), and a novel supplementary graduated income-tax on freehold lands and offices, plus a grant renewing the customs dues for another two years. Payments were also made to a number of Exchequer officials for their diligence in making extracts from the Receipt and Issue Rolls of the Lower Exchequer and transcripts of customs accounts from the ports. Tresham's and his lawyer-colleagues' services had evidently been of a political as well as administrative character.[21]

For once in a while, Tresham was not re-elected to the next Parliament which met in January 1437. But during this year, along with Richard Woodville of Grafton Regis, he was appointed by Henry V's feoffees (in those parts of the Duchy of Lancaster set aside as long ago as 1415 for the fulfilment of his will) as their steward in Northants, Hunts, Beds, and Bucks. In this office Tresham was to be confirmed for life on 27 November, 1443, when his son Thomas became his fellow-steward instead of Woodville.[22] In the accounts of the Duchy of Lancaster Receiver-General for the year February 1438-9, William Tresham appears, too, as one of the apprentices-at-law retained as counsel to the Duchy, a function which he was still discharging in 1444-5.[23]

It was in the Parliament eventually summoned to meet at Westminster on 12 November

---

[20] E403/712, mem.9; Accounts of the Controller of the Household, P.R.O., E101/409/9, p. 37, *ibid.*, 409/11, p. 38; Enrolled accounts of the Keeper of the Great Wardrobe of the Household, E101/409/18, 410/4.

[21] Issue Roll, E403/715, mem.9; E403/721, mems.6, 10, 12.

[22] By November, 1447, William was Duchy steward in the lordship of Higham Ferrers as well. R. Somerville, *History of the Duchy of Lancaster*, I. 586.

[23] P.R.O., D.L. 28/5/2.

1439 that, once more elected for Northamptonshire and sitting for the seventh time, he was elected by the Commons to his first speakership. The first session lasted until 21 December, when the Parliament was adjourned to Reading where it continued to meet for about a month from 14 January 1440. The sessions were made especially difficult by the demands of the Commons for measures designed to discourage the trade of foreign merchants in England, with the result that peculiarly stringent "hosting" regulations were imposed on them as the price of a grant of supplies, and these supplies, too, included a poll-tax on resident alien traders. The remainder of the Commons' grant comprised a whole and a half tenth and fifteenth (minus £6,000) to be spread over the next two years, and an extension of the wool subsidy and tunnage and poundage for three years.

Tresham's choice as Speaker is more likely to have been connected with the concern expressed in this Parliament for the deplorable financial state of the royal Household and with the measures designed to remedy the crisis. How important the Commons in 1439-40 regarded an appropriation of funds to the charge of the royal Household was further indicated by their successful petition that the quarter of the subsidy payable by their grant at midsummer 1440 should be delivered to the Treasurer of the Household 'to pay redie money in hand for expenses of your said Householde as ferre as the said money will atteyn or stretch to.' Tresham's links with the administration of the Duchy of Lancaster were perhaps especially important in this regard. Following 'great murmour and clamour' because of the non-payment of the expenses of the Household and the abuses of purveyance, it was further provided that the income from the unenfeoffed portions of the Duchy of Lancaster as well as from the Duchy of Cornwall should be diverted for the next five years (Michaelmas 1439-44) to the satisfaction of Household debts; Henry V's surviving feoffees (Cardinal Beaufort, Archbishop Chichele and Lord Hungerford), in spite of the incomplete execution of Henry V's will, also expressed their readiness on certain conditions to put their surplus revenues at the disposal of the Treasurer of the Household.

The Commons assented to both these arrangements which were, in fact, no more than a regularization and extension, so far as the Duchy of Lancaster was concerned, of an existing partial appropriation of its revenues to 'state purposes.' For from February 1425 the Receiver-General of the Duchy had been under orders to pay his surplus to the Exchequer, and from Michaelmas 1437 he had been required to deliver to the Household as much as 5,000 marks a year and from Easter 1439 all his issues. In the Parliament of 1442, when Tresham was again functioning as Speaker, and when the enfeoffments of Henry V were resumed into Henry VI's hands and subjected to the appropriation of 1439, the Commons were to press for a continuation of this appropriation until 1447, and, when he was again Speaker in the November 1449 Parliament, and by that time Chancellor of the Duchy, arrangements were made for the Household to enjoy the net issues of the Duchy for seven years from May 1450.[24]

Since his first speakership of 1439-40 Tresham's connection with the royal administration and with the Duchy of Lancaster had been considerably strengthened. In September 1440 he was made one of the feoffees of all the estates of the alien priories then in the King's hands. During the January-March 1442 Parliament, when Tresham was Speaker, one of their acts was to grant the advowson of the priory of Goldcliff to Tewkesbury Abbey. Following the 1442 Parliament, on 3 July of that year, he was granted the reversion of the offices of Chancellor of

[24] R. Somerville, op. cit., i. 204-5, 215; Rot. Parl., v.7; 62, 175 (Somerville says from May 1451, but 1450 is the correct date).

the Duchy and Chancellor of the County Palatine of Lancaster after the death of the then occupier, Walter Shirington, clerk, who had held since 1432. When it materialized, the appointment was to be for life. He did not succeed Shirington before the latter's death on 2 February 1449, but was certainly in possession by 10 June 1449, when John Say, an esquire of the body and Speaker in February 1449, was given the next reversion, and Tresham continued in possession until the day of his death, 23 September 1450. His fee was the same as Shirington's: £40 a year.[25]

In the meantime, while waiting for these offices to come his way, Tresham continued to act as counsel to the Duchy. Moreover, by a series of patents of 29 November 1443, 7 July 1444, and 23 February and 29 June 1445 (under the seal of the Duchy), the terms of which were eventually confirmed by authority of Parliament in a comprehensive patent (under the Great Seal as well as the Duchy seals) of 6 April 1446, Tresham had been included in a large committee of 31 feoffees in certain portions of the Duchy (estimated as worth £3,395.11s.7d. a year) to fulfil the will of Henry VI. Additions to the enfeoffment and the appointment of new feoffees were subsequently made in Parliament on 16 July 1449. Although these estates were not detached from Duchy control, the feoffees were to appoint their own administrative officials. Tresham was, however, appointed as Chancellor for the estates in feoffment directly by the King on 10 December 1447, with an annual fee of £40. The seal in his custody was applied to Henry VI's will on 12 March 1448, along with the Great Seal of England, the Duchy seal, the royal signet, and the signet of the eagle. Whether Tresham retained this chancellorship for the feoffment after he came into the office of Chancellor for the Duchy proper in February 1449, is not certain, although he had been given the former office on 12 March 1448 for life. But if he was superseded in the chancellorship of the feoffment, it is likely to have been only by his son Thomas, who was occupying it in 1453. The Duchy estates comprised in this enfeoffment of Henry VI included Higham Ferrers and other property in Northants, of which William and Thomas Tresham had been joint stewards for life since 1443.[26]

Before 1430 William Tresham had been successful in securing a share in occasional royal wardships of a minor sort.[27] The years of his increased official importance and influence inevitably brought their rewards in the shape of control of other property temporarily in royal hands, as well as fees and other monetary payments. As early as June 1433 he shared with Walter Green esquire of Hayes (Middlesex)[28] a grant of the wardship of Green's young kinsman, Henry Green; the latter was to be shire-knight for Wiltshire in 1442 and for Northants (along with Tresham) in 1447, and Tresham was later to be one of his feoffees at Warminster (Wilts.).[29] Tresham's payments for Exchequer work in 1434 and for special work in Parliament in 1435 have already been noted. His membership of the investigation into the value of the Crown lands in Northants in May 1439,[30] and especially into the state of Kingsthorpe, King's Cliffe, Brigstock, and Geddington, manors lately held in dower by Queen Joan, Henry IV's widow, seemingly soon stood him in good stead. On 1 March 1440, shortly after the end of his first Speakership, he and the abbot of the Augustinian abbey of St. James outside Northampton, and Richard Willoughby, as executors of Thomas Woodville, were granted £40 a year from

[25] C.P.R., 1436-41, 471; Cal. of Papal Registers, Papal Letters, viii. 242; R. Somerville, op. cit., i. 390; Duchy of Lancaster, Accounts Various, P.R.O., D.L. 28/5/3-7.

[26] Rot. Parl., v. 70-3; Somerville, op. cit., i. 211-2, 586; N. H. Nicolas, Testamenta Vetusta, i. 23.

[27] See above, pp 139, 140.
[28] Walter Green had already been Knight of the shire for Middlesex five times since 1414, and was to be so again in 1435, 1439 and 1445.
[29] C.F.R., 1430-7, 150; C.P.R., 1446-52, 124.
[30] See above, p. 141.

Kingsthorpe until a royal debt to Woodville dating from 1424-5 and amounting to £619 (for his custody of two French prisoners of war, the Sires de Stuteville and de Gaucourt) was paid off.[31]

A little later, on 15 May 1440, Tresham was himself granted a royal annuity of £40 for life (from Michaelmas 1439) charged on the manor of King's Cliffe, for good services to Henry V and Henry VI. And a year later, on 27 May 1441, he and Isabel Thorley shared a grant in survivorship of an annuity of £20 from the manor of Brigstock; Isabel, who had been one of Queen Joan's waiting women, had previously had sole benefit from the annuity since Henry IV's reign.[32] On 22 September following, Tresham shared with John Hampton, a royal esquire for the body,[33] a grant of the wardship of the Beds. and Northants estates of the lately deceased Thomas Wood-hill esquire, a wardship which had only just been granted to John Lord Fanhope. On 10 November 1441, Tresham secured a royal charter granting him rights of free warren in his demesnes and reversions in Northants, especial mention being made of Rushton, Sywell, and Hannington.[34] Less than two years later, by patent of 21 July 1443, he secured a royal licence for life to hunt in season in the royal forests, parks and hays in Northants and Bucks., and to kill and take away one buck and two does in any forest. In February 1445 Tresham surrendered his grant of the £40 annuity charged on the manor of King's Cliffe, but only so that it could be converted into a grant in survivorship to him and his son, Thomas. Little more than a year passed before the father and son shared a further grant in survivorship (on 17 March 1446) of another £40 annuity chargeable on the Receiver-General of the Duchy of Lancaster as from Michaelmas 1445.[35]

By this time William Tresham's son was in the Household of Henry VI as an esquire of the King's Hall and Chamber. In April 1446 he was made a J.P. for Hunts along with his father. In the following year, when William Tresham was again (for the third time) Speaker in the Bury St. Edmund's Parliament summoned to meet on 10 February 1447, Thomas sat as knight of the shire for Bucks. The Parliament was evidently intended to witness the impeachment of Humphrey, Duke of Gloucester, the fallen enemy of the Court party (now so largely under the control of the Marquess of Suffolk), and Gloucester was arrested on his arrival at Bury but died on 23 February. Little was done during a short session of no more than three weeks, and there was no grant of supplies forthcoming.

Although a week before Parliament began Tresham had been given a special reward at the Exchequer for certain diligent labour by him undertaken which especially concerned the profit of the King, there is no record of any special payment for his services as Speaker.[36] It is possible, however, that Tresham used his position as Speaker to promote a petition, addressed in the first place to the Commons and offered by them in this Parliament to the King, on behalf of himself and his fellow-executors of the will of John Brokley, late alderman of the city of London. Their co-executrix, the widow of the testator who had now married again, had received in the neighbourhood of £8,000 but had done little for the testator's soul, so that the other executors now requested that she and her present husband should be summoned to appear in Chancery, and that the Chancellor should make provision for the soul of the testator according to his discretion. Thomas Burgoyne, another of the executors, a lawyer and under-sheriff of London, was parliamentary burgess at this time for Bridgwater. The petition was successful.[37]

In February 1449 Tresham came into the enjoyment of his nearly seven-year-old grant

[31] C.P.R., 1436-41, 387; C.C.R., 1454-61, 4.
[32] C.P.R., 1436-41, 430, 554. For Isabel's relationship with Joan of Navarre, see P.R.O., E101/407/11.
[33] Hampton was Knight of the shire for Staffs. in 1437, 1439, 1442, 1445, 1449 and 1453.
[34] C.P.R., 1441-6, 2; C.Ch.R., vi. 30.
[35] C.P.R., 1441-6, 192; P.R.O., D.L. 28/5/6.
[36] P.R.O., E403/765, mem.15.
[37] Rot. Parl., v. 129.

of the reversion of the Chancellorships of the Duchy and of the County Palatine of Lancaster. This was just before the opening of the February-July Parliament of 1449, the first Parliament to meet for two years,—that is, since the short Bury St. Edmund's session. Although as usual returned for Northants, Tresham was not re-elected Speaker.

The second Parliament to meet within the year sat at Westminster or the Blackfriars in London from 6 November to 17 December 1449, at Westminster from 22 January to 30 March 1450, and at Leicester from 29 April to about the end of the first week in June. To this Parliament William Tresham was re-elected for Northants, and his son Thomas—who, when elected, was escheator in Northants and Rutland—for Hunts. In these important sessions, William Tresham once more acted as Speaker for the Commons (for the fourth time in ten years), after Sir John Popham, an old friend of Richard, Duke of York, had declined to accept election to the office. It was in the first session of this Parliament that the Commons successfully brought in a bill asking that an allegedly murderous attack on Lord Cromwell in Westminster Hall on 28 November by William Tailboys esquire of Kyme (Lincolnshire) should be met with Tailboys's imprisonment in the Tower for a year, pending his prosecution in the King's Bench. Tailboys was a supporter of the Duke of Suffolk, whom Cromwell charged with instigating the offence. And the first week of the second session of the Parliament saw the beginning of a direct attack against Suffolk himself, which soon developed into his impeachment for treason and other offences by the Commons on 7 February 1450. Another month passed before, on 9 March, the Commons presented the Lords with a second bill of charges of misprision, and Suffolk was brought to answer. But the trial resulted in no judgement, and Suffolk was finally banished on the King's sole authority. Going into exile in May 1450, the Duke was waylaid at sea and murdered on ship-board.

As Speaker, Tresham had been required to play a leading rôle in these developments which virtually amounted to a 'court-revolution.' Already personally connected (as one of his feoffees) with the Duke of York, who had perhaps most to gain by the elimination of Suffolk, it has been generally assumed that Tresham was in complete sympathy as a "Yorkist" with the attack on William de la Pole. But Tresham had risen as a careerist lawyer to the chancellorship of the Duchy of Lancaster during the years when Suffolk had been 'priviest of the King's counsel' and (as steward of the Duchy in the North) had held an important place in the Council of the Duchy. And it will not do to write Tresham off as an out-and-out Yorkist partizan any more than as a quondam devotee of Suffolk's who had turned coat. It would be over-reaching the evidence to suggest that, as Speaker, he engineered the down-fall of Suffolk. The part he played was doubtless one that he was assigned to play by the Commons, and their temper in this crisis was informed by a sense of national frustration at the collapse of Suffolk's policy regarding France, rather than, at this point, by any belief in the saving graces of the Duke of York, who was in virtual exile in Ireland as the King's Lieutenant there. Tresham's own allegiances are likely to have been in a state of flux and confusion in this time of national calamity and threatening strife. That he was not an unacceptable Speaker to the government of the day on personal grounds, is suggested by his retention of the chancellorship of the Duchy of Lancaster until his death on 23 September 1450, which followed Suffolk's by nearly five months, and also by the way in which he figured as an esquire of the Household among those exempted from the Resumption Act of this parliament of 1449-50.

That the Parliament of 1449-50 ran to a third session, and that by prorogation this took place at Leicester, was doubtless due to the antipathy of the Commons to the Court party, resulting in their refusal before Easter to grant the royal demand for a subsidy for the defence of Normandy. The Commons withstood, says Dr. Thomas Gascoigne, threats from the King and his young councillors, refused to be intimidated by the rumoured prospect of Parliament being indefinitely continued, and in the end, at Leicester, voted a graduated income-tax instead of a normal subsidy, and that only in return for an Act of Resumption. This latter measure, necessitated by the King's financial insolvency, was to apply (with certain exceptions) to royal grants of sources of income, lands, annuities, offices, etc., made since the beginning of the reign.

Tresham came out of this business of the resumption with no very serious discomfiture to himself. His appointment in December 1447 as Chancellor of those Duchy of Lancaster estates enfeoffed for the eventual fulfilment of Henry VI's will had brought him a fee of £40 a year, over and above the annuity of £20 from Brigstock (the one originally shared with Isabel Thorley), and the annuities of £40 from King's Cliffe and £40 from the Receiver-General of the Duchy of Lancaster, both shared with his son Thomas. In addition, on 8 June 1448 he had secured a grant of a parcel of wood in the royal forest of Salcey (saving pasture for the King's deer), the right to have his own woodward and to sell timber, and a grant of 12 trees a year for fuel; by the same patent he secured the view of frankpledge, the rights of jurisdiction formerly associated with the sheriff's tourn, and the assize of bread and ale and victuals in the manor and vill of Sywell, the homages and services of the King's tenants there and at Hannington, together with £1 a year from the fee of the priory of St. Andrew in Sywell and Sulgrave.[38] In February 1449 he had become Chancellor of the Duchy as well as of the County Palatine of Lancaster. None of these royal grants or offices did the Resumption Act of 1450 touch, except the annuity of £20 charged on the manor or vill of Brigstock which was now resumed; a proviso to the Act exempted all the rest.[39] This proviso was the outcome of a single petition submitted by a group of prominent Household esquires, of whom Speaker Tresham was one, claiming a general exemption from the Act, except for certain specified items of income from royal sources which each was resigned to losing. He had also used his influence to secure a proviso on behalf of the collegiate church of St. Mary, Leicester, continuing its grant of a tun of wine from the royal prisage in the port of Hull: the college's petition for exemption is subscribed 'per Willelmum Tresham.' His is the only commoner's name subscribed on any of these petitions submitted to the Lords for their consideration and subsequently approved by the King.[40]

On 10 and 15 August 1450 Tresham was among those indicted at Rochester before Cardinal Kemp, Archbishop Stafford and the Duke of Buckingham: many of those so indicted were to be included in a list of persons charged in a bill, which the Commons presented to the King in the next Parliament, with 'misbehaving about your royal person and in other places.' The bill did not, of course, include Tresham because by then he was dead, but his indictment at Rochester suggests that he was then generally recognized to be one of the foremost members of the Court party.[41]

In the years covered by his parliamentary career the services of William Tresham as an up-and-coming lawyer had been in increasing demand for participation in work of a private character. On 18 February 1432 he and Nicholas Ratford were appointed by Cardinal Beaufort as his attorneys-general (pending his return to England), with especial reference to the action

---

[38] C.P.R., 1446-52, 162.

[39] Rot. Parl., v. 190b.

[40] ibid., 189a; P.R.O., Chancery, Parliament and

Council, C49/58/11.

[41] C. L. Kingsford, English Historical Literature of the Fifteenth Century, App. 'A Yorkist Collection, 1447-52,' p. 365.

under a writ of Praemunire obtained by the Duke of Gloucester against the Cardinal in November previous but respited until the King's recent home-coming from France. On 29 April 1433 Tresham and John Hody were made his general attorneys by the abbot of St. Albans who had the King's licence to visit the General Council of the Church then being held at Basel.[42]

Tresham, too, very frequently acted as feoffee and executor on behalf of notables of his own shire and region and even further afield. In 1423-4 he had been a feoffee in the Hunts manor of Waresley in a settlement by final concord in the Court of Common Pleas. By 1432 and thenceforward he was one of a group of feoffees making presentations to the provostship of the collegiate church of Cotterstock. In 1434-5 he was a feoffee in the Huntingdonshire manor of Abbotsley. In 1437-8 he was party to a final concord relating to the Cambridgeshire manor of Swaffham Prior.[43] In the same year he was a feoffee to John Neville esquire in the Buckinghamshire manor of Gayhurst, and in 1439 to Sir Ralph Rochford, a former captain of the castle of Hammes near Calais, in his reversion of the manor of Newton Longueville in the same county and of other lands of the French priory of St. Faith, Longueville, which in 1441 went to New College, Oxford. In 1440 he was acting as executor to Thomas Woodville esquire who had been knight of the shire for Northants in the Leicester parliaments of 1414 and 1426.[44] By this time he was feoffee of lands in Cheshunt (Herts.) and of the manor of Brampton (Northants.). By 1441-2 he was feoffee to Sir Robert Bulmer in Harlestone and Heyford and elsewhere in Northants, and to Sir Thomas Green in a tenement near Wakefield.[45] In November 1442 he was one of the feoffees of the Leicestershire manor of Lubenham. In the following month he appears as one of the feoffees of Elizabeth, a younger daughter and coheir of Ralph, Lord Basset of Sapcote and the widow of Richard, Lord Grey of Codnor, in all her estates in the shires of Northampton, Leicester, Derby, and Lincoln, for the performance of her will; the committee of feoffees, who included the Earl of Somerset, Bishop Alnwick of Lincoln, and Lords Willoughby, Zouche, Lovell, and Cromwell, was in 1445 ordered to sell the lands in order to execute the trust.[46]

After the death of John Lord Fanhope, in December 1443 Tresham became a feoffee in all his Bedfordshire manors, apparently on behalf of Ralph, Lord Cromwell who claimed the right of purchase against Fanhope's step-son, the Duke of Exeter. By April 1445 he was one of the feoffees of a justice of the Common Pleas who also had connections with Lord Cromwell and was eventually to be one of his executors: John Portington, who held South Conesby and Gunness (Lincs.).[47] By the end of 1448, that is within two years of his death, William Tresham was also feoffee to Henry Green esquire, who had been his fellow knight of the shire in the Parliament of Bury St. Edmunds in the previous year, in his Wiltshire manor of Warminster;[48] to William Catesby of Ashby St. Legers, a fellow esquire of the royal Household, who was to be knight of the shire for Northants with Tresham in the next Parliament (that of February 1449);[49] to John Hampton, esquire of the body and an old associate, in his Staffordshire manors of Kinver and Stourton and in his offices of keeper, ranger, and bailiff in the royal forest of Kinver;[50] and to Margaret, widow of John Beaufort, Duke of Somerset, in

[42] *Foedera*, x. 500, 551.
[43] *Cambridge Antiquarian Society Procs.*, xxxvii, 'Cal. of Feet of Fines relating to Huntingdonshire, 1194-1603,' ed. G. J. Turner, pp. 103, 106; *Procs.*, xxvi, 'Feet of Fines relating to Cambridgeshire,' ed. W. Rye, p. 152; G. Baker, *Northants*, ii 439-40.
[44] *C.P.R., 1436-41*, 227; 359; 387.
[45] *C.C.R., 1435-41*, 376; Baker, *op, cit.*, ii. 283; i.

520; *C.P.R., 1436-41*, 565.
[46] *C.C.R., 1441-7*, 117; 313-7, 466-71.
[47] *C.P.R., 1441-6*, 267; *C.C.R., 1441-7*, 219, 222-3; 297.
[48] *C.P.R., 1446-52*, 124.
[49] *Catalogue of Ancient Deeds*, iv. A.10387.
[50] *C.C.R., 1447-54*, 170-1.

her manor of Overstone (Northants).[51] Another aristocratic connection Tresham enjoyed as feoffee was with William Lord Zouche of Harringworth, to whose daughter, Margaret, his son Thomas was married.[52] But perhaps the most important attachment he formed in his later years was with Richard, Duke of York, to whom, by February 1449, he was feoffee in the Rutland manor of Hambleton, a possession which had come to the Duke through the Mortimers.[53]

Whether this link with York was the dominant factor determining Tresham's political outlook in the last Parliament to which he was elected and in which he served as Speaker for the fourth time (the Parliament of November 1449 to June 1450), is open to question. He himself had close connections with the Household, the Duchy of Lancaster administration, and with members of the Court party, and his son was also, and remained, an esquire of the royal Household and was to become its Controller during the next decade. It seems, nevertheless, to have been the Yorkist tie which was the immediate cause of his tragic end within four months from his last Speakership. This occurred when he was going with his son to meet Duke Richard on the latter's return from Ireland in the late summer of 1450. His motive may well have been no more than that of a feoffee seeking out his principal on matters of private business. Or, if it had a political significance, it may have been no more than an act of self re-insurance against any possibly dangerous eventualities: as Chancellor of the Duchy of Lancaster, Tresham had much to lose from a shift in the control of the royal administration. However this may be, York, after his landing in Anglesea, had been denounced as a traitor, had gathered supporters in the Welsh Marches, and, when Tresham set out to meet him, was on his way to London, where he did not scruple to 'beat down the spears and walls' in the King's chamber to secure an audience. Moreover, the Kentish revolt in the previous spring, which had brought Tresham's last Parliament to a hasty end, had perhaps been mainly engineered by Yorkist sympathisers. Whatever his motive, in going to *rendez-vous* with the Duke in these circumstances Tresham was inviting trouble. It was, in fact, disaster that befell him.

III

According to the petition to the King exhibited by Tresham's widow in the next Parliament to meet after his death—the session began on 6 November 1450—Tresham was at 'his owen place' at Sywell (Northants) on 22 September, purposing 'to mete and speke' with the Duke of York who had written to him. That day 'toward nyght' a Rutland esquire, Simon Norwich, and a group of 'yeomen' of Beds and Northants with some from Wales, sent one of their number—a Kislingbury man—to Tresham, to pretend that he wanted him to be his 'good maister' in a feigned suit he had with the Duke. This was in order to learn the time of Tresham's departure. When this information was gained the conspirators assembled a gang of over 160 armed men at 'a place called Thorplandclose[54] in Multon,' which was some four miles from Sywell, on the road to Northampton. There they waited for Tresham who came by early on the following morning, 'seiying matyns of oure Lady,' and out of their ambush they set upon and killed him, robbing him of a collar of the royal livery, a chain of gold, his signet, certain jewels, £20 in money, and his horse. They also severely wounded the ex-Speaker's son, Thomas, who was accompanying his father, and robbed him too. A Welshman, Evan ap Rice, who killed William Tresham with a lancegay, was alleged to have continued to ride his victim's horse,

[51] Baker, *op. cit.*, i. 460.
[52] *Ancient Deeds*, iv. A.6637, A.9098.
[53] *C.P.R.*, *1446-52*, 218.

[54] Thorpelands, as it is now called, is on the main Northampton-Kettering road, about 3 miles from the centre of Northampton.

and a child, Thomas Tresham's. The miscreants, said the petition, were still at large, boasting of their crime, in spite of the petitioner's request to the sheriff—actually her own brother, William Vaux of Harrowden—to arrest them. This he dared not do, and a jury impanelled by the coroners had been subjected to threats, so that process by common law was impossible. The petition went on to ask that, by authority of Parliament, a writ of Chancery should go out to the sheriff ordering proclamation for the appearance of those charged to answer for their crime on a bill of appeal before the Court of King's Bench on the quindene of Hilary next; that they be not granted bail or mainprise; that, if they sought to bar the appeal, the issue might be tried by jurors of Northamptonshire, each with income of £20 a year from land; and that conviction should go by default of appearance. The petition suggested, too, a heavy fine of £200 for future remissness on the part of the sheriff and a warning against those who might have received the miscreants. In case the widow's appeal were disallowed, it was asked that William's next heir might take her place as appellant. The petition was granted as requested.[55]

Tresham was important enough for his murder not to go unnoticed in one or two of the chronicles of the time. William Gregory's London Chronicle supplies no more than the brief statement that in 1450 'was slayne Tresham, the man of lawe, that was Speker of the Parlyment, and hys sone was soore woundyde in Northehampton schyre.' The set of historical notes of another Londoner, with perhaps connections with Stony Stratford, followed a reference to the arrival of the Duke of York in this town on his way south on 23 September—the day of Tresham's death—with an unflattering allusion to the murder of 'Tresham of Northamton shire, an extorcioner, under Multon parke.' Another contemporary annalist, William of Worcester, the secretary of Sir John Fastolf, K.G., also knew the place and date of the incident and that Tresham was riding to meet the Duke of York, and gives the additional information that Tresham was killed 'per gentes domini Gray de Ruthyn.'

Whence the Tudor antiquary, John Leland, derived his information is not clear, but he embodied a tradition of the murder in his *Itinerary:* mistakenly he described Tresham as being on his way from Northampton to Sywell (instead of in the reverse direction), and his story that Tresham's 'route of servants cumming by chaunce half a myle behynd him, and they hering the scry cam and cut of eche end of the spere yn hym, bringging him back to Northampton, where after the truncheon was pullid oute he dyed,' may have been only a piece of later embroidery. But Leland, too, attributed the ultimate responsibility for the deed to servants of Lord Grey of Ruthyn.[56]

The contemporary William of Worcester's allusion to the implication of Lord Grey's men is at any rate reasonably safe evidence. One of the yeomen named in Tresham's widow's parliamentary petition of 1450 as partly responsible for his murder was stated to belong to Castle Ashby, a manor some six miles east of Northampton then in possession of the Grey family, and Lord Grey of Ruthyn was a great landlord in Northants as well as in Bedfordshire. On his mother's side a great-grandson of John of Gaunt, Edmund Lord Grey of Ruthyn was to be a prominent member of the Lancastrian party until his desertion to the Yorkists at the battle of Northampton in 1460.

There is no knowing whether some local quarrel lay behind this putative share of Lord

[55] *Rot. Parl.*, v. 211-3.
[56] Camden Society, *Collections of a London Citizen in the Fifteenth Century*, ed. Jas. Gardner, III. 'William Gregory's Chronicle of London,' 195;

C. L. Kingsford, *English Historical Literature in the Fifteenth Century* 372; *Wars of the English in France*, ed. J. Stevenson (Rolls Series), ii. 769 (Willelmi Wyrcester Annales); John Leland, *Itinerary*.

Grey in Tresham's death, or whether it was suspicion, ill- or well-founded, of Tresham's connection with Richard of York, and of a political significance in their projected meeting on 23 September which the ex-Speaker's murder forestalled. It should be remembered that Thomas Tresham was also attacked in the affray of his father's murder: there was no break in his career of service at Henry VI's court, where he continued as an esquire of the Hall and Chamber to enjoy the ever deeper confidence of the King, until by 1461 he was Controller of the royal Household, having been in the meantime Speaker in the openly royalist Parliament at Coventry in 1459. If Thomas Tresham did not come under suspicion at Court, there is perhaps no reason to think of his father as an out-and-out Yorkist partizan at the time of his death.

7

SIR JOHN SAY OF BROXBOURNE

The parliamentary career of Sir John Say of Broxbourne extended over the last fourteen years of the reign of the Lancastrian Henry VI and for the greater part of the reign of the Yorkist Edward IV. It was not an unbroken career, even though Say represented more than one constituency. But he sat in at least eight out of the thirteen parliaments which met between 1447 and his death in 1478. It was as burgess for Cambridge that he was first returned to parliament in 1447. To the next parliament of 1449, when he was first to act as Speaker for the Commons, he was elected for Cambridgeshire, the county of his first wife's family rather than his own. But from then on, when Say again sat in parliament—in 1453–54, 1455–56, 1463–65, 1467, 1472–75, and 1478—in every case but one it was Hertfordshire, the county in which he made his home, that he represented, the exception occurring in 1472 when he was reduced to sitting for the Devonshire borough of Tavistock.[1] It is possible that he was also elected in 1460 to the last parliament of Henry VI's reign and to Edward IV's first parliament in 1461, the Hertfordshire returns to both of which parliaments have been lost. In the parliaments of 1463–65 and 1467 he was again elected Speaker, so that he served the office three times in all. Only five previous Speakers had acted so often as this. Say is unique in having been Speaker in both Lancastrian and Yorkist parliaments.

Sir John Say's politically active life was lived in a time of danger and violence, when to be involved in affairs of State was very hazardous. His career inevitably had its ups and downs. But, generally, his political speculations and investments " paid off ", and at his death in 1478 his stock stood as high as at any time in his life. He had first come into prominence in the 1440s as a member of Henry VI's Household, seemingly owing his advancement to the position of Esquire of the Body to the patronage of the all-powerful William de la Pole, Duke of Suffolk. But it was after Suffolk's fall and murder that Say was made Chancellor of the Duchy of Lancaster (in 1450) and became a member of the royal Council (in 1454). That he held these offices through the period of commotion and civil war which resulted in the supersession of the Lancastrian by the Yorkist dynasty in 1461 suggests that he was tough and far-sighted, and that he had a good head and sound nerves in time of crisis. Having survived the dangers of association with Suffolk, Say eventually showed that he had learned the importance of re-insurance against personal disaster by allying himself with those who were strong enough not to commit themselves irrevocably in the struggle for the Crown until their support could command its highest price. Such were the Bourchiers. And there is no doubt that Say's connection with this family was an important cause of his surviving the crisis of 1460–61 and being able to do much more then merely live down his Lancastrian past. He owed his occupation of the office of Under-Treasurer of the Exchequer in 1455–56, 1461–64, and 1475–78, on each occasion, to this Bourchier connection.

Say's own ability as an administrator and man of affairs must not, however, be left out of the reckoning. The supple resilience which he showed in coming through the events of 1460–61 and the brief Lancastrian restoration of 1470–71, suggests a subtlety and a capacity for accommodation that are not out of place in an administrator or " civil servant ". Certainly his mastery of the technique of management was likely to be useful to any government, if we may judge by the substantial rewards he won by his conduct as parliamentary Speaker.

*   *   *

It is not known for sure who were John Say's parents or when he was born, but it is possible that he was descended from the family of Geoffrey, Baron de Say (c. 1305–59), himself a descendant of William de Say and his wife Beatrice, sister of Geoffrey de Mandeville, Earl of Essex. On one occasion he is referred to as " Fiennes the Speaker ", and it seems likely that he was closely connected with the family of James Fiennes, Lord Saye and Sele, who was himself descended from a younger daughter of Geoffrey, Baron de Say.[2] He may have been the son of John Say of Podington (Beds).[3] He was certainly the brother (probably the younger brother) of William Say, doctor of theology, formerly of New College, Oxford, who by 1449 was Dean of the King's Chapel and Master of the Hospital of St. Antony in London, and who retained these preferments, even after his election as Dean of St. Paul's (in 1457) and his appointment as Archdeacon of Northamptonshire (in 1464), down to his death in 1468, when John Say acted as his executor. It is probable that the Speaker, as well as his brother, had attended the schools at Oxford as a member of the University.[4]

John Say was already well established as a member of the Household of Henry VI when, apparently late in 1446, he allied himself with the family of Cheyne of Fen Ditton (Cambs) by marrying Elizabeth, daughter of the Laurence Cheyne esquire who had represented Cambridgeshire in the parliaments of 1431, 1432, 1435, and 1442, and been sheriff of Cambridgeshire and Huntingdonshire in 1429–30 and 1435–36. At the time of her marriage with John Say, Elizabeth was the widow of Sir Frederick Tilney of Ashwellthorpe (Norfolk). By this first husband she had had a daughter, Elizabeth, whose marriages were later to be of some significance to John Say and his family. His stepdaughter and also his ward, Elizabeth Tilney first married Sir Humphrey Bourchier, the first-born son of John Lord Berners, and a nephew of Henry Bourchier (whom Edward IV in 1461 raised from a viscountcy to the Earldom of Essex) and of Thomas Bourchier, Archbishop of Canterbury (1454–86). After Humphrey was killed fighting for Edward IV at the battle of Barnet in 1471, Elizabeth then (in April, 1472) married Thomas Howard, who was to be created Earl of Surrey in 1483 when his father, John, was made Duke of Norfolk.

After his first wife's death on 25th September, 1473, John Say married again, his second wife being Agnes, a daughter of John Danvers of Cothorpe, near Banbury (Oxon). Agnes Danvers had been twice married already : firstly, to Sir John Fray, Chief Baron of the Exchequer (1436–48), who died in 1461, and secondly, to John Lord Wenlock, Speaker for the Commons in 1455, who was killed fighting as a Lancastrian at the battle of Tewkesbury in May, 1471.[5] Agnes's own family was of some importance : one of her brothers, Sir Robert Danvers, had been a Justice of the Common Bench (from 1450 to 1467), and another, William, was later to be a Justice of the King's Bench (from 1488 to 1504). Agnes's half-sister Jane, moreover, married Richard Fowler, Solicitor for the King (1461-70), Chancellor of the

Exchequer (1469–71), Under-Treasurer of England and Chancellor of the Duchy of Lancaster (1471–77). Whereas Say's first marriage clearly had taken him into connection with the aristocracy, his second wife came out of a mainly bureaucratic and judicial *milieu* : something of a reflection of the development of his own political career, which he began as a " young courtier " type and ended as an administrator of first-rate executive importance, albeit always, necessarily, in more or less close touch with the Court.

We first meet John Say in an account-book of the Controller of the King's Household for the year Michaelmas, 1443–44, where he is listed as one of some forty *valetti camere domini Regis*, in annual receipt of robes worth 13s. 4d. and with an allowance of 3s. 8d. for hose.[6] It is quite likely that at this point, and for some time yet to come, he owed advancement to William de la Pole, Earl (later Marquis and then Duke) of Suffolk, for in a satirical poem (written soon after Suffolk's murder in 1450) Say, who is listed there among a number of " traitors ", is made to contribute to the blasphemous " office " for the dead duke the words *Manus tue fecerunt me*.[7] However this may be, on 19th February, 1444, when Say was paid at the Receipt of the Exchequer an advance of £21, he was standing ready to accompany, as one of its members, the embassy, which Suffolk was to lead, authorized to negotiate *pro materiis pacis* and for the marriage of Henry VI and Margaret of Anjou. His wages were to be five shillings a day.[8] It was on the next day that Suffolk secured from the Council an indemnity from any blame for what he might do in the conduct of this diplomatic business. Starting from Portsmouth, the embassy landed at Harfleur on 13th March : not until 27th June did it return to London, having failed to arrange a permanent peace but having succeeded in arranging for a truce and the royal marriage. It was possibly in recognition of these diplomatic services, or perhaps because of his growing status in the large group of Household servants attending on the person of the young King, that on 6th October following, as king's serjeant, John Say got the promise of a grant for life of the office of Coroner of the Marshalsea of the Household when its then holder should die. A fortnight later, as a yeoman of the Chamber, he was entitled by patent to receive £10 a year for life charged on the royal alnage receipts in Norfolk. On 16th January, 1445, as a yeoman of the Crown, he was given 6d. a day from the issues of Staffordshire (expressly notwithstanding his other recent grants and his share of a small part of the petty custom in Bordeaux forfeited by a Gascon rebel), and on 8th March following he was granted for life the keeping of the privy palace of Westminster.[9]

Perhaps a cause, perhaps a consequence, of his interest in Elizabeth the young widow of Sir Frederick Tilney, whom he was soon to marry for his first wife, John Say was appointed royal escheator in Cambridgeshire and Huntingdonshire on 4th November, 1445. The day on which a year later (4th November, 1446) his term of office as escheator expired and he was succeeded by his future brother-in-law (John Cheyne), Say himself was given the same administrative post in the adjacent bailiwick of Norfolk and Suffolk, an office which he held until November, 1447.[10] A week after this appointment he surrendered his own grants of annuities charged on the alnage of cloth in Norfolk and Norwich, and then with his fiancée, Elizabeth Tilney, received instead an increased annuity, granted in survivorship, of £32 10s. from the same subsidy. By 1st December, 1446, John Say and Elizabeth were married, for Say's feoffees then undertook (with the bride's father, Laurence Cheyne, and others) to settle land worth 50 marks clear per annum upon them and their issue before Candlemas, 1453.[11]

Say's marriage obviously gave him an entrée into Cambridgeshire society, and on 3rd February following (1447) he was elected to parliament for the first time as one of the burgesses chosen to sit for Cambridge in the parliament that was to meet a week later at Bury St. Edmunds. Here, following charges of treason, the arrest of the King's uncle, Humphrey, Duke of Gloucester, took place, and the duke shortly afterwards died (on 23rd February). But little else happened during a brief session of three weeks. On the day of his election at Cambridge, Say, as a yeoman of the King's Chamber, had been paid at the Lower Exchequer £20 which (the Issue Roll states) the King had ordered him to have *de dono suo per viam regardi*, and on 21st February, 1447, during the parliamentary session at Bury, he procured a royal patent giving him the wardship and marriage of his step-daughter, Elizabeth Tilney the younger, who was her late father's heir, and four days later (on 25th February, 1447) a grant for life of the manor of Lawford near the Stour estuary in north-east Essex, his right being ratified by a patent, issued on 10th October following, in which he was described as gentleman-usher of the Chamber.[12]

By this time Say had clearly been recently promoted in the Household service, because, whereas the account-book of the Treasurer of the Household for Michaelmas, 1446–47, lists him among the *valetti camere regis*, the next one (1447–48) lists him as one of 268 *scutiferi aule et camere domini regis*. His new rank carried with it a livery of robes worth £1 a year, but his status was obviously still inferior to the great majority of the *scutiferi*, whose robes were worth £2 a year.[13] Another mark of favour he received about this time was in the form of a grant (by patent of 14th September, 1447) of a third share of the right to present to the parish church of Cottingham (near Hull); Say and his fellows presumably immediately acted, for their presentee, Robert Stillington, D.C.L., a canon of Wells, the same who was to be Bishop of Bath and Wells from 1466 to 1491 and Chancellor of England from 1467 to 1473 (except during the brief Lancastrian Readeption), was refused institution by the Official and the Vicar-General of York, and before 18th March, 1448, the Abbots of St. Albans and Bury St. Edmunds and the Prior of St. Mary Overy, Southwark, were acting in the case as papal judges-delegate, following an appeal to the Roman Curia.[14] Particular signs of the closeness of Say's connection with the King were the latter's grant to him from the jewel-house, on 17th February, 1448, of a cup of silver and gilt, and the payment at the Lower Exchequer on 24th October, 1448, to the King in his Chamber of £20 for his private expenses, *per manus Johannis Say.*[15]

In the meantime, it was doubtless Say's new interests in Cambridgeshire, arising from his marriage, that had prompted his inclusion on 8th February, 1448, in a royal commission of inquiry in that county and in Huntingdonshire into cases of concealment of wardships, reliefs, and other sources of casual royal income, and four days later (on 12th February) he was made a J.P. in Cambridgeshire, an office which he continued to hold without a break until November, 1458.[16].

It was for Cambridgeshire that John Say was elected for the first time as knight of the shire. This was to the parliament summoned to meet next after the Bury session of 1447 ; the parliament which met in 1449 for two sessions at Westminster (from 12th February to 4th April and from 7th to 30th May) and for a third and last session at Winchester (from 16th June to 16th July). It was in this parliament that John Say served the office of Speaker for the Commons on the first of three occasions. It says much for the solidarity and strength of the Household element in the Commons that he was so elected, for he had been associated with the diplomacy of the peace-policy, which since then had been tarnished by the surrender of Maine. (Before this first of the two parliaments of 1449 was dissolved, Charles VII of France declared war.) Suffolk's reputation suffered and, with it, that of the party at Court supporting him, of whom John Say was a member or was believed to be at the time. The first session realized a financial grant of no more than a half-tenth and half-fifteenth, although a subsidy of tunnage and poundage was then granted for an unusually long period of five years and, in the third session at Winchester, another half-tenth and half-fifteenth were allowed plus an extension of the wool-subsidy for over four years. Even so, in view of the dire military threat to Normandy, the two half-subsidies, the collection of which was even spread over the next two years, were a niggardly grant, and the wool-subsidy was largely earmarked by the mercantile interest for the defence of Calais alone.

Of special concern for the Household (and possibly for Say himself) were the bills sent into parliament by its gentlemen and yeomen and by the staff of the Royal Chapel. To these bills, claiming heavy arrears of pay and asking that they should be met out of the feudal revenues of the Crown, the Commons agreed, but the King only accepted them with a reservation of his right to withhold any grants until August. Another bill in which Say certainly had a particular interest was one requiring parliamentary authority for letters-patent establishing a new committee of feoffees in certain parcels of the Duchy of Lancaster. These estates had already been appropriated to the fulfilment of the King's will in the parliament of 1445–46, but replacements in the committee had since then been necessitated by the death of some of the original trustees ; and both John Say and his brother William, now Dean of the King's Chapel, were among the new patentees.[17] That Say's Speakership had not completely absolved him from his domestic duties in the King's Chamber is clear from the fact that only three days after his formal presentation as Speaker, at the very outset of the first session, he was attending on Henry VI when a bill was presented on behalf of a Glastonbury monk (for a pardon for the unlicensed purchase of a papal bull of migration).[18]

Say's exercise of his duties as Speaker was evidently regarded as satisfactory from the point of view of the Court, because on 3rd April, 1449, the eve of the first prorogation of parliament, he was granted for life a further annuity of 50 marks (as from the previous Christmas), charged on the farm of Southampton and the issues of the county of Devon ; the patent described him as Esquire for the Body. In the middle of the second parliamentary session, by patent of 16th May, he and his co-feoffees in a number of Herts and Essex manors secured pardon of their trespass in making, without royal licence, certain unspecified conveyances. And towards the end of the same session a licence was procured by Say's

father-in-law (Laurence Cheyne) for a settlement of certain estates in the
east midlands on feoffees, of whom Say was one.[19] These last were trivial
and, in any case, hardly personal concessions. On 10th June, 1449, however,
less than a week before the third session of this parliament began at
Winchester, Say was given the reversion of the offices of Chancellor of the
Duchy and of the County Palatine of Lancaster and Keeper of the seals of
these offices, immediately upon the decease or resignation of the then
Chancellor, William Tresham. When he came into possession Say was to
hold for life, with fees of 100 marks a year, and with authority to appoint
deputies.[20]

Neither to the next parliament, which sat between November, 1449,
and June, 1450 (and in which Say's brother-in-law, John Cheyne, sat
for Cambridgeshire), nor to the parliament of November, 1450, to May, 1451,
was Say elected. The fall of Normandy, late in 1449, entailed the dissolution
of an administration which was largely dependent on the personal prestige
and authority of the Duke of Suffolk. And early in 1450, Suffolk was himself impeached in parliament and, when exiled by the King, murdered at
sea on his way to the continent. Kent now became the centre of armed
disaffection, and here, in June, 1450, came Jack Cade's revolt, the rebels
demanding (*inter alia*) " an Act of Resumption, the dismissal and punish-
ment of Suffolk's ' false progeny and affinity ', the recall of York, the
formation of a new government of ' true ' barons " (McFarlane). It seems
clear that John Say was one of Suffolk's " progeny "—only the duke's
complaisance could have secured him his appointment as sheriff of Norfolk
and Suffolk on 20th December, 1449 [21]—and although Say remained sheriff
for the usual annual term (until 3rd December, 1450), the year was without
doubt one of upset and strain for him. In March and April, 1450, he was
authorized to sit on inquiries into treasons in London, Hampshire, and
Northants. He came well out of the Resumption Act passed at Leicester
in June, 1450, being penalized by it only to the extent of surrendering
an annuity of £9 2s. 6d. and losing the keepership of the privy palace of
Westminster ; he was allowed by the King to retain grants worth £65 8s. 4d.
a year.[22] But in one lampoon that has survived, produced immediately
after the murder of Suffolk, he was referred to as one of the duke's creatures
and a traitor, and in a satire, made in the form of a dirge by the Commons
of Kent at the time of their rising under Cade in June, 1450, he was noticed
in similarly disparaging terms. The rebel movement was at its height when,
among others of the Court party, John Say was indicted of treason by the
insurgents at the Guildhall in London.[23] Perhaps he was out of the way,
because he escaped the fate of his kinsman, Lord Saye, whom the rebels
executed.

On top of all this, Richard, Duke of York, returned from Ireland on his
own initiative to demand reform and to change the membership of the
royal Council. The Commons in the parliament which met in November,
1450, were favourably disposed to York's ideas, but the Lords doubtless
saw the dynastic issue in all of his schemes and were obstructive. John
Say, again not elected as knight of the shire—indeed, York's own Chamberlain, Sir William Oldhall of Hunsdon, was returned for Herts—came through
all this crisis for the royal Household with comparatively little bother.
William Tresham, Chancellor of the Duchy and of the County Palatine of
Lancaster, had been murdered on 23rd September, 1450, when on his way

to confer with York, and Say's former grant of the reversion of these offices for life became operative and was not apparently challenged. He was to continue to hold these Duchy appointments without a break until June, 1471.[24] It is true that on 16th December, 1450, just before the end of parliament's first session, his 1444 grant of the reversion of the office of Coroner of the Marshalsea of the royal Household was waived aside in favour of the existing official's son. But a Commons' bill to the King, demanding the removal from Court of the Duke of Somerset, the Duchess of Suffolk, the Bishop of Coventry and Lichfield, Lords Dudley and Hastings, and some twenty and more other members of the Household, of whom John Say was one, for *misbehaving about your royal person*, would seem not to have affected him, because the King excepted those who were used to wait on him,[25] and, moreover, Say was one of the esquires of the Hall and Chamber who figured in the Controller of the Household's accounts for the whole of this year, September, 1450–51.[26] In any case, we have the testimony of William of Worcester that, in general, nothing came of this bill. With others who had been indicted of treason in the City by the rebels in the previous summer, Say was also now acquitted; this was presumably not long before the end of the second session of the parliament of 1450–51, the commission of oyer and terminer to the Lord Mayor and other justices issuing on 10th March 1451.[27] On 19th September, 1452, accounts were squared when the keepership of the privy palace at Westminster, which Say had been compelled to surrender by the Resumption Act of 1450, was granted to him and a yeoman of the pantry (in survivorship). This office Say almost surely held until his death in 1478; he was certainly still occupying it in 1471.

Appointed in January, 1453, as a commissioner in Hertfordshire for the raising of a royal loan for the war in Aquitaine, John Say was elected for the first time as knight of the shire for that county to the parliament which first sat at Reading in March, 1453, and then at Westminster from the end of April to the beginning of July, and again from mid-February to mid-April, 1454. His fellow shire-knight was a companion usher of the King's Chamber and another of those of the Household who, like Say, had been denounced in 1450: Bartholomew Halley of King's Langley. This parliament of 1453–54 was again one in which the Household interest was particularly well represented among the Commons. It was during the autumn of 1453 that (by patent of 18th October,) Say shared with his brother-in-law, John Cheyne, and a Hertfordshire lawyer, Ralph Grey, a grant of the wardship of John Boteler, Say's wife's stepbrother. (The ward was only three years short of his majority, but the estates were extensive.[28]) Precisely how Say was affected by Henry VI's mental illness, which made him from August, 1453, to Christmas, 1454, incapable of transacting state business, is not known. It was, however, possibly because of his long and close attachment to the King's person that, soon after York was named Protector and two days before parliament was dissolved, Say was appointed on 15th April, 1454, to be a member of the royal Council at a fee of £40 a year. On the very next day he was one of the two commoners summoned to a Council meeting for a discussion of the defence of Calais (the other commoner being Sir Thomas Stanley, Controller of the Household), and there are a few scattered references extant to Say's acting on later occasions as a royal councillor right down to the end of the reign.

In a list of members of the Household, attached to a series of Household ordinances which passed a Great Council in November, 1454, he still appeared as one of the four royal Esquires for the Body. By this time he and his brother William were among the feoffees of Ralph Lord Cromwell, the Chamberlain of the royal Household, for the fulfilment of his will relating to Tattershall and his other estates, a business in which Say still retained an interest until his death. Incidentally, this feoffeeship was likely to strengthen his ties with the Bourchiers, for Henry Viscount Bourchier's third son, Humphrey, married one of Cromwell's two nieces and coheirs and, in fact, was to be summoned to parliament as Lord Cromwell in 1461.[29]

In the meantime, on 10th June, 1454, John Say had been appointed as a J.P. for Hertfordshire as well as for Cambridgeshire, and during the next few years he occasionally acted as a justice of gaol delivery at Hertford and on other commissions in the county.[30] (He was to retain his office as J.P. in Hertfordshire—except between 13th January and 1st December, 1455—until his death, although he dropped out of the Cambridgeshire commission in November, 1458.) His local interests now seem to have been centred more closely on Hertfordshire than on the county of his wife's family, and it was for Hertfordshire again that he was re-elected to the parliament which met at Westminster on 9th July, 1455, seven weeks after the Yorkist victory at St. Albans, the first battle in the " hot war " between the Yorkist and Lancastrian parties.

In this conflict John Say was clearly ready for most eventualities, so far as his own personal situation was concerned. Esquire for the Body, Chancellor of the Duchy of Lancaster, and member of the royal Council, not unnaturally he was with the King himself at Kilburn on 21st May, 1455, the day before the clash at St. Albans ; and, in fact, it was he who there presented for the King's consideration a letter which York and his fellow-rebels (the Earls of Warwick and Salisbury) had sent to Henry VI from Royston on the day before *via* Archbishop Thomas Bourchier, the Chancellor, who probably had the goodwill of both sides. Knowledge of this letter and of another missive of the next day, dated at Ware and sent direct, in which the rebel lords requested access to the King's presence in order to vindicate their loyalty, was later alleged to have been withheld from King Henry, principally by the Duke of Somerset, the battle at St. Albans thereby resulting.[31] Say was presumably with the King in the battle.

It is possible that when he presented the first of these letters to Henry VI at Kilburn, Say was acting as a messenger from the Primate. If this was so, it would help to explain an interesting development in his career at this tricky stage. For on 29th May, 1455, a week after the Yorkists made themselves masters of the King, the Primate's elder brother, Henry Viscount Bourchier, brother-in-law of the Duke of York, was made Treasurer of England, and probably immediately, certainly by 15th July, John Say occupied the office of Clerk to the Treasurer, *alias* Under-Treasurer. Henry Bourchier was formally responsible for the Exchequer until October, 1456, when he relinquished office in favour of the Earl of Shrewsbury, Say himself having just been replaced as Under-Treasurer, apparently at the end of the previous month (September, 1456).[32] He continued all this while, of course, in his Duchy of Lancaster offices and also retained his membership of the royal Council. On 9th July, 1456, the Exchequer was authorized to pay him £80 for his wages as councillor up to Easter, 1456.[33]

The coincidence of the dates of Say's Under-Treasurership with those of Henry Bourchier's appointment does more than merely suggest a connection between the two men, because Say had had no previous official link with the Exchequer. There was not necessarily anything unnatural in this connection from Say's point of view. Admittedly, Viscount Bourchier was brother-in-law to York, but he and his brothers seem to have been inclined to hold a place near the fulcrum or centre of balance between the two parties, and Archbishop Bourchier retained the Great Seal, as his brother did the Treasurership, until October, 1456. By this time Queen Margaret and her supporters had gained such ground since the beginning of the year that she could secure the dismissal of the Bourchiers from office—the signal perhaps for an abandonment of the " mediating policy ", which they and their half-brother, Buckingham, represented, in favour of a policy of open and determined opposition to York. Say was possibly one of those who had genuine misgivings about this tougher royalist policy, for not all those who shared them were Yorkists. A policy of accommodation was, for one thing, nearest the King's own mind. It was most likely Say's connection with the Bourchiers and a known feeling of sympathy for their point of view rather than any sudden access of affection for the Yorkist party (or any bid on their part for his support) which had brought about his new appointment as Under-Treasurer at the Exchequer and his retention of his existing offices in 1455.

Certainly, Say's connection with the Bourchiers was antecedent to these administrative changes occasioned by the Yorkist victory of May, 1455, a victory from which he seems to have profited rather than lost. In July, 1451, Sir John Bourchier of West Horsley (Surrey), the younger brother to Viscount Bourchier and Thomas Bourchier (then Bishop of Ely) who was to be first summoned to parliament in 1455 as Lord Berners, undertook to pay 100 marks a year for six years to John Say and his father-in-law, Laurence Cheyne, the two parties then entering into bonds, each for £500, to guarantee the deed. This transaction may very well have had to do with arrangements for the marriage between Humphrey, John Bourchier's son and heir, and Elizabeth Tilney, Laurence Cheyne's granddaughter and John Say's stepdaughter and (since 1447) his ward. When this marriage took place is not known, but Humphrey Bourchier was near to being (if he was not already) of full age in 1451, and the marriage certainly came to pass.[34] This tie with the Bourchiers perhaps does something to explain or rationalize Say's position in 1455 and subsequently under Edward IV, even before whose accession the Bourchiers had turned into Yorkist partisans.

There is little detailed knowledge of Say's activities in the last five years of Henry VI's reign. He remained Chancellor of the Duchy of Lancaster, after ceasing to be Under-Treasurer of the Exchequer in the early autumn of 1456, and presumably he also continued to be a member of the royal Council, because his attendance is recorded at one of its meetings in March, 1458, and he was summoned to another in the following October.[35] In the autumn of the previous year, 1457, he had served on a few local commissions, a commission of array in Hertfordshire and Cambridgeshire, a commission to arrest a soldier who was giving the prioress of Rowney (Herts) some trouble, and a commission to apportion a parliamentary levy of archers for royal service among the hundreds and vills of Hertford-shire.[36] And on 26th November, 1457, after a delay of some four years since the death of the previous holder, Say's grant (of 1444) of the reversion of the office of Coroner of the Marshalsea of the Household was recognized, so that he now obtained a patent giving the office to him and his younger son, Thomas, in survivorship. They held this office jointly until the end of Henry VI's reign and, thereafter, Thomas Say alone until 1470.[37]

In the autumn of 1459, the uneasy peace between the Court and the Yorkists broke down. The royalists were defeated at Bloreheath but successful in the " rout of Ludford ", and parliament was summoned to Coventry for 20th November, in order to register the momentary Lancastrian superiority by proscribing the Yorkist leaders and their chief active supporters. The parliament was certainly packed, and Say's re-election for Hertfordshire would almost surely have been a foregone conclusion, had the county court met between the sheriff's receipt of the writ and the beginning of the parliament ; a return was made by the sheriff of Essex and Hertfordshire for the former but not for the latter shire, and Say was not elected. There can be little doubt, however, that he was in attendance on the King during the month's session (20th November to 20th December, 1459). On 21st December, the day after the parliament ended, he was included in the Hertfordshire one of a number of precautionary anti-Yorkist commissions of array, and on 29th December he profited by the recent disturbances to the extent of being granted for life the Stewardships of the lordships of Hitchin and Anstey (Herts), forfeited by the attainted Duke of York, and of the lordships of Ware, Bushey, Shenley (Herts), Weald Bassett, Clavering, and Ham (Essex), similarly forfeited by Richard Neville, Earl of Salisbury.[38] In view of all this and especially because of John Say's undisturbed occupation of the Chancellor-ship of the Duchy of Lancaster, it is difficult to account for his exclusion (along with his brother William) from the committee of feoffees in the duchy estates set aside for the fulfilment of Henry VI's will, when this committee underwent a considerable reshaping by an act of the Coventry parliament. Both brothers were, however, to be re-established as feoffees in a new settlement arranged in the very next parliament, which met on 7th October, 1460.[39]

To this parliament, the last of Henry VI's proper reign, John Say may well have been returned for Hertfordshire, but the returns are lost, and his election must remain conjectural. When parliament was summoned and when it met, the Yorkists were enjoying the ascendancy won for them by their military victory at Northampton in July, and the King was under their control. Say's own position at this moment was probably somewhat equivocal. Henry Viscount Bourchier, whose Under-Treasurer Say had been in 1455–56, and with other members of whose family he had ties, had fought as a Yorkist at Northampton, and his elder brother, the Primate, had recently favoured the rebel party, although he was not likely to go so far as to favour a change of royal line. Henry VI, whom Say had long served, was in Yorkist hands, but his Household was still his own. It is possible that Say still hoped for moderate dealings and for the sort of political compromise that the Bourchiers had long advocated. Whatever his feelings, he certainly did not play the part of a Lancastrian die-hard. In August, 1460, he was attending meetings of the Council, and on the day after the beginning of the parliament of 7th October, 1460, he lent £2,000 to the new administration at the Lower Exchequer.[40] The killing of York and Salisbury at the end of the year was to prove only a temporary set-back for the Yorkist cause, but between the Lancastrian successes in the battles of Wakefield and St. Albans, Say saw fit to take out on 14th January, 1461, a pardon, warranted by the King himself, of all felonies and trespasses.[41] Certainly by the beginning of February, 1461, he was once more acting at the Exchequer as clerk to Viscount Bourchier, who had been again appointed Treasurer of England on 28th July, 1460 ; indeed, it is probable that Say had been Under-Treasurer from the earlier date. The Lancastrian victories in the field made no difference to the Yorkists' control of London, and Bourchier, and with him Say as his clerk, was able to continue to administer the Exchequer until Edward IV's accession on 4th March, 1461, when both were reappointed, Say now taking a fee of £20 a term.[42] The latter had severed all ties with Henry of Windsor when the King joined the Queen and their son after the second battle of St. Albans (17th February, 1461).

With Edward IV's accession, Say's conversion to the Yorkist cause was complete. On 5th June, 1461, he was reappointed for life as Chancellor of the Duchy and on 16th June as Chancellor of the County Palatine of Lancaster as well. These offices Say was to retain uninterruptedly for the next ten years, until June, 1471.[43] His office of Under-Treasurer of the Exchequer he continued to hold under Bourchier (now created Earl of Essex) until April, 1462, under Bourchier's successor, John Tiptoft, Earl of Worcester, until June, 1463, and under Edmund Lord Grey of Ruthin, until Easter, 1464. From the very beginning of the reign he was again a member of the royal Council with a fee of £40 a year, and he was still a counsellor in 1468.[44] That he had very early won Edward IV's confidence is indicated by the terms of a letter dated at Bristol on 9th September, 1461, and written to John Say himself, possibly by the Earl of Essex : in it the writer informs Say that *the King maketh grete bostes of you for the truest and the feithfullest man that any christen Prince may have, of the whiche I am right glad and joyeux that ye have soo borne you.*[45] And service under the Yorkists was paying John Say good dividends. In fact, less than three weeks after the sending of this letter, he was paid 100 marks at the Receipt of the Exchequer (on 26th September) as a special reward for his vacation work as Under-Treasurer on the collection of a clerical tenth, and on 23rd May, 1462, he received another 50 marks as special reward for work in and out of court-time. Occasionally, however, he made considerable loans to the administration : £100 on 7th December, 1461, £45 on 11th December, 100 marks on 28th April, 1462, and so on. But early repayment seems to have been normal in his case.[46] And on 18th March, 1462, he shared with Lord Wenlock and the Treasurer and Controller of the Household (Sir John Fogge and Sir John Scot) the right to administer (under Exchequer control) the estates of John, Earl of Oxford, who less than a month before had been executed and had incurred forfeiture for treasonably arranging for a Lancastrian landing on the east coast.[47]

Since the beginning of Edward IV's reign, Say had continued to serve as a J.P. in Hertfordshire and had been authorized to act on one or two casual local commissions as well ; at midsummer, 1461, he had been put on a commission to urge the men of Suffolk, Essex, and Hertfordshire to raise (at their own costs for half a year) a squadron of six ships, equipped with 700 men, for use against the Scots and French, and on 14th March, 1462, he was appointed to serve on a special assize of novel disseisin, relating to lands in Essex, in which the King's late father had been implicated.[48]

In all probability John Say had been elected as knight of the shire for Hertfordshire to Edward IV's first parliament of 4th November to 21st December, 1461, but the returns have been lost, and there is far from certainty. With at least one item of the business of this parliament he was personally concerned : the Act of Attainder against Robert Lord Hungerford and Moleyns who, since his return in 1459 from a six years' exile in France as a prisoner-of-war, had been and still was a Lancastrian partisan under arms. Hungerford's mother was later to claim that, though his ransom had stood at nearly £8,000, more than twice that sum had been expended in all, directly or indirectly, on securing his liberation, and there had been much conveyancing and mortgaging of land to raise loans to meet these cash transactions. Say was one of a group of creditors and mortgagees of this Lord Hungerford's father (who had died in 1459) and one of the feoffees of a considerable number of Hungerford estates, which now required special parliamentary authority to exclude them from the general forfeiture of family lands.[49]

The electoral returns for Hertfordshire to the next parliament, which sat (with four prorogations) from 29th April, 1463, to 28th March, 1465, have also been lost, but Say was Speaker for the Commons in this parliament and almost as certainly sat for Hertfordshire. Chancellor of the Duchy of Lancaster and member of the royal Council, when this parliament began he was still also Under-Treasurer of the Exchequer. In fact, it was little more than a month before parliament assembled that, on 23rd March, 1463, he was paid £4 as Under-Treasurer for his hire of men and horses to ride with money in the previous December to the King at Durham, where Edward then was during the northern campaign which resulted in Harlech castle alone remaining in Lancastrian hands. In the course of the first session, which lasted from 29th April to 17th June, 1463, he was granted at the Lower Exchequer (on 13th May) 200 marks as a special reward for his labours as Under-Treasurer on different occasions, *in tempore curie* and in vacations, and for expediting scrutinies and searches on behalf of the Treasurer, and five days after the session (on 22nd June) he was granted an assignment of £200 at the Exchequer, expressly as a special reward and recompense for his great labours, diligence, and good and faithful service as Under-Treasurer of England from the first day of the reign until then, *ad domini Regis proficuum et incrementum viis multimodis per ipsius Johannis policiam discretionem ac sapientiam*, and also for all the labour and costs borne by him in this instant parliament. And on the same day he and the Treasurer (the Earl of Worcester) and John Wode, a former Under-Treasurer, were repaid a loan of £200 which they had made at the Receipt four weeks earlier. A fortnight later, a warrant under the Privy Seal ordered Say to be repaid loans that he had made for expenditure against the Lancastrian rebels in the north, including one of £200 for which he now received an assignment on the recently granted parliamentary aid.[50]

Say's reward for his services as Speaker had presumably been well deserved, for the Commons in this first session of the parliament had been prevailed upon to grant an " aid " of £37,000 for defence, although they were to ask in the next session (on 4th November, 1463) that £6,000 of it should be remitted and that the levy of half of the truncated grant should be postponed. Parliament was then prorogued to meet on 20th February, 1464, at York, when it was immediately adjourned to 5th May. It was then immediately prorogued again to 26th November following, when it reassembled only to be ordered to come together on 21st January, 1465, at Westminster. Here it sat until 28th March, when it was dissolved. In this second normal session the Commons granted tunnage and poundage and the wool subsidy to Edward IV for life, as they had previously done to Richard II in 1398, to Henry V in 1415, and to Henry VI in 1453. This session also saw the passage of an Act of Resumption from which the Speaker's brother, William Say, Dean of the Royal Chapel and Dean of St. Paul's, was exempted regarding his Wardenship of the Hospital of St. Antony in London. [51] Whether John Say received any further financial recognition of his performance of the Speaker's office is not known. But certainly, in 1463 and throughout 1464, he was in regular receipt of his fee of £40 a year as a King's counsellor, and in November, 1464, the Exchequer was authorized to pay him the fee annually as long as he remained a counsellor.[52]

At Easter, 1464, that is, during the long interval between the two normal sessions of the parliament of 1463–65, John Say had been superseded as Under-Treasurer of the Exchequer by Hugh Fenn, an auditor of long-standing in the department.[53] And it was during the same interval that on 7th October, 1464, when at a feast given by the serjeants-at-law the seat of honour was allotted to the Treasurer so that Matthew Philip, goldsmith, the Mayor of London, abruptly left rather than countenance this breach of his right of precedence, Say the Speaker, Sir John Clay (a Knight of the Body), John Dinham, and Hugh Fenn (the Under-Treasurer) formed a deputation to the Guildhall to see the Mayor to assure him that the affront to his dignity was disapproved of by the lords present, and to ask him to dine with them next day. What was the upshot of this incident, or what lay behind it, it has not been possible to discover.[54]

Nearly two months after the dissolution of the parliament of 1463–65, namely, on Whit-Sunday (26th May), 1465, Elizabeth Wydeville, to whom Edward IV had been secretly married over a year before, was crowned at Westminster. Three days before the ceremony, in the Queen's honour the King had created at the Tower nearly fifty Knights of the Bath, and on the eve of her coronation they preceded her through the city : among the officials to be so singled out was the late Speaker, John Say. On 16th August following, he was reappointed (as Sir John Say) Chancellor of the Duchy and of the County Palatine of Lancaster, with a readjustment of his fees presumably resulting from his new rank.[55]

Other indications about this time of Say's continuing influence are his feoffeeships to uses. In March, 1465, he was named in this capacity in a patent granting to John Donne, Esquire of the Body, certain estates forfeited by the son of Say's predecessor in his Duchy of Lancaster offices,

Thomas Tresham of Rushton (Northants).[56]   In September, 1466, he was one of the feoffees of Anne, eldest sister of Edward IV, who had married Henry Holand, Duke of Exeter (a staunch Lancastrian who had been attainted in 1461), in certain lands granted for her support, including especially Holand properties in Essex and Northants and also estates in these counties held by the King in right of his Queen, the property of her former husband's family of Ferrers of Groby. Say was still a feoffee in the Essex manors in 1473 when they were settled on the Duke of Exeter's daughter and her husband, the King's stepson, Thomas Grey (Lord Ferrers of Groby), soon (in 1471) to be created Earl of Huntingdon and later (in 1475) Marquis of Dorset, to whom (in 1476) the feoffees granted a life-interest in the former Holand estates comprised in the original enfeoffment.[57]   In March, 1467, Say was a feoffee of John Lord Dinham and his wife Elizabeth (widow of John Radcliffe, Lord FitzWalter) in thirteen East Anglian manors, his co-feoffees being Sir Richard Illingworth (Chief Baron of the Exchequer) and Thomas Urswick (Recorder of London).[58] At the time of Say's death, Lord Dinham was one of his feoffees in Paddington Bray (Surrey). In this same year (1467) Say was also a feoffee to John Young, then Mayor of London and a brother of Thomas Young (Justice of the Common Bench), who had recently bought land near to Say's place in Hertfordshire.[59] In 1468 he was also one of the trustees of Ralph Lord Sudely in estates in Derbyshire, Nottinghamshire, and Rutland.[60]

Between Say's being knighted in May, 1465, and his re-election as Commons' Speaker in June, 1467, when he was again acting as knight of the shire for Hertfordshire, there is little to record of him. He was, of course, still Chancellor of the Duchy of Lancaster and a royal counsellor. Late in January, 1466, together with the King's Secretary and an Esquire of the Body (Thomas Prout, the Duchy of Lancaster Steward in Hampshire and Berkshire), he was given the collation to the next vacant prebend in the College of St. George, Windsor.[61] And then, a year or so later, on 9th January, 1467, he was appointed a member of a royal embassy which included the Queen's father, Earl Rivers, appointed to treat with commissaries of the Duke of Burgundy for a truce and also *de intercursu mercandisarum*. This was part of Edward IV's scheme for cultivating friendship with Burgundy rather than France which soon resulted in the Earl of Warwick's alienation from the King.[62]

Parliament next met on 3rd June, and sat until 1st July, 1467, Sir John Say being re-elected as Speaker. Following successive prorogations at Reading on 6th November, 1467, and 5th May, 1468, the parliament again sat at Westminster for its second proper session from 12th May to 7th June, 1468, when it was dissolved. In the meantime, on 24th July, 1467, Say had been granted, for 100 marks (payable in the Exchequer), the wardship and marriage of the heiress of Walter Raleigh.[63]   The parliamentary session of 1468 saw the laying of information in the Lower House against the Keeper of the King's Exchange and one of the governors of the Tower Mint for overcharging for coining and for devaluing the silver coinage ; and a commission of oyer and terminer was set up at the Commons' request, comprising certain lords, justices, and nominees from among the Commons themselves, Speaker Say at their head.[64] In the 1467 session no grant of funds had been demanded, and its chief financial item of business had been an Act of Resumption. The second session (in 1468) resulted, however, in a grant of two whole tenths and fifteenths. Say's own work as Speaker had evidently been regarded as highly satisfactory, judging from the fact that on 25th July following there issued a privy seal warrant to the Lower Exchequer requiring him to be paid £200 *in consideracion of the great costes, charges, and expenses, born and had* by him during the recent parliament *by occasion of thoffice of speker for the Commons of this our Reaume in the same assembled*. The grant, which describes him as *counsellor*, was to be made *by way of rewarde in recompense* either in cash or in the form of Exchequer assignments by tally without further charge.[65] It was in the following autumn, on 29th October, 1468, that Say secured a royal letter patent confirming a previous charter of 1406 which had licensed the emparking of 800 acres adjoining his Hertfordshire manors of Bedwell and Little Berkhampstead and granting rights of free warren in his demesnes of Essendon, and also another patent confirming a charter of 1253 granting rights of free warren in his neighbouring manors of Baas and Hoddesdon and a weekly market and yearly fair at Hoddesdon.[66]

During 1469 nothing is known of Sir John Say except that on 29th October he was appointed a royal commissioner of array in Hertfordshire, a capacity in which he was to act again under a patent of 14th February, 1470.[67] This was a time of political uncertainty, inconclusive revolts, and a breach of relations between Edward IV and the Nevilles, culminating in the King's flight to Holland in September, 1470. Sir John Say seems so far to have kept out of trouble and to have been faithful to the King: on 7th April, 1470, he had secured a privy seal warrant for repayment of a loan to the King of 100 marks[68]; on 25th April, his son John was a commissioner to sequestrate the landed property of the Earl of Warwick and the Earl's son-in-law, George, Duke of Clarence, the King's brother; and his eldest son William was allowed a general pardon on 22nd May.[69] It is nevertheless likely that Sir John Say supported the re-establishment of Henry VI and possibly attended the Lancastrian " re-adeption " parliament of 1470–71: certainly, on 4th December, 1470, he was included once more in the re-formed Hertfordshire commission of the peace, a fortnight later (17th December) was put on a commission to make arrests at Ware (Herts), and on 24th February, 1471, was confirmed in the Keepership of the privy palace at Westminster, first granted him in 1445.[70] By 11th April, 1471, Edward IV was back in London and, after the battles of Barnet and Tewkesbury and the suppression of the rising under the Bastard Falconbridge, by the end of May was safer on the throne than ever before. And so he was to remain. That Sir John Say had been complaisant towards the government of the Lancastrian Readeption (or at any rate no cause of embarrassment to it) is suggested by the fact that on 8th June, 1471, he saw the need to get a general pardon, and this impression is strengthened by the fact that two days later (on 10th June, 1471) he was superseded as Chancellor of the Duchy and of the County Palatine of Lancaster by Sir Richard Fowler, Chancellor of the Exchequer and soon to be Under-Treasurer, to whom, on 4th June, Say had already quitclaimed all title in the Chancellorship of the County Palatine.[71]

In the summer of 1471, Sir John Say's political career was not at an end, although he had lost all offices of profit. It is worth noting that in July (1471) he was continued as a J.P. in Hertfordshire, and that in August his son Leonard was given by the King for life the free chapel of the Duchy of Lancaster castle of Tickhill.[72]   And Sir John was still influentially connected.   Sir Humphrey Bourchier, the husband of his stepdaughter and former ward (Elizabeth Tilney), had been killed fighting at Barnet for Edward IV, but now, in April, 1472, she was to marry Thomas, son and heir of John Lord Howard, who had himself been badly wounded at Barnet and was an Esquire of the Body to Edward IV : Sir John Say was the first of her feoffees.[73]   He was also still one of the feoffees of the Duchess of Exeter, the King's sister, whose daughter had married the Queen's son by her first marriage, Thomas Grey, who was now created Earl of Huntingdon.   Moreover, his friends, the Bourchiers, were still a great force at Court : Henry Bourchier, Earl of Essex, was once again made Treasurer of the Exchequer in 1471, and retained the office until his death in 1483 ; and both he and his brother, the Primate, had done much to bring about Edward IV's restoration in 1471.   That Say had already formed the connection with Lord Hastings, the King's Chamberlain, which is evidenced in his will, seems not to be capable of proof, but it is possible.   The Speaker in the parliament of 1472–75 was Sir John Say's wife's kinsman by marriage, William Allington, a member of the royal Council.

To this first parliament to be convened after Edward IV's restoration, both Sir John Say himself and his eldest son William were returned. The latter, who had married into the family of Hill of Spaxton (Somerset), was elected for Plympton in Devon, his father, Sir John, for Tavistock. That Sir John Say's own county of Hertfordshire had evidently preferred two lesser men of the royal Household, and that he had now condescended to the status of parliamentary burgess, suggests a lowering of his political stock, even locally.   And little is known of him in the two and a half years of this seven-sessioned parliament.   He acted in January, 1473, as a feoffee in a settlement of estates in Essex on Thomas Grey, Earl of Huntingdon.   On 18th August, 1473, he was made a commissioner of inquiry in Essex and Hertfordshire regarding lapsed royal farms and profits due to the Exchequer.[74]   In the third session of the parliament (October to December, 1473) an Act of Resumption was passed covering not merely grants of land and fees but also assignments for royal debts, and an arrangement was now to be made for the payment of these debts to be spread over the next twenty years.   Sir John Say was exempted from the Act, but only to the extent of any grant or assignment under the seal of the Duchy of Lancaster and any other payment made to him by a grantee of forfeited estates up to a yearly value of 20s.[75]

It was during the course of this 1472–75 parliament, just before the third session began, that on 25th September, 1473, Sir John Say's wife Elizabeth died, and that, presumably shortly afterwards, he married for his second wife, Agnes, daughter of John Danvers of Cothorpe, near Banbury (Oxon).   Agnes Danvers had already been twice widowed, her former husbands having been Sir John Fray, who had been Chief Baron of the Exchequer from 1436 to 1448 and had died in 1461, and John Lord Wenlock who had been killed on the Lancastrian side at the battle of Tewkesbury in 1471.   She was a member of an important legal family, being sister of Sir Robert Danvers, Justice of Common Pleas from 1450 to 1467, of Sir William Danvers, Justice of King's Bench from 1488 to 1504, and of

Thomas Danvers, a retainer of Bishop Waynflete of Winchester : the two latter brothers represented respectively Taunton and Downton in the 1472–75 parliament.[76] Certainly, Sir John Say had married Agnes Danvers by 29th April, 1476, when he himself, his late wife Elizabeth, his present wife Agnes, and his children were granted letters of confraternity by the Abbot and Convent of St. Albans.[77]

Just when Sir John Say secured political rehabilitation by way of reinstatement as a member of the royal Council and reappointment to his former office of Under-Treasurer of the Exchequer cannot be precisely determined. Certainly, on 12th December, 1475, he was described as " Counsellor and Under-Treasurer " in a signet warrant ordering him to make a payment to the Clerk of the Sessions at Winchester and Salisbury. But it is most likely that he was given the Under-Treasurership soon after the dissolution of the 1472–75 parliament which befell in March, 1475. A grant to him and the Treasurer (Henry Bourchier, Earl of Essex) on 25th June, 1475, allowing them or their factors to export Staple commodities and import other merchandise free of customs and subsidies to the value of £4,000, suggests an official connection between the two men at that date. Be this as it may, Say was now to remain Under-Treasurer and a member of the royal Council for the last three years of his life. In the meantime, on 13th October, 1476, he was also appointed (during royal pleasure) as Keeper of the Great Wardrobe of the Household. As Clerk to the Treasurer, *alias* Under-Treasurer, Say had replaced the man who had superseded him in the Chancellorships of the Duchy and County Palatine of Lancaster in 1471, Sir Richard Fowler. Incidentally, the latter's wife and Say's second wife, Agnes Danvers, were half-sisters. Fowler continued to hold the Duchy Chancellorships until his death on 3rd November, 1477, but these offices were then immediately given once again to Say in a grant for life.[78]

Presumably much of Sir John Say's time in 1475–77 was taken up with administrative work at the centre of affairs. He was still a J.P. in Hertfordshire, but otherwise he served on few local commissions. On 23rd November, 1476, he and John Sturgeon, an usher of the Chamber and Master of the Ordnance on Edward IV's expedition to France in 1475, were granted by royal patent the Stewardship and Parkership of the lordship of Walkerne (Herts) along with the offices of Steward, Surveyor, Receiver, and Parker of Hallingbury Morley (Essex) during the minority of Henry (Lovel) Lord Morley, then a boy of ten who was to marry the King's niece, Elizabeth de la Pole. And on 13th February, 1477, Say was made a royal commissioner for sewers along the river Lea (in Essex and Herts).[79]

Member of the Council, Under-Treasurer, Keeper of the Great Wardrobe, and by the end of 1477 once again Chancellor of the Duchy of Lancaster, Sir John Say was for the first known time for over ten years elected as knight of the shire for Hertfordshire to the short-lived parliament which met between 16th January and 26th February, 1478. His fellow shire-knight was his co-steward in the Morley lands, John Sturgeon. William Allington, a fellow-member of the royal Council, was the Speaker. One of the main political reasons for the holding of the parliament was the need to secure the attainder of George, Duke of Clarence. The session had still twelve days to run when, on 14th February, 1478, along with the Treasurer of the Chamber (Sir Thomas Vaughan, knight of the shire for Cornwall), the Treasurer and the Controller of the Household (respectively, Sir John Elrington, knight of the shire for Middlesex, and Sir Robert Wingfield), and the Recorder of Coventry (Henry Boteler, parliamentary burgess for the city), Sir John Say as Under-Treasurer of the Exchequer was commissioned to examine the accounts of Clarence's lands, and on 16th March, 1478, he was made a member of the Hampshire and Essex part of the general inquiry into Clarence's estates.[80]

Sir John Say was presumably still engaged in these administrative repercussions of Clarence's forfeiture when he died on 12th April, 1478. He was buried in the church of Broxbourne (Herts), the place that he had made his principal residence, where his first wife had been buried less than five years before. The still extant " brass " effigy on his tomb bore the Yorkist collar of suns and roses.[81] The royal writs of *diem clausit extremum*, authorizing inquiries into his lands, were issued from the Chancery on 24th April, 1478, to the escheators in Norfolk and Suffolk, Essex and Hertfordshire, and Rutland.[82]

On 10th April, 1478, only two days before his death, Sir John Say had made his will. It was very much a family affair : there were bequests of plate to his three sons and five daughters, provision for the completion of a chantry for his brother, William Say, the late Dean of St. Paul's, and another at Broxbourne for himself and his late wife Elizabeth, for twenty years after his death at a cost of 10 marks a year. His confessor, an Austin friar, was to receive £5. His executors were to have £20 each. The latter were not to be vexed by his present wife, Agnes, who was to acquit them and his heirs. After all legacies, bequests, and debts had been paid off, the residue of his movables was to be expended on prayers for the welfare of the souls of himself, his late wife, and his late brother William, for the prosperous estate of Edward IV, and for the soul of Henry VI *in whos service I was brought up and preferred.* Say's executors were John Russell (Bishop of Rochester and Keeper of the Privy Seal), Master John Morton (the later Archbishop and Cardinal who was then Master of the Rolls), his eldest son William, Thomas Say his brother, and John Pulter. The overseer of the will appointed was the testator's *singuler and speciall goode lorde*, William Lord Hastings, Chamberlain of Edward IV's Household. When Say's connection with Hastings had begun, is not known ; but it is worth noticing that, when Sir John's widow (who survived him by less than three months) drew up her will on 11th June, 1478, she also made Hastings her overseer.[83]

The choice of Bishop Russell and Master John Morton as executors was probably a result of their own and Sir John Say's connection with Archbishop Bourchier. Certainly Say's link with the Bourchiers had been an important aspect of his political career, and it was clearly to be of some significance in the career of his heir. Sometime after his father's and stepmother's deaths in 1478 (when he was twenty-six years old) William Say married (as his second wife) his stepmother's daughter by her first husband, Sir John Fray : Elizabeth, widow of Sir Thomas Waldegrave of Smallbridge (Suffolk). One of their two daughters, Elizabeth, married William Blount, Lord Montjoy, and by him had issue, Gertrude, who married (as his second wife) Henry, Marquess of Exeter, who was to be executed for treason in 1539. But Sir William Say's elder daughter Mary married Henry Bourchier, second Earl of Essex, grandson of the first

Earl, and nephew of Elizabeth Wydeville, Edward IV's Queen. In the year of his father's death William Say became sheriff of Somerset and Dorset (1478–79), and he was also sheriff of Essex and Hertfordshire in 1482–83. He was made a Knight of the Bath by Richard III on the Sunday before his coronation. Understandably perhaps, he achieved little under Henry VII except family alliances. He did, however, sit for Hertfordshire in the parliaments of 1491–92 and 1495.

Of Sir John Say's other two surviving sons, Thomas settled at Liston Hall (Essex), and Leonard, who had taken priest's orders, just before his father's death had secured cathedral prebends at York and Lincoln. Anne, the eldest of Sir John's daughters, had married the heir of an old colleague in the Household of Henry VI : Henry Wentworth of Nettlestead (Suffolk), who was first an esquire of the King's Household from 1468 to 1485 (despite the devotion to the Lancastrians of his father who had been executed for it at Hexham in 1464) and then a Knight of the Body to Henry VII from 1489 to 1499. Say's daughter Elizabeth had married a Thomas Sampson, probably the same who was parliamentary burgess in 1485–86 for Ipswich, where he was customs-collector throughout the reign of Henry VII. Another daughter of Say's, Katherine, married a near neighbour, Thomas Bassingbourne of Hatfield Woodhall (Herts). And his fourth surviving daughter, Mary, married the cousin of her sister Anne's husband, Sir Philip Calthorpe of Kerdiston (Norfolk), who in 1521 was to become Chamberlain to the royal heir-presumptive (as she then was), the Princess Mary.[84]

By careful attention to the need to establish and maintain himself and his family by courtly and then by administrative office, Sir John Say had risen from being a mere yeoman of the King's Chamber to a combination of moderately important offices in Crown service. In early life attached to the Court, he had then held aloof from war-service when there was " no future " in it and it was likely to prove financially embarrassing or at best unprofitable. Reconciling himself, apparently with no great difficulty and certainly with alacrity, to the change of royal dynasty in 1461, he had almost always been close to Crown sources of financial profit, and his periods of office as Under-Treasurer in 1455–56, 1461–64, and 1475–78, must have been especially productive in view of all the opportunities for special rewards and for speculations of one kind and another which membership of the Exchequer staff provided. That Sir John Say accumulated considerable wealth is suggested by the object of some of its expenditure : his acquisitions of landed property were quite important, especially in south-east Hertfordshire. Here, in 1448, he acquired the manor of Baas (in Broxbourne) where he normally lived when not at Court.[85] In 1466 he got the manor of Bedwell,[86] and by 1468 he had also the neighbouring manors of Little Berkhampstead and Hoddesdon.[85] In this latter year he purchased the manor of Sawbridgeworth from Philip Malpas, a yeoman of the Crown.[87] By the end of his life he had also secured the manors of Boxes, Foxtons, Geddings, Langtons, and Marions (in Broxbourne) and Perrers (in Cheshunt),[88] and in north-east Essex three manors in Liston Overhall and the manors of Lawford-Says (granted him for life only in 1447), Carbonells in Foxearth, and Little and Much Wendon.[89] In Rutland he held at his death the manor of Market Overton.[88] From 1456 he had a life-interest in Bigrave (Herts),[90] and from 1467 he shared a lease at farm of the manor and advowson of Barnes (Surrey) by grant of the Dean and Chapter of St. Paul's.[91]

The following abbreviations have been used :—

CCR	Calendar of Close Rolls.
CFR	Calendar of Fine Rolls.
CPR	Calendar of Patent Rolls.
DNB	Dictionary of National Biography.
H.M.C.	Historical Manuscripts Commission.
PPC	Proceedings and Ordinances of the Privy Council, ed. N. H. Nicolas.
P.R.O.	Public Record Office.
Rot. Parl.	Rotuli Parliamentorum.
R.S.	Rolls Series.
V.C.H.	Victoria County History.

[1] *Official Return of Members of Parliament*, 1, 335, 338, 348, 350, 358, 364, xxv ; J. C. Wedgwood, *History of Parliament, Register*, 411.

[2] R. Clutterbuck (*The History and Antiquities of the County of Hertford*, iii, 196) makes John son of Sir John Heron, nephew and heir of William Lord Say, manorial lord of Sawbridgeworth, to be father of Sir John Say, but this John Heron was only nine years old in 1420, much later than which date the Speaker is hardly likely to have been born. *DNB*, xvii, 876.

[3] Wedgwood, *op. cit., Biographies*, 744.

[4] *CPR, passim* ; Le Neve, *Fasti, passim* ; *CPR, 1477–85*, 185. After Dean Say's death in 1468, the Chancellor and University of Oxford wrote to his brother, Sir John, referring to the fact that the Dean had owed £5 to the University from the time when he had been one of its proctors and asking that the debt should be paid. They referred to both William and John as *child of this same modyr*, which seems to mean that John had been at Oxford like his brother (British Museum, Vespasian F XIII, fo. 121). Certainly by Edward IV's reign it was possible for a page at Court, once he had grown too big for his duties, to be given a place by the King's influence at one of the Oxford or Cambridge colleges.

[5] J. E. Cussans, *History of Hertfordshire*, ii, 141, 310 : R. Clutterbuck, *op. cit.*, iii, 196 ; G. Baker, *The History and Antiquities of the County of Northampton*, i, 714 ; *Collectanea Topographica et Genealogica*, i, 326.

[6] Exchequer Accounts, P.R.O., E 101/11/p. 38[V].

[7] Camden Society, vol. 67, *Trevelyan Papers*, ed. J. Payne Collier, pp. 72–4.

[8] Exchequer, Issue Rolls, P.R.O., E 403/751, mem. 5 ; Privy Seal warrants for issue, E 404/60/128.

[9] *CPR, 1441–6*, 295, 310, 347, 330.

[10] P.R.O., Typescript List of Escheators, 14, 87.

[11] *CPR, 1446–52*, 23 ; *CCR, 1441–7*, 441.

[12] Exchequer, Issue Rolls, E 403/765, mem. 14 ; *CPR, 1446–52*, 43, 105.

[13] Exchequer, Household Account Books, P.R.O., E 101/409/16, p. 35[V] ; E 101/410/1.

[14] *CPR, 1446–52*, 103 ; *Cal. Papal Registers, Papal Letters*, x, 13.

[15] *PPC*, vi, 326 ; Exchequer, Issue Rolls, E 403/773, mem. 3.

[16] *CPR, 1446–52*, 140, 587.

[17] *Rot. Parl.*, v, 165.

[18] *PPC*, vi, 67.

[19] *CPR, 1446–52*, 246, 253, 259.

[20] R. Somerville, *History of the Duchy of Lancaster*, i, 391 ; Duchy of Lancaster, Accounts Various, P.R.O., D.L. 28/5/7.

[21] P.R.O., *Lists and Indexes*, ix ; *List of Sheriffs*, 87.

[22] *Rot. Parl.*, v, 192a ; Exchequer Miscellanea, Q.R., P.R.O., E 163/bundle 8, no. 14, mem. 2 ; *ex inf.* Dr. B. Wolffe ; *CPR, 1446–52*, 377, 320, 383 ; *ibid., 1452–61*, 15.

[23] Camden Society, vol. lxvii. *Trevelyan Papers, op. cit.*, pp. 72–4 ; Camden Society, *Three Fifteenth Century Chronicles*, ed. J. Gairdner (1880), p. 101 ; *Wars of the English in France* (R.S.), ed. J. Stevenson, ii, 768.

[24] R. Somerville, *op. cit.*, i, 391. Strictly speaking, as sheriff of Norfolk and Suffolk, Say was ineligible as knight of the shire.

[25] *Rot. Parl.*, v, 216ᵇ.

[26] P.R.O., E 101/410/6.

[27] *Wars of the English in France, op. cit.*, ii, 770 ; *CPR 1446–52*, 443.

[28] *CPR, 1452–61*, 15, 53, 155 ; *ibid.*, *1467–77*, 244.

[29] Exchequer, Issue Rolls, P.R.O., E 403/807, mem. 9 ; *PPC*, vi, 175, 233, 257, 258, 260, 295, 297, 306 ; *ibid.*, 223 ; *CPR, 1452–61*, 200, 341 ; *ibid.*, *1477–85*, 48, 107 ; *H.M.C. Report, MSS. of Lord de l'Isle and Dudley*, i, 174 ; *CCR, 1468–76*, 246, 321.

[30] *CPR, 1452–61*, 178, 436, 662, 667.

[31] *Rot. Parl.*, v, 282.

[32] Exchequer, Issue Rolls, P.R.O., E 403/801, mem. 6 ; P.R.O., typescript List of Officials. Among the recipients of liveries at the hands of the Keeper of the Great Wardrobe in the year 28th September, 1455–56, only John Say appears as " Clerk of the Treasurer ".

[33] Privy Seal warrants for issue, E 404/70/3/81.

[34] *CCR, 1447–54*, 270, 282–3 ; N. H. Nicolas, *Testamenta Vetusta*, ii. 482 ; *The Complete Peerage*, ii, 153.

[35] *PPC*, vi, 295, 297.

[36] *CPR, 1452–61*, 402–3, 408.

[37] *ibid.*, 399 ; P.R.O., *Lists and Indexes*, no. xi, 55.

[38] Wedgwood, *History of Parliament, Register*, 258 ; *CPR, 1452–61*, 559, 571.

[39] *Rot. Parl.*, v, 355b, 387.

[40] *PPC*, vi, 306 ; Exchequer, Issue Roll, E 403/820, mem. 1.

[41] *CPR, 1452–61*, 646.

[42] Exchequer, Issue Roll, E 403/820, mem. 6 ; E 403/822, mem. 4.

[43] R. Somerville, *op. cit.*, i, 391.

[44] Issue Rolls, *passim* ; Privy Seal warrants for issue, E 404/72/3/20 (a warrant, dated at Windsor on 16th April, 1463, authorizing the Exchequer to pay Say, *oon of Counsail*, a reward of £80 for his *attendance unto our Counsail by the space of two yeres last past*, i.e. from 4th March, 1461).

[45] *Original Letters illustrative of English History*, ed. Henry Ellis (London, 1824), 1st series, vol. 1, p. 15.

[46] Issue Rolls, E 403/822–5.

[47] *CPR, 1461–67*, 229.

[48] *ibid.*, 33, 180.

[49] *Rot. Parl.*, v, 482b ; *CPR, 1461–67*, 182, 284, 363–5 ; *H.M.C. Report, MSS. of R. R. Hastings*, i, 24.

[50] *Rot. Parl.*, v, 497 ; P.R.O., E 403/827, mem. 18 ; E 403/829, mems. 2, 5, 6 ; Privy Seal warrants for issue, E 404/72/3, no. 54.

[51] *Rot. Parl.*, v, 520b.

[52] Issue Rolls, E 403/829, mem. 8 ; E 403/832 ; Privy Seal warrants for issue, E 404/72/4, no. 68.

[53] P.R.O., *List of Officials* (typescript).

[54] R. R. Sharpe, *Letter Books of the City of London*, L, p. 7. The date of the incident here given, 1463, is incorrect. The Mayor, Matthew Philip, was not elected until 13th October, 1463. Stow (*Survey of London*, ed. C. L. Kingsford, ii, 36) says that the feast took place in Michaelmas term, 1464, and names Lord Grey of Ruthin as being the Treasurer in question. The London Chronicle of William Gregory (*op. cit.*, p. 222) says that the dinner took place about midsummer, 1464, and names the Earl of Worcester as having supplanted the Mayor at a time when he had ceased to be Treasurer. The fact that Hugh Fenn is described as Under-Treasurer is conclusive proof that the incident should be dated 1464 and not 1463, for it was only at Easter, 1464, that Fenn assumed that office.

[55] *Wars of the English in France, op. cit.*, ii, 784 ; C. L. Scofield, *The Life and Reign of Edward IV*, i, 376 ; R. Somerville, *op. cit.*, i, 391.

[56] *CPR, 1461–67*, 431.

[57] *ibid.*, 533 ; *ibid, 1467–77*, 373, 582 ; *Rot. Parl.*, vi, 75.

[58] *CPR, 1467–77*, 12.

[59] O. Manning (and W. Bray), *The History and Antiquities of the County of Surrey*, ii, 141.

[60] *CCR, 1468–76*, 25. In 1460, Say had attested a conveyance by Lord Sudeley of the reversion of the manor of More, etc. (Herts), to St. Albans Abbey (*Registrum Abbatie J. Whethamstede* (R.S.(, i, 367).

[61] *CPR, 1461–67*, 476.

[62] T. Carte, *Catalogue des Rolles Gascons, etc.*, ii, 357.
[63] *Rot. Parl.*, v, 572 ; *CFR, 1461–71*, 204.
[64] *Rot. Parl.*, v, 634.
[65] Privy Seal warrant for issue, P.R.O., E 404/74/1, no. 53.
[66] *CPR, 1467–77*, 114, 123.
[67] *ibid.*, 195, 199.
[68] P.R.O., E 404/74/3, no. 6.
[69] *CPR, 1467–77*, 218 ; 205.
[70] *ibid.*, 616 ; 250 ; 244.
[71] *ibid.*, 262 ; R. Somerville, *op. cit.*, i, 391 ; *CCR, 1468–76*, 203.
[72] *CPR, 1467–77*, 616, 446.
[73] N. H. Nicolas, *Testamenta Vetusta*, ii, 482.
[74] *CPR, 1467–77*, 373, 407.
[75] *Rot. Parl.*, vi, 83.
[76] P. Morant, *History and Antiquities of the County of Essex*, ii, 320 ; Cussans, *op. cit.*, ii, 141, 310 ; Clutterbuck, *op. cit.*, iii, 196.
[77] T. Madox, *Formulare Anglicanum* (London, 1702), 336.
[78] Privy Seal warrant for Issue, P.R.O., E 404/72/5, no. 6 ; *CPR, 1467–77*, 532, 597 ; *ibid., 1477–85*, 138 ; R. Somerville, *op. cit.*, i, 391.
[79] *CPR, 1467–77*, 603 ; *ibid., 1477–85*, 22.
[80] *CPR, 1477–85*, 64, 109.
[81] Cussans, *op. cit.*, ii, 183.
[82] *CFR, 1471–85*, 149.
[83] Somerset House, Register Wattys, fos. 34–5.
[84] Cussans, *op. cit.*, ii, 141 ; *Wedgwood, Biographies, passim*. For William Say's being made a knight, see B.M., Harley MS. no. 293, fo. 208[v].
[85] *CPR, 1467–77*, 114, 123 ; *V.C.H., Herts*, iii, 433.
[86] *V.C.H., op. cit.*, iii, 460.
[87] *CPR, 1477–85*, 116.
[88] *CCR 1476–85*, 101.
[89] Morant, *op. cit.*, i, 436 ; ii, 320, 327, 593.
[90] Cussans, *op. cit.*, i, 52.
[91] Manning (and Bray), *op. cit.*, iii, 326.

8

SIR WILLIAM OLDHALL, SPEAKER IN THE PARLIAMENT OF 1450-1

Occasionally under Richard II and Henry IV the Speaker for the Commons had been one whose closest political allegiance was to some member of the royal family who was not in sympathy with the King and was critical of his policy. But more usually the Speaker had been a member of the King's own Household and sometimes a member of the royal council. Under Henry V, perhaps to stand well with him and at the same time to improve the conduct of their own business, the Commons soon got into a fairly regular habit of electing as their Speaker a professional lawyer who was employed in some branch of the royal administration and also had considerable experience of parliament. This habit had persisted and grown stronger under Henry VI. But, although for the Commons to elect as Speaker a lawyer acceptable to the King was becoming common practice, there was no rule about it. And at a parliament which promised a political "show-down," an election outside the normal trend was especially liable to take place. Whom the Commons then chose would mainly depend upon their own political complexion and temper, and who was available qualified by political affiliation to reflect their attitude. But the King had a right to admit and therefore to reject a Speaker. If a Speaker were a "King's man," obviously his election would pass without question; and normally the King needed to have no qualms. If he accepted a Speaker known to belong to a party opposed to the régime, this was almost certainly because the hostility which such a Speaker's election represented could be neither ignored nor for the moment countered. It was just such a situation in which Sir William Oldhall, when first elected to Parliament (for Hertfordshire), became Speaker in November 1450.[1]

When the previous parliament had first met a year before, in November 1449, the little that still remained in northern France of what had once been won by Henry V and painfully held together by his brother, the Duke of

[1] *Official Return of Members of Parliament*, i, 344.

Bedford, was in process of being rapidly lost. The situation was already virtually hopeless. Since 1435, the year of Bedford's death and the defection of Burgundy from the English alliance, military inefficiency and strain had taken heavy toll of English resources. Costly diplomatic efforts had failed to contain the French recovery. One of the few results of negotiation, Henry VI's marriage with Margaret of Anjou, the French Queen's niece, had come to be regarded in England as no more than a successful French "take-over bid" for Anjou and Maine, a cause of suspicion against the English diplomats principally the Duke of Suffolk. Either just before or early in the parliament of 1449–50 those at the head of the Lancastrian administration had resigned office. Financially shaky, administratively unstable, and politically moribund, the Lancastrian government could not protect even its own former leaders: first the former Keeper of the Privy Seal (Bishop Moleyns) was done to death, and then the Duke of Suffolk himself, after being impeached by the Commons, was murdered at sea when on his way into exile. Moreover, the royal marriage had not so far produced an heir: the only descendant of Henry IV now alive was Henry of Windsor himself. As long as this was the case, a state of dangerous uncertainty over the royal succession was inevitable. Richard, Duke of York, as both heir-male and heir-general of Edward III, had a claim stronger by hereditary right than even the King's. Edmund Beaufort, Duke of Somerset, grandson of John of Gaunt, was York's keenest rival; but his family had been associated with the policy of peace with France, and he himself with the military débâcle in Normandy. York was bound to be the focus and, being the man he was, the natural leader of any opposition to the discredited party of the Court. He was all the more dangerous for having personal grounds for discontent: in 1445 he had been replaced by the Duke of Somerset as King's Lieutenant-General in France, and his appointment as King's Lieutenant in Ireland in 1447 was one which he had accepted only with reluctance and regarded as tantamount to banishment. At the beginning of the parliament of 1449–50 the Commons had chosen Sir John Popham as Speaker, an old campaigner under Henry V and Bedford, now for some time a member of York's affinity; but, with York out of the country, the government had been able, seemingly, to overrule this election. Between then and the opening of parliament in November 1450 much had happened. The régime of the Duke of Suffolk had collapsed. The Commons, who had impeached the Duke and brought about his fall, had continued unruly and hostile to the government, even after the parliament's place of meeting was changed in April 1450 from Westminster (where it was open to pressure from the City) to Leicester. Then, in the summer months of 1450, came the brief but savage revolt of Jack Cade, in which the rebels demanded a reconstitution of the government and the Duke of York's recall from Ireland, presumably so that he could head the new administration. Hardly had this insurrection been suppressed when news came through of the fall of Cherbourg, which meant that nothing, save Calais alone, was left to the English in northern France. It was now that Richard of York returned from Ireland. And with him came his Chamberlain, Sir William Oldhall, who was to be Speaker in the parliament which Henry VI had already summoned. This parliament of 1450 was bound to provide the severest test to which the Lancastrian dynasty had yet been exposed.

Oldhall's part in this crisis inevitably was important and justifies a full consideration of his career. A biographical article by C. F. Johnston, published in *The English Historical Review* as long ago as 1910, covered much of the ground. Even so, it has been possible to put together a fuller, more detailed account not only of Oldhall's activities about the time of his Speakership, but also of his earlier career as one of the great professional captains of the French wars, from which he and many like him, some of them his fellow-members of York's retinue, emerged as disappointed, sour, and unforgiving men, shut off from profit in 1450 both at home and abroad, even then ready for mischief, and soon to be eager to bring down a dynasty which had failed itself and them too.

*   *   *

When William Oldhall was born, probably in the last decade of the fourteenth century (but before 1395), his father's family had been settled for over a century in Norfolk and, especially by favourable marriages with suitable heiresses, had accumulated a number of estates in this county.[2] It was in one such west Norfolk manor at Little Fransham, a score of miles west of Norwich, that Edmund Oldhall, William's father, who had acquired the place by his first marriage with Alice, daughter and coheir of Geoffrey de Fransham, was evidently living at the turn of the century. Alice was presumably William Oldhall's mother, but she was dead by January 1395 when Edmund Oldhall's wife was called Mary.[3] All the Norfolk estates which eventually were to come into William Oldhall's possession were in west and north-west Norfolk. A group of them was within very easy reach of Little Fransham: the manors of Bodney (later given by William to Thetford Priory) and Narford (both of these certainly acquired by William's father), the manor of Great Fransham, and land in Scarning and Dillington (all held of the Duchy of Lancaster), the manor of Creke's or Oldhall's manor (their own family's place) in East Dereham, and the manor of Belhouse in North Tuddenham.[4] To the north-wards, halfway between East Dereham and the coast, were lands at Little Ryburgh and Stibbard, subsequently granted by William to Walsingham Priory.[5] Near King's Lynn and the Wash was the manor of Brookhall (or Oldhall) in Dersingham,[6] and then, further round the coast to the eastwards,

[2] *Archaeologia*, XXXVII, pp. 335–50.
[3] *CCR, 1396–99*, 518; *Catalogue of Ancient Deeds*, i, B/1235.
[4] F. Blomefield, *An essay towards a topographical history of the County of Norfolk*, VI, 16, 232; IX, 496; X, 208; *CPR, 1452–61*, 102; *Feudal Aids*, iii, 596, 626; *Rot. Parl.*, VI, 435a; Sir William Oldhall's will, in Somerset House, Stockton Register, fo. 21.
[5] *CPR, 1452–61*, 68.
[6] Blomefield, *op. cit.*, VIII, 399; *Rot. Parl.*, VI, 435.

the manor of Nowers in Saxlingham.[7]   An important group of estates in east Cambridgeshire—the manor of Ditton Valence and its appurtenances in Ditton Camoys, New Market, Cheveley, Saxton, Kirtling, and Stetchworth—had come into the possession of William Oldhall's father Edmund just before the end of the fourteenth century, and these in due course became William's.[8]   Also, in the early years of his career, in the 1420's, William was already holding lands in south-east Yorkshire at Skipwith and Menthorpe, and lands in north Lincolnshire at Laceby near Grimsby, and, further south in the same county, at Grainthorpe, Wragholme, Covenham, Walmsgate, Little Cawthorpe, Ketsby, and Ormesby.   These estates undoubtedly had come to him with his wife Margaret, a daughter of William Lord Willoughby of Eresby, as a result of her previous marriage with Sir Thomas Skipwith.   Oldhall is once (in 1423) described as resident at South Ormesby and in 1431 as "late of Ormesby," and he and his wife were still occupying these estates in 1441.[9]   It was undoubtedly by purchase, presumably in the 1440's, that Oldhall came into possession of a little but compact collection of property in the south-east corner of Hertford-shire.   The most important of these Hertfordshire estates was the manor of Hunsdon, which he bought from his lord, the Duke of York, and then proceeded to build upon and occupy as his main residence.   From York he had already got a grant for life of the nearby manors of Standon and "Pleshy's" (in Standon) and, very close to Hunsdon itself, he soon acquired the manors of Eastwick and Pishobury (in Sawbridgeworth).   Also by grant of the Duke he came to hold for life the manor of Swanscombe near Gravesend, in Kent, and, in Buckinghamshire, the manor of Hambledon near Henley.[10]

William Oldhall's estates were sufficiently extensive to supply something of a basis upon which to build and develop a career.   His father's life, too, had been an extremely busy one and can only have brought his family useful contacts, although these would appear to have been mainly influential in East Anglia.   In the last year of John of Gaunt's life (1398-9), Edmund Oldhall was the receiver (or local financial agent) for the Duchy of Lancaster estates in Norfolk, an office which he retained under Henry IV and Henry V.   Certainly under Henry IV, and perhaps later, he was duchy receiver in Cambridgeshire and Suffolk as well.[11]   At the time of the death of Margaret, Duchess of Norfolk, in 1399, Edmund was also one of her receivers, and he later became an executor to Alexander Tottington, Bishop of Norwich (who died in 1413) and to Isabel Ufford, Dowager Countess of Suffolk (who died in 1416).[12]   In the

[7] Blomefield, *op. cit.*, IX, 433.
[8] *Ancient Deeds*, i, B/1235, B/1244, B/3779; *Feudal Aids*, i, 177; *Rot. Parl.*, VI, 435a.
[9] *Feudal Aids*, iii, 262, 341, 363; *CCR, 1435-41*, 476.
[10] *VCH, Hertfordshire*, vol. iii, 327, 353, 318; *CPR, 1436-41*, 531; *ibid., 1452-61*, 34; *CFR, 1454-61*, 138.
[11] R. Somerville, *History of the Duchy of Lancaster*, i, 596; *HMC Report, MSS. of Marquess of Lothian at Blickling Hall, Norfolk*, p. 59.
[12] *CCR, 1399-1402*, 50; *CPR, 1416-22*, 16 (Lambeth Palace Library, Arundel Register, Pars II, 165a); *The Register of Archbishop Chichele*, ed. E. F. Jacob, ii, 96.

meantime Edmund had served the Crown in a variety of local offices: he had been a collector of tunnage and poundage and of the wool subsidy at Ipswich, had twice been sheriff of Norfolk and Suffolk (in 1401–2 and 1413–4), three times escheator in these same counties (in 1405–6, 1411–2, and 1416–7), a J.P. in Cambridgeshire (in 1394) and in Norfolk (from 1406 to 1418), and five times M.P. for Norfolk (in the parliaments of October 1404, 1411, 1413, March 1416 and 1417).

William Oldhall did not, however, owe to his father the arrangement of his marriage with a niece of William Ufford, Earl of Suffolk. For, although there is evidence that William was married before 1423 to this lady—Margaret, a daughter of William Lord Willoughby K.G. of Eresby and sister of Robert Lord Willoughby K.G.—her first husband, Sir Thomas Skipwith, died early in 1418, shortly after the death of Edmund Oldhall.[13] This new family connection is bound to have been profitable, apart from the lands that the marriage brought into William Oldhall's control. William Lord Willoughby had died in 1410. But his son and heir, Robert, had a very active and eventful career: summoned to parliament between 1411 and his death in 1452, he shared in the expeditions for the conquest of France (in 1415 and 1417 and later) under Henry V, fought at Cravant and Verneuil (in 1423 and 1424), was in Normandy in 1426, on the Somme in 1433 (with 1,600 men under his command), in charge of the Paris garrison after the Congress of Arras in 1435 until he was forced to surrender the city in 1436, and was still in France (under the Duke of York) in 1442, when he defeated the French with great loss near Amiens. Lord Robert married, firstly, the sister of Thomas, Earl of Salisbury, and, secondly, a niece and coheir of Ralph Lord Cromwell. That the connection between Oldhall and Lord Willoughby was a close one is suggested by the fact that Willoughby in January 1431 had recently granted his brother-in-law and sister an annuity of £80 (chargeable on his lands in Norfolk and Suffolk) in return for funds which Oldhall had lent to or paid for him at need.[14]

So far as can be ascertained, William Oldhall did not take part in Henry V's expedition to Normandy in 1415, but the beginning of his long military career is not to be dated later than the following winter (of 1415–16) when his name heads a list of *homines ad arma equitantes* retained by the King's uncle, Thomas Beaufort, Earl of Dorset, for service at Harfleur, where, as soon as the place had surrendered in the previous September, Beaufort was appointed captain. At the end of February 1416 Beaufort was made Lieutenant of Normandy and in November following was created Duke of Exeter.

Henry V's second French expedition left England for Normandy in the summer of 1417. The Duke of Exeter did not join it until May 1418. But,

[13] *Paston Letters* (Library Edition), ed. Jas. Gardiner, vol. ii, p. 33; *CCR, 1435–41*, 476; *DKR*, XLVIII, 226. (In June, 1423, Oldhall is described as of South Ormesby, a Skipwith manor.)

[14] *Paston Letters, loc. cit.* (Robert Lord Willoughby and his sister, Oldhall's wife, were on their mother's side great-grandchildren of Edmund FitzAlan, Earl of Arundel.)

although he was a member of Exeter's company, Oldhall seems to have preceded the duke overseas and to have been in Normandy at the time of his father's death in the autumn of 1417. He was certainly present, as was the duke himself, at the long siege of Rouen, which surrendered early in 1419, and he was still a member of Exeter's retinue when on 1 and 6 June 1421 he took out royal "letters of protection" as about to return from England to France.[15] Clearly, Oldhall had crossed to England when Henry V himself came home early in this year, although Exeter had stayed on in France and had had the misfortune to take part in the battle of Baugé where his nephew, the Duke of Clarence, was killed and he himself captured.

The reason for Oldhall's brief interruption of his military service in France in 1421 was evidently trouble over part of his inheritance. According to the petition which William presented to the King in the parliament of May 1421, Edmund Oldhall had died about the time of All Saints 1417, he himself, the son and heir, being then (as before and since) overseas in the Duke of Exeter's retinue. Edmund had made no written will, and one William Shelton had applied successfully to the Archbishop of Canterbury for the administration of Edmund's property, had then represented to one of Edmund's feoffees-to-uses in the Norfolk manors of Narford and Bodney that the heir had died on military service overseas, had prevailed upon the feoffee to sell these estates to his nominees, and since then had fraudulently appropriated the revenues. No remedy—it was alleged by William Oldhall in his petition—lay at Common Law, and unless the King ordained remedy by authority of parliament, Oldhall stood to be disinherited. The formal answer to the petition was that Shelton should be summoned before the King for examination. The ultimate outcome can only have been favourable to Oldhall, for certainly later on he enjoyed possession of the lands in question.[16]

After this visit to England in 1421, William Oldhall, Esquire, returned to France and presumably rejoined Exeter's retinue, the Duke having now regained his freedom. But he seems to have been soon back in England where he may have remained for the time being. He was certainly in this country in October and November 1421, in February 1422 (when he stood surety in Chancery for Robert Lathbury, "gentleman," when the latter undertook to fulfil his indenture of military service with the King), and in July following (when he stood surety for Sir Edward Stradling regarding a grant of a royal wardship).[17] Nothing more is known of Oldhall until the summer of 1423, when on 1 June he took out royal "letters of attorney" and on 11 July following "letters of protection," as once more going abroad. He was again a member of the

[15] PRO, E101/47/39; *Rot. Parl.*, IV, 158b; *DKR*, XLIV, 627, 629; *Itinerarii Symonis Simeonis et Willelmi de Worcestre*, ed. J. Nasmith (Cambridge, 1788), "Itinerarium Willelmi de Worcestre," 370, 374.

[16] *Rot. Parl.*, IV, 158b; *Archaeologia*, XXXVII, 335-50.

[17] *CCR, 1419-22*, 220; *ibid., 1422-29*, 55; *ibid., 1419-22*, 227; *CFR, 1413-22*, 441.

Duke of Exeter's retinue,[18] but fought in the battle of Cravant on 31 July 1423 with the Earl of Salisbury's force, as did his brother-in-law, Lord Willoughby.[19] It was seemingly here that he was knighted.

The chivalry of England was no longer maintaining its previous interest in the French war, and there was now a correspondingly greater reward to be won by those who were still prepared to continue an overseas military career. Sir William Oldhall was one such, and he clearly soon established himself as one of the high-ranking military captains of the next two decades. In the spring of 1424 he was recruiting a large retinue of his own, comprising 44 men-at-arms and 135 archers, and on 29 May was advanced at the Lower Exchequer the sum of £616 odd for their next half-year's pay.[20] He took an active part in the important campaigns of this year's summer: a member of a force operating in eastern France in July under the Earl of Salisbury, he was at the taking of Ivry and Montsoer, being appointed constable of the latter place, and on 17 August he fought in the Duke of Bedford's great engagement at Verneuil (in Perche).[21] Oldhall's rapid emergence in these opening years of Henry VI's reign is most clearly attested by his appointment in the following November as Seneschal of Normandy, an office he held for just a year (until 16 November 1425).[22] In the course of 1425 he was engaged in the Earl of Salisbury's expedition into Anjou and Maine. In 1426 he was appointed captain of the castle of St. Laurence de Moitiers in Anjou, and about this time he was also made captain of Argentan and Essey.[23]

Because of a serious quarrel between the Duke of Gloucester and Bishop Beaufort of Winchester, in 1426 the Duke of Bedford was in England and acted as Protector. And during this year Oldhall was certainly for a time in England too. The Duke of Exeter, his old master, was in failing health and no longer very active (although he was still the chief of the guardians of the infant Henry VI), and already Oldhall was becoming more firmly attached to the Bedford group, a natural development in view of their main pre-occupation with the military situation in France. It was probably owing to this growing association with the Regent of France (and heir-presumptive to the throne) that Sir William was included, along with Bedford's own Chamberlain of Household, Richard Wydeville, Esquire, in an embassy to Flanders that

[18] *DKR*, XLVIII, 225–6.

[19] *Wars of the English in France* (RS), ed. J. Stevenson, vol. ii, part ii, 385; J. Anstis, *Register of the Most Noble Order of the Garter*, 170; *BIHR*, XVIII, 39; BM, Harleian Ms. no. 782, fo. 51.

[20] *DKR*, XLVIII, 230; Warrants for issue, PRO E404/40/188; Exchequer, Issue Roll, PRO, E403/666, mem. 4.

[21] *Archaeologia*, XXXVII, *loc. cit.*; C. L. Kingsford, *English Historical Literature in the Fifteenth Century*, App., p. 321 (The Latin Brut); *Itinerarium Willelmi de Worcestre, op. cit.*, 161, 282; *Three Fifteenth Century Chronicles* (Camden Society, 1880), ed. J. Gairdner, p. 164; *Wars of the English in France, op. cit.*, vol. ii, part ii, p. 394; J. Anstis, *Register of the Order of the Garter, op. cit.*, p. 170.

[22] *BIHR, loc. cit.*; *Archaeologia*, XXXVII, *loc. cit.*

[23] *Wars of the English in France, op. cit.*, vol. ii, part ii, p. 412; J. Anstis, *loc. cit.*; *Archaeologia, loc. cit.*

was presumably designed to bring about a betterment of relations between the Duke of Burgundy and his cousin, Jacqueline of Hainault, the wife of the Duke of Gloucester. For Duke Humphrey's support of his wife's claims in Hainault was threatening to undermine the Anglo-Burgundian alliance, upon which English success in France, military and political, depended. On 17 July 1426 Oldhall was advanced £50 at the Lower Exchequer, by warrant of the royal Council, to enable him to take part in an embassy to the Duke of Burgundy and the Duchess of Gloucester, expressly, *pro certis materiis eisdem ducisse et duci ex parte ipsius domini Regis exponendis*, alias, *pro certis negociis rem puplicam* [sic] *ipsius domini Regis et regni sui maxime concernentibus*. With an escort of 41 horsemen, Oldhall and his fellow-envoys left London on 1 August 1426. They did not return before 10 October following, having had long to wait for an answer to their proposals. Twenty years later, Oldhall was still owed £24 8s. for his additional expenses.[24] The diplomatic results of the enterprise have not been discovered.

All that is known of Sir William Oldhall in 1427 is that on 11 March he and his wife (Margaret) received a papal indult to have a portable altar.[25] But at this time he was probably back in France with the Regent, Bedford. In May 1428 he assisted John Lord Talbot in the rescue of Le Mans. It was perhaps in October of this year that he was sent by the Council of Normandy to strengthen Argentan, after news had come in that there was to be an attempt to betray the place to the Duke of Alençon.[26]

How highly at this time Bedford valued Oldhall as a support for his efforts to maintain and extend the English Conquest across the Channel, is suggested by part of a *detail* which the Regent put together sometime between February and April 1429. The despatch was intended to serve as a guide in the event of elections being made to the Order of the Garter, and Bedford catalogued the military actions of no more than five knights then employed in France under his command. In this communication Oldhall is mentioned as having been knighted in 1423 at the battle of Carence (Cravant?), where he proved himself a good knight, and as having fought at Verneuil (in 1424), served continually on the frontiers of the conquered areas in Anjou and Maine (in 1425), and assisted Lord Talbot at Le Mans (in 1428). One special exploit was noticed in his favour: he had once ridden with 3 *speres* and 14 *bowes* from one fortress to another, his men, when ambushed by 20 French men-at-arms (without mention of others), having killed 14 men-at-arms, taken 9 prisoners, and *discomfited* the rest.[27] Nothing came of the recommendations, so far as Oldhall was concerned.

[24] Issue Roll, PRO, E403/675 mem. 9; E403/765, mem. 4; Exchequer,, Accounts Various, E101/322/14; Enrolled Foreign Accounts, E364/60; *PPC*, iii, 201, 244.
[25] *Cal. of Papal Registers, Papal Letters*, VII, 551.
[26] J. Anstis, *loc. cit.*; *Wars of the English in France, op. cit.*, vol. ii, part i, p. 85.
[27] J. Anstis, *loc. cit.*

In view of the absence of any record showing him to have been in England, it may fairly be presumed that for most of the time between 1429 and June 1433 (at the earliest) Sir William Oldhall was on Bedford's staff in France. In these four years nothing certain is known of him, except that on 6 July 1431 he and his wife received from Eugenius IV another papal indult to have a portable altar and a privilege granting them a plenary indulgence.[28]   When Bedford returned to England in June 1433 (after an absence of six years), Oldhall possibly returned with him.   But it is not until April 1434 that we are afforded any record of Sir William's presence in England: he was then summoned to a Great Council which met at Westminster between 24 April and 8 May 1434.[29]   During the proceedings, Gloucester questioned his brother Bedford's conduct of the French war and himself offered to serve instead; the offer was rejected on financial grounds, and Bedford, after justifying his policy in France, went overseas again in July.   Oldhall either accompanied or soon followed him: on 12 July, as proceeding to Normandy, he procured royal "letters of general attorney."[30]

In 1435 occurred the three-fold disaster, so far as English interests in France were concerned, of the failure of the Congress of Arras, the ensuing withdrawal of Burgundy from the English alliance, and, on 14 September 1435, the death at Rouen of the Duke of Bedford.   It is most probable that Oldhall, who by this time was a knight-banneret, now came home again to England for a space: on 5 December following he and some others (including Sir John and Sir Robert Clifton who had both been with him as *logeyng felowys* at the siege of Rouen in 1418–9, and of whom the former had since served with Bedford in France) were given a year's custody of the Norfolk manor of Newton-by-Castle Acre; and, in Hilary term 1436, he and his second cousin, Richard Bozon, were plaintiffs in a suit in the Court of Common Pleas against the prior of the house of Austin canons at Pentney (Norfolk) over the manor of West Bilney.[31]

It was about this time (in January 1436) that Richard, Duke of York, was appointed to follow Bedford in controlling and defending what was left of the English conquests in France.   When York crossed the Channel, Paris had just been surrendered by Oldhall's brother-in-law, Lord Willoughby, and a great part of Normandy had been recovered by the French.   It is very likely that Oldhall agreed to continue to serve with York as he had done under his predecessor: certainly, on 1 November 1436 Oldhall was granted royal "letters of attorney" as leaving the country, and nearly a year later, on 24 October 1437, by which time York had been superseded by the Earl of Warwick, Oldhall was granted "letters of protection" as being then about to go to Bayeux.[32]   His service overseas was evidently punctuated by occasional

[28] *Cal. of Papal Registers, Papal Letters*, VIII, 365–6.
[29] *PPC*, IV, 212.
[30] *DKR*, XLVIII, 298; T. Carte, *Rolles Gascons etc.*, ii, 280.
[31] *CFR, 1430–37*, 256; *The Genealogist*, N.S., XVII, 249.
[32] *DKR*, XLVIII, 315, 320.

reappearances in England as before: he was, for example, one of those five "professional" soldiers who attended a great council of Lords called to Westminster on 24 February 1439 to discuss the war. Another of the five knights was Sir John Popham, soon to be a member of York's council, and a third was Sir Henry Inglose, a Norfolk neighbour of Oldhall's and a former Deputy-Admiral of Bedford's, for whose daily appearance in Chancery (pending a dispute with the abbot of St. Benet's, Hulme) Oldhall was to enter bail on 15 May following.[33]

In 1439 and 1440 the military rear-guard action in France continued, as did diplomatic exchanges. On 2 July 1440 York was once again appointed as the King's Lieutenant-General in France and Normandy (in succession to the Earl of Somerset), this time for five years. He did not, however, cross the Channel until June 1441, by which time enemy successes had reduced the English council at Rouen to despair. Sir William Oldhall was now a member of the Duke's *chieff councelle* in Normandy, and his own indentured retinue numbered no fewer than 42 lances and 146 archers, a force slightly larger than he had produced in 1424.[34] His connection with the Duke of York was already on a more than purely military basis: along with two other members of the Duke's military council, Sir John Fastolf and Sir William ap Thomas (as well as with Bishop Alnwick of Lincoln, Viscount Beaumont, and Lord Cromwell), Oldhall had been made one of the Duke's feoffees-to-uses in over ten manors or vills in Dorset, Gloucestershire, Suffolk, Essex, and Surrey, and lands in East Anglia, whose conveyance had been authorized by letters patent for which the Duke had petitioned the King on 16 March 1441[35]; and, exactly two months later (on 16 May 1441), Oldhall himself secured a licence under the Great Seal regularizing his tenure of the manors of Standon and Plashes (Herts), Hambledon (Bucks), and Swancombe (Kent), which the Duke had granted him for life. It is probable that York also gave Oldhall those estates in Ireland which he was certainly holding by July 1444.[36]

One chronicle account of this time criticized York's inactivity in his first period of office as Lieutenant-General of France and Normandy in 1436–7, ascribing it to the fears of his counsellors for his personal safety.[37] Now, in 1441, two other sets of annals were doing the same: one complained, however, that the Duke, young himself, was ruled by young men's counsel, the other that he was governed by Oldhall's counsel: incompatible opinions, in view of

[33] *PPC*, V, 108; *CCR, 1435–41*, 274.

[34] *Wars of the English, op. cit.*, vol. ii, part ii, 585; PRO, E101/53/33.

[35] *PPC*, V, 136.

[36] *CPR, 1436–41*, 531; *ibid., 1441–6*, 273. (Oldhall was granted on 23 July 1444 a royal patent licensing his absence from Ireland and allowing the administration of his estates there through bailiffs who were allowed to send all the profits to him, presumably to France if need be.)

[37] *Incerti scriptoris chronicon Anglie de regnis trium regum Lancastrensium* (London, 1848), ed. J. A. Giles: *Chronicon Henrici VI*, p. 18.

Oldhall's age and experience.[38]   But of the Duke's lack of success in 1441, there can be no doubt: the English lost their last hold on the Ile de France; and there were further reverses in Normandy itself.   Certainly in 1442 a singular lack of initiative was shown, and for this real or pretended reason the Duke of Somerset was given military control in Guienne and in other areas of France not actually under York's control.   York formally protested, but, unfortunately for his case, Dieppe had been added to the places recently wrested from the English, even before Somerset crossed the Channel.   Doubtless the farce of Somerset's campaign of 1442-3 was some consolation to York and his council.   But negotiations for peace were continuing: in 1443 they received an added impulse with the proposal for a marriage between Henry VI and Margaret of Anjou, a niece of Charles VII's Queen; in 1444, after the royal betrothal, a truce for two years was agreed; and in 1445 Queen Margaret came to England.   York had conducted her to the Normandy coast; he was himself in this year negotiating with Charles VII for the marriage of his heir with Charles's infant daughter; and at home in England, in parliament in June 1445, one of his foremost supporters, William Burley, in his capacity as the Commons' Speaker, was congratulating the Marquis of Suffolk on his successes in diplomacy.   York seems not to have had much difficulty in accepting the inevitable.   He himself came home at the end of 1445.

In these years of York's absence overseas—from 1441 to 1445—nothing substantial is known of the part which Oldhall played in military matters in France, and but little regarding any other of his affairs.[39]   It is evident, however, that he remained a very influential member of the Duke of York's council at Rouen, and that the ties between the two men were becoming very intimate.   It would appear that, hardly later than the beginning of 1444, Oldhall had been appointed by the Duke as his Chamberlain: to about this time is almost certainly to be attributed a signet letter from Henry VI to York in which the Duke was asked to spare for a time the services of his Chamberlain, Sir William Oldhall, so as to enable the latter to cross to England and, regarding *the treete that is now at hand to be made betwix us and our uncle of France*, advise the King and Council *in such things as shalbe occurrent and touche our Reaume of France and Duchie of Normandie, as he that of reason shuld have mooste perfite knowlege in the same, considering his longe abode with you there, and of your*

---

[38] C. L. Kingsford, *op. cit.*, App. VI, pp. 339, 341.   (The name given is Sir *John* Oldhall, but there is no other mention of anyone of this name, and the name *John* must be regarded as a slip for *William*, for Sir William Oldhall was certainly a member of York's council in Normandy in 1441.)

[39] On 24 July 1443 Oldhall and his wife received a papal indult to have low mass celebrated by their own priest before daybreak or early in the afternoon, if their business required it, without blame attaching to them or the priest (a peculiar practice, but one enjoyed by the Carmelites), and on 17 August, in another papal privilege, their confessor was authorized to dispense them from the requirement not to eat flesh-meats in Lent or on other days of prohibition (*Papal Letters, op. cit.*, IX, 369, 374).

Conseil.[40] In July 1446, after York's return to England, Oldhall was still a member of his council and, expressly as his Chamberlain, attested one of his deeds on 28 February 1447, that is, during the parliament of Bury St. Edmunds.[41] This was only four days after the mysterious death of Duke Humphrey of Gloucester, that die-hard opponent of a compromise-peace with France, following his arrest by members of the royal Household. York came into some of Gloucester's estates and offices, and, had there not been a more eminent candidate available for the late Duke's stall in the chapel of the Order of the Garter at Windsor (namely, King Alfonso V of Portugal), Sir William Oldhall himself might conceivably have filled it; certainly, in the next chapter of the Order, held on the eve of the patronal feast (22 April 1447), Oldhall was the first of the Duke of York's three nominees for election to the vacancy.[42]

Perhaps it was about this time that Oldhall bought from his lord of York the manor of Hunsdon, where he now began to build and castellate on a considerable scale: the height of the *turris manerii* was over 100 feet, and the principal hall 80 feet by 24; and William of Worcester, Sir John Fastolf's secretary (who is the source of these details), had it from a member of Oldhall's wardrobe-staff that the works cost in the neighbourhood of 7,000 marks (£4,666 odd). These extensive building operations can only have been retarded by the later vicissitudes of Oldhall's career, and they were not, in fact, to be completed by him.[43] In this same year, on 28 October 1447, he was granted by York a lease for life (rent-free) of the meadow, pasture, and castle-garden on the Duke's estate at Clare in the valley of the Stour, roughly half-way between Oldhall's main Norfolk properties and his newer acquisitions in south-east Hertfordshire: they were worth 46 shillings a year.[44]

Of Oldhall's activities in 1448, nothing is known. In the autumn of 1447 his master, York, had been mortified by the success of the Marquis of Dorset, Edmund Beaufort, Cardinal Beaufort's nephew, in securing the Lieutenancy of France, for which York had competed, and by the way in which, at this same time, he himself was being shuffled off into the wings of the stage by his appointment as Lieutenant of Ireland for a ten years' term, an appointment tantamount to exile. He made a hard bargain of the terms of his office and, moreover, delayed his departure for a year and a half. On 20 February 1449 Oldhall took out royal "letters of protection" valid for a year, as going in York's company to Ireland; and in July of this year, when York eventually crossed the Irish Sea, Oldhall presumably sailed with him.[45]

[40] *Letters of Queen Margaret of Anjou, Bishop Beckington and others*, ed. C. Munro (Camden Society, 1863), p. 70.

[41] *PPC*, VI, 52; *CPR, 1446–52*, 231.

[42] J. Anstis, *Register, op. cit.*, 132–3. (York's other nominees were Sir Andrew Ogard and Sir William Bonville.)

[43] *Itinerarium Willelmi de Worcestre, op. cit.*, 88; *Archaeologia*, XXXVII, *loc. cit.*

[44] Westminster Abbey Muniments, no. 12165. (This account refers to Oldhall as the Duke's Chamberlain.)

[45] *CPR, 1446–52*, 233.

At this time Oldhall's connections with important soldiers who had served either with the Duke of Bedford or the Duke of York (or with both) were securing him feoffeeships-to-uses on many sides: by 1450 he was, for example, a trustee of estates belonging to Sir John Fastolf (for the eventual performance of his will),[46] to Sir Andrew Ogard, a Danish knight, once Chamberlain to Bedford but now a member of York's council,[47] to Sir Edmund Mulsho, another member of York's council,[48] to Sir John Clifton of Old Buckenham, once a retainer of Bedford's,[49] and to John Flegge, Esquire, another retainer of York's.[50] Oldhall, as well as being the Duke of York's Chamberlain, was still of course one of his feoffees-to-uses and remained so until his death.[51]   York and his retainers were clearly a compact and closely interdependent group of men.

In the summer or early autumn of 1449—during this "last act" of the French war—the castle and fortress of La Ferté (at the mouth of the Somme), of which Oldhall was *seigneur*, was among those many places that fell to the French when Charles VII seized the opportunity to declare war afforded him by the sack of Fougères, a *débacle* which culminated in the surrender of Rouen itself at the beginning of November 1449.[52]   On 12 August 1450, when Cherbourg fell, an end was put to English rule in northern France (save at Calais).

Earlier in the year, when England was seething with indignation at the rapid adverse turn of events abroad, the Duke of Suffolk had first been impeached in parliament and then murdered on his way to exile, and Archbishop Stafford of Canterbury had given place at the Chancery (after an eighteen years' custody of the Great Seal) to Archbishop Kemp of York.   In June and July 1450 Jack Cade's rising in Kent, Surrey, and Sussex gave a new form and direction to the general disgust at the government's ineptitude; and whether York, who was all this time in Ireland, was or was not behind this movement, "the Yorkists considered Cade's cause their own" (Ramsay).   Certainly, the rebels demanded Duke Richard's recall.   York needed no recalling: he came.

With the King childless and his administration discredited, for York to be given control of the government (as he most probably intended) would be hazardous in the extreme for the Court, especially in view of his claims to the Crown.   If the claims of Edmund Beaufort, now Duke of Somerset, as heir-male of John of Gaunt, were seriously considered—assuming the continued childlessness of the royal pair—York's position would be equally perilous, despite his strong backing in the nobility, especially among the Nevilles. Returning from Ireland, York landed at Beaumaris in North Wales, late in August or early in September 1450.   Oldhall had very probably been with

---

[46] *HMC Report, MSS. of Marquess of Lothian*, 54; *CPR, 1446-52*, 301, 314.
[47] *ibid.*, 112; *Calendar of Charter Rolls, 1427-1516*, 38; *VCH, Herts.*, iii, 370.
[48] *CPR, 1461-7*, 180.
[49] *CCR, 1454-61*, 91.
[50] *CPR, 1461-7*, 45.
[51] *Somerset Record Society*, xxii (Feet of Fines, Henry IV–VI), 113, 201; Westminster Abbey Muniments, no. 12168.
[52] *Wars of the English in France, op. cit.*, vol. ii, part ii, p. 622.

him in Ireland recently, having renewed his royal "letters of protection" as late as April 1450.[53]   It was later asserted by the Lancastrians, however, that he had given help to Jack Cade.[54]   This is most likely true, but it is all but certain just the same that he went to Ireland in the summer of 1450 and re-crossed to England in York's retinue.   For when, soon after his return and with an army at his back, the Duke forced his way into the royal palace at West-minster, he complained in an audience with the King of attempts to arrest him at his landing made by a groom of the King's Chamber, *which* [who] *had in charge . . . to take me and put me into your castell of Conwaie and* [also] *to strike off the head of Sir William Oldhall*, as well as to imprison two others of his retinue, Sir Walter Devereux and Sir Edmund Mulsho.[55]   It was then, on the occasion of this protest, that the King agreed to the Duke of York's being included in a newly constituted royal Council.   There can be no doubt of Oldhall's participation in the Duke's *coup*.   When, over a year-and-a-half later, in Easter term 1452, following the failure of York's *putsch* at Dartford, the political pendulum had swung decisively in favour of the Court party, and legal proceedings began to be taken in the Court of King's Bench against York's supporters for some of their actions in 1450, a jury was to present that at Westminster on 27 September 1450 Sir William Oldhall of Hunsdon, *pro magnificencia et exaltacione dicti Willelmi*, had plotted the death of the King and to bring about discord between him and the lords, and between the lords and men assembled for rising in war against the King.[56]

Of Oldhall's pre-eminence in York's counsels at this moment, there can be little question.   In a letter of 6 October 1450, in which Justice Yelverton's clerk wrote to John Paston that the Duke had applied to the King by bill to have a number of his opponents (who had been indicted) arrested without option of bail, it was told how Oldhall had had an affable conversation with the King (at Westminster, on 5 October) which had lasted *more thenne to* [two] *houres*.   Henry VI had there and then asked Oldhall—the letter stated—to speak to and secure the favour of the Duke for John Penycok, one of his own Esquires of the Body who had been denounced by the Kentish rebels in the previous June, with the object of ensuring that the Duke's tenantry would permit Penycok's bailiffs to collect rents from such of his lands as lay among the Duke's own lordships.   Oldhall seemingly put the King off by saying that York's tenants would disobey any such instructions; the temper of the *western men* was such, Oldhall added for good measure, that when he himself had intervened to protect Lord Hoo from their hands at a meeting between this ex-Chancellor of France and York near St. Albans, it was only at the risk of his own life.

[53] *CPR, 1446–52*, 324–5.
[54] *Rot. Parl.*, V, 265b.
[55] Raphael Holinshed, *Chronicles of England, Scotland and Ireland* (London, 1808), vol. iii, 231.
[56] Coram Rege Roll, PRO, K.B. 27/777, Rex roll, mem. 7[v].

Another of those of the Court group who in the autumn of 1450 still stood to lose much by the new turn of events was Sir Thomas Tuddenham of Oxburgh (Norfolk). A close adherent of the late Duke of Suffolk, Tuddenham had been an object of Cade's hostility and in June 1450 had lost his office as Keeper of the Great Wardrobe of the Household. But, although since then he had been indicted, he still held on to his posts in the administrative system of the Duchy of Lancaster, in which he was Chief Steward north of Trent and (jointly with John Heydon, a Norfolk lawyer and another official who was suspect to the Yorkists) Steward in Norfolk, Suffolk and Cambridgeshire. According to the letter of Justice Yelverton's clerk of 6 October, both these men were then working through the Yorkist lawyers, William Burley and Thomas Young, to have Oldhall's "good lordship," and were prepared to *profyr more thanne to* [two] *thousand pownde* in order to secure it. It was in just this situation that, in another letter to John Paston, who was personally embroiled with Tuddenham and Heydon in Norfolk, Paston and others were advised to wait on the Duke of York when he moved from Walsingham to Norwich, to *cherse* [cherish] *and wirchep well Sir William Oldhalle*, and to *spende sum what of your good* [wealth] *now and gette yow lordshep and frendship ther, quia ibi pendet tota lex et prophetae*. Thomas Lord Scales, who had assisted the government against Cade in London in the previous June and was a fairly sound loyalist, had already come to know where he also could best make headway: the letter of 6 October stated that he and Oldhall *arne made fredys*. Sir Thomas Tuddenham apparently had no such luck: sometime in November 1450 Justice Yelverton was alleging in correspondence that Tuddenham had been telling *the falsest tales* of Oldhall and himself; not surprisingly, Yelverton gave it as his opinion that *it wer ful necessarye and profitable to the Kyng and to his pepil for to have othir officers in his duche* [of Lancaster].[57]

Apparently even before York thrust himself into the presence of Henry VI at Westminster and forcibly secured appointment as a member of the royal Council, parliament had been summoned (on 5 September 1450) to meet on 6 November following. In the interval York and his friends busied themselves in influencing local elections to parliament, especially in the shires where their authority was likely to be an important factor. At Bury St. Edmunds on 16 October, York arranged with his wife's nephew, the Duke of Norfolk, who should be knights of the shire for the two East Anglian counties of Norfolk and Suffolk. Already on the previous day (15 October), the county court of Hertfordshire had met at Cheshunt, and here, for the first time, Oldhall had been elected as knight of the shire. In East Anglia the Yorkist nominations had not been altogether successful. But, when parliament assembled on 6 November, Oldhall found himself one of a respectably sized group of at least ten shire-knights whose Yorkist attachments were already clearly defined: from Suffolk had been returned Sir Roger Chamberlain and Sir Edmund

[57] *Paston Letters* (Library Edition, 1904), ed. Jas. Gardiner, vol. ii, p. 174, 176, 180, 191.

Mulsho; Thomas Mulsho, Edmund's brother, was one of the Northants knights; Henry Gray from Norfolk was a Mowbray candidate; from Herefordshire and Shropshire in the Welsh Marches, where York's influence was naturally and directly powerful, came respectively Sir Walter Devereux and William Burley the lawyer, both retainers of the Duke; one of the Yorkshire knights was Sir John Savile of Thornhill near Wakefield; Robert Poynings, Esquire, elected by Sussex, had been sword-bearer to Cade in the recent revolt; and William Haute, another sympathiser with Cade, was shire-knight for Kent. And from Bristol, whose trade with Gascony was going to be hard-hit if that province followed Normandy into French hands, were returned the Yorkist lawyer, Thomas Young, and his half-brother, William Canynges, the greatest of the merchants of the port.

There must have been many more who were favourable to York's claim to be included in the government and also hostile to the Court party (especially to the Duke of Somerset), but who were yet not so strictly bound to York's support as this nucleus of known retainers and political sympathisers. For, without doubt, York enjoyed the backing of the parliamentary Commons. This much may be inferred from their election and presentation (on 9 November 1450) of his Chamberlain, Oldhall, to be their Speaker, over a week before York and his nephew, the Duke of Norfolk, themselves came up with their great retinues to Westminster.

The first session of the parliament ran until a week short of Christmas (18 December), the second from 20 January 1451 to 29 March, and the third and final session from the fifth to sometime during the last week of May following. Presumably York's arrival on 18 November was a signal for greater parliamentary activity, and to the weeks between then and the adjournment for Christmas is probably to be attributed the initiation of the most striking proposals and acts of the parliament: the Bill of Attainder against the dead Duke of Suffolk, which the King refused; the unsuccessful attack on the Dowager Duchess of Suffolk, who was a second cousin to the Duke of Somerset; the bill for the removal from the verge of the Household of a number of persons who had misbehaved about the King, the Duke of Somerset at their head, a bill from which the King removed the sting by excluding Somerset, such other peers as were named, and any who waited on his person; and the bill for an Act of Resumption of royal grants since the beginning of the reign in 1422. This first session also saw a "great division" between York and Somerset: on 1 December an attempt was made to arrest Somerset and, although the Duke himself escaped, his house and, on the next day, the houses of Thomas Lord Hoo and Sir Thomas Tuddenham were plundered. In the spoiling of Somerset's property at the London Blackfriars, Oldhall himself seems to have taken a hand. What is more, in Easter term 1452 Oldhall was indicted in the King's Bench of having, on that very same day (1 December 1450), incited men of Kent and others to kill the lords and magnates, so that, in the great hall of pleas of the King (Westminster Hall), the courts of King's Bench, Chancery, Common Bench, and Exchequer openly sitting, they committed their treasons and felonies "to the final destruction of these courts and of the laws and customs of the land," appearing there arrayed in manner of war and shouting, "Justice, justice."[58]

Something of a revulsion of feeling in favour of the Court seems to have occurred during, if not even before, the Christmas recess. Cade had been posthumously attainted of treason, and on 14 December York himself received a commission to try the rebels of the previous summer in Kent and Sussex, a "harvest of heads" being the result. Somerset was not only soon appointed Captain of Calais, but clearly regained some measure of control: in February 1451 his friend Abbot Bowlers of Gloucester, who, a member of the royal Council until the recent changes, had been imprisoned by York at Ludlow, was now preferred to the vacant see of Hereford, a diocese in York's own peculiar sphere of influence in the March of Wales. When, during the third session of the parliament, perhaps as a last and reckless throw by the Yorkists, Thomas Young, the lawyer-burgess for Bristol, moved in the Lower House for the recognition of the Duke of York as heir to the throne (a motion perhaps more particularly directed against Somerset than at the childless King), parliament was immediately brought to a close, and Young committed to the Tower. The parliament clearly had settled nothing to York's advantage.

Of Oldhall's Speakership, or rather of the manipulative and managerial services which as Speaker he performed in the Yorkist interest during the parliament, nothing precise is known. He had perhaps used his influence to further certain private matters, for example, a Chancery suit against the Crown brought in December 1450 by himself and other feoffees of Sir John Clifton, a cousin of Lord Cromwell and the father-in-law of Sir Andrew Ogard, a member of York's private council; the suit went in the feoffees' favour in Easter term 1451, the estates in question having been meanwhile committed to their custody.[59] And Oldhall also seems to have secured for himself the Duchy of Lancaster office of Steward of the honour of Clare in Suffolk in this year.[60] However, he must soon have lost it. For, in the next two years, the political pendulum swung away from the Yorkist interest.

Early in 1452 York was back where he had been at the time of his return from Ireland in 1450: solemnly insisting on his loyalty, but prepared to use armed force to get a hearing in order to state his case. On 1 March 1452 he and his private army were at Dartford, threatening the capital; but he was outwitted and disbanded his men and, instead of the Duke of Somerset being arrested to stand trial (as he demanded), York found himself a prisoner, although the Council let him go after certain undertakings.

[58] Coram Rege Roll, PRO, K.B. 27/777, Rex roll, mem. 7v.
[59] *CPR, 1454–61*, 91; *CFR, 1445–54*, 184.
[60] *DKR*, XLIII, 317.

Oldhall was privy to the Yorkist movements of disaffection which reached this culmination. In Easter term 1452 he was indicted in the Court of King's Bench of assembling with other traitors on 20 July 1451, again in the great hall of the palace of Westminster, of intending to rise in rebellion in mid-September following and come to the King's presence to take and rule him and the kingdom *ad eorum libitum* (so the charge ran), and of conspiring how to deprive him of his crown and royal power and secure possession of the Great Seal. Again, in Michaelmas term 1452, at Peterborough, before the Earl of Wiltshire and other justices investigating cases of treason in Northants, a jury presented an indictment of Oldhall and others, describing how at Fotheringhay on 11 November 1451 they had met to encompass the King's death by war and discord, had conspired to depose him, and how to this end, arrayed in manner of war, they had risen against their allegiance in favour of the Duke of York. A week or so before this incident, on 3 November 1451 at Hunsdon —according to an indictment laid before the Duke of Somerset on 16 October 1452 at Hitchen (Herts)—Oldhall had been promoting a rising of Hertfordshire men which came to a head at Hitchen on 20 February 1452.[61]

It was not long after this that, on 23 November 1451, Oldhall had entered the sanctuary of the royal chapel of St. Martin-le-Grand in London. Here he remained, except for brief intervals, until after the Yorkist victory in the first battle of St. Albans in 1455. Attempts to have him removed were made by Lancastrian agents, but these attempts failed on account of the Dean of St. Martin's determination to preserve the sanctuary rights of his church. Certain of Somerset's party actually broke into the sanctuary on 18 January 1452 and abducted Oldhall to Westminster. The Dean, however, pressed for his return and, after Oldhall had been detained for two days, obtained it[62]. But, according to an indictment presented in the King's Bench in Easter term 1452, Oldhall was able to help prepare the abortive Yorkist rising of February 1452: a jury presented that on 27 February 1452 at Westminster he had conspired to excite a rising in order to take possession of the Great Seal and discharge the Chancellor, and that on the following day a thousand men accordingly came together at Hounslow with banners unfurled (*cum vexillis apertis*) and levied war in the field. It was only a day later that York was outwitted at Dartford into disbanding the main body of his forces.

As is made clear in the Bill of Attainder preferred against Oldhall in the Reading parliament of 1453, he was not himself in the field with the Duke of York at Dartford. He was alleged in the bill, however, to have aided and counselled those who were. And, even after this failure, he was soon once

[61] Coram Rege Roll, PRO, K.B. 27/777, Rex roll, mem. 7. (The occurrences at Fotheringhay are dated in the roll as taking place on 11 November 1450, but on 9 November 1450 Oldhall was presented at Westminster as Speaker. The events fit better the circumstances of the following year, and the regnal year of the record is doubtless a slip.
[62] *EHR*, XXV (1910), C. E. Johnston, "Sir William Oldhall," pp. 717–8; A. J. Kempe, *Historical Notices of the Collegiate Church of St. Martin-le-Grand, London* (1825), pp. 140–4.

again active in the Duke's interest: according to an indictment in the King's Bench (on 19 May) he was plotting at Westminster on 12 April 1452 to raise the Welsh March, for which treason one of his fellow-conspirators, John Sharp, Esquire, of Brentford, who immediately went off to Ludlow to put the plan into action, was convicted and hanged at Tyburn a year later.[63] After the Dartford business, the King issued a proclamation promising a general pardon in honour of Good Friday (6 April), and York and many of his supporters, Oldhall among them, availed themselves of it. But the pardon only extended to offences committed before Good Friday, and Oldhall had offended after that date. It was doubtless for this reason that pleas in the King's Bench were entered against him in the Easter term. On 27 June Oldhall was allowed to produce in Chancery a dozen sureties (mainly London citizens) prepared to offer bail in £100 for his good behaviour. But the pardon he had taken out would seem to have been rescinded or ignored, because about this time the King's half-brother, Jasper, Earl of Pembroke, got a grant of all his landed estates.[64] Oldhall himself appears to have now remained in sanctuary. It was probably on this account that, on 29 August 1452, he was granted a safe-conduct under the Great Seal to communicate with John Lord Beauchamp of Powick.[65]

However, in Michaelmas term following, as has been seen, criminal proceedings were resumed against him, and, after he had been once more indicted of treason-felony in the Court of the King's Bench, and a writ of exigent had been issued against him on 25 November 1452, he was outlawed in March 1453. As he was to plead when (in Trinity term 1455) he secured a reversal of these proceedings, at the time of his outlawry he was "in prison" in the custody of two yeomen of the Crown, that is to say, in sanctuary under the guard of royal officers responsible for preventing his escape.[66] In the meantime, on 13 December 1452, an esquire of the royal Household, Walter Burgh (M.P. for Downton in 1450–1), who, in January 1452, had been "beaten up" by three unknown men in the London streets (by Oldhall's connivance, as it was believed at Court) for accusing Oldhall of stealing the Duke of Somerset's goods during the pillage of December 1450, had been granted all the arrears of some Lincoln-shire rents due to Oldhall from his step-son, Sir William Skipwith, the arrears of a yearly fee of £80 which Oldhall had been given (for life) by his late brother-in-law, Lord Willoughby, and also all his goods and chattels, including stocks of brick and timber at Oldhall's places in Hertfordshire (Hunsdon, Eastwick, and Pishobury) and Norfolk, the whole of which money and property was stated to be forfeit to the King on account of Oldhall's treason. It was on 25 March 1453, towards the close of the first session of the parliament which met early in that month at Reading (away from the possibility of interference

[63] PRO, K.B. 27/768, Rex roll, mem. 7.
[64] CCR, 1447–54, 363; CPR, 1446–52, 557.
[65] CPR, 1446–52, 569.
[66] PRO, K.B. 27/777, Rex roll, mem. 3; EHR, op. cit., p. 718.

from the citizens of London), that the Earl of Pembroke received a (presumably) confirmatory concession to him and his heirs of all Oldhall's real estate and feudal rights. On 6 May, early in the second session of the parliament (now at Westminster), there was excluded from the forfeiture the two contiguous manors of Little Ryburgh and Stibbard (Norfolk) which Oldhall had released in frankalmoign to the Augustinian priory of Walsingham two years before; on 24 May following, the Duke of Somerset, in a grant to him and his heirs, acquired the manors of Hunsdon and East Wick (Herts); and on 23 June the manor of Bodney (Norfolk) was released to the Augustinian house at Thetford, which was stated to have purchased the place from Oldhall long ago before ever he committed treason.[67]

A proceeding calculated to regularize Oldhall's forfeiture had just been initiated in parliament on 22 June 1453 (during the second session). This had taken the form of a Bill of Attainder presented by the Commons. The Lower House, where there was a sitting a goodly sample of men of the royal Household, and whose composition was heavily weighted towards the Lancastrians, had requested that all ungranted petitions presented in the parliament of 1450–1 should be put into oblivion as purposed against God and Conscience and the Kings Regality and unreasonable. The Commons now proceeded against the ex-Speaker himself, asking that, in consideration of his *fals, cursed, and trayterours disposition*, as exemplified by his undutiful and faithless conduct in supporting Jack Cade and other traitors and giving counsel and aid to those in the field at Dartford, he should be attainted of high treason by parliamentary authority and incur forfeiture, saving any grants of his properties already made or to be made by the King.[68] Needless to say, the bill passed.

Some prospect of a turn for the better in Sir William Oldhall's affairs came in the following year: at Westminster, on 27 March 1454, during the third and last session of the parliament of 1453–4, the Duke of York, contrary to the Queen's aim to be Regent for as long as Henry VI was incapacitated by his mental illness, was chosen by the Lords as Protector. Since just before Christmas 1453, the Duke of Somerset had been in the Tower, awaiting trial, and he remained in custody until March 1455. But by Christmas 1454, when the King recovered his faculties, York's Protectorate had already ended, and, although Oldhall had secured a writ of error in the previous October to begin the process of the annulment of his outlawry, evidently there had not been time to procure his rehabilitation at law, and so he remained in sanctuary.[69]

In the first few months of 1455 Richard of York found himself once more utterly excluded from any share in the government, so that he and the Nevilles gave vent to their exasperation by again taking up arms. The result was the first battle of St. Albans of 22 May 1455, in which Somerset was killed. York was now appointed Constable of England, and with his friends he assumed

[67] *CPR, 1452–61*, 34, 111, 75, 103, 102.
[68] *Rot. Parl.*, V, 265.
[69] *EHR, op. cit.*, p. 719.

control of the administration. Oldhall's situation almost immediately changed complexion. In the next week or so, York's nephew by marriage, Richard Neville, the young Earl of Warwick, with Somerset's heir in his custody, was at Oldhall's place at Hunsdon, awaiting the meeting of parliament, and, as a letter to Sir John Fastolf's secretary (William Worcester) stated, Oldhall *abydeth no lenger in Seyntwery* [sanctuary] *than the Chef Juge* [Fortescue, C.J.,K.B.] *come, for that tyme he shal goo at large and sewe all his maters himself.* Oldhall did, in fact, surrender himself to the King's Bench in the Octave of Trinity (1–8 June). His case was re-opened on a writ of error; his plea—that in the earlier process of outlawry between November 1452 and March 1453 he had been forcibly detained in sanctuary and had therefore been unable to appear to defend himself—was admitted by the King's Attorney-General and the coroner of the Court under instructions from the Council; his outlawry was quashed; and before June gave way to July he had been acquitted on all the charges brought up in 1452. Two days before parliament met on 9 July, William Worcester was able to write to John Paston that Sir William's process in the King's Bench was reversed.[70]

This alleviation of Oldhall's troubles was doubtless the circumstance which prompted John Paston's efforts to get him to marry his sister, Elizabeth Paston. Sir William's wife, Margaret Willoughby, who was still alive in the autumn of 1450 (when he and she had together received a papal plenary remission of all sins when at point of death), had probably died when he was in sanctuary, for she was buried in the church of the Greyfriars in London.[71] Mistress Paston was willing for the match, but nothing came of the proposal, and the lady subsequently married Sir Robert Poynings, Jack Cade's erstwhile sword-bearer, who, at the same time as Oldhall's outlawry was annulled, was also acquitted and delivered (so William Worcester wrote) of all treasons.

A letter from Agnes Paston to her son John, then at the Inner Temple, mentioning his proposal to marry off his sister to Oldhall, shows that the Pastons were in some doubt whether as yet *his lond standyt cler*,[72] in other words, whether Oldhall had recovered his forfeited lands. In fact he had not. But he now took advantage of the Yorkist ascendancy to present to the Commons in the July 1455 parliament a petition demanding restitution. In it he pointed out that he had been a faithful liegeman to each of the Lancastrian kings, and had *dispended his yong daies in the service of theym and of othir Princes of theire blode* in France, Normandy, Guienne, and elsewhere. He had intended, he stated, to live out his days supported by his inheritance and the property acquired by *his long contynuel labour*, but, after being indicted by an intimidated jury and subsequently outlawed, on the ground that he had given *fals untrewe Counsaill* to Jack Cade and other rebels, in the parliament of 1453 he had been

[70] *Paston Letters*, iii, p. 33, 41; *EHR, loc. cit.*; PRO, K.B. 27/777, Rex roll, mem. 3.
[71] *Papal Letters*, IX, 71.
[72] *Paston Letters*, ii, p. 301; *Archaeologia*, XXXVII, *loc. cit.*

declared a traitor by *malicious labour* and attainted. His outlawry had now been reversed, following his acquittal in the King's Bench on the oath of another jury, and he therefore requested that the Act of 1453 should be annulled by authority of parliament, that he should be restored to *name, fame, and worship* and to possession of his estates and other property, and that his own and his heirs' title to his lands should be affirmed. His bill was adopted by the Commons, passed by the Lords, and granted by the King.[73] On 23 October 1455 his forfeited estates were farmed out by the Exchequer to Richard Jenny and Thomas Petwyn (one of his own servants and later his executor) for two years as from Easter 1455; and on 21 November 1455, during the second session of the parliament, only four days after the Duke of York had again become Protector (following the King's relapse into madness), Oldhall requested and secured a royal patent exemplifying the recent parliamentary reversal of the attainder of 1453. All seems now to have been well, or at least for the time being: in February and March 1456 his three London tenements in Mugwell Street in Cripplegate Ward and his Hertfordshire manor of Eastwick were quitclaimed to him; by 22 October 1456 his Cambridgeshire manors were once more in his possession; and, clearly by the time when he made his will in November 1460, so were his other Hertfordshire lands and his Norfolk estates as well.[74]

Early in 1456 Henry VI recovered his health somewhat, and York's Protectorate came to an end on 25 February. However, the Duke remained chief counsellor for a time, and presumably one manifestation of his continued influence was Oldhall's first appointment, on 7 May 1456, to the office of justice of the peace in Norfolk, a position which he retained through the vicissitudes of the next four years. It is very improbable that Oldhall had resumed his old office of Chamberlain to the Duke of York. He evidently retained close contacts with his master and with old friends in the ducal household—in May 1458, for example, Sir Edmund Mulsho, an old colleague and a member of York's council, made him one of the executors of his will.[75] But in this time of more or less acute tension and hollow peace between the Yorkist and Lancastrian parties, there are some slight indications that Oldhall recognized his need to trim sail to catch other political breezes: it was almost certainly late in August 1458 that a correspondent of John Paston's told him that Archbishop Thomas Bourchier and his brother Henry, Viscount Bourchier, were to go down to Oldhall's place at Hunsdon *and hunte and sporte theym* there as his guests.[76] Lord Bourchier was married to the Duke of York's sister, but the Bouchiers were inclined to adopt a middle position between the Yorkists and the Court party. When, however, in the summer of 1459 the two main

[73] *Rot. Parl.*, V, 451; Ancient Petitions, PRO, S.C. 8, file 29, no. 1409.
[74] *CFR, 1454–61*, 138; *CPR, 1452–61*, 282; *CCR, 1454–61*, 115, 390; *Cat. of Anc. Deeds*, I, B/1244.
[75] *CPR, 1452–61*, 672; J. C. Wedgwood, *History of Parliament, Biographies*, p. 618.
[76] *Paston Letters*, iii, 133.

parties were preparing to resort to arms, there was no doubt where Oldhall's sympathies lay.

York's brother-in-law and supporter, Richard Neville, Earl of Salisbury, on 23 September 1459 met and defeated a Lancastrian force at Blore Heath (Staffs) when on his way to join York at Ludlow. But, faced with a powerful royalist army, the Yorkists gave way at nearby Ludford on 12 October and dispersed, their leaders fleeing overseas. A packed parliament subsequently met at Coventry on 20 November to register the Lancastrian victory, attaint York and his foremost supporters, and confirm the title to the throne of the six years old Prince of Wales. Sir William Oldhall was among those twenty-three lords and commoners singled out to be proscribed for treason, he himself being particularly charged with having, on 4 July previous at London in the parish of St. James at Garlickhithe, imagined and encompassed Henry VI's death and stirred the leaders of the Yorkist party to the treasons of Blore and Ludford.[77] Forfeiture of Oldhall's estates and other property followed automatically: on 5 January 1460 all his lands, goods and chattels were given to Humphrey, Duke of Buckingham, and on 13 February and again on 20 March royal commissions were set up in the Home Counties and East Anglia to find out what these were and to seize them; and on 12 March a similar commission of inquiry and sequestration was instituted regarding Oldhall's property in London. On 16 March Buckingham's grant was confirmed, the lands and goods (including debts) being now made over to him and his heirs. On the same day, however, another writ gave control of all the chief forfeitures for the next three years to a group of specially appointed royal receivers, Oldhall's lands included, and his estates were certainly in *their* hands by 20 May.[78] Meanwhile, he was naturally dropped from the Norfolk commission of the peace when fresh patents of appointment were issued in March 1460.

Oldhall's new misfortune directly profited at least two men who had been objects of his displeasure. One was a Richard Wenlock who was now pardoned by the Crown 31 marks, which sum he had been condemned to pay the Earl of Warwick by the *malicious labour* of Sir William Oldhall, and on account of which he had been in Newgate gaol for two years.[79] The second was none other than Oldhall's own son-in-law, Walter, the son of Sir Theobald Gorges of Wroxhall (Somerset) and husband of Sir William's daughter and heir, Mary. There had evidently been a serious quarrel between father and son-in-law which had resulted in legal process, a dispute arising (according to Walter's petition) out of Sir William's failure to honour the marriage settlement. A promised entailed estate, in an annual rent of 40 marks, had been withheld. Subsequently, it was alleged, Oldhall and his servants had been only prevented by his daughter from murdering her husband at Little Fransham (Norfolk).

[77] *Rot. Parl.*, V, 349.
[78] *CPR, 1452–61*, 535, 562, 606; 605; 571, 572; *CCR, 1454–61*, 409.
[79] *CPR, 1452–61*, 581.

This attack by Oldhall had been followed by the extortion from his son-in-law of an oath to submit all matters between them to his judgement, and later by an action in the Court of King's Bench, which resulted in Walter Gorges being condemned in 500 marks; and then, afterwards, when Walter was still being kept in the prison of the King's Bench by Oldhall's influence, as it was alleged, the latter sued a feigned action against him on a charge of detinue of evidences and so had him condemned in a further sum of 300 marks. On 9 February 1460, when these damages stood to be regarded by the Crown as part of Oldhall's forfeited personalty, Walter Gorges received a royal pardon.[80]

What had been Oldhall's whereabouts since the Rout of Ludford in October 1459, there is no knowing. Clearly he was at large, and he may well have accompanied the Duke of York in his flight to Ireland and not come back to England until early in September 1460, when York himself returned (after the Yorkist victory at the battle of Northampton). Oldhall was certainly in London on 12 October 1460,[81] two days after the Duke's arrival at Westminster and four days before the Duke (in parliament) claimed the throne by hereditary title. This Yorkist parliament, summoned in Henry VI's name, after settling the reversion of the Crown on York and his heirs, automatically reversed the attainders of the Coventry parliament of the previous year. And so, legally, Oldhall's estates were once more his own. But time can hardly have been afforded him to regain possession.

By this time Oldhall must have been about seventy years of age, and the excitements of the previous ten years, especially of the last year, can only have told heavily on his constitution—his conduct towards the husband of his only child suggests a growing lack of judgement in family affairs and a failure of self-control, perhaps to be put down to feelings of frustration or hardening arteries. However this may be, although he survived to hear of his master, York, being proclaimed heir-apparent on 8 November 1460, he did not live to hear of the Duke's death at the battle of Wakefield just over seven weeks later. For, in spite of the fact that on 24 November 1460 his name was once more included in the list of those appointed to the Norfolk commission of the peace,[82] it is clear from other evidence that he was already dead by that date. He died, in fact, sometime between 17 November (when he had added a codicil to a will made two days before) and 20 November, when a writ was issued from Chancery instructing the royal escheator for Norfolk and Suffolk to make inquisitions post mortem regarding his estates. (A similar inquiry in Cambridgeshire and Huntingdonshire was authorized on 26 November.[83])

It may safely be assumed that Sir William Oldhall died in London, for his will was made on 15 November 1460 in the city. By it he provided for his

[80] *ibid.*, 541.
[81] *Paston Letters*, iii, 234.
[82] *CPR, 1452–61*, 672.
[83] *CFR, 1454–61*, 282.

body to be buried, under a flat tomb of grey marble, in the chapel of St. John the Evangelist in the parish church of St. Michael called Whittington College, according to the discretion of the Master and his own executors. Here was to be established a chantry of two chaplains at a charge of 10 marks a year to be divided between them, and to the church Oldhall also left stuffs for vestments and all his military pennons and banners. The monetary bequests of the testament are set forth in considerable detail. They included small bequests for forgotten tithes to the churches of Little Fransham (£1), St. James in Garlickhithe in the City (£1), and Hunsdon (1 mark), and further sums to these churches, and to the church of Ditton Valence (Cambs), for masses for his soul. The Carmelites in Fleet Street, in whose church Sir William's father had been buried, were to receive £5 for masses and a gold herse-cloth, and every Franciscan, Dominican, and Austin friar in London was to have 2 marks. Every chaplain present at his interment was to have a shilling, every clerk, 6d., and every boy knowing how to read and sing, 4d. 15 marks were to go to lazars and other poor men. The Premonstratensian house at Wendling (Norfolk) and Bermondsey Priory (Surrey) were to receive other vestments. Members of Oldhall's personal household did pretty well out of the will: his chaplain and ten servants were named as beneficiaries, altogether receiving over £100 in money. Mention is made in the will of the testator's sister, Margaret Lexham, his niece, Agnes Cheyne, and William Lexham, his kinsman (perhaps nephew): the two ladies each received plate worth 20 marks, his kinsman Lexham 100 marks.

A somewhat surprising omission from the list of Oldhall's beneficiaries is that of the Duke of York himself, but the Duke's two elder sons, Edward, Earl of March, and Edmund, Earl of Rutland, received bequests: the former, Oldhall's grey walking-horse, and the younger brother, the horse's value in money. Archbishop Bourchier of Canterbury, whom Oldhall appointed as one of his executors, was left a great bowl of silver which was to be called the *bolle of Caunterbury*, and to another of his executors, Thomas Young, the Yorkist lawyer of Bristol, the same who had moved in parliament in 1451 for the recognition of the Duke of York as the King's heir and who was now (in 1460) sitting in parliament for Gloucestershire, Oldhall left the very large sum of £200, which was to be raised from moneys due to him from Richard Lord Willoughby and from the father of his son-in-law, Sir Theobald Gorges.

The will also contained instructions, regarding certain of Oldhall's manorial and other estates, to his feoffees: the priory of Pentney was to get Oldhall's manor of "Belhoushall" in North Tuddenham for the support of a perpetual chaplain in the priory church; an estate in the manors of Great and Little Fransham was to be created for his kinsman, William Lexham; the rents from the manor called "Oldhall's" in East Dereham and from Ditton Valence were to go to his executors until all his debts were paid, and then to his daughter Mary; his lands in fee simple in East Dereham and all his other estates in

England not mentioned specifically were to be sold by his executors, the money being used to content his legatees; and the rest of his wealth was to be distributed for the good of souls. An estate in the manor of Scarning, called "Drayton Hall," was to be created for Denise, wife of Edmund Buckenham, Esquire, so a codicil of 17 November provided. In addition to Archbishop Bourchier and Thomas Young, Oldhall's executors included Justice William Yelverton (of the King's Bench), John Heydon, William Lexham, his kinsman, and his servant, Thomas Peytewyn. Young, Heydon, and Justice Yelverton in 1457 had been among his feoffees in his Cambridgeshire estates and probably elsewhere as well.[84]

Not all of Oldhall's dispositions were observed: "Belhoushall" and Great and Little Fransham passed to his daughter Mary, and her husband died seised in 1466. The future of Hunsdon and Eastwick (Herts) was not specifically provided for in the will (except that a tenement in the former manor was to be given to one of Oldhall's servants by his feoffees there). But Hunsdon soon passed into royal hands, being bought for 2,000 marks by Edward IV from Archbishop Bourchier (doubtless acting as Oldhall's executor) sometime before July 1471. (In Henry VIII's reign, it was one of the houses where the royal children lived.) It is probable that Eastwick was also sold. Certainly, this estate was not mentioned in a petition presented to parliament in 1489 in which Oldhall's grandson, Sir Edmund Gorges, requested the annulment of the royal grant of his grandfather's forfeited estates (made originally in 1453 and confirmed in 1488) to Jasper Tudor, uncle to Henry VII and now Duke of Bedford, and his own restitution. It was only Great and Little Fransham, "Oldhall's manor" in East Dereham, Brookhall in Dersingham (Norfolk), and Ditton Valence (Cambs) that Jasper Tudor now relinquished. But then he may never have secured more than these to relinquish. Competition for forfeited lands had been keen in the 1450's.[85]

In looking over Oldhall's career, it would appear that he was unfortunate in the date of his birth: he was too young to profit as much as he might have done from Henry V's wars. Never did he receive any royal annuity for his long service overseas. And, though he served under John, Duke of Bedford, and Richard, Duke of York, when competitors for promotion were fewer, the greater part of that time was one in which the English were on the defensive in France, even in Normandy itself, so that the profits of war were no longer what they had once been. He was for long periods overseas, and so never was in a position to reap the advantages of appointment to local office: not until the last four years of his life was he even a J.P. in his native county, and he never held the positions of sheriff and escheator as his father had done. Moreover, he died just before the Yorkist party, to which for twenty years he had been closely attached, triumphed with the accession of Edward IV.

[84] Somerset House, Register Stokton, fo. 21; *Cat. Ancient Deeds*, i, B/1244.
[85] *Rot. Parl.*, VI, 435a; *EHR*, XXV, p. 721; *CCR, 1468–76*, 191.

9

THOMAS THORPE, SPEAKER IN THE PARLIAMENT
OF 1453-4

It may perhaps be said that the career of the Lancastrian civil servant, Thomas Thorpe, reached its climax not in 1453, when he was Speaker for the Commons and was made a Baron of the Exchequer, but in 1455. For it was then that he was accused of being responsible, along with Edmund Beaufort, Duke of Somerset, for the battle of St. Albans (the first battle in the Wars of the Roses), in which Somerset was killed: they were alleged, in the parliament which followed, to have kept Henry VI in ignorance of certain letters by which Richard, Duke of York, and the chief supporters of his rebellion had intended to explain the innocence of their intentions. Thorpe's career seems even generally to have followed the ups and downs of the Beaufort party during the political turbulence of the middle decades of the century; and it was at least partly to his membership of this group that he owed his election as Speaker in the parliament which met at Reading in March 1453.

The previous two parliaments had been actively hostile to the Lancastrian régime. The parliament of 1449-50, hurriedly dissolved because of Cade's Rebellion, had helped to bring about the fall of Henry VI's chief minister, the Duke of Suffolk. The parliament of 1450-1, when the Duke of York's chamberlain had been Speaker,[1] had witnessed a serious, even violent, collision between York and the Duke of Somerset and his friends. Coming to an end in fiasco, with an unsuccessful proposal from a Bristol lawyer that York should be recognized as heir to the throne, it had settled nothing to York's advantage. The Lancastrian régime had not, however, won back much ground; and, even though in 1451 the French overran Gascony, parliament neither met again during that year nor was summoned in 1452.

In the meantime, Yorkist disaffection had persisted, culminating early in 1452 when York and his supporters rose in arms and assembled at Dartford. This insurrection did little to encourage York to hope for a successful outcome to his vendetta with Somerset. The Earl of Worcester, a friend of York's, became Lord Treasurer in April, an appointment which was the source of

The following abbreviations have been used in the references:

C.C.R.   = *Calendar of Close Rolls.*
C.F.R.   = *Calendar of Fine Rolls.*
C.P.R.   = *Calendar of Patent Rolls.*
D.N.B.   = *Dictionary of National Biography.*
P.P.C.   = *Proceedings and Ordinances of the Privy Council,* ed. N. H. Nicolas.
P.R.O.   = Public Record Office.
Rot. Parl. = *Rotuli Parliamentorum.*

[1] See my paper, "Sir William Oldhall, Speaker in the Parliament of 1450-1,"
      The parliament of 1450-1 was the immediate predecessor of that of 1453-4, and that paper and this should be read in conjunction.

considerable annoyance to Thomas Thorpe as an Exchequer official. But that Somerset and the Court party continued to enjoy the upper hand is made clear by the translation of Cardinal Kemp, the Lord Chancellor, from the see of York to Canterbury in July, and of William Bothe, the Queen's Chancellor, from Lichfield to York. The régime, however, continued to stand in great need of popular support, and it was partly in an effort to win it that the government despatched an expedition to the Bordelais under the old Earl of Shrewsbury as Lieutenant of Aquitaine. It was in the spirit of easy optimism to which Talbot's deceptively quick success gave rise that Henry VI, on 20 January 1453, summoned to meet at Reading on 6 March the parliament in which Thomas Thorpe was to act for a time as Speaker.

To say that Thorpe, when elected Speaker by the Commons at Reading, was a friend of the Duke of Somerset, should not be taken to imply that he was foisted on them from above. For the parliament at any rate began as an assembly sympathetic to the Court and at first did well by the government in making substantial grants of taxes. This support proved, however, unequal to the strain caused by happenings later in the year. Admittedly, in October the Queen was delivered of a son. But already (in July) her husband had become mentally deranged, and within days of the royal birth Bordeaux, and with it the whole of Guienne, had fallen to the French. Before the end of the year Somerset was imprisoned pending an enquiry into his conduct of affairs at home and abroad; and before the parliament ended York was made virtual regent with the title of Protector, despite the opposition of the Queen. In the meantime, perhaps as a consequence of Somerset's disgrace, Speaker Thorpe had been imprisoned early in 1454 for acts, hostile to the Duke of York, committed by him in another capacity during the previous summer, and at the beginning of parliament's last session in February he was superseded in the Speakership. The Commons' protest against the infringement of their privilege of freedom from arrest availed them nothing, even though it was their Speaker who suffered from it.

It is on account of this breach of parliamentary privilege, which was excused on the ground that the arrest had been made in time of parliamentary vacation, that Thomas Thorpe is chiefly remembered among constitutional historians. His career, however, is of interest for other reasons. It is mainly remarkable for the light it throws upon the weakness of the royal administration in the later years of Henry VI; for one of the causes of this weakness was the distraction, from their proper functions, of too many of the government's executive officials, lesser as well as greater, because of involvement in political intrigue and manoeuvre.

It is not possible to trace with any confidence the ancestry of Thomas Thorpe. (The commonness of the surname is the reverse of helpful.) There is, however, little doubt that his family was connected with Northamptonshire, where he himself had lands and interests. It is doubtful whether he was related to the Sir William de Thorpe who had a royal licence to crenellate the

Northamptonshire manor-house of Maxey in 1374 and was keeper of the castle and steward of the forest of Rockingham under Richard II; but it is very probable that he was a descendant, perhaps the grandson, of the Thomas Thorpe who was elected (but not returned) as M.P. for Rutland to the parliament of January 1404, during which he was appointed sheriff of this county.[2] Certainly, the lands which Speaker Thorpe held in Northamptonshire, at Barnwell All Saints and Lilford, neighbouring places in the valley of the Nene in the north-east of the county, were divided only by this river from Pilton, the place where the earlier Thomas Thorpe had lived. It has not been possible to identify the Speaker's father, unless he was the Thomas Thorpe who appears as a "king's serjeant" under Henry V and as a porter in the royal household in the early years of Henry VI.

All this is purely conjectural, and the most that can safely be said regarding Speaker Thorpe's origins is that they should almost certainly be sought in Northamptonshire, the county for which he first sat in parliament and where he undoubtedly held property. His manor at Barnwell All Saints at the end of the reign of Edward III had been in the possession of Sir Richard Stury, a knight of the King's Chamber, and remained in Stury's family until it passed in 1435–6 to John Sturdys, who sold it in 1446–7 to Thomas Thorpe.[3] Just when Thorpe acquired his property at nearby Lilford is not known. Neither is it known when he got his estates in Essex, but he certainly was holding some of them by 1451. His main place in Essex was not far from the city of London, being at Great Ilford: here he had seemingly purchased from Isabel, the dowager countess of Oxford, the manor of Clayhall and a messuage and 81 acres, and here eventually he also possessed two tenements, the Swan and the Bell. In Essex, too, he came to hold 2 messuages, 348 acres, and 50s. rent in Barking and Chigwell, and a little further northwards still, up in the Epping Forest area, he had another estate, called the Bellhouse, at Stanford Rivers.[4] In London itself he had a messuage, called the Walnut Tree, in the parish of St. John Zachary in Aldersgate Ward, in the north-west corner of the City. It was in the church of this parish that Thorpe's wife, Joan, was buried in 1453.[5] Her identity is not known, but very likely she came of a City family.

Thomas Thorpe's connections with London men were undoubtedly numerous. Frequently in the course of his career he appears as a member of small groups of assignees of the goods and chattels of various citizens. In fact, it was as Thomas Thorpe "gentilman," one of the assignees of the goods and chattels belonging to a London vintner, that he makes his first known appearance in a Chancery record on 4 May 1434; he acted in a similar capacity in July 1438 to a skinner, in February 1446 to an ironmonger, in September 1447 to a girdler,

[2] J. Bridges, *The History and Antiquities of Northamptonshire*, ii. 522; *D.N.B.*, XIX. 802.

[3] J. Bridges, *op. cit.*, ii. 214; *C.C.R.*, *1447–54*, 484; *Catalogue of Ancient Deeds*, I. B.201; *C.P.R.*, *1461–7*, 134.

[4] *C.C.R.*, *1447–54*, 255, 483; *Rot. Parl.*, VI. 294.

[5] *C.C.R.*, *1447–54*, 484; Weever, *Antient Funeral Monuments*, 179.

in September 1453 to a haberdasher, in June 1454 to a notary, each of whom was a citizen of London.[6] All of these transactions are recorded on the dorse of the Close Rolls of the Chancery, and there were probably many more in which he participated which are not. It is tempting to conjecture that such conveyances of chattels were intended to secure to the assignor a state of temporary freedom from the pursuit of pressing creditors and perhaps represented a stage in his withdrawal into an ecclesiastical sanctuary. If this is so, it may well be that Thorpe was chosen so frequently to act as an assignee because he lived close by the most important of London sanctuaries, that of St. Martin the Great in Aldersgate Ward itself. It was to this very same sanctuary that Thorpe himself retired (or contemplated retirement) during his trouble with the Duke of York in the autumn of 1453.[7]

When Thorpe became attached to the royal Exchequer, presumably as a subordinate clerk in one of its sub-departments, is not precisely known. It is reasonable to suppose that he was "on the strength" of the Exchequer when, on 1 April 1438, he and another Exchequer clerk, both of them described as "gentilmen of London," acted as sureties for a short Exchequer lease of some small Buckinghamshire estates (forfeited to the Crown because of an unlicensed alienation) to a small syndicate of London tradesmen, headed by one of the King's goldsmiths of the City.[8] It was another two Londoners who, on the self-same day, went surety for Thorpe and a Dutchman in the royal service, Derrick Pile, when they were granted (for seven years) two-thirds of the profits of a crane and some tenements (presumably warehouses) in the parish of St. Martin in the Vintry, at a rent still to be arranged in the Exchequer. (Some two years later, the grant was restricted to the Dutchman alone and made rent-free.) The loan of £2 which Thorpe made to the King at the Lower Exchequer in March 1439 was probably a temporary remission on his part of fees that were due to him as an Exchequer clerk.[9]

Similarly, the Crown wardship (together with the marriage of the heir) of certain estates in Essex, Kent and Surrey, which was surrendered by Lord Scrope of Masham and on 2 November 1439 granted to Thorpe and a yeoman of the King's Chamber (Thomas Scargill), was probably given to recompense them for their official fees being in arrears. This was a time of acute financial embarrassment to the royal administration and of special hardship among its employees. The grant, however, profited Thorpe and his partner but little if at all, for early in the following month they surrendered it in favour of a royal esquire, a *protégé* of the Earl of Stafford, who was M.P. for Staffordshire at the time (Thomas Arblaster).[10] Favourably placed at the Exchequer for knowing what was passing down that main conduit of Crown patronage, Thorpe could afford to disregard such a reverse, if reverse it was.

[6] *C.C.R.*, *1429–35*, 311; ibid., *1435–41*, 192; ibid., *1441–7*, 369; ibid., *1447–54*, 29, 466.
[7] *Ibid.*, *1447–54*, 484.
[8] *C.F.R.*, *1437–45*, 33.
[9] *Ibid.*, 34; Exchequer, Issue Roll, E403/743.
[10] *C.F.R.*, *1437–45*, 110, 121.

Some equally (or even more) profitable source of income could be relied upon to come into early view, and this, in fact, is what seems to have occurred. On 2 February 1440 Thorpe was appointed (on the Treasurer's warrant) as weigher of wool exported from Berwick-on-Tweed, and on 19 May following to the same office at Newcastle-on-Tyne. The Berwick office he only managed to keep to himself until 27 October in the same year, when a fresh grant of it (in survivorship) was made to him and William Grendon, a man with Northamptonshire connections, and even together they did not retain the office beyond July 1443. The Newcastle office Thorpe lost to a Boston merchant in October 1442.[11] In the meantime, on 12 April 1440 he had shared (with two others) a grant of the subsidy and aulnage of cloth in Hertfordshire for the period Michaelmas 1439-46 at an annual farm, payable in the Exchequer, of 7 marks (£4   13s.   4d.).[12]

Although Thorpe's employment in the Exchequer in 1440 and even in the years immediately preceding that date may be safely assumed, it is not until February 1441 that evidence is forthcoming of what its nature was. By that time he was one of the summoners (*summonitores*) of the Exchequer and, as such, in receipt of a fee of £4 a year, £2 for each of the Michaelmas and Easter terms of the Exchequer year.[13]

It is very likely that, politically, Thorpe was already attached to the Beaufort family which in the years following the end of Henry VI's minority (in 1437) came virtually to control English government policy, the royal Council degenerating into an instrument whose own proper authority had become somewhat unreal. Cardinal Beaufort, in spite of the "sniping" tactics of his nephew, Humphrey, Duke of Gloucester, who detested his policy of peace with France, was the chief source of authority in the government from 1439 until his death in 1447. This was a time during which the Cardinal's family gained a great deal of influence, however incapably they exercised it: both his nephews, John and Edmund Beaufort, at first had some success in France, in their attempts to "freeze" English territorial assets there, pending a settlement by diplomacy; and the younger of the two brothers, Edmund, was first (in 1442) created Earl and then (in 1443) Marquess of Dorset, and the elder, John, was shortly afterwards elevated in the peerage from Earl to Duke of Somerset. John died in disgrace after the military fiasco of 1443-4, but his brother and heir, Edmund, succeeded him in his earldom, became Lieutenant and Governor-General of France in 1447 (superseding the Duke of York), and in 1448 was also created Duke of Somerset. After the death of Duke Humphrey of Gloucester early in 1447 and before the birth of Edward of Lancaster in 1453, the problem of the royal succession was largely one at

---

[11] *C.P.R., 1436-41*, 442, 570; *ibid., 1441-6*, 194, 128. (There is no question of this Thomas Thorpe's identity with the Exchequer official. Cf. the latter's revived Newcastle-on-Tyne grants of 1448-9.)

[12] *C.F.R., 1437-45*, 155.

[13] J. C. Wedgwood, *History of Parliament, 1439-1509, Biographies*, 849; Issue Roll of the Exchequer, P.R.O., E403/743.

issue between Somerset, in whose niece Margaret the Lancastrian claim might be said to have resided, and the Duke of York, who represented the strictly legitimist Mortimer claim to the throne. Somerset not only incurred some of the odium which attached itself to the Duke of Suffolk on account of the unfortunate and inconclusive settlement with France of 1444, but in 1449 and 1450 personally associated himself with the ignominious loss of the most important towns then still held by the English in Normandy, Rouen and Caen. His influence with Henry VI remained always strong, but his reputation in the country at large never recovered from this connection with the last military humiliations in northern France; and if ever he had hopes of re-establishing an English ascendancy in Guienne, they died at Châtillon in 1453.

There is no doubt of Thomas Thorpe's later close attachment to the Duke of Somerset; but his connection with the Beaufort party in the days of his obscurity in the early 'forties in all probability rested on no firmer basis than his association with Master John Somerset, physician to the King, and also Chancellor of the Exchequer, Keeper of the Exchange, and Master of the Mint in the Tower. It is not known what was the precise nature of Master Somerset's kinship with the Beauforts, but there can be no doubt that some tie of kinship existed. It was by Thorpe's hands that on 9 December 1441, and again on 16 October 1442, Master Somerset's half-yearly fee as Chancellor of the Exchequer (20 marks) was disbursed at the Lower Exchequer.[14] That Thorpe owed to Master Somerset his association, on 22 September 1442, with Henry Ragley, a goldsmith of London, in the office of Controller, Changer, and Assayer of the Tower Mint with fees of 40 marks, an office held by Ragley alone since November 1438, is no more than highly probable. But on 19 May 1443 Thorpe and John Hampton, Master of the Royal Ordnance and an Esquire of the Body to Henry VI, shared with Master Somerset the wardship and marriage of a tenant of the Archbishop of Canterbury, these being at the disposal of the Exchequer because the see of Canterbury had been recently left vacant by Archbishop Chichele's death and its temporalities were in the King's hands.[15]

In the meantime, on 18 April 1442, Thomas Thorpe had been given a royal patent under the Great Seal granting him for life an annuity of £10. This grant proved profitless, and on 21 December following he received another grant for life of the same annual income (charged on the issues of Essex and Herts) which was back-dated to 20 January 1437, that is, made payable from the death of the previous patentee (a yeoman of the cellar of Queen Anne of Bohemia) who had been granted a confirmation on each royal accession since the original grant by Richard II.[16] Perhaps Thorpe's tenure of the office of royal escheator in Essex and Herts in the current administrative year

[14] Issue Roll, E403/743; E403/747, mem. 1.
[15] C.P.R., 1441–6, 125, 193; C.F.R., 1437–45, 262.
[16] C.P.R., 1441–6, 396; ibid., 137, 357.

(November 1442-3) had brought this potential source of income to his notice.[17] Earlier in 1442 (on 22 April), in his capacity as a subordinate officer in the Exchequer, Thorpe was appointed (by warrant under the Signet) to receive all the proceeds from a royal general pardon and apply them to the provision of a maritime force for defence and to the safe-keeping of Calais.[18]

It was towards the end of Ralph Lord Sudely's first year of office as Treasurer of the Exchequer that, on 25 April 1444, Thomas Thorpe was promoted in that department of State to the post of Treasurer's Remembrancer, which carried with it an annual fee of 40 marks; he was to hold office as from 3 February 1444. On 16 September following he was granted a royal patent ratifying his appointment with the assent of Lord Sudely, but now conferring the office for life and the right to act by deputy. Although the position was one normally regarded as within the Treasurer's gift, Thorpe was not to be removable by him. He was to receive the usual fee of 40 marks a year and money for parchment from the Lower Exchequer, and his vesture of livery from the Great Wardrobe; and he was also granted for life an annual Christmas allowance of one tun of red Gascon wine or two pipes of other red wine, as he pleased, to be taken in the port of London.[19] (In this office Thorpe had two Exchequer clerks under his immediate surveillance, the senior of whom received £5 a year, the other £4.) Less than two years later, on 8 January 1446, in addition to his customary fee as Remembrancer, by special royal grace he was granted for life an annuity of 50 marks, in consideration of the charges of his office, together with an annual livery at Christmas of a cap, gown, and tabard of the kind worn by a Baron of the Exchequer. Moreover, this fresh annuity, chargeable on the Lower Exchequer, was to be back-dated to 31 March 1442 to recompense him for the annuity of £10 then granted, from which he had had no profit. When, acting on a writ of 21 January 1446, the Exchequer came to make its first payments of arrears, it went no further back than Michaelmas term 1442; but, of the £116 13s. 4d. (175 marks) due to Thorpe, it paid him as much as £65 15s. 3d. in ready money, the rest by tallies of assignment.[20] His fees as Remembrancer, customary and special together, now amounted to £60 a year.

Thus far, with the exception of his occupation of the escheatorship of Essex and Herts in 1442-3, Thorpe's administrative energies seem to have been predominantly expended in work at the Exchequer itself. Nothing is known of his doings in 1447, but early in 1448 he began to be employed in royal commissions in the counties where he had private, landed interests, and elsewhere. The commission set up on 8 February 1448 to investigate in Middlesex all cases of concealment of royal revenue from feudal rights, non-observance of sureties of the peace, non-payment of customs, and such like,

[17] C.F.R., 1437-45, 241.
[18] P.P.C., V. 186.
[19] C.P.R., 1441-6, 363; Enrolled Accounts of the Keeper of the Great Wardrobe, P.R.O., E101/409/13, 18; 410/4, 7; Issue Roll, E403/751, 753.
[20] C.P.R., 1441-6, 396; C.C.R., 1441-7, 336; E403/759.

was very much an Exchequer concern, the commission being headed by the Chief Baron and including another Baron and the Under-Treasurer, as well as Thorpe, the Treasurer's Remembrancer. So were the two commissions to which Thorpe was appointed on 9 July 1448: one, a multi-articled commission, enforceable in twelve counties in the south of England, authorized an inquiry into all kinds of concealment of royal revenue; the other appointed, for the next twenty-one years, a group of assessors of the Duchy of Cornwall estates in Devon and Cornwall, of whom Thorpe was to be especially associated with the Receiver-General of the Duchy.[21] Meanwhile, on 28 March and 5 May 1448 he had been made a J.P. in Essex and Northants respectively (for the first time in each case); he was to be a member of the commission of the peace in Essex without a break until January 1457 and in Northants until December 1458.[22] Only two days after his appointment to the revenue commissions of 9 July 1448 he was re-appointed to the office of weigher of wool for export at Newcastle-on-Tyne, a sinecure which he had first taken in May 1440 but lost in October 1442; and on the very next day (12 July 1448) he received for himself alone a grant of the offices of Controller, Exchanger, and Assayer of the Tower Mint, which since September 1442 he had shared with the goldsmith, Henry Ragley. These offices at the Tower he was to keep until May 1450, the Newcastle place until December 1450.[23] In the meantime he added to his Northumbrian interests when, on 29 January 1449, he and his son Roger together procured a grant in survivorship of the office of porter of the royal castle at Newcastle-on-Tyne (with the usual fees, including two shillings a day from the issues of the county).[24] This office father and son held together until April 1453. Further, on 8 May 1449, his sureties being his own two subordinate clerks at the Remembrancer's office in the Exchequer, Thomas Thorpe received a grant of the royal manor of Brigstock (Northants) at a farm of £40 a year, for ten years as from 9 July next following. Here Thorpe was less fortunate than with his other grants, because before this concession became operative the right to farm the manor had been given for the next forty years to a group of its own tenants.[25]

Despite this *contretemps*, Thorpe's reputation in Northamptonshire was evidently well established, for on 23 October 1449 he was for the first time elected as one of its knights of the shire to the parliament summoned to meet at Westminster on 6 November, his fellow (and senior) knight of the shire being William Tresham, who had been Speaker for the Commons in 1439–40, 1442, and 1447, and was now to be re-elected to this office.

The parliament threatened to be a stormy one. Thorpe's latest administrative chief, Bishop Lumley of Carlisle, had resigned the Treasurership in September. On 13 December, shortly before the end of the first session of the

[21] *C.P.R.*, *1446–52*, 139, 190–1.
[22] *Ibid.*, 589, 592; *ibid.*, *1452–61*, 665, 673.
[23] *Ibid.*, *1446–52*, 180(418), 180(334).
[24] *Ibid.*, 226.
[25] *C.F.R.*, *1445–54*, 110.

parliament, Thorpe made a loan to the Exchequer of £50 for which a week or so later he received re-payment by assignment.[26] This may well have been no more than a fictitious loan, representing a postponement of the payment of his official salary. On 23 March 1450, a week before the end of the second session of the parliament, during which the Duke of Suffolk had been impeached and banished, Thorpe was included in a commission of oyer and terminer authorized to inquire in London, which had been recently much disturbed by seditious activity, about treasons against the King's person and other offences committed by a London vintner, John Frammesley; and on 26 April, at the end of the next recess and only three days before parliament re-assembled at Leicester, he was put on a similar commission regarding the treason of John Harries, a Yorkshire "shipman," who, when Henry VI and his lords passed through Stony Stratford on their way to Leicester, had used a threshing flail in front of them "to show that the Duke of York then in Yreland shuld in lyke manner fight with traytours at Leicester Parliament and so thrashe them downe as he had thrashed the clods of erthe in that towne."[27]

The Leicester session opened on 29 April 1450, the day before Suffolk sailed from Ipswich, ostensibly into exile, in fact to his death by murder at sea. In parliament, meanwhile, the Commons resisted the demands for a subsidy made by Lord Saye and Sele, the new Treasurer, and they brought in a bill requiring an Act of Resumption which was to cover all royal grants since the beginning of the reign, a measure for which they had already pressed. On 6 May the King agreed on condition that all exceptions, put into writing before parliament ended, should be allowed; and then the Commons conceded a subsidy for the French war, in the form of a graduated income-tax, the revenue from which was to be in the care of special treasurers (the first of their kind to be appointed since 1406). The final Act of Resumption contained a clause exempting Thorpe from its operation, apart from an annuity of £10, the one charged on the issues of Essex and Herts which, originally granted him in December 1442, was now resumed.[28] Although by 21 May Thorpe had also surrendered his offices in the Tower Mint and the office of porter of the castle of Newcastle-on-Tyne, he had to some extent offset these losses by securing on 13 May a grant, which he shared with Ralph Lord Cromwell, Chamberlain of the Exchequer, of the wardship and marriage of the son and heir of Sir Henry Pleasington, a wardship which in December 1452 the Duke of Somerset took over.[29]

At about the end of the first week in June 1450 the Leicester parliament was cut short by news of Jack Cade's rising in Kent and the threat to London. The Court returned in haste to Westminster, Thorpe with it. (On 12 June

[26] Issue Roll, E403/777, mem. 7.

[27] C.P.R., 1446-52, 320, 383; C. L. Kingsford, English Historical Literature in the Fifteenth Century, App. XII, p. 371.

[28] Rot. Parl., V. 199b.

[29] C.P.R., 1446-52, 334; ibid., 1452-61, 64; C.F.R., 1445-54, 155.

he was at the Lower Exchequer where he received 25 marks as part-repayment of a loan of 40 marks which he had recently persuaded the Abbot of Peterborough to contribute.[30]) The disorders in London and nearby counties lasted for over a month. In the meantime, the Treasurer, Lord Saye and Sele, shortly after resigning, was arraigned by the rebels on 4 July at the Guildhall and beheaded in Cheapside. A new Treasurer, John Lord Beauchamp of Powick, had already been appointed on 22 June. Thorpe came through this commotion unscathed, but he had evidently been in some danger. A dirge for the late Duke of Suffolk, in which certain alleged traitors are featured, perhaps belonged to this time of turbulence. And one of its couplets runs:

> "Arys up, Thorp and Cantelowe, and stond ye togeder
> And synge *Dies illa, dies ire.*"[31]

Moreover, Thorpe seems to have been indicted before a royal commission sent to Rochester some time during the rising with the object of appeasing the rebels.[32]

The government had survived Cade's revolt, but with considerable loss to its already diminished prestige. No part of northern France was now in English control except Calais. Internally, misgovernance and lack of order were rife. The King had begotten no heir after five years of marriage, so that the problem of the royal succession, for which York and the Beauforts were in competition, was in the mind of every man. It was to a chaotic situation that both York and Somerset now returned, the former from Ireland to be treated as a rebel, the latter from Calais to be appointed Constable of England (on 11 September). York forced his way through to London but, although fairly treated by the King, had to wait for parliament's meeting on 6 November 1450.

Whether Thomas Thorpe tried to secure re-election to this parliament as knight of the shire for Northamptonshire (where the senior knight chosen was Thomas Mulsho, elder brother of a member of the Duke of York's council) we do not know. But certainly, if he did so, he failed. He managed, however, to get himself returned for the Wiltshire borough of Ludgershall, being substituted for an earlier nominee, the son of William Yelverton (JKB), who was put in for Old Sarum instead.[33]

Once met together, the Commons showed their bias towards the Duke of York by electing his chamberlain (Sir William Oldhall) as their Speaker, and matters at first went York's way. During the first session the Duke of Somerset and a few of his supporters had a hazardous time; and at the beginning of the

[30] E403/779, mem. 6; E404/67/92. (Thorpe himself lent the Exchequer 160 marks in 1449–50.)
[31] *Three Fifteenth Century Chronicles*, ed. Jas. Gairdner (Camden Soc., 1880), 103. There seems to be no particular reason for Thorpe's name being linked with that of Cantlowe, who was presumably the William Cantlowe who was a merchant-stapler and alderman of London.
[32] C. L. Kingsford, *op. cit.*, App. A ("A Yorkist Collection, 1447–52"), p. 365.
[33] J. C. Wedgwood, *History of Parliament, 1439–1509, Register*, 171–2.

second session, in January 1451, he and a number of prominent members of the royal household staff and other loyalists, thirty in all, were petitioned against by the Commons for "mysbehaving" about the King's person and elsewhere, and their banishment from Court for life was requested, a demand which the King contemptuously dismissed. The Chancellor of the Exchequer, Master John Somerset, was the only officer of that department to be so proscribed by the Commons. Thorpe himself was not even mentioned and probably had no difficulty in retaining his Exchequer post. It is true that on 22 December 1450, immediately after the end of the first session of the parliament, he lost his office of troner at Newcastle-on-Tyne to one of the parliamentary burgesses for that town, Richard Weltden, a client of the Nevilles.[34] But on 20 November he had already received a writ authorizing the Exchequer to repay the 160 marks (£106 13s. 4d.) which he had lent to the King in the previous year, and on 8 April 1451, early in the recess between the second and third parliamentary sessions, he received at the Lower Exchequer an assignment of £10 paid to him in his capacity as Treasurer's Remembrancer. This grant was a special reward for the adjudication of claims in his office, for the abnormal diligence he had been required to show during the Michaelmas term in scrutinizing the valuations of the lands of the late Duke of Suffolk now in royal hands—he had discovered that the old extents were £136 a year above the latest valuations—and for extra duties connected with the Resumption Act of 1450.[35] Only two days after this later payment, the widow of a London fishmonger and a retainer of the Duke of York released to Thorpe and his feoffees all actions relating to his Ilford and other Essex estates.[36]

This year, 1451, saw considerable local disorder and disturbance, but the hostility between York and Somerset was temporarily suspended, the King doing his best to keep up the pretence of peace between them. Little is known of Thomas Thorpe's activities during the year, outside his official Exchequer routines. It is worth noting, however, that on 11 and 15 December 1451 payments to Master John Somerset, still Chancellor of the Exchequer, amounting to £120, were made at the Lower Exchequer by the hand of Thomas Thorpe's servant, Thomas Cross.[37] That Thorpe had influence as well as friends in his own department is also suggested by the fact that on 5 February and 17 March 1452 he received grants of the wardship of the lands of John Helion, a modest Essex landowner who had recently died, together with the marriages of two of his daughters and coheirs, paying for them 340 marks in all.[38] Shortly afterwards, however, there occurred a change of Treasurer, John Tiptoft, Earl of Worcester, succeeding Lord Beauchamp on 15 April 1452.

[34] C.P.R., 1446-52, 418.
[35] P.R.O., E404/67/92; E403/781.
[36] C.C.R., 1447-54, 255.
[37] P.R.O., E403/786, mem. 6.
[38] C.F.R., 1445-54, 259, 263.

This change at the Exchequer was doubtless part of the price which the Somerset group paid for the pacification with the Duke of York that followed the Yorkist rising which recently (at the beginning of March) had culminated in an encounter between the Duke's supporters and the King's forces at Dartford. For the Earl of Worcester was a friend of York's. And Thorpe now ran into heavy weather for a time. Not until December 1453, when Thorpe was in trouble again, did Thomas Combe, clerk to John Holmes, one of the Barons of the Exchequer, get paid his 5 marks as special reward for the work, but it was in Trinity term 1452 that this clerk was ordered by the new Treasurer to write divers rolls of defects found in the memoranda and other records in the office of the Treasurer's Remembrancer by the scrutiny of his master, John Holme, and of another Baron, John Durham.[39] Clearly, soon after his appointment Tiptoft had begun to search for some cause or pretext to remove Thorpe from the office which, granted for life, he had now been occupying for over eight years. Treasurer's Remembrancer though he was, Thorpe evidently considered that his original grant was proof against interference, even by the Treasurer himself: the grant itself had expressly rendered him immune from removal. He put up a strong fight to retain his tenure which thus far had witnessed three changes of Treasurer.

Tiptoft's eventual success proved something of a Pyrrhic victory. Sometime in Michaelmas term 1452 Richard Forde, until then Clerk of the Pipe, succeeded Thorpe as Treasurer's Remembrancer.[40] We may conjecture that this disturbance of Thorpe's Exchequer position occurred sometime before 22 November 1452, when he secured a grant of the reversion of the office of Chancellor of the Exchequer for life, on the death of Master John Somerset, with a promise of an annual fee of £40 and a confirmation of his Christmas livery of Gascon wine in the port of London. By that time this crisis in Thorpe's affairs was doubtless over: on 30 November a Privy Seal warrant authorized the Exchequer to pay him £200 of the King's especial grace, "considering the good and agreeable service done . . . and also the greet costes, charges, troubles and vexacions that he hath hadde and suffred for us," and on 12 December an assignment of revenues was made to him.[41] He did not get the office of Chancellor of the Exchequer, at least not when Master Somerset died; but then he did not need to. Presumably soon after 22 November 1452 and certainly before the end of April 1453, Thorpe had defied the Earl of Worcester, ejected his competitor for the office of Remembrancer, and re-occupied the place, refusing to relinquish it unless he were promoted to be Third Baron of the Exchequer. We know of these circumstances from the petition which Richard Forde presented in the parliament of July 1455, when he took advantage of the recent Yorkist victory in the first battle of St. Albans to protest against Thorpe's advancement. The petition went on to

[39] P.R.O., E403/796, mem. 10.
[40] P.R.O., E403/791.
[41] C.P.R., 1452–61, 43; Privy Seal warrants for issue, P.R.O., E404/69/74.

describe how Forde, having given up his office as Clerk of the Pipe, was left destitute after his removal from the Remembrancership, and how in order to secure his re-instatement certain well-disposed colleagues in the Exchequer had had to contrive the retirement of William Fallan from his office as Third Baron, so that Thorpe might succeed him. But this was only managed on the understanding that Forde paid Fallan a pension of 40 marks a year for life (the equivalent of his fee as Baron) unless the King made similar provision.[42] By 26 April 1453 Thorpe was Third Baron.[43] It may perhaps be presumed that he began the Easter term in the office, but whether his promotion had already taken effect when the parliament summoned to Reading met on 6 March 1453, is a matter of doubt. Elected for the first time as senior knight of the shire for Essex, Thorpe was chosen Speaker for the Commons on 8 March.

Among the knights and burgesses who met at Reading, well away from the Yorkist pressure of the City of London, was a goodly number of members of the royal household and other supporters of the administration. The political tone of the Lower House was even predominantly Lancastrian. The Exchequer itself was represented by a few of its subordinate clerks, including Thomas Cross, Thorpe's servant, who was returned for Heytesbury. Roger Thorpe, the Speaker's son, sat for Truro. Another connection of Thomas Thorpe's to be elected was Richard Strickland, Esquire, master (for life) of the King's harriers, who was returned for East Grinstead; for Thorpe was one of Strickland's feoffees-to-uses in the manor of Haversham (Bucks).[43a]

This opening session at Reading lasted only from 6 to 28 March. One of its first acts was to decide that the petition of 1450, in which the Commons had asked that the Duke of Somerset and his supporters might be banished from the Court, should be "put in oblivion." Further, the Commons in another petition asked for a resumption of all grants made to those who had been with the Duke of York in the field at Dartford. This short session also resulted in the first grant of a regular parliamentary subsidy of a tenth and fifteenth to be made since 1449, and this tax was backed up by a grant to the King for life of the wool subsidy, tunnage and poundage, and the poll-taxes on aliens, and by a novel grant of 20,000 archers for six months service when required.

The value of Thomas Thorpe's managerial qualities may be gathered from the personal profit which he himself extracted from this phase of Lancastrian ascendancy in the course of the parliament's second session, which was held at Westminster between 25 April and 2 July 1453. The office of porter of the castle of Newcastle-on-Tyne, which Thorpe and his son had lost by the Resumption Act of May 1450, was first given to Roger on 29 April and then, on 17 May, was granted once more (as in January 1449) to Thomas and Roger

[42] *Rot. Parl.*, V. 342b, no. 25.
[43] P.R.O., E404/69/134; *C.P.R., 1452-61*, 64.
[43a] *Catalogue of Ancient Deeds.*, iii. B4220.

together (in survivorship).[44] On 23 May the Speaker also received a fresh grant confirming him in his right to hold the Helion wardship, which within the next three weeks he proceeded to sell to Sir Thomas Tyrell, and on the same day he and some associates took out a pardon under the Great Seal of all actions, amercements, and arrears of accounts.[45]

In parliament itself this second session saw a scaling down of the grant of archers and also its suspension for two years. But this was on condition that the Commons made a grant for Guienne, and in fact they made a further grant of a half $\frac{1}{10}$ and $\frac{1}{15}$ for which the King personally thanked them. The continuance of a strong Lancastrian political bias in the parliament is indicated by a bill (first presented in the Lords) securing to the Duke of Somerset a lien on all the revenue from import and export trade through the port of Sandwich, together with a grant of a noble (6s. 8d.) on every sack of wool exported elsewhere. This appropriation was to ensure repayment of the £21,648 due to Somerset as Captain of Calais, after the Duke of Buckingham had first been contented of £19,000 charged on the same sources. The Commons themselves, moreover, successfully petitioned for the attainder of Sir William Oldhall, the Yorkist Speaker of the previous parliament of 1450–1, who was now in a London sanctuary, and accordingly he incurred forfeiture.

During the closing stages of this session, on 23 June 1453, Thorpe's wife, Joan, had died, and had been buried in the City church of St. John Zachary. The inscription on her tomb described her as *uxor Thome Thorp, unius baronum de scaccario domini Regis, prolocutoris parliamenti tenti apud Reding anno Regis Henrici sexti xxxi*.[46] How successfully, despite this personal trouble, Thorpe had acted as Speaker in the royalist interest is made abundantly clear by the fact that on 24 July he received at the Lower Exchequer an assignment for £200 which the King, "for certain causes and considerations moving him," had ordered (on 11 July) to be delivered to him as a gift. The assignment was made by the hands of Thomas Bourne, then M.P. for Steyning, who on the same day was the recipient of payments on behalf of the Duke of Somerset himself.[47] By this time Thorpe was a member of the King's Council: his first recorded appearance at a council meeting was on 11 July, and there are half-a-dozen other notices of his attendance between then and the middle of August.[48] It is possible that he had been a councillor for some time. (The records of the Council are unfortunately very imperfect in this period, and the date when Thorpe joined it cannot be precisely stated.)

During the late summer and autumn of 1453, Thorpe's position as Baron of the Exchequer naturally occupied him in other than conciliar duties; on 12 August he was appointed a member of a commission authorized to compel the payment of arrears of farms in Merionethshire owing to the Exchequer

[44] *C.P.R., 1452–61*, 64, 81.
[45] *Ibid.*, 78, 82, 113.
[46] Weever, *Antient Funeral Monuments*, p. 179.
[47] P.R.O., E403/793, mem. 8; Privy Seal warrants for issue, P.R.O., E404/69/179.
[48] *P.P.C.*, VI, 143, 144, 152, 154, 156–7, 331.

of North Wales and to treat with the tenants for a subsidy in satisfaction of their arrears; and a month later he was made a member of a board of inquiry into trespasses, including cases of concealment of sources of royal revenue, in Caernarvonshire, Merionethshire, and Anglesey.[49] He was one of a small but evidently financially powerful syndicate, also comprising the Treasurer (the Earl of Worcester), John Wode (the Under-Treasurer), Sir Thomas Brown (the previous Under-Treasurer) and Sir William Lucy (another member of the King's Council), which syndicate on 20 October made a loan of as much as 2,000 marks to the Exchequer; four days later they received payment in the form of an assignment.[50]

By this time yet another political crisis of first magnitude was brewing. During the summer of 1453, seemingly in July, the King fell ill of a mental malady which rendered him incapable of maintaining even a semblance of control of the administration for the ensuing year and a half. Added to this, on 13 October the Queen gave birth to a son, Edward, about whose paternity ugly rumours were soon afoot. With the problem of the regency (during the King's illness) still unsolved, parliament met at Reading on 12 November, as previously arranged, only to be immediately prorogued again to re-assemble there on 11 February 1454. By the end of November the Duke of Somerset had been imprisoned in the Tower, following a demand, laid before the Council, for an inquiry into his conduct of affairs at home and also overseas, where the whole of Guienne had fallen into French hands with the loss of Bordeaux on 19 October 1453.

What now befell Speaker Thorpe may perhaps be regarded as a repercussion of Somerset's disgrace. In the middle of November 1453 Thorpe was still occupying his office as Baron of the Exchequer.[51] Before the end of the month, however, he seems either to have sought refuge in the London sanctuary of St. Martin the Great in his own ward of Aldersgate, or to have had this step in mind: on 25 November he made a grant of all his goods and chattels to Master Richard Cowdray (the Dean of St. Martin's), Master Laurence Bothe (the Queen's Chancellor), and eleven others, including the under-sheriff and an alderman of London and two Exchequer clerks.[52] Whether or not he took sanctuary, he was soon afterwards imprisoned in the Fleet prison. From the explanation offered by the Duke of York's counsel to the Lords when parliament re-assembled in February 1454 and when Thorpe's imprisonment came up as a question of the Commons' privilege of freedom from arrest, it appears that sometime during the previous year, and presumably during the second session of the parliament at Westminster, Thorpe had gone to the London inn of the Bishop of Durham (Robert Neville) and there attached certain unspecified goods and chattels belonging to the Duke of York. According to a petition

[49] C.P.R., 1452–61, 124, 173.
[50] P.R.O., E403/796, mem. 15.
[51] P.R.O., E403/796, mem. 12.
[52] C.C.R., 1447–54, 484.

submitted over thirty years later, in Henry VII's first parliament of 1485, by Thorpe's son Roger, these goods and chattels were "certain harness and apparatus of war" which Thorpe had arrested by the King's order. A conflation of the two accounts yields the information that, prompted by Thomas Colt, Esquire, who was "nigh of councell with the said . . . duke" (and incidentally, M.P. for Warwick in 1453–4), York began an action by bill in the Exchequer, where Thorpe, by demanding privilege of court, could insist his trial should be held. Thorpe appeared and, having "had diverse daies to emparle atte his requeste and desire," pleaded not guilty. A writ of *venire facias* was addressed to the sheriffs of Middlesex returnable in the Exchequer, and there, by a jury that passed between the Duke and Thorpe (was acceptable to both?), it was found that Thorpe was guilty of the trespass stated in the bill. Roger Thorpe later alleged that this was done "by speciall labour and untrue means" on Colt's part. However this may be, judgement was given for the Duke of York, the jury assessed damages in his favour at £1,000 and costs at £10, and Thorpe was committed to the Fleet pending payment.[53] This action probably came on after 19 January 1454 when, in a letter from London, it was stated that "Thorpe of th'escheker articuleth fast ayenst the duke of York, but what his articles ben it is yit unknowen."[54]

If this was so, Thorpe cannot have been long imprisoned in the Fleet when parliament re-assembled. It met at Reading on 11 February 1454 only to be told by York's friend, the Treasurer (the Earl of Worcester), that the session would begin at Westminster three days later. The question of the regency during Henry VI's illness was still unsettled. The Queen felt herself entitled to it, but York secured the initiative when on the eve of the session he was allowed the right to open and conduct parliament's proceedings.

Thorpe being the Commons' accredited Speaker, the session began with a petition from the Lower House requesting his liberation as a matter of privilege. The Judges declined to deal with the matter, on the ground that any privilege of parliament was for the Lords and not them to determine. The Chief Justice, however, while admitting that there could be no general *supersedeas* when parliament was sitting, gave it as his opinion that it was usual for any person under arrest who was "a membre of this high court of Parliament" to be free to attend, provided that he had not been arrested for treason, felony, surety of the peace, or upon a charge made in parliament. But York's counsel had urged upon the Lords that the trespass committed by Thorpe had taken place since the beginning of the parliament, that the Duke's whole action against him had been both begun and terminated in time of parliamentary vacation, and that if Thorpe were released by privilege before payment of damages and costs, the Duke would be deprived of remedy; and so they demanded that Thorpe should be kept in custody until he had fulfilled the award of the Court of Exchequer. Notwithstanding the privilege

[53] *Rot. Parl.*, V. 239; VI. 294.
[54] *The Paston Letters, 1422–1509* (Library edition, 1904), ed. J. Gairdner, ii. 296.

and the fact that Thorpe was Speaker, the Lords ruled that he should remain in prison and that the Commons should elect another Speaker. An explanation was made to the Lower House by one of the King's serjeants-at-law in the presence of Bishop Bourchier of Ely and other lords; and on the third day of the session (16 February) the Commons accepted the *fait accompli* and elected one of the Middlesex knights, Sir Thomas Charlton, to the Speakership.

This last session of the parliament ended on 17 April 1454. In the meantime, although the infant Edward of Lancaster was recognized on 15 March as Prince of Wales and Earl of Chester, the Duke of York was appointed on 27 March as Protector during the King's infirmity, and on 2 April the Duke's brother-in-law, Richard Neville, Earl of Salisbury, was appointed Chancellor in succession to the late Cardinal Kemp. The Commons, however, could not be induced to add to the financial grants they had made at Reading. It was an unquiet time, but York seems to have remained in virtual control of the administration until Henry of Windsor came to his senses about Christmas 1454. Soon afterwards the Protectorship ended. And early in February 1455 Somerset was released from custody.

Thomas Thorpe had had nothing like so long to wait to be liberated. Just when he left the Fleet prison is not known, but it seems very likely that he secured his release during the parliamentary session in which he had been deprived of the Speakership: on 6 March 1454, described still as one of the Barons of the Exchequer, he was made one of the feoffees of an Essex glover in a croft at Leyton; on 20 June he and a fellow-Baron were among the assignees of the goods and chattels of a London notary; and on 17 July Thorpe was paid his terminal fee as one of the Barons of the Exchequer.[55] Temporarily at any rate, he came to terms with the Duke of York when on 26 July 1454 (before the Mayor of the Staple at Westminster) he entered into a "statute-staple" for a debt of 200 marks payable to the Duke on 1 November 1455.[56] This was not the whole of the sum still outstanding from the award of damages made in the Exchequer of Pleas in January or February 1454—there was £210 of this still unpaid in July 1455—but the transaction at least points to some sort of accommodation between Thorpe and the Duke. There seems to be no doubt that Thorpe by this time had recovered (if ever he had lost) his office as a Baron of the Exchequer, and on 28 November 1454 he was appointed as a justice of oyer and terminer in Essex regarding treasons, felonies, and other offences, including breaches of alliances and truces with foreign powers by Norfolk shipmen.[57]

The recovery of the King resulted in the Duke of Somerset's liberation early in February 1455, and then, a month later, in his political rehabilitation. At the same time Richard of York was relieved of his command of Calais, which was immediately given to Somerset. On 7 March the Earl of Salisbury

[55] *C.C.R., 1454-61*, 353; 46; P.R.O., E403/798, mem. 11.
[56] *C.C.R., 1454-61*, 108-9.
[57] *C.P.R., 1452-61*, 222.

was dismissed from the Chancellorship, and it was Archbishop Bourchier, a moderate man, who was then entrusted with the Great Seal. On 15 March an important change at the Exchequer took place, when the strongly royalist Earl of Wiltshire followed the Earl of Worcester. This was evidently an appointment of immediate significance for Thomas Thorpe who, on 24 March, was granted for life the office of Chancellor of the Exchequer, of which he had secured the reversion in November 1452.[58] He continued in office as a Baron of the Exchequer. It is, moreover, highly probable that he had been now re-instated as a member of the royal Council. He certainly was in intimate contact with the King at this time.

When the Duke of York had had time to react to the new situation he collected his allies, the Earl of Salisbury and his son, the Earl of Warwick, in the North, and together their forces marched towards London. From Royston on 20 May 1455 they wrote a letter to Archbishop Bourchier, the Chancellor. In it they stressed their loyalty and their intention only to act with him and all the other lords, complaining of the suspicion that they had meant harm to the King's person. They also declared their purpose, which was to put down those guilty of creating such a mistrust and to remove "the ambiguitee and th'occasion" of it. A copy of this manifesto was enclosed with another letter, written at Ware on the following day and addressed to the King: this second letter affected to complain of the King's being estranged from these Yorkist lords by their enemies who, being "of approved experience . . ., abide and kepe theim self undre the wynge of your Mageste Roiall"; and the letter requested that its authors be admitted to the King's presence as faithful subjects. Neither the letter to the Chancellor, which Archbishop Bourchier forwarded to the King at Kilburn, nor the letter and enclosure addressed to the King direct, which reached the Court at Watford, was allowed to come to Henry's personal notice (so the Yorkists asserted in the next parliament), and even the purport of these letters was allegedly suppressed by the Duke of Somerset, Thomas Thorpe, and the King's Secretary, William Joseph, once they had read them. This embezzlement of their missives, the King's ignorance of their intentions, and the resistance offered at St. Albans on the following day (22 May) by Somerset, Thorpe, and Joseph to their offer to make a personal explanation to the King, were later represented by the Yorkist leaders as their excuse for fighting the first battle of St. Albans.[59] The engagement resulted in the death of the Duke of Somerset, the Earl of Northumberland, and Lord Clifford, and the virtual capture of the King himself, whom the Yorkist lords then led back to London. Thorpe, rumour had it, and doubtless on this occasion rumour did not lie, had fled from the field with the new Treasurer, the Earl of Wiltshire, and others, "and left her harneys behynde hem cowardly."[60] Only a week later Wiltshire was superseded

[58] *Ibid.*, 230.
[59] *Rot. Parl.*, V. 280–2.
[60] *Paston Letters*, iii. 28.

at the Exchequer by Henry Viscount Bourchier, brother of the Chancellor
and brother-in-law of the Duke of York. Nevertheless, it is almost certain
that Thorpe was not immediately dismissed from his Exchequer posts.

Parliament was summoned on 26 May 1455 to meet at Westminster where,
despite indisposition, the King opened its proceedings on 9 July. Formalities
over, the session began with a consideration of the reasons for "the male
journey of Seynt Albones." The outcome of this discussion was that the
Yorkist rebels were exonerated, the blame for the battle being put squarely
on the dead Duke of Somerset, Thomas Thorpe, and William Joseph. The bill,
which, when agreed by both Lords and Commons and approved by the King,
gave parliamentary authority to this conclusion, was passed on 18 July, but
to it "mony a man groged full sore nowe it is passed."[61] Apart from alluding
to the culprits' obstruction of the letter forwarded by the Chancellor (Bourchier)
and the letter sent by the Yorkist leaders direct to Henry VI, this parliamentary
declaration of the fidelity of the Duke of York and his friends referred to the
way in which the King had been "moved and sollicited" by Somerset, Thorpe,
and Joseph "to mistrust oure seid cousyns and to instraunge theym from
oure favour and good grace," the result being that he had been provoked "to
have proceeded with grete might of people under colour of oure matiers,
where noon we hadde, to the avansyng of theire owne matiers and quarelles."
The Yorkist lords had been forced, they alleged, to seek the King's presence
to declare themselves his true subjects especially because Somerset, Thorpe, and
Joseph had "enforced thaim[selves] with grete might of men in diverse
Countreyes, moche harneys, and grete habilamentes of werre."[62]

So far as Thorpe was concerned, there were to be important repercussions
from this Act. The Commons requested that both he and William Joseph
should suffer a resumption of all the offices and grants they had received
during the reign, that all their letters patent be annulled, that neither should
be retained by the King, Queen, or Prince of Wales or come within seven
miles of them, and that they should both be imprisoned for twelve years, any
pardon or breach of prison to result in forfeiture of lands and tenements and
a fine of £1,000 payable to the Treasurer of Calais. The Lords seemingly passed
the bill, but the King rejected it, perhaps acting on the advice of the judges,
who are not likely to have responded favourably to the suspension of the
royal power of pardon or to the procedural abnormalities which the bill
recommended.[63] This bill and its defeat almost certainly belong to the
parliament's first session which ended on 31 July.

Parliament was to meet again on 12 November 1455. When the time came
round, the King's mental health had suffered another relapse and the Duke of
York was commissioned to re-open the parliament. Immediately, the Commons
began to press for the Duke's re-appointment as Protector. Twice they repeated

[61] Ibid., iii. 44.
[62] Rot. Parl., V. 280-2.
[63] Ibid., 332-3, no. 9.

their demand, and on 19 November York assumed the Protectorship with the usual safeguards and, as in 1454, with a proviso for the rights of the Prince of Wales.

To this second session, which ended on 13 December 1455, is probably to be attributed a renewal of the attack on Thomas Thorpe and William Joseph. For as late as 8 November the former was still occupying his office as Baron of the Exchequer,[64] and not until 16 December was his successor as Chancellor of the Exchequer appointed.[65] But certainly the Commons' petition against him and Joseph described Thorpe as "*late* one of the Barons of the Exchequer." Perhaps it was one of York's first acts as Protector to dismiss him from office. However this may be, the Commons requested again that all Thorpe's and Joseph's offices, fees, and annuities should be altogether resumed, whether held by them singly or jointly, on the grounds that they had both demeaned themselves unbecomingly in the King's presence with "inordinate and presumptuouse malepertenesse," and because Thorpe had committed certain (unspecified) offences and misprisions in the Exchequer. This bill contained no demand for their imprisonment. It was granted that it should take effect from 13 December, the last day of this session.[66] Evidence of Thorpe's extravagances in the Exchequer had probably already come to the Commons' notice in the private bill which Richard Forde, Thorpe's successor in the office of Treasurer's Remembrancer, asked them to sponsor, the petition (remarked above) which had alluded to Thorpe's defiance of the Earl of Worcester in 1452–3 and to the disreputable means he had employed to come by his office as Third Baron in April 1453.[67]

Certainly, by the end of 1455 Thomas Thorpe stood bereft of all his offices[68]; but not all hope of recovery was lost. Only half of the lords summoned to parliament had attended during the recent autumn session, and even these had needed pressure from the Commons before they would agree to appoint York as Protector: clearly the Duke's position, outside the ranks of his kinsmen, was not without obvious weaknesses. When parliament resumed its sittings on 14 January 1456, there were prospects of the King's health improving; and, although it was believed that Henry was prepared to retain York as Chief Councillor, there were those who trusted the Queen to put an end to any nonsense of that sort. Not until 25 February, however, did the King sufficiently recover to be able to attend parliament, an event which automatically concluded York's Protectorship.

Before this occurred, at Northampton on 27 January the Duke had given

[64] P.R.O., E403/806. Privy Seal warrants dated 26 April 1455 and 1 October 1455 authorized the Exchequer to pay Thorpe the terminal instalments of his fee as Baron (P.R.O., E404/70/2, no. 65; E404/70/3, no. 10).
[65] *C.P.R., 1452–61*, 276. First appointed on 10 July 1454 but replaced by Thorpe on 24 March 1455, Thomas Witham was re-appointed on 16 December 1455 and confirmed on 11 May 1456.
[66] *Rot. Parl.*, V. 342, no. 23.
[67] *Ibid.*, 342, no. 25.
[68] *C.P.R., 1452–61*, 365.

an acquittance for 500 marks to Thomas Thorpe, "late one of the Barons of the Exchequer." The Duke's receipt mentioned a petition which he himself had made in parliament in July of the previous year, drawing attention to the fact that Thorpe was indebted to him in £210, to ensure payment of which Thorpe had delivered an obligation drawn up in his own name and that of William Benyngton, "gentilman" of Walthamstow (Essex). (Presumably, the sum referred to was the unpaid residue of the fine of £1,000 imposed for Thorpe's trespass of 1453.) York stated that he had relied on this obligation, "trustying of the trouth and worshipp to be stabblisshed of presumpcion in persones called [to] the office of any baron and the honnour that belongeth thereunto," but that later it was discovered that Benyngton had no knowledge of the obligation. The Duke, therefore, had petitioned in parliament for execution on the body of Thomas Thorpe by writ of Chancery, as if he had been bound by a statute-staple, and requested that all Thorpe's lands, after being valued, should be surrendered to him until the sum in question, *plus* damages and costs, had been received. The petition had evidently been successful, and action taken. Thorpe settled the account on 31 January, and the business ended with the enrolment of its details on the Close Roll of the Chancery on 2 February 1456. That the final transaction took place at Northampton suggests that Thorpe had taken himself off to his county of origin during this period of adversity.[68a]

Perhaps to the third and final session of the 1455-6 parliament, which lasted from 14 January to 12 March 1456, should be attributed a private petition calling attention to "sinistre labour" governing Exchequer appointments and asking the Commons to promote legislation safeguarding Exchequer officials against dismissal except for offences against their oath or personal incapacity, and to secure the restoration to office of all those dismissed since Easter 1454 before Lady Day next (25 March), provided that the Act did not apply to Thomas Thorpe. The bill was adopted by the Commons, but rejected by the King.[69]

Although the end of York's Protectorship did not bring about any immediate change in the direction of affairs, there are signs that Thorpe's case was no longer desperate: on 7 February 1456 he was granted for 24 years the custody of the honours of Peverel, Boulogne, and Haughley in Buckinghamshire, Northamptonshire, and Leicestershire, together with the castle and honour of Huntingdon, all of which had escheated to the Crown on the death of John de Hastings, Earl of Pembroke, in 1389. On 3 July following, the estates of the three honours in East Anglia, Cambridgeshire, and the Home Counties were added to the lease for 20 years, at a farm to be agreed with the Exchequer.[70] Moreover, by Michaelmas 1456 Thorpe's son and heir, Roger, had been taken on to the establishment of the King's Chamber, where

[68a] *C.C.R.*, *1454-61*, 108-9.
[69] *Rot. Parl.*, VI, 338-9, no. 18.
[70] *C.F.R.*, *1454-61*, 147, 163.

he was now one of the King's four "Henxmen" or personal grooms,[71] and a month after this time Roger was appointed as troner at Berwick-on-Tweed, an office held by his father from 1440 to 1445.[72]

In the early autumn of 1456 certain important changes in the control of the royal administration took place. First, on 24 September, Lawrence Bothe, Queen Margaret's Chancellor, became Keeper of the Privy Seal; then, on 5 October, Viscount Bourchier, York's brother-in-law, was replaced as Treasurer by the Earl of Shrewsbury, a Lancastrian; and finally, on 11 October, Archbishop Bourchier gave up the Great Seal to Bishop Waynflete of Winchester. The Bourchiers were men for the middle of the road; but because they had been put or continued in office by York, their dismissal represented something of a recovery of the initiative by the royalist party. Thomas Thorpe, however, did not get back his Exchequer offices at this time; nor, perhaps, was he likely to do so as long as there was any hope of the Court party reaching an accommodation with his enemy, the Duke of York. And for a year, from July 1456 to August 1457 he was even removed from the commission of the peace for Essex. That his son Roger was safely in favour, however, is made clear by his being granted in April 1457 the porter's office at the castle of Newcastle-on-Tyne, although his own and his father's former grant of 1453 had been annulled during the parliament of 1455–6.[73] This grant significantly referred to Thomas Thorpe as "*then* [i.e. in 1453] one of the Barons of the Exchequer." Clearly, Thomas Thorpe had not recovered the office of Baron at the time of his son's grant. On 1 August 1457, however, he was re-appointed as a J.P. in Essex, and then, on 16 November following, he was granted for life the office of the Keeper of the Privy Wardrobe in the Tower, an office recently held by no more important a person than an usher of the Chamber at a wage of only a shilling a day.[74] He now began to serve once more on occasional local commissions, being appointed on 17 December 1457 to serve in Essex on a commission to apportion the county's share of a force of archers (voted in the parliament of 1453) among the hundreds and lesser divisions of the county, and then on 25 February 1458 he was authorized to commandeer workmen for the manufacture of bows, acting doubtless in his capacity as Keeper of the Privy Wardrobe.[75] At this time a Great Council of the lords was meeting in London, and the City and its environs were swarming with the retinues of the leaders of the factions.

Whether Thomas Thorpe figured in the great "love-day" in London Cathedral on 25 March 1458, when there was a solemn reconciliation of the feuds set going at the battle of St. Albans nearly three years before, is not known. The policy of appeasement had no lasting value. This being so,

[71] P.R.O., E101/410/14 (enrolled account of the Keeper of the Great Wardrobe, Michs. 1456–7).
[72] C.P.R., 1452–61, 329.
[73] Ibid., 365.
[74] Ibid., 392.
[75] Ibid., 406, 416.

Thorpe's personal position was likely to improve, especially since the young Duke of Somerset, Henry Beaufort, now aged twenty-two, was already coming to the fore in the Lancastrian party. Thorpe had been very close to the late Duke, and so it seems he was to his son. In 1457 Somerset had been made Lieutenant or Warden of the Isle of Wight. On 10 September 1458 Thorpe was put on a commission of inquiry into wastes and alienations of royal estates in the island, especially in the lordship of Carisbrooke, and into the whereabouts of all stores and artillery. Such a commission came his way perhaps because he was Keeper of the Privy Wardrobe, but another commission issued at the same time, of which he was also a member—to muster the retinue of the Duke of Somerset for service in the Isle of Wight—suggests a personal connection with the Duke.[76] It was only two days later, on 12 September, that the Council authorized Thorpe's re-instatement as a Baron of the Exchequer. Described in his letter patent as "late third Baron," he was now appointed to occupy the place of second Baron during royal pleasure, and on 30 November following he received a grant of an annual fee of 50 marks, chargeable to the farm of London and Middlesex.[77] In the course of this Michaelmas term of 1458, along with the other Barons he received at the Lower Exchequer a payment (by assignment) of £10 as a special reward for diligent labour undertaken at the Treasurer's order for the King's profit, and for expediting royal business in the Exchequer and elsewhere; on 17 February 1459, by the hands of his clerk, Thomas Bourne, he received another assignment for £20 as a reward additional to his fee for Easter term 1453 and Michaelmas term 1453-4; two months later (on 17 April 1459) he was allowed another assignment of £40 as a reward additional to his fees for the four main terms between Easter 1454 and Easter 1456. Further, on 9 May 1459 he was given an assignment of £10 over and above his fee for the current term, and on 6 July following he received further Exchequer tallies amounting to £50 13s. 4d., after returning tallies (dating back to 1452 and 1454) which he had been unable to cash.[78] These assignments of annual rewards of £20 were not peculiar to Thorpe: his fellow Barons of the Exchequer received them, too. But the Exchequer terms for which he was to draw them make clear that from sometime in the term beginning Michaelmas 1455 until Michaelmas 1458 he did not occupy the office of Baron.[78a]

It is Thorpe's return to the preoccupations of official life at Westminster which accounts for his having been dropped from the Northamptonshire commission of the peace in December 1458.[79] Another indication of Thorpe's return to the proximity of Exchequer channels of royal patronage had come on 20 February 1459, when he secured a grant of a manor in Bulmer (Essex) and a messuage in Hadley (Suffolk) which he was to hold (as from Michaelmas

[76] Ibid., 488.
[77] Ibid., 458, 477.
[78] P.R.O., E403/817, 819 (mems. 1, 3, 6).
[78a] Privy Seal warrants for issue, P.R.O., E404/71/3, no. 67.
[79] C.P.R., 1452-61, 673.

1458) as long as they were in the King's hands for a yearly farm of £7 13s. 4d. plus an increment of 3s. 4d.; the former estate had belonged to a customs-official at Ipswich who had died a debtor to the Crown, the Hadley property to a farmer of the aulnage of cloth in Suffolk and Essex who had similarly died owing money at the Exchequer.[80] At the end of the same month (on 28 February) Thorpe's son Roger received a grant for life of the keeping of the stank or water of the Fosse at York, an office which carried with it 6d. a day in wages, drawn from the issues of the county of York.[81] During this term, Thomas Thorpe was also involved in some semi-private, semi-official business: he was appointed on 21 February 1459 to act as one of the two arbiters in a dispute between the widow of John Troutbeck, a former colleague in the Upper Exchequer (King's Remembrancer in 1447–50), and her step-son, William Troutbeck.[82] The latter was to be killed in the Lancastrian defeat at Bloreheath in Staffordshire eight months later.

Open civil war between the Lancastrian and Yorkist parties broke out in the early autumn of 1459, the result of which—the end of the Lancastrian rule and the accession of Edward IV, a year and a half later—Thorpe was never to see. Not since early in 1456 had parliament met, so that the emotions of the factions had been denied any expression by constitutional methods. The government's policy of appeasement had only been spasmodic, having alternated with passages of inept provocation, and both parties spent the year 1459 openly preparing for a show-down. On 7 May 1459, "considering thennemies on every syde aproching upon us as wel upon the see as on land, willing and entendying to resiste theym to their grete rebuke with the grace of Jhe [Jesu]," the King authorized the purveyance of 3,000 bowstaves and stuff to make 3,000 sheaves of arrows and their delivery for safe-keeping until further order to Thomas Thorpe as Keeper of the Privy Wardrobe in the Tower.[82a] At this juncture, the Yorkist plan was doubtless to re-create the situation of 1455 and possibly extract from it a recognition of Richard of York's claim to the royal succession; and in September 1459 the Earl of Salisbury moved down from Yorkshire to join the Duke at Ludlow in the Welsh March, the old home-ground of the Mortimers. On 23 September the Earl defeated a Lancastrian force of interception at Bloreheath (Staffs.); but at Ludford on 12 October the Yorkist coalition itself was routed, so that its leaders scattered and left the country. Already, on 9 October parliament had been summoned to meet at Coventry on 20 November.

A single session of a month's duration sufficed to register the Lancastrian triumph, attaint the Yorkists, and guarantee the right of the six-years-old Prince of Wales to the throne. The Commons' Speaker on this occasion was Thomas Tresham, Controller of the King's Household, a Northamptonshire

[80] C.F.R., 1454–61, 228.
[81] C.P.R., 1452–61, 479.
[82] C.C.R., 1454–61, 354.
[82a] Privy Seal Warrants for issue, P.R.O., E404/71/3, no. 77.

man, and, what with irregular or rigged elections and the prestige of their party's victory in the field, the Lancastrians had it all their own way. Whether Thomas Thorpe was returned to the parliament, is not known. He certainly did not sit for Essex; but it is just possible that he represented Northamptonshire along with the Speaker, for the returns of the election at Northampton have not survived. It is an idle speculation. Not long before the parliament met, however, Thorpe was almost certainly with the King at Coventry. And very probably he was in the retinue of the Duke of Somerset. For on 10 November 1459 a Privy Seal warrant authorized him to be paid at the Exchequer £40 for shipping and £4 for messengers,[83] the shipping being for service with the Duke of Somerset whose purpose it was to attack Calais, where the Earls of Salisbury and Warwick had taken refuge a week or so before. A month had passed since Somerset's appointment as Captain of Calais, but he was now, of course, refused admission to the town and had to be content with taking nearby Guînes and making himself a nuisance to Calais in the winter months.

During the Coventry parliament it must have been a source of some irritation to Thorpe that Thomas Witham, who had replaced him in his office of Chancellor of the Exchequer in December 1455, managed to secure an exemption from an Act directed against those officials who, appointed by Yorkist influence after the battle of St. Albans, had not given clear proof of loyalty to Henry VI in the recent upsets. The proviso took account of Thorpe's continuing reversionary rights in the office, but permitted Witham to retain it until death or until Michaelmas 1465 if he lived so long.[84] At this time, however, Thorpe had few other causes for complaint. On 8 January 1460 his appointment as Second Baron of the Exchequer was rendered more secure when the Council not only ratified it but also now allowed him to hold the office *quamdiu bene gesserit* instead of *quamdiu regi placuerit*.[85]

Thorpe served at the end of 1459 and early in 1460 on a number of local and other commissions arising out of the commotions of the previous autumn: for example, on 21 December 1459 (the day after the dissolution of the Coventry parliament), he was put on a commission of array for his own county of Essex. The threat of Yorkist reprisals was an ever-present one in what proved to be only a lull between hostilities. Kent, ever likely to support the Yorkist cause, was bound to be regarded by the Lancastrians as a tender spot, especially in view of the use being made of Calais by the Earl of Warwick, and on 15 March 1460 Thorpe was made a member of a commission of oyer and terminer regarding all cases of treason and rebellion in this county.[86] On the following day (16 March), as Second Baron, he was set at the head of a group of five Exchequer officials appointed to act for the next three years as receivers of revenues from all the estates forfeited by the Yorkist leaders

[83] E404/71/4, no. 18.
[84] *Rot. Parl.*, V. 366.
[85] *C.P.R., 1452–61*, 549.
[86] *Ibid.*, 558, 611.

and those of their supporters who had been attainted in the Coventry parliament. For this work the members of the commission were to take an annual sum provided by the Council. Thorpe, however, on 9 April following secured to himself (as from the end of the Coventry parliament) a special grant of an annual rent of £40 charged on˙the forfeited estates of the Duke of York and the Earl and Countess of Salisbury.[87] Further to these satisfactory developments, on 17 May 1460 he and Sir Thomas Tyrell (M.P. for Essex in the Coventry parliament and now sheriff of Essex and Herts) were granted a twenty-year lease of the royal lordship of Havering-at-Bower (as from Michaelmas 1459) at an annual farm of £102 payable in the Exchequer.[88] It was about this time that Thorpe was acting as chief member of a small group of Exchequer and Household officials concerned with the collection of the wool-customs and the subsidies of tunnage and poundage, his fellow-members being the Treasurer of the King's Chamber, the Keeper of the Great Wardrobe, and the previous Under-Treasurer of the Exchequer.[89] On 23 May he was also put on a commission authorized to muster troops intended to reinforce the Duke of Somerset at Guînes in the Pas de Calais.[90] Only a month before, at Pont de Neullay, the Duke had suffered a serious defeat from the Yorkist force at Calais. Thorpe's own son, Roger, was at this time in Somerset's service and with him at Guînes.

This order of 23 May 1460 was Thomas Thorpe's last royal commission. Some five weeks later, York's eldest son (Edward, Earl of March) and the Earls of Salisbury and Warwick crossed the Channel, landing at Sandwich, where they were met friendly-wise by Archbishop Bourchier. They then moved, through an enthusiastic Kentish countryside, up to London, which they reached on 2 July. According to a London chronicle,[91] Thorpe was one of those who then took refuge in the Tower with Lord Scales, Lord Lovell, and Lord Hungerford. These Lancastrian magnates surrendered on 18 July. Thorpe, however, must already have got away: in the account of his troubles (given in a petition presented by his son Roger to Henry VII in 1485) he is stated to have been with Henry VI at the Lancastrian defeat at Northampton on 16 July, there taken prisoner, brought back to London, and kept in custody, first in the Newgate prison and then in the Marshalsea.[92] Certainly, he was in Newgate early in October,[93] and it was presumably there that, on 2 October, he surrendered his office as Keeper of the Privy Wardrobe to John Parr, a Yorkist whose father had been attainted at Coventry in 1459.[94] We may take it for granted that Thorpe had also been deprived of his office as Second

[87] *Ibid.*, 572, 585.
[88] *C.F.R.*, *1454–61*, 275.
[89] *Ibid.*, 254.
[90] *C.P.R.*, *1452–61*, 609.
[91] *D.N.B.*, XIX, 802; *Three Fifteenth Century Chronicles*, ed. J. Gairdner (Camden Society, 1880), p. 75.
[92] *Rot. Parl.*, VI. 294.
[93] *Paston Letters*, iii. 228.
[94] *C.P.R.*, *1452–61*, 624.

Baron of the Exchequer. From the account of the same London chronicle, it appears that he managed to escape from prison in disguise, but "he was take and brought to London ayene [again] with a newe shave crowne, and so brought to the Erle of Salysbury place and afterwarde sent to the Toure of London."

Thomas Thorpe was still in prison at the end of the year when his old enemy, the Duke of York, recently recognized in parliament as Henry VI's successor, met his death in the battle of Wakefield on 30 December. Thorpe's son, Roger, took part in this engagement, probably as one of the retinue of the Duke of Somerset who led the Lancastrian force to victory. Meanwhile, Queen Margaret was recruiting support in Scotland and, despite the Lancastrian reverse at the battle of Mortimer's Cross, moved with the Lancastrian lords south, defeating the Earl of Warwick in the second battle of St. Albans on 17 February 1461. The Lancastrian cause might then have been saved, at least for a time, if the loyalist army had advanced immediately on London; but, even if so, it would have profited Thomas Thorpe nothing. It was on the very day of the battle that, again escaping from prison (presumably in an effort to make contact with the Queen's army), he was caught by a party of Londoners in Harringay Park, to the north of the City, where (as his son was to state in his petition of 1485) "contrary to all law and conscience he was cruelly beheaded, his goods and chattels being spoiled from him."[95] There can be little doubt that Thomas Thorpe's estates were subjected to forfeiture as soon as Edward IV established himself as King: on 20 July 1461 a commission was appointed to seize into the King's hands all the lands and possessions he held in Barnwell (Northants).[96]

Certainly, his son and heir, Roger, fared ill under the Yorkists. In February 1462, for taking part in the battle of Wakefield he was sued in the King's Bench by his father's old enemy, Thomas Colt, who, fighting on the Yorkist side, had fallen wounded. Colt, pretending in his plea that the engagement was a private encounter between them, claimed £2,000 as damages for the trespass he had suffered. By "sinister labour" the case was tried at *nisi prius* before the justices of assize in Yorkshire, where the jury found for Colt, who then secured judgement in the King's Bench for recovery of his damages. Roger Thorpe was imprisoned for execution of judgement until he released to Colt and his feoffees his possession of an estate-in-reversion in certain properties in Essex, including tenements in Ilford, the evidences relating to which were secured by Colt from the Blackfriars in London and other places. Excluded from a royal pardon in July 1463, Roger Thorpe was not able to secure an annulment of these proceedings until 1485 when he successfully made petition to that end in Henry VII's first parliament.[97]

[95] *Rot. Parl.*, VI. 294.
[96] *C.P.R., 1461-7*, 134.
[97] *Ibid.*, 292; *Rot. Parl.*, VI. 294.

10

JOHN LORD WENLOCK OF SOMERIES

I

The story of the life of John Wenlock of Someries is likely to be of some interest to Bedfordshire historians. His family, while retaining property in their native Shropshire, had settled in Bedfordshire in the fourteenth century. John's father and another member of the family, perhaps an elder brother, had now and then represented the county in Lancastrian parliaments. So did John himself, six times in all : in 1433, 1437, 1439-40, 1447, 1449 and 1455-6. On the last of these occasions he acted as Speaker for the Commons.[1]

Wenlock's election as Speaker, in the parliament which met soon after the Yorkist victory in the first battle of St. Albans, was the culmination of his career as an occasional member of the Lower House. It was not the acme of his career more widely regarded. Even so, by 1455 he had come far. In the 1430s closely connected with a Bedfordshire magnate, Lord Fanhope of Ampthill (a great-uncle of Henry VI by marriage), it was in the 1440s that Wenlock moved quickly forward, first, as an usher of the King's Chamber, and then, after diplomatic services in the cause of an Anglo-French peace and the King's marriage with Margaret of Anjou, as an usher of the Queen's Chamber and, later (by quick promotion), as her Chamberlain. Perhaps partly as a result of being a victim of Henry VI's chronic financial insolvency, by 1459 Wenlock had cut adrift from intimate association with the Lancastrian Court and thrown in his lot with the Yorkists.

Care has been taken not to confuse John Wenlock the Speaker with the John Wenlock esquire who was attorney to the Earl of Shrewsbury in 1442 in a conveyance of Talbot lands in Salop and Herefordshire (*C.C.R., 1441-7*, 155-6), as an esquire witnessed the will of the heir of the Earl in 1452 (Lambeth Palace Library, Kemp's Register, fo. 312ᵛ), acted as surety for the Dowager Countess of Shrewsbury in December 1460, again as esquire (*C.F.R., 1454-61*, 295), and who survived until 1477 when he made a will, many of whose details recall his close connexion with the Talbot family (Somerset House, Register Wattys, fo. 33).

1. *Official Return of Members of Parliament*, i, 323, 329, 335, 338, App. xxiii; *C.F.R., 1437-45*, 140 (for 1439); *Rot. Parl.*, v, 280; *Lords' Report on the Dignity of a Peer*, IV, 958-74.

Wenlock took a very active part in those movements of Yorkist rebellion whose final outcome was the displacement of Henry VI and the accession of Edward IV in 1461. His help to the Yorkist cause had been worth having, and clearly still was. And Wenlock got his price : immediately, Edward IV made him a member of his Council, raised him to the peerage, and appointed him as Chief Butler of England, Chamberlain of the Duchy of Lancaster, and Treasurer of Ireland. Much reliance was also put on his obvious flair for diplomacy with the French, and in the last ten years of his life never a year went by but Wenlock crossed the Channel as a member of some embassy. This brought him into constant touch with the great Earl of Warwick ("the Kingmaker"). It also gave him scope for re-establishing contact with the exiled Lancastrians. Eventually, with Warwick himself, Wenlock supported the Lancastrian restoration—the Re-adeption—of 1470-1.

Perhaps Wenlock's *volte-face* in 1470 was made for the same basic reasons as Warwick's : disgust at Edward IV's growing independence of the Yorkist "old guard" and the King's preference for the family of his Queen, the Wydevilles, and hope of further self-aggrandisement. Wenlock's profits from one dynastic revolution had been considerable; he had no reason to doubt that a successful counter-revolution would prove at least equally advantageous. But the Lancastrians miscalculated, Wenlock with them, and his life (however minimal its social value) was part of the crippling price exacted in the disasters which befell their cause at Barnet and Tewkesbury in 1471.

To criticize Wenlock's record as one of dishonour and turpitude towards first his Lancastrian patrons and then the Yorkist King would be largely beside the point, considering that the period was one of extreme political complication, upset, and strain. If self-preservation had ever a right to be dignified as a rule of natural law, it was then. And better men than Wenlock had worn a collar of livery of the Lancastrian esses, only to discard it for a collar of the Yorkist suns and roses. None the less, Wenlock seems to have been a born intriguer, and perhaps more objectionable than some. Moreover, that there is a striking lack of evidence of his employment as a feoffee-to-uses and as an executor of wills (except in the case of Lord Fanhope) does not suggest that he was generally regarded as very trustworthy by members of his own set in their everyday concerns. At the end of his career, his actions point to a singular superabundance of faith in himself, and perhaps, therefore, to a failure of judgment. And yet he had undoubted ability and experience.

Perhaps we ought to consider that for long he had contended with certain natural disadvantages, which may have had a real, if incalculable, effect on his political career. He was without close kinsmen to advise him in its later and more dangerous phases. Also, though married twice, he had no children of his own, and at his death his next heir was only a distant cousin. The possession of direct heirs might have steadied him at the time of what proved to be the last crisis in his affairs. Had Wenlock had children married off into other families of substance, such alliances might have served to consolidate his own position in different ways. The present and future interests of children alone, for example, might have made him give pause before he committed himself to support the Lancastrian Re-adeption, a course of action which resulted in his death and the forfeiture of his estates. It was perhaps a disadvantage that he had nothing to lose but his own.

II

The family of Wenlock (alias Wynell) to which John Wenlock belonged had clearly had its origin in Much Wenlock in Shropshire. It was to be with his support that the incorporation of this town (as a free borough with representation in parliament) was secured by royal charter in 1468. Moreover, in 1448 John himself petitioned for 16 messuages and 80 acres of land there (along with 4 acres of meadow in Callaughton) that had been alienated in Richard II's reign (without royal licence) to the Cluniac priory of Much Wenlock by his great-uncle.[2] The latter, William Wenlock, canon of St. Paul's from 1362 and archdeacon of Rochester from 1376, had seemingly been beneficed and resident in Bedfordshire, for at his death in 1391 he was buried in the church of St. Mary and All Saints, Luton.[3] Other members of the family also seem to have moved across the midlands, for the canon's nephew and executor, William Wenlock, the father of John Wenlock, as early as 1377 had acquired a quarter of a sixth part of the manor of Luton,[4] and other lands in the county also came into his occupation when he married a

2. *C.Ch.R.*, VI, 229; *C.P.R., 1446-52*, 247; *C.C.R., 1405-9*, 327.
3. Somerset House, Register Rous, fo. 6; *V.C.H., Beds.*, ii, 372.
4. *V.C.H., Beds.*, ii, 351-2.

Bedfordshire heiress, Margaret, sister and heir of John Briton. These estates included the manor of Upper Stondon,[5] which the Briton family had been holding in the early thirteenth century, and the manor of Britons (alias Grove Manor) in Houghton Conquest.[6]

To his father's estates John Wenlock made considerable additions either by his own first marriage or by purchase : he built up a compact group of estates at or within easy reach of Luton, including the manors of Fennels Grove in Hyde, Great-hampstead, Someries, and Luton Mortimer,[7] land in Stopsley, and (over the county boundary) more property at Kimpton and King's Walden in Hertfordshire. In mid-Bedfordshire, his first marriage (about 1441) with Elizabeth, widow of Christopher Preston and daughter and coheir of Sir John Drayton, brought John Wenlock possession of Drayton's manor in Kempston. And by the end of his life he had also acquired the manor of Aspley and lands in the "parishes" of Barton-in-the-Clay, Ion, Gravenhurst, and Lower Stondon. He also held the Bedfordshire hundred of Flitt. In London, he possessed a messuage called "le Ryall".[8] Following proceedings in the Court of Common Pleas, Wenlock's estates in Bedfordshire and Hertfordshire and his messuage in London were sold in 1477 to Bishop Rotherham of Lincoln, Chancellor of England. From the fact that John Cornwall, illegitimate son of John Lord Fanhope, in 1488 quit-claimed to the bishop's feoffees, it would appear that at least some of Wenlock's estates had been purchased by him either from Lord Fanhope himself (who had died in 1443, when Wenlock was one of his executors) or his feoffees.[9]

The date of the death of Wenlock's first wife is not known, but some time in the last ten years of his life he married (as his second wife) Agnes, a daughter of John Danvers of Cokethorpe (Oxon.), the widow of Sir John Fray, a former Chief Baron of the Exchequer (1436-48) who died in 1461. Agnes was herself a member of an important legal family. She was a sister of Thomas Danvers (a servant of Bishop Waynflete of Winchester) and of William Danvers (Justice of the King's Bench from 1488 to 1504), and half-sister of Robert Danvers (Justice of the Com-

5. Ibid., 305; *C.C.R., 1389-92,* 240.
6. *V.C.H., Beds.,* iii, 292.
7. Ibid., ii, 358, 364; *C.C.R., 1461-8,* 186.
8. *C.C.R., 1476-85,* 65.
9. *C.C.R., 1476-85,* 65; *Notes and Queries,* 5th Ser., vol. VIII, p. 462; vol. IX, p. 373.

mon Bench from 1450 to 1467).[10] If either of his two wives bore Wenlock children, none is recorded. Certainly, none survived him. And his heir at his death in 1471 was the son of his second cousin, namely, Thomas Lawley esquire of Much Wenlock.

When first John Wenlock was elected as knight of the shire for Bedfordshire in 1433, his family was well established in this county. His father, William Wenlock, had acted in a similar capacity in the "Unlearned Parliament" which sat at Coventry in the autumn of 1404, and a Sir Thomas Wenlock, who was probably John's elder brother, had more recently represented the county in the first four parliaments of Henry VI's reign (in 1422, 1423, 1425, and 1426). This Sir Thomas Wenlock had served in Henry V's campaigns in France, almost without interruption, as a member of the retinue of the King's uncle by marriage, Sir John Cornwall of Ampthill (later Lord Fanhope), with whom he was already connected and to whose service he remained attached, presumably until his death in 1429.[11] It is perhaps well to remember that Lord Fanhope had important estates in the Wenlocks' home county of Shropshire.

John Wenlock himself had also served in Henry V's expeditions into France and, at the time of the King's death in 1422, he was constable of Vernon-sur-Seine (half-way between Rouen and Paris).[12] At that date there is no evidence to connect him with Sir John Cornwall, but when next John Wenlock appears in the records it is as a witness to a grant to Cornwall (now Lord Fanhope), in January 1433, of lands in the north and south fields of Ampthill and of a grove at Steppingley (Beds.).[13]

It was in the following summer, in July 1433, that John Wenlock was first returned for Bedfordshire to parliament, seemingly after a disputed election. And then he began to be put on local commissions of royal appointment. On 27 December following he was commissioned (along with Lord Grey of Ruthyn and his own fellow-knight of the shire) to apportion among the poorer vills of Bedfordshire the county's share of the general deduction from the recently granted parliamentary subsidy. On 20 January 1434 he and his fellow shire-knight were ordered to submit lists of the notables of the county who should

10. J. C. Wedgwood, *History of Parliament, Biographies,* 256-8. Thomas Danvers was M.P. for Downton in 1459, 1472-5, and 1478, and for Hindon in 1467-8; William Danvers, M.P. for Taunton in 1467-8 and 1472-5, and for Hindon in 1478.
11. J. S. Roskell, *The Commons in tne Parliament of 1422,* p. 235.
12. *D.K.R.,* XLII, 452.
13. *Ancient Deeds,* VI, C 5812.

swear an oath (already taken by the Lords and Commons in the recent parliament) to maintain the King's peace;[14] and on 1 May following, Wenlock and his fellow-knight (along with Bishop Alnwick of Lincoln and Lord Fanhope) were instructed to act as commissioners to administer the oath.[15] After the next parliament of 1435, to which Wenlock was not re-elected, he was appointed on 29 January 1436 as a commissioner to make assessments in Bedfordshire for a graduated tax on incomes of over £5 from freehold lands and offices. A year later, in January 1437, he was back at Westminster as knight of the shire, and on 20 May following (along with his fellow-knight and again with Lord Grey of Ruthyn) was once more commissioned to share among the vills of the county its part of the general and now recurrent rebate of direct taxation.[16]

In the spring of 1437 Bedfordshire was seriously disturbed by acute tension between two rival local factions. One supported Lord Fanhope, himself a member of the King's Council, and the other, Lord Grey of Ruthyn. There was no actual violence occasioned. But the dispute led to a cleavage among the justices of the peace for the county. The reasons for the dispute are difficult to seek : it may have arisen, as one account puts it, because of the "marriage of a womman and for certain goodes", meaning perhaps a quarrel arising out of a conflict of feudal rights, or (as was more likely) on account of circumstances connected with the marriage of Lord Grey's son and Constance Holland, Lord Fanhope's step-daughter, who was a sister of the Earl of Huntingdon. However this may be, the closeness of the Bedfordshire estates of Grey and Fanhope, centred in Wrest Park near Silsoe and Ampthill respectively, gave their tenants ample opportunity to make reprisals on one another.

The immediate occasion of a threatened riot at Silsoe in May 1437, of which the King's Council had to take account in June and July following, arose out of the appointment of a royal commission, of which the members were mainly attached or favourable to Lord Fanhope. When, with Fanhope giving his personal support, they came to sit in Lord Grey's manor of Silsoe, one of Grey's council told them that their patent was procured to indict his lord's tenantry and that he proposed to hold the sessions of the peace after the special commission had sat. Grey himself was also there with a force of several hundred

14. *C.F.R., 1430-7*, 187; *C.C.R., 1429-35*, 271.
15. *C.P.R., 1429-36*, 373.
16. *C.F.R., 1430-7*, 261, 351.

men, so that Fanhope sent off to his place at Ampthill for his armour (*harneys*) and for reinforcements. But a J.P. who was one of the *quorum* refused the suggestion that there should be a session for the peace, and finally the two lords submitted to arbitration.[17] John Wenlock was present at Silsoe on the day of trouble as a member of Lord Fanhope's party. For one deponent before the King's Council (on 28 July) stated that in the end Lord Fanhope had a backing of 120 men, among whom there were no habergeons (*haberjons*) except two, one of which was worn by Wenlock.[18]

Arbitration or no, the quarrel between the two most important resident peers in Bedfordshire did not die down yet awhile. On 3 July 1438, described as "of Someries", John Wenlock was one of Lord Fanhope's sureties in Chancery when the latter undertook to keep the peace.[19] And when, on 12 January 1439, there occurred in Bedford itself something of a repetition of the Silsoe disturbances, and the supporters of the two magnates so collided at the sessions-house there as to prevent any peaceful execution of the commission of the peace, Wenlock was again involved as a member of Fanhope's affinity. The certifications of both parties were regarded as malicious by the royal Council, which again had to intervene, but Fanhope and his foremost adherents, Wenlock and a servant of his among them, were the first to receive, on 7 March 1439, a general pardon and release of all securities of the peace,[20] whereas their leading opponents were not pardoned until the end of May. Moreover, Fanhope's supporters among the J.P.s were reappointed on 12 March, when Grey's were not.[20]

At the time of this *émeute*, Wenlock was the King's escheator in Bedfordshire and Buckinghamshire, having been appointed on 6 November 1438.[21] He held the position for roughly a year (as was usual), and at the end of it was elected to represent Bedfordshire at the parliament which sat, first at Westminster from 12 November to 21 December 1439 and then at Reading from 14 January into the second half of February 1440. Along with his fellow-knight of the shire, William Peck, a lawyer, a former governor of Lincoln's Inn, and a member of Lord Fanhope's faction in Bedfordshire, and also with Lord

17. Roskell, op. cit., pp. 176-7.
18. *P.P.C.*, V, 59.
19. *C.C.R.*, *1435-41*, 186.
20. *C.P.R.*, *1436-41*, 246, 282, 578.
21. *P.R.O.*, *List of Escheators*, p. 5.

Fanhope himself, Wenlock was soon afterwards (on 20 April 1440) commissioned to make the usual apportionment of the county's share of the reduction of the parliamentary subsidies voted.[22]

John Wenlock esquire remained attached to Lord Fanhope. And he became his executor on 10 December 1443, on which day (or the next) Lord Fanhope died.[23] But Wenlock had already become a member of the King's Household. Here the dominant party of Cardinal Beaufort and William de la Pole, Earl of Suffolk, was now in a fair way to reduce the King's Council into being a mere instrument for the pursuance of its policy : at home, to control the royal authority in its own interest; abroad, to reach an accommodation with France. In this situation, Wenlock was very rapidly to attract attention and develop his own career. Just when he joined the corps of esquires in the King's pay is not known. It is possible that he had already done so by 5 June 1439, when as John Wenlock, *gentilman of London*, he made a grant to a London barber and Joan Wenlock of all his personal property, there and elsewhere, and of his debts.[24] By September 1441, certainly, he was *scutifer aule et camere Regis*.[25] Just as certainly, however, he was attached to the Court by the end of the previous June, when he began to be concerned with English diplomatic activities in France that were designed to bring an end to the war. In one way or another, on and off, such enterprises were to occupy his attention for the next four years.

III

Since 1439, the peace-party in England, directed by Cardinal Beaufort, had put its faith in the mediation of Charles, Duke of Orleans (a prisoner-of-war since 1415), once his liberation could be arranged. In November 1440 the Duke was set free to enable him to work for a peace, and this step was immediately followed by negotiations for a treaty with Duke John VI of Brittany. Lord Fanhope was a member of the English party which accompanied Orleans across the Channel. Wenlock may very well have gone with his lord on that occasion. This would perhaps explain how now he first came to take part in the

22. *C.F.R., 1437-45*, 140.
23. Lambeth Palace Library, Stafford Register, fo. 119[v].
24. *C.C.R., 1435-41*, 273.
25. Account Books of the Controller of the Household, P.R.O., E 101/409/nos. 9, 11, 16.

long series of diplomatic exchanges which ended (so far as he personally was concerned) with the marriage of Henry VI and Margaret of Anjou in 1445.

On 30 June 1441 Wenlock left England by the port of Poole for Cherbourg, not returning until 2 December. He came home apparently only to report progress, and on 20 December he went back again by the same route to rejoin his embassy. It was already in contact with the Duke of Brittany, the Duke of Alençon, and those other French princes whose discontent with Charles VII's government it was the object of the Dukes of Orleans and Burgundy to fan into a new *Praguerie*. These princes came together at Nevers in March 1442. The French King was, meanwhile, militarily very active in both Poitou and Gascony.

Wenlock next returned from France on 29 May 1442.[26] Again, he was not in England for long. On 16 July, as a year before, he was personally paid at the Lower Exchequer three months' wages at the rate of one mark (13s. 4d.) a day, that is £56, now as being about to accompany Ralph Lord Sudeley to the Duke of Orleans, who was expected to be in the marches of Brittany.[27] And, on 9 September, he was appointed a member of the embassy formally instructed to treat for peace with France, at the head of which were the Duke of York (in his capacity of Lieutenant-General of France and Normandy), the Cardinal of Luxembourg, the Archbishop of Rheims (the Chancellor of France), the Bishops of Lisieux and Bayeux, and the Earl of Shrewsbury.[28] Wenlock was clearly still involved in this business early in February 1443, when an assignment of £20 was arranged for him at the Exchequer. But he was himself then probably back in England, because on 8 March the Council authorized a further Exchequer grant of £4 (this time in cash) towards his sea-passage, when soon he should go out again. On this occasion, we are told, he was to carry correspondence to the Duke of Orleans. The payment was made on the very next day.[29] By 26 July following he was back once more in England, being now advanced at the Exchequer another quarter's wages— £60 13s. 4d.—as about to be sent overseas *pro materiis pacis*.

The war was going badly, and the Beaufort-De la Pole *bloc* at Court was preparing to make an effort to negotiate peace,

26. Enrolled Foreign Accounts, L.T.R., P.R.O., E 364/77, m. N.
27. Issue Rolls, E 403/745, m. 10.
28. T. Rymer, *Foedera*, XI, 13.
29. *P.P.C.*, V, 238; E 403/747, m. 13.

again with Orleans as intermediary, but now on the basis of a renunciation of the French Crown in return for the recognition of an English possession of Normandy and Guienne in full sovereignty. Such a pact, if it could be achieved, was to be cemented with a marriage between Henry of Windsor and the French Queen's niece, Margaret, daughter of René, Duke of Bar and Lorraine, Count of Provence, and titular King of Sicily and Jerusalem. In September 1443, about a month after an army under the Earl of Somerset had crossed to Cherbourg to undertake what proved to be a particularly disastrous expedition, Wenlock also landed there, having sailed from Poole (as usual) about 10 September. This time he stayed in France until the early summer of 1444, only returning to England on 27 June.[30] On 19 November 1443 he had already been given an Exchequer prest for £20, this sum being paid into the hands of Lord Fanhope, who died some three weeks later, leaving Wenlock (as we have seen) as one of his executors.[31]

Although Wenlock had gone over to France in the late summer of 1443, it must have been mainly "secret service" and other preliminary diplomatic work that engaged his time, because the Earl of Suffolk, the head of the main embassy *pro materiis pacis*, did not leave Portsmouth for Harfleur until nearly the middle of March 1444. The Earl's ambassadorial colleagues were Adam Moleyns (the new Keeper of the Privy Seal), Dr. Richard Andrew (the King's Secretary), Sir Robert Roos, and two esquires of the King's Chamber, John Say and John Wenlock himself.[32] (In the meantime, on 27 February 1444, the Council had warranted an Exchequer prest of £40 in Wenlock's favour.[33]) The English party, Wenlock among them, were at Tours by 16 April 1444. Here, on 24 May, Margaret of Anjou was betrothed to Henry VI, Suffolk acting as the King's proxy, and on 28 May the English ambassadors, finding the French adamant on the issue of sovereignty, arranged for a truce to last from 1 June 1444 to 1 April 1446.[34] A month later, on 27 June, Suffolk and his colleagues reached England, the two years' truce being immediately ratified.

Wenlock's work as courier and ambassador during the previous three years had entitled him, at a daily wage-rate of a

---

30. Enrolled Foreign Accounts, loc. cit.
31. P.R.O., E 403/751, m. 1, and see footnote 23.
32. E 403/751, m. 5.
33. *P.P.C.*, VI, 315.
34. *C.C.R., 1441-7*, 232; T. Carte, *Catalogue des Rolles Gascons, etc.*, ii, 310.

mark (13s. 4d.), to £427 odd, including some £21 for travelling charges : about half of this amount, £214 odd, was still owing to him, and, although repayment at the Lower Exchequer was promptly authorized on 17 July 1444, he had to wait until 17 February 1445 before he got a tally of assignment, and even then £100 was left out of the reckoning until, on 16 November 1445, another tally of assignment for that amount came his way. In February and July 1448, however, first one and then the other, he returned these tallies to the Exchequer as uncashable and took out two fresh ones, one of which again he had to renew in November 1448.[35] Precisely when, or even whether at all, Wenlock received final satisfaction on the score of his ambassadorial wages, is not known. But what was lost in one direction might be regained in another. And this (as we shall see) was to be so in Wenlock's case. Nevertheless, it is very likely that his position as one of many royal creditors occupied some of his time in the summer following his return from Tours in 1444.

Another matter which then closely concerned Wenlock was the administration of the affairs of his late master, Lord Fanhope, of whose executors he was one. His colleagues in this business included Archbishop Stafford of Canterbury, Ralph Lord Cromwell (the ex-Treasurer), and two serjeants-at-law. Already, in mid-May 1444, they had come to some arrangement about the disposal of Fanhope's Bedfordshire manors and estates in view of his having left no legitimate issue. This had been done in Wenlock's absence, but he was made party to it on his return. Now, however, there was trouble over the contrary claims of Fanhope's step-son, John Holland, Duke of Exeter, and Lord Cromwell. Cromwell sued one of Fanhope's feoffees, who was also one of the executors (Nicholas de Assheton, serjeant-at-law), for not selling him some of the property in accordance with Fanhope's will, and the case between the claimants had to be submitted to arbitration.[36] Another matter of concern to Wenlock in his capacity as an executor was the negotiation of a loan to the Crown of 4,000 marks out of Fanhope's estate, for which on 13 July 1444 he and his colleagues received a patent authorizing repayment from the customs of Southampton (but only after Cardinal Beaufort had been repaid *his* loans).[37]

In the autumn of 1444 John Wenlock again crossed over to

35. Enrolled Foreign Accounts, loc. cit.; Issue Rolls, E 403/755, m. 8; E 403/759, m. 6; E 403/769, m. 4; E 403/771, m. 7; E 403/773, m. 5.
36. *C.C.R., 1441-7*, 218-9, 229; *V.C.H., Beds.*, iii, 272.
37. *C.P.R., 1441-6*, 273.

France, this time as a member of the large party (nearly 300 strong) which accompanied Suffolk to bring back the new Queen. On 6 November, the day after Suffolk himself left London, Wenlock was appointed sheriff of the joint-bailiwick of Bedfordshire and Buckinghamshire, an office which he held for the next twelve months, being for much of this time, however, an absentee.[38] A week later, Suffolk's party crossed the Channel and made their way to Nancy, where the French Court was. Margaret of Anjou herself, however, was at Angers, a circumstance which may have been used by the French to help extract from Suffolk a promise to surrender English claims to Maine and Anjou. Margaret was, then, to come to England as a reminder of the policy of peace with France, a policy which went so crooked in its execution that England eventually lost all save Calais : the Queen was thus doomed to an unpopularity which her later adoption of an attitude of enthusiastic partizanship in English politics did nothing to lessen.

Agreement was reached about the marriage-settlement, but not until February 1445 did Margaret arrive in Nancy. Early in March the marriage was celebrated by proxy, and then, by way of Paris and Rouen, Margaret and her entourage came to the Channel coast, crossed from Honfleur, and landed at Portsmouth on 9 April. Suffolk's party's excursion to France and back had lasted exactly five months. By then, or at any rate before the Queen's coronation on 30 May 1445, Wenlock had secured his appointment among the select little group of the ushers of her Chamber, with pay of 1s. 6d. a day for himself and an extra allowance of 6d. for a *valettus*.[39]

Wenlock's recent diplomatic activities abroad had evidently given him contacts in Brittany. In November 1444 he was acting as an attorney for the Breton owner of a ship of Légue plundered of her wine-cargo on the Cornish coast. And it would appear that he acted as host to the Secretary of the Duke of Brittany and one of the Duke's pursuivants when, sometime in the spring of 1445, they came to England on official business; certainly, payments amounting to £20 were made to the two Bretons *per manus Johannis Wenlock*.[41]

Wenlock was himself still quite unsatisfied, as we have seen, of all that was due to him at the Exchequer for his own diplo-

38. *P.R.O., Lists and Indexes,* IX, *List of Sheriffs,* 2.
39. British Museum, Add. ms. no. 23938, fo. 14ᵛ.
40. *C.P.R., 1441-6,* 339.
41. E 403/757, m. 6.

matic work. But his membership of the Queen's entourage put
him in a highly favourable position for watching what went down
the drain of royal patronage, and, very shortly, circumstances
allowed him to take advantage of it. The prospective value of a
grant (in survivorship) to Wenlock and another usher of the
Queen's Chamber (Edmund Hampden) of certain royal lands
in County Dublin and of the offices of Treasurer of Ireland and
Constable of the castles of Dublin and Wicklow by a royal patent
of 16 May 1446 was somewhat doubtful, because it was made
contingent upon the death or retirement of Giles Thorndon,
who was then occupying them. Moreover, the reaction of Thorndon and the attitude of the Earl of Shrewsbury, the Lieutenant
of Ireland, who felt his control of the Irish administration
jeopardized by the manner of Wenlock and Hampden's reversionary grant, were unfavourable to it, and on 22 July 1446
Thorndon was confirmed in possession.[42]

The year 1446 was not, however, entirely an unsuccessful
one for Wenlock, so far as royal grants were concerned. A
profitable grant, and one made to Wenlock alone, was the one
which (as an usher of the Queen's Chamber) he received on 13
June 1446. This comprised the constableship of Cardiff castle,
together with the perquisites of the stewardships of the lordships of Glamorgan and Morgannok and the master-forestership
of all the forest there. These estates had belonged to Henry
Beauchamp, the late Duke of Warwick. On his death, a year
before (11 June 1445), the lands and the various offices attached
had come into the King's control because of the minority of
Anne, the Duke's infant daughter and heir, and Wenlock's grant
was for the period of her nonage. The Queen secured the wardship and marriage of the child herself on 15 June 1446, and
immediately some other members of her household were set up
with a number of offices on estates of the Beauchamp inheritance.
Within the next three months, however, this wardship passed
to William de la Pole (now Marquis of Suffolk), and the farm
of the Beauchamp lands in Warwickshire, Gloucestershire and
Worcestershire went to De la Pole, Ralph Lord Sudeley
(Treasurer of England and Chamberlain of the King's Household), and Sir John Beauchamp; and the farm of all the other
Beauchamp property in England and at Calais went to the same
men *plus* Richard Neville, Earl of Salisbury, the infant heiress's
grandfather (on her mother's side). But this rearrangement was

42. *C.P.R., 1441-6*, 424, 457.

not to prejudice any grants of offices made to Wenlock and four other members of the royal Household. Wenlock's grant, therefore, presumably held good until the infant heiress's death in January 1449, when the next heir to the Beauchamp estates was her aunt, another Anne, the wife of Richard, the eldest son of the Earl of Salisbury, who *jure uxoris* now became Earl of Warwick.[43] In comparison with this grant from the Beauchamp wardship, another grant, which Wenlock received on 7 November 1446, was of but minor significance : the wardship of William, the son and heir of Robert Ford of Hanslope (Bucks.) and an idiot from birth, and the custody (during William's life) of two messuages there and another two at Dunstable (Beds.), together worth 14 marks a year. This grant was to be confirmed to Wenlock, expressly for good service to the King and Queen, on 30 April 1448.[44] Another unimportant grant, but presumably worth the getting, was one which Wenlock shared on 15 January 1447 with a yeoman-usher of the Queen's Chamber : the custody of four Irish rebels then at Southampton, where they had put in with merchandise without a royal safe-conduct or licence.[45]

It was about this time that, having perhaps missed an opportunity of being returned to parliament in 1442 and 1445 because of absence abroad, Wenlock was again elected as knight of the shire for Bedfordshire to the parliament summoned to meet on 10 February 1447, first at Cambridge and then at Bury St. Edmunds (where Suffolk's personal influence was especially strong). Here died Duke Humphrey of Gloucester, still the heir-presumptive to the throne but long an enemy to the policy of peace with France. The government had intended his impeachment, and he died in custody. Some contemporaries imagined that he had died too conveniently (for his enemies) for his death to have been natural. They were probably wrong. But it is hardly likely to have raised the government's reputation that the single short session of 22 days came to an end on 3 March, only a week after Gloucester's demise.

Some two years later, to the parliament which met at Westminster on 12 February 1449, Wenlock was re-elected for Bed-

43. Ibid., 437; ibid., *1446-52*, 1. Richard Neville (the Kingmaker) had married Anne, daughter of Richard Beauchamp, Earl of Warwick (ob. 1439) by his second wife (Isabel Despenser), in the same year that her brother Henry married Richard Neville's sister Cecily. The constableship of Cardiff and the chief forestership of Glamorgan and Morgannok reverted to John Nanfan, an old Beauchamp retainer who had formerly occupied these offices, by royal patent of 7 July 1449.
44. *C.P.R., 1446-52*, 5, 152.
45. Ibid., 28.

fordshire. In the meantime, the domestic and foreign situation had seriously deteriorated : the surrender of Maine had become public knowledge, and the appointment of Edmund Beaufort, Duke of Somerset, to the Lieutenancy of France had had no result except to antagonize the Duke of York and his friends, and to allow the French to cast doubt on the honesty of English professions of a desire to make peace. All was immediately going well, however, with Wenlock, for by this time he had been made Queen Margaret's Chamberlain. Precisely when he was appointed to this office is not known. But certainly his promotion from his post as usher of the Chamber, which he was still holding in January 1447, had been secured before 15 April 1448. Then, described as occupying the office of Queen's Chamberlain, Wenlock had laid the first stone of the chapel of the Queens' College in the University of Cambridge.[46] The Queen was patron of the college, one of the few evidences of Margaret's compatibility with her husband being the interest she shared with him in educational schemes.

It is very probable that Wenlock's appointment as Queen's Chamberlain had been made the occasion of his being knighted. He was certainly a knight by the end of April 1448.[47] It was also in this year that, on 26 June, he was for the first time made a justice of the peace in Bedfordshire.[48] A fortnight later, it was expressly as Chamberlain of the Queen and as "King's knight" that he was granted for life (by patent of 9 July) the office of constable of the castle of Bamborough in Northumberland when the then constable, John Heron esquire, died. But nothing ever came of this grant.[49] Something more tangible came his way on 24 March 1449, shortly before the end of the first session of the 1449 parliament, in the form of a share in the wardship of John, the heir of Drew Barentyne, an Oxfordshire lawyer, the mother of the boy being Wenlock's own first wife's sister (Joan, another daughter of Sir John Drayton).[50]

The first parliament of 1449 sat at Westminster from 12 February to 4 April, from 7 May to 30 May, and then at Winchester from 16 June to 16 July. All summer, affairs were going badly in France : the English sack of Fougères gave Charles VII of France the pretext for formally declaring war, and by the

46. *D.N.B.*, XII, 1027.
47. *C.P.R., 1446-52,* 152.
48. Ibid., 586.
49. Ibid., 165, 526.
50. Ibid., 244; *V.C.H., Berks.,* IV, 387.

Addition to notes 46 and 47: *Catalogue of Manuscripts of St. George's, Windsor*, ed. J. N. Dalton, p. 200: 7 January 1448, John Wenlock, *knight*, Chamberlain of Queen Margaret.

end of the year Rouen and Harfleur had been won by the French. The parliament had granted a subsidy, and Wenlock, as an ex-knight of the shire, was commissioned on 1 August (along with his companion and Edmund Lord Grey of Ruthyn) to apportion the now usual rebate of taxation in Bedfordshire; on 25 September he was put on a commission to raise Crown loans in the county.[51] It was shortly after this time that the government incurred a remarkable indebtedness to Wenlock. On 18 December 1449 he received royal letters patent granting that he should be repaid a loan to the Crown of 1,550 marks (£1,033 6s. 8d.) from the issues of parliamentary and clerical subsidies, with a proviso that if such payment was not forthcoming the debt should be discharged at the rate of 500 marks a year from the customs of Southampton. In view of the fact that only two days later (on 20 December) the Lower Exchequer was ordered to deliver to an esquire of the Duke of Somerset, for the raising of a loan of £1,000 for the Duke's expedition to Normandy, certain jewels lately delivered to the Exchequer by Wenlock as one of the executors of the late Lord Fanhope, it is just possible that this deposit of Fanhope's jewels constituted Wenlock's loan. However this may be, nearly ten years later (as we shall see) it was still entirely unrepaid.[52]

Wenlock had not been re-elected to parliament, which, because of the critical situation in Normandy, had met again early in November 1449. Being one of the diplomatic agents who had engineered the French marriage and also the Queen's Chamberlain, Wenlock was probably more than content to watch the business of this parliament from the "side-lines". Adam Moleyns, Bishop of Chichester, a member of the embassy of 1444, on 9 December 1449 saw fit to resign his custody of the Privy Seal and shortly afterwards was murdered. And when, after the Christmas recess, parliament resumed its sittings on 23 January 1450, the Duke of Suffolk, the only important friend of the Queen, was impeached, and Archbishop Stafford gave place to Archbishop Kemp at the Chancery. The government was utterly discredited. Suffolk was banished on 17 March and, subsequently, on his way to exile, was murdered on shipboard on 2 May. Parliament was still in session, but now at Leicester, far away from the turbulence of the capital. Nothing is known of Wenlock's doings in the interval, except that on 22

51. *C.F.R., 1445-54,* 122; *C.P.R., 1446-52,* 298.
52. *C.C.R., 1454-61,* 154, 162, 318; *Wars of the English in France* (RS), *ed.* J. Stevenson, i, 504.

January 1450, the eve of the second session of the parliament, he had been commissioned by Henry VI to deliver to Bishop Aiscough of Salisbury certain jewels, sent by the Queen to the King by Wenlock's hands, in pledge for a loan of 1,000 marks.[53] At Leicester, the Commons succeeded eventually in extorting a Resumption Act from the government, but most of those who commanded influence at Court secured exemptions. And Wenlock was one of them.[54] Unlike so many other members of the royal Household, he seems not to have excited any particular animosity among those who took part in Jack Cade's Revolt in June and July 1450. The rebels were, however, entirely hostile to the Queen : before the revolt was put down, Bishop Aiscough, the King's Confessor, who had performed the royal marriage-service, was murdered down in Wiltshire, and Margaret's Chancellor, Bishop Bothe of Lichfield, and her own Confessor, Bishop Lehart of Norwich, were the object of threats to their safety.

There was as yet no issue of the King's marriage, and it was probably uncertainty regarding the royal succession which encouraged some to think of the claims of the Duke of York, who now returned from virtual exile in Ireland, forced his way through to the royal presence, and then awaited parliament's meeting in November 1450. The political history of the next four-and-a-half years is largely one of the Yorkists' attempts to make head against the alliance between the Duke of Somerset (Suffolk's successor in the task of propping up the Lancastrian dynasty) and Queen Margaret, whose political position was much strengthened by the birth of her son Edward in October 1453. Largely unsuccessful in getting his share of the control of affairs, except from March 1454 to the end of the year, when he acted as Protector during Henry VI's bout of insanity, Richard of York took up arms in the spring of 1455. His victory in the first battle of St. Albans on 22 May 1455, when Somerset lost his life, was the immediate outcome.

During these years of increasing tension and strain, surprisingly little is known of Sir John Wenlock's personal activities. In the summer of 1450, by a royal letter patent of 8 August, he was appointed to help assess in his own county of Bedfordshire those liable to pay a graduated income-tax on lands, wages, and fees.[55] On 10 September following he took out letters patent nominating as his agents in Ireland, where he evidently still

53. *C.P.R., 1446-52,* 311.
54. *Rot. Parl.,* V, 193a.
55. *C.F.R., 1445-54,* 171.

entertained hopes of becoming Treasurer, two attorneys who in 1448 had been jointly granted the offices of Chancellor of the Green Wax and Clerk of Common Pleas in the Dublin Exchequer.[56] On 1 October 1450 he and his wife, Elizabeth, procured a papal indult granting full remission of their sins when at point of death.[57] On 2 March 1451 he was involved in the negotiation of a ransom of £2,500 : to help liberate John Ormond esquire, the second son of the Earl of Ormond and next younger brother of the Earl of Wiltshire, who had been taken prisoner by John, Bastard of Orleans, at the surrender of the castle of Vernon in August 1449. How Wenlock came to be implicated in this business is not clear, but he seems to have been associated in it with Lord Scales.[58] As a King's Knight, he was granted on 15 June 1451 a patent authorizing the repayment (from the customs and subsidies of the port of London) of a loan of £200 that he had made to the Crown. A month or so later, on 18 July, he was one of a commission ordered to arrest and bring into Chancery (to answer certain charges) the vicar of Standon (Herts.), where the Duke of York's Chamberlain, Sir William Oldhall, was lord of the manor, and later in that same summer, by a royal patent of 2 September 1451, he was appointed as a member of a commission set up in Middlesex to investigate riots, unlawful assemblies, and all trespasses committed at the Abbey of St. Mary Graces and the Hospital of St. Katherine, which were both situated near the Tower.[59]

It was only a fortnight after this that Wenlock and his wife's brother-in-law, Drew Barentyne, a lawyer of Little Haseley (Oxon), were creating trouble for themselves. They were the opponents of the feoffees-to-uses of Alice, the widowed Duchess of Suffolk, and her son John, Duke of Suffolk, in an assize of novel disseisin relating to a tenement in Nuneham (Oxon). According to an information laid by Lord Lovell and other local J.P.s and by the sheriff and under-sheriff of Oxfordshire, Wenlock and Barentyne collected 3,000 men at Henley-on-Thames to impede the taking of the assize on 16 September 1451 and threatened their opponents and the assize-judges with death. On 15 March 1452 Wenlock was party to a recognizance for 500 marks, undertaking to produce Barentyne in Chancery or surrender him to the Fleet prison by 9 May, and on 20 March

56. *C.P.R., 1446-52*, 400.
57. *Cal. of Papal Registers, Papal Letters*, X, 70.
58. *C.C.R., 1447-54*, 266.
59. *C.P.R., 1446-52*, 452, 478, 533.

both men undertook (Wenlock in another recognizance for 2,000 marks and Barentyne in one for £2,000) to behave themselves while the assize was pending. The assize seems to have been taken at Henley before no less than the two Chief Justices.[60]

It was in relation to these happenings that on 21 April 1452, at the petition of the Queen, Wenlock secured a royal pardon of all trespasses, misprisions, riots, routs, contempts, congregations and other offences, and of any consequent outlawries. And this pardon he pleaded when, in the Court of King's Bench on 31 May 1454, he answered a plea of trespass against the peace and was accordingly acquitted. The pardon describes him as the Queen's Chamberlain, and he was certainly still occupying the office and receiving a fee of £40 a year by the hands of her Receiver-General at Michaelmas 1453.[61] Just when he ceased to be Margaret's Chamberlain is not known. Nor is there any information about him during the next year, which is remarkable. But it was on the King's side that Wenlock fought in the first battle of St. Albans on 22 May 1455, and it is at least possible that he was still the Queen's Chamberlain then and even later.

It was reported at the time that he was carried off from the engagement at St. Albans in a cart, "sore hurt".[62] If this was so, he soon recovered, for he was re-included in the Bedfordshire commission of the peace on 23 June 1455.[63] And, also about then, he was elected (for the sixth time) as knight of the shire,[64] parliament having been summoned on 26 May to meet at Westminster on 9 July. This parliament sat from then until 31 July, from 12 November to 13 December, and from 14 January to 12 March 1456.

It has been assumed, perhaps because there is some evidence to support the view that "the Yorkists openly rigged the elections" (McFarlanc), that the Commons in the 1455-6 parliament were wholly Yorkist in their political sympathies, and, this being the case, that Sir John Wenlock, whom the Commons chose as their Speaker on 1 July 1455, must have already changed sides and gone over to the Yorkist party. The changes in the govern-

60. Coram Rege Roll, K.B. 27/772, Rex Roll, m. 7; *C.C.R., 1447-54*, 338-9; *C.P.R., 1452-61*, 98.
61. *C.P.R., 1446-52*, 530; Duchy of Lancaster, Accounts Various, D.L. 28/5/8, fo. 12.
62. *Paston Letters*, iii, 28.
63. *C.P.R., 1452-61*, 660.
64. The returns to this parliament for Bedfordshire (and some other counties) have been lost. It is hardly likely that Wenlock sat for any county but Bedfordshire.

ment that followed closely upon the Yorkist victory at St. Albans do not, in fact, warrant us in assuming without question that York and his friends were now so comfortably and securely invested with the control of the royal authority as to be able to dominate the parliament. Archbishop Bourchier of Canterbury retained the Great Seal and, although his brother, Henry Viscount Bourchier, who was now appointed Treasurer, was brother-in-law to both the Duke of York and his friend the Duke of Norfolk, the chief members of the Bourchier family were regarded as holding a sort of middle place between the two main contending parties. Their brother, John Bourchier, now personally summoned to parliament for the first time (as Lord Berners), had been on the King's side at the battle of St. Albans, and so had their half-brother, Humphrey, Duke of Buckingham. More important than these indications is the fact that in their reluctance to accept York as Protector in the following November, the parliamentary peers in general were to show themselves by no means enamoured of York's ascendancy. Indeed, although during the first session of the parliament an Act was passed indemnifying the Yorkist leaders of responsibility for "the male journey" of St. Albans, it was reported that "to the . . . bill mony a man groged full sore nowe it is passed", and the first session also saw a fresh oath of allegiance taken to Henry VI. Simply to regard the parliament of 1455 as a partizan assembly operating in the Yorkist interest requires a considerable faith in some large assumptions.

Regarding the Commons, although the Yorkists worked hard to secure a favourable Lower House, the elections seem to have resulted in a far from disproportionate unbalance between their supporters there and its loyalist elements. Wenlock's election as Speaker confirms this impression. For, although there is no direct evidence at all to suggest that he was already a turncoat, there is at least some sort of evidence to suggest that he was still a loyal Lancastrian, apart from the fact of his having recently taken the King's part at St. Albans. It may very well have been, in fact, a connection of Wenlock's with the Bourchiers, whose policy was doubtless to prevent either party from going to extremes, which prompted the Commons or their steadier elements to choose him as their Speaker in July 1455 : only five days after the parliament finished on 12 March 1456, he and John (Bourchier) Lord Berners were the chief recipients of a royal licence to found a gild in the chapel of the Holy Cross in the parish church of St. Mary, Staines, together with a chantry where mass was to be celebrated expressly for the good estate of King Henry and Queen Margaret as well as of the founders, and for their souls after death.[65] That Wenlock was as yet no convert to Yorkist pretensions is perhaps also suggested by the fact that when, immediately after the beginning of the second session of the 1455 parliament on 12 November, by which time the King's mind had again given way, the Commons persistently pressed the obviously reluctant Lords to recognize York as Protector, they did so, not through their accredited Speaker, Sir John Wenlock, but through a member of York's own council, William Burley, a lawyer and knight of the shire for Shropshire. After Christmas the King was to recover, and, with York's Protectorship *ipso facto* brought to an end, the parliament was to be dissolved on 12 March 1456 with the chief contesting parties in a state of uneasy equilibrium.

Wenlock's own part as Speaker in the proceedings of the parliament of 1455-6 it is not possible to discern. The Commons made no money grant, and perhaps were not asked for one. But Wenlock at least did his best for himself. During the third and last session of the parliament two Acts were passed confirming arrangements for the repayment to the merchants of the Calais Staple of advances of cash for the defence of the place. This repayment was to be out of the customs and subsidies. It was, however, agreed that it should not prejudice the repayment out of the Southampton customs of the loan of £1,033 6s. 8d., which Wenlock had made prior to December 1449. (The whole of *this* loan was still unpaid.) He was now to receive preference. Moreover, in the Resumption Act which was passed in this same session, one of the Commons' own provisos of exemption safeguarded the Speaker's grant undertaking the repayment of his loan. Nothing, however, had been repaid by 7 December 1456, when the collectors at Southampton were warned that Wenlock's letters patent were still in force, nor by 31 May 1457 when, following a petition from Wenlock, they were instructed to pay him 500 marks a year until he was satisfied of the debt. Another two years went by and still nothing had been done, the order of May 1457 being repeated on 1 March 1459.[67] The government's attitude to Wenlock with regard to this loan may have been one factor among others eventually disposing him to transfer his support to the Yorkists.

65. *D.N.B.*, *sub* Sir John Wenlock.
66. *C.P.R.*, *1452-61*, 287.
67. *Rot Parl.*, V, 300b, 302b; *C.C.R.*, *1454-61*, 154, 162, 318.

After Henry VI's recovery from his breakdown and the end of York's Protectorship in February 1456, an uneasy state of tension existed between the Yorkist and Lancastrian parties for the next two years. Sir John Wenlock was authorized on 26 September 1457 to act on a commission of array in Bedfordshire, and on 17 December following he was appointed to a commission for sharing out in the county an obligation to supply 201 archers, its contribution to the force of archers voted in the parliament of 1453-4, now ostensibly to be used for the King's personal protection.[68] One of the useless "reconciliations" in this interlude before the final outbreak of open civil war occurred on 25 March 1458, when the chief antagonists walked together in procession to St. Paul's, the object of the demonstration being to suggest that the feuds set going or exacerbated by the first battle of St. Albans were at an end. Three weeks before this (on 4 March), Wenlock had been present as a member of the King's Council at one of its meetings at the Blackfriars in London.[69] This was at a time when the Lords were concerned to resolve the disputes between the Percies and the Nevilles, whose private war of the previous year was still threatening upheaval in the North. Just when he had joined the royal Council is not known, and it is impossible safely to say what interest his membership represented.[70] That on 14 May 1458 Wenlock was appointed as an ambassador (along with the Earls of Salisbury and Warwick and Viscount Bourchier) to treat with commissioners of Duke Philip of Burgundy about breaches of the Anglo-Burgundian truce suggests—because one of the mission's real objects may very well have been to establish private relations between York and foreign powers—that by this time Wenlock was moving towards Duke Richard's support, if, indeed, he was not already committed to it. He was an influential member of the embassy and was at Calais certainly to the end of June.[71]

Wenlock was still a member of the King's Council when on 26 August following he was ordered to come to a meeting at Westminster called for 11 October.[72] Before then, however, he was probably out of England again, receiving a safe-conduct on 29 August as going to Antwerp and elsewhere in the Burgundian

68. *C.P.R., 1452-61*, 403, 407.
69. *P.P.C.*, VI, 295.
70. On 13 May 1458 Wenlock undertook to abide the award of arbiters regarding all actions between himself and Archbishop Tregurry of Dublin, and the Archbishop was similarly bound in a recognizance for £400 (*C.C.R., 1454-61*, 276-7).
71. T. Carte, *Catalogue des Rolles Gascons, etc.*, ii, 342; *C.C.R., 1447-54*, 451.
72. *P.P.C.*, VI, 297.

lands on royal affairs, presumably a continuation of the previous
Anglo-Burgundian business.[73] This mission appears to have been
made an opportunity for opening up discussions for a series of
marriages between the sons of Henry VI and the Dukes of York
and Somerset and daughters of the Count of Charolais (the son
and heir of Philip of Burgundy) and the Dukes of Bourbon and
Guelders, or, alternatively, between these English boys and
daughters of Charles VII, the Duke of Orleans, and the Count
of Maine. These last proposals of marriage were seemingly
offered by Wenlock to the representatives of Charles VII at
Rouen in December 1458 and January 1459. Both sets of offers
were politely but firmly turned down.[74] The historian Ramsay is
disposed to treat these negotiations of Wenlock's as a private
mission on behalf of York.[75] There is no need to follow him so
far. Nevertheless, the fact that a Yorkist marriage abroad was
projected suggests the dynastic drift in York's intentions at this
time, and Wenlock's concern with it perhaps presupposes some
contact with York on his part. If this were so, it would go far
to explain how in the following year Wenlock came to be completely committed to membership of the Yorkist party.

IV

Next to nothing is known of Sir John Wenlock's activities in
1459 before the civil war broke out, a conflict for which both
Lancastrians and Yorkists had clearly been preparing.[76] The
open breach came when the Earl of Salisbury led a large Yorkist
force from Middleham across the northern midlands to join
up with York and Warwick at Ludlow. Intercepted by a Lancastrian force under Lord Audley at Bloreheath (Staffs.) on 23
September 1459, Salisbury won the day and got through. The
Yorkists' next move would probably have been to compel an
audience with the King, as they had done at St. Albans four-and-
a-half years before. The plan badly misfired, for a royal army
centred at Coleshill moved westwards against the numerically
inferior Yorkist forces, and at Ludford, in front of Ludlow,
after no more than a skirmish, the Yorkist leaders dispersed on

73. *D.K.R.*, XLVIII, 429; T. Carte, loc. cit.
74. *Wars of the English in France* (RS), *ed.* J. Stevenson, i, 361-77.
75. J. H. Ramsay, *Lancaster and York,* ii, 210-11.
76. Sometime in the late spring or early summer of 1459 a royal messenger went
down to Beds. with a writ of privy seal for Wenlock, probably summoning him
to a Council at Coventry (Issue Roll, P.R.O., E 403/819, m. 4; the messenger was
paid on 2 July 1459).

12 October. Certainly by this time Wenlock had gone over to the rebels, and while York fled to Ireland, he accompanied the Nevilles and York's eldest son, Edward, Earl of March, to Devon. From here they escaped (via Guernsey) to Calais, where Warwick had refused to give up his command, landing there on 2 November.[77] Two days after the rout of Ludford, on 14 October, a royal commission had already issued from Ludlow authorizing the seizure and retention of all Wenlock's goods and chattels as forfeit to the King.[78]

In the ensuing parliament, held at Coventry between 20 November and 20 December 1459, Wenlock was attainted of high treason and condemned to forfeiture along with twenty-two other Yorkist leaders and notables who had been under arms, the specific charge against them being that they had "imagined" the King's death by giving out that he was dead and causing mass to be said for him, "to make the people the lesse to drede to take the feld". On 16 March 1460 a committee of receivers was appointed for three years to administer the forfeited estates of the leading Yorkists, including Wenlock's.[79] In the meantime, on 3 February, Sir Baldwin Fulford, who had been entrusted with the keeping of the sea for the next three months, had been offered 500 marks for Wenlock's capture, half the sum offered for the capture of any one of the traitor peers. What had provoked this special offer was probably a surprise raid on Sandwich early in January, led by Sir John Dinham and Wenlock, when they had carried off to Calais Lord Rivers and his son, who had been guarding the Cinque Ports against the threat of a Yorkist landing. They repeated the raid in the spring when Osbert Montford esquire, who was about to take a force over to Guînes to assist the Duke of Somerset, was seized, carried off to Calais, and executed there on 25 June.[80]

It was on the very next day that the young Earl of March, Salisbury, and Warwick—and Sir John Wenlock with them—crossed the Channel and landed at Sandwich. Here they were met by Archbishop Bourchier. Within a week, gathering forces as they went through Kent, they were entering London. On 10 July the Earls of March and Warwick defeated the disheartened

77. *Collections of a London Citizen, William Gregory's Chronicle* (Camden Society, 1876), *ed.* J. Gairdner, p. 205; *Three Fifteenth Century Chronicles* (Camden Society, 1880), *ed.* J. Gairdner, p. 72.

78. *C.P.R., 1452-61,* 555.

79. *Rot. Parl.,* V, 348b; *C.P.R., 1452-61,* 572.

80. *Wars of the English in France,* op. cit., ii, 514, 772; Waurin, *Chroniques, etc.* (RS), vol. VI, pp. 283-4; Ramsay, op. cit., ii, 222.

Lancastrian army at Northampton. The Lancastrian lords left to guard the capital (including Lord Hungerford and Lord Scales), who had taken refuge in the Tower and stood a siege of over a week, surrendered on the following day. And a day later again, Wenlock, who (with the Earl of Salisbury) had been investing the Tower, took possession. He was ordered to arrest the Lancastrian lords whom he found there, but Lord Scales, "prevely" sent away, was done to death by the Thames watermen, and some of the Duke of Exeter's followers were later tried in the Gildhall by the Earl of Warwick and executed.[81] On 16 July Henry VI was brought to London; nine days later Warwick's brother, George Neville, Bishop of Exeter, became Chancellor; and on 30 July writs went out summoning parliament for 7 October. The Yorkist magnates were declared loyal on 8 August. And Wenlock acted during August and was still acting in November as a member of the royal Council, which was now, of course, largely Yorkist in its composition.[82] Whether Wenlock was elected to the parliament, and, if so, whether for Bedfordshire, is not known. It is, however, quite likely that he sat. His attainder was annulled at the beginning of the session, when the acts and proscriptions of the Coventry parliament were all repealed. On 10 October York claimed the throne, but a fortnight later had to be content with a compromise whereby the reversion of the Crown was settled on him and his heirs, an arrangement which Henry VI accepted on 31 October. A month later (on 1 December) parliament was prorogued to meet in January 1461. Already, on 14 November 1460, Wenlock had been granted for life the office of Chief Butler of England.[83]

The Duke of York was killed in the batcle of Wakefield on 29 December 1460, and the Earl of Salisbury was captured and without delay beheaded at Pontefract. Warwick was then in London with the King. Edward, York's heir, was at Ludlow. So was Wenlock, and he probably fought with Edward in his victory at Mortimer's Cross. Shortly afterwards, at the time of the second battle of St. Albans (17 February 1461), when Warwick was defeated by Queen Margaret's forces, Wenlock was still with Edward in Gloucestershire.[84] In the meanwhile, on 11 January, he had been put on a royal commission, appointed in

81. *Wars of the English,* ii, 773 ; *Three Fifteenth Century Chronicles,* op. cit., p. 75, 169 ; Ramsay, op. cit., ii, 229.
82. *P.P.C.,* VI,, 304, 306-7.
83. *C.P.R., 1452-61,* 644.
84. *Wars of the English,* op. cit., ii, 773.

Henry VI's name but in the Yorkist interest, ordered to imprison all those guilty of unlawful assembly and combination in the eastern and central midlands and to gather forces for this purpose, and on 16 January he was himself alone commissioned to suppress Lancastrian adherents in the south-east midlands.[85] On 15 January he had been appointed Steward for the Duchy of Lancaster estates in Middlesex, Essex, Herts., Beds., and Bucks.[86] And on 8 February, nine days before the second battle of St. Albans, along with the Earl of Warwick, and also with Lord Bonville and Sir Thomas Kiriell, both of whom were to be captured and executed after the battle, he had been elected a Knight of the Garter in a special chapter of the Order held in the Bishop of London's palace in the City.[87] Being with Edward of York in Gloucestershire, Wenlock escaped the risks of the battle of St. Albans. But when the Mayor of London ordered victuals and funds to be sent to the Queen, it was Wenlock's chief cook who helped the commons of the City to prevent this by taking possession of the supplies : Wenlock's cook was a "grete doer of thys mater".[88]

Presumably Wenlock returned to London with Edward of York on 26 February 1461. A week later and Edward declared himself King. He lost no time in following after the Lancastrian army, which had now withdrawn towards the north. Wenlock went with him : he was in command of the rear-guard in the skirmish at Ferrybridge on 28 March and, on the next day, fought in the crowning Yorkist victory at Towton, after which Henry VI and his Queen fled farther northwards, and eventually into Scotland, with a handful of the survivors of the battle. Three days later, on 1 April, Wenlock was commissioned to besiege the Lancastrian Duke of Exeter's castle at Thorpe Waterville (Northants) with forces which he was authorized to gather in that and the surrounding counties. And this he certainly did.[89] He was evidently at York after Edward IV's return from Newcastle upon Tyne when, on 10 May, he was made a member of

85. *C.P.R., 1452-61*, 655, 657.
86. R. Somerville, *History of the Duchy of Lancaster,* i, 605.
87. J. Anstis, *Register of the Order of the Garter,* 166-7. Wenlock was present at chapters held at Windsor in April 1463 and April 1467.
88. *Collections of a London Citizen, William Gregory's Chronicle,* ed. J. Gairdner (Camden Society, 1876), p. 214.
89. *C.P.R., 1461-7,* 28; Issue Roll, P.R.O., E 403/822, m. 6. (On 23 July 1461 Wenlock was owed £252 odd for the expenses of himself and his men between 17 March and 15 May "tam bene durante expectatione sua ante Thorpwatervyle per preceptum domini Regis quam in partibus borealibus et aliis locis in comitiva ipsius domini Regis".)

a commission of oyer and terminer to deal with the treason of the future Cardinal and Archbishop, John Morton, LL.D., then Chancellor to the young Prince Edward of Lancaster, who had fled with the Lancastrians. Wenlock had possibly been at Newcastle himself, for there on 1 May he had been confirmed, again by a grant for life, in his office of Chief Butler of England.[90]

By 14 June 1461 Edward IV was back in London. Already, on 23 May, during the King's absence in the north, writs had been issued summoning his first parliament to meet on 6 July. Wenlock was eventually (on 26 July 1461) summoned as Lord Wenlock to the Upper House. This was after the parliament had been adjourned to meet on 4 November.[91] He was already once more a proper member of the royal Council. In anticipation of Edward IV's coronation on 28 June, Wenlock was soon busy receiving bills of claims to render services during the great coronation feast. In this business he was acting, along with the Bristol lawyer, Thomas Young, on behalf of the King's brother George, who was too young to discharge his office of High Steward himself : the mayor and six burgesses of Oxford, among others, met Wenlock in this capacity when they claimed to do service in the royal buttery.[92] In the week following the coronation he secured the appointment of a yeoman in his own Chief Butler's office to purvey wines for the Household, on the ground that he was too busy to attend to this duty himself.[93]

Lord Wenlock's overload of administrative work is not difficult to understand. Not only was he Chief Butler of England and a member of the royal Council : on 26 July 1461 he was also appointed Chamberlain of the Duchy of Lancaster for life (as from the beginning of the reign), continuing to hold his local Duchy stewardships in Bedfordshire and Buckinghamshire, Essex, Herts., and Middlesex.[94] He soon began to engross offices on a considerable scale, along with other perquisites of his influential position. On 2 November 1461, two days before he sat in the Lords for the first time, he was given for life the office of Steward of the Duchy of Cornwall castle and lordship of Berkhamstead and, on 16 December, the stewardship of the royal lordships and manors of Langley Marish, Wyrardisbury, and Bledlow (Bucks.), to which group of estates in February

90. *C.P.R., 1461-7*, 30 ; 8.
91. *Lords' Report on the Dignity of a Peer*, IV, 958.
92. *Munimenta Civitatis Oxonie*, ed. H. Salter (Oxford Hist. Soc., LXXI), p. 222.
93. *C.P.R., 1461-7*, 14.
94. R. Somerville, op. cit., i, 417, 605.

1462 was added the lordship of Ruislip (Middlesex).[95] Having already been reappointed (in May 1461) as a J.P. in Bedfordshire, Wenlock was included in the commission of the peace for Buckinghamshire on 2 January 1462. And he was later also to be made a J.P. in Berkshire (on 28 February 1463) and in Herts. (3 October 1464).[96] The grant of the reversion of the office of Treasurer of Ireland, originally made to him in 1446, had become for the first time a reality when, on 21 December 1461, the last day of the parliament of 1461, he and Sir Roland Fitz-Eustace were appointed jointly to the office for life at a fee of £60 per annum, being also given the custody of the royal manors of Newcastle-by-Lyons and Saggart in County Dublin. Wenlock was still Treasurer of Ireland in March 1466.[97]

Grants of wardships and other custodies, especially of the lands of those disinherited as a result of sheer loyalty or political miscalculation in the recent dynastic revolution, soon came Wenlock's way. Only four days following the death of John, Duke of Norfolk, on 6 November 1461, Wenlock was appointed by the King to be governor of the seventeen-year-old heir and given control of all his estates and their official staff during his minority. (On 20 October 1462 Wenlock was granted 70 marks a year in aid.) The late Duke had been a firm Yorkist, but in the present situation it was agreed that Wenlock should have young Mowbray stay where he thought best.[98] On 15 March 1462 he was also made governor of Eleanor Beaufort (the eldest daughter of Edmund, late Duke of Somerset, and widow of the late Earl of Wiltshire who had been beheaded at Newcastle upon Tyne on 1 May 1461 and afterwards attainted for treason) and was given control of her jointure, with authority to appoint and dismiss her officials. Wenlock was then, too, made keeper of Eleanor Moleyns (the wife of Robert Lord Hungerford, who had also recently been attainted and was now a member of Queen Margaret's band of Lancastrian exiles) and of her two younger sons and only daughter, and he was given control of all the lands which had been held by Eleanor's husband in her right. Simultaneously, he was also made keeper of Anne, Baroness Hungerford's mother, who was now the wife of another attainted Lancastrian supporter, Sir Edmund Hampden, a former colleague of Wenlock's among the first ushers of Queen Margaret's

95. *C.P.R., 1461-7*, 54, 88.
96. Ibid., 560, 565.
97. Ibid., 84, 517.
98. Ibid., 105, 112.

Chamber who recently had been Chamberlain to Prince Edward of Lancaster and was now in exile at Bordeaux.[99]

On 12 March 1462, three days before these ladies were put into Wenlock's charge, he was given the wardship and marriages of the three daughters and coheirs of the widow of Robert Danvers and the management of her lands in Abbeyfield (Berks.). And on 14 March he was also granted the custody of the Norfolk estates of Sir Thomas Tuddenham, a recent Treasurer of Henry VI's Household (1458-60), who had been executed for treason in London some three weeks before. The custody of Tuddenham's other lands in Suffolk and elsewhere was made over to Wenlock in the following August. On the eve of his execution, Tuddenham had made Wenlock one of his executors, granted him for life a quarter of the barony of Bedford and his Norfolk manors of Oxborough, Shingham and Sparham, and instructed him to sell his Suffolk manors of Wangford and Elveden.[100] On 18 March Wenlock shared (with the Treasurer and the Controller of Edward IV's Household and with John Say) a grant of the custody of all the forfeited estates of John de Vere, Earl of Oxford, who, on 26 February, only six days after the execution of his son and heir (Aubrey), had himself been executed for treason on Tower Hill. This wardship presumably lasted until January 1464 when a younger son (who married the Earl of Warwick's daughter) was given royal licence to enter his estates.[101] The grant of the temporalities of the Cluniac priory of Much Wenlock in Shropshire, which, by a royal patent of 20 March 1462, Wenlock shared with John Lawley (his second cousin) and William Clerk (a local man who was an auditor of the Exchequer and constable of Bridgnorth), proved to be a custody of only short duration, for the vacancy in the priorate ended less than four months later (on 11 July).[102]

The above grants, though substantial, were necessarily temporary in character. On 12 March 1462, however, the Hertfordshire and Middlesex lordships and manors of the ex-Chief Justice of King's Bench, Sir John Fortescue, who had been recently attainted for his fidelity to Henry VI and was now in exile in Scotland, had been conveyed in an out-and-out gift to Lord Wenlock and the heirs of his body, along with the reversion of the

99. Ibid., 178, 181. (In December 1463 Wenlock was in possession of Hungerford estates at Hungerford (Berks.) as well. Vide Ancient Deeds, VI, C 6191.)
100. C.P.R., 1461-7, 178, 184, 195; N. H. Nicolas, Testamenta Vetusta, i, 297.
101. C.P.R., 1461-7, 229.
102. C.F.R., 1461-71, 79.

Gloucestershire manor of Ebrington. This grant was not only
to be exempted from the parliamentary Resumption Act of June
1467, but a year later was to be substantially enlarged when (on
28 June 1468) Wenlock was given (as from Easter 1467) Fortescue's estates in Wiltshire and Somerset. All these Fortescue
lands were, moreover, now conveyed to him and *his heirs or
assigns*. The conversion of the estate from one in tail to one in
fee simple was an important concession, in view of Wenlock's
failure to beget an heir.[103]

Lord Wenlock doubtless remained a member of Edward
IV's Council until he joined the great Lancastrian attempt at
restoration that was launched in 1470.[104] All his offices were
exempted from the Resumption Act of 1467, and he was then
still Chief Butler of England, Treasurer of Ireland, and Chamberlain of the Duchy of Lancaster. Regarding the first two of
these offices, his activities as executor to Lord Fanhope and Sir
Thomas Tuddenham, his governorship of the Duke of Norfolk,
and his custodies of the Hungerford, Fortescue, and Hampden
forfeitures, he had taken out a royal pardon of all offences on
24 March 1466.[105] Although still Chief Butler in July 1468, he
was replaced in this office, probably early in 1469 (certainly by
5 May 1469), by the Earl of Wiltshire. When he relinquished
the Chief Butlership, he was still actively engaged in Yorkist
diplomacy, and evidently still retained Edward IV's confidence.
There is nothing to suggest that he did not retain his other offices
until the Yorkist breakdown of 1470.

The north of England remained unpacified for over three
years after Edward's seizure of the throne in 1461. The Lancastrians, assisted by the Scots, enjoyed during this time a more
or less uninterrupted occupation of the most important of the
Northumbrian castles. It was in December 1462, when the King
himself went north, that Wenlock, along with Lord Hastings,
was in charge of the siege of Dunstanborough castle. The place
was won, but it was soon recovered by the Lancastrians and not
regained for Edward IV until the summer of 1464.[107] Apart from
this military interlude, Wenlock's most important services were
of a different order.

Shortly after the beginning of Edward IV's reign Wenlock

103. *C.P.R., 1461-7*, 183; *Rot. Parl.*, V, 581b; *C.P.R., 1467-77*, 99.
104. Lord Wenlock was certainly a member of the Council in the years 1461-3
(Issue Rolls, *passim*) and attended when his diplomatic services did not prevent it.
105. *Rot. Parl.*, V, 607b; *C.P.R., 1461-7*, 517.
106. Issue Roll, E 403/840, m. 9.
107. *Three Fifteenth Century Chronicles,* op. cit., p. 159.

had resumed activity in the diplomatic field, and from the summer of 1461 until his death he spent some time of every year overseas on ambassadorial work. At first this work was connected with the Earl of Warwick's obstruction of the foreign alliances attempted by the exiled Lancastrians. To begin with, there was special need for the Yorkists to nurse the Burgundian alliance : in the summer of 1461 Warwick began to negotiate for Edward IV's marriage with Philip of Burgundy's niece, Katherine of Bourbon, and on 8 August Wenlock was put at the head of an embassy sent to treat about English trade with Burgundy.[108] He and his fellows were at Calais early in October, after waiting three weeks for safe-conducts to visit the new King of France, Louis XI, as well.[109] The change of ruler in France temporarily eased the Yorkists' difficulties, and an Anglo-French truce could be arranged. A month later, on 12 November 1461, Wenlock was given power to decide cases of breach of the truce with Burgundy.[110]

Working in another direction, the Earl of Warwick managed to excite a revolt in the Scottish Highlands and detached the Scottish Queen-Mother, Mary of Guelders, from active support of the Lancastrian exiles, himself meeting her at Dumfries and Carlisle early in .1462. In this quarter also Wenlock was employed : on 8 February 1462 he was made a member of an embassy to the Earl of Ross; he may well have been involved in the Dumfries meeting; and he was certainly in Scotland in June and July 1462 with an embassy led by Warwick himself.[111] On 18 September following, he was again appointed to treat in Flanders with Burgundian commissioners for the continuation of truces and the establishment of mercantile intercourse, a *modus operandi* being arranged in December 1462 to last until November 1463.[112] As has already been noticed, Wenlock returned to spend Christmas on the Scottish borders, staying with Warwick at Warkworth and besieging Dunstanborough.

In August 1463, by which time Margaret of Anjou had been compelled for want of funds and support to leave Scotland for first Flanders and then France, Wenlock acted as a member of the English embassy sent to the conference at St. Omer, a meeting convened by the Duke of Burgundy to compose differences

108. T. Carte, op. cit., ii, 351.
109. *Paston Letters*, iii, 312.
110. *C.P.R., 1461-7*, 102; Waurin, *Chroniques, etc.* (RS), vol. VI, 412.
111. *C.P.R., 1461-7*, 115; *Archaeological Journal*, XVII, 53; *Paston Letters*, IV, 50.
112. T. Carte, op. cit., ii, 352-3.

between France, England, and himself; and Wenlock afterwards
went on to Hesdin to conclude a year's truce with France (as from
20 October), the first Anglo-French truce since 1449. This embassy was led by Warwick's brother, George, Bishop of Exeter
and Chancellor of England, and Henry Bourchier, Earl of
Essex. Wenlock is noted as having been present at Dover Priory
on 21 August 1463 when the Chancellor surrendered the Great
Seal for the time of his absence. At a meeting of the royal
Council on 4 July previous he had himself been present when
voted in advance a reward of £80 for his services on the embassy.[113] This work was no sinecure. From St. Omer Wenlock
was personally in touch with Edward IV, letters from him on
at least one occasion being sent direct from Picardy to the King
at Pontefract. In 1464 he was again much involved in cross-
Channel negotiations : he and Warwick were empowered on
28 March to treat for a continuation of the truce with France
and for friendship with Burgundy, the result of which was that
on 24 April orders could be given to proclaim a maritime truce
with France to last until 1 October. On 8 June Wenlock's
authority to work for extending the truce with France was
renewed.[114]

All these diplomatic *démarches* upset the Lancastrians'
calculations of foreign assistance. Moreover, their last military
bid for the time being was defeated at Hedgeley Moor and
Hexham in April and May 1464. Warwick's foreign schemes,
including a plan for a marriage between Edward IV and Louis
XI's sister-in-law (Bona of Savoy), nevertheless, were all but
frustrated by the King's secret marriage with Elizabeth Wydeville on 1 May 1464. If faced with a choice between the two
alternatives, Warwick himself would have preferred an alliance
with Louis XI rather than with Burgundy, where the pro-
Lancastrian sympathies of Charles, the Burgundian heir-
apparent, seemed to bode ill. And so Edward IV's marriage
removed an important diplomatic counter from Warwick's
board. Although Edward's position in England was now safe,
Warwick's mortification at being duped by the King, and their
pursuit of different policies abroad, destroyed the solidarity of
the Yorkist party. On 8 March 1465 Wenlock was once again
associated with Warwick as a keeper of the truce with Brittany,
and a couple of months later the two men were members of an

---

113 Privy seal warrants for issue, E 404/72/3, no 84; *C.C.R., 1461-8,* 202, 210;
Wars of the English, op. cit., ii, 781; Issue Roll, E 403/832.
114. T. Carte, op. cit., ii, 354; *C.C.R., 1461-8,* 259.

embassy charged to treat about a peace and for trade with the Duke of Brittany, and also to discuss matters with Louis XI and the Burgundian heir.[115] Whether Wenlock shared Warwick's continued aversion to the rapprochement with Burgundy, which eventually resulted (in July 1468) in the marriage between Charles of Burgundy and Edward's sister Margaret, is not known for sure. It is, however, very likely that he did. The two men were much together. In March and June 1466 and in May 1467 Wenlock was again associated with the Earl in diplomatic exchanges with both Burgundy and France.[116] Moreover, when, in December 1467, Louis XI's emissary, Sir William Monypenny, came to England to encourage Warwick in his by now rebellious attitude to the Court, an attitude which was giving the exiled Lancastrians great hopes, Wenlock was one of Warwick's own council in London with whom the Frenchman conferred.[117] Again, when at Whitsuntide 1468 a bearer of letters from Margaret of Anjou was captured at Queenborough and he "appealed" John Hawkins, a servant of Wenlock's, of receiving letters from Margaret, Hawkins is alleged to have said many things against his own lord before he was condemned for treason and executed at Tyburn.[118] If this was so, the charge seems to have been passed over at Court. At least it did not prevent Wenlock from getting important additions to his already considerable holdings of Chief Justice Fortescue's lands shortly afterwards.

Wenlock is just as likely as Warwick to have resented Edward IV's attempts, exemplified in his partiality for members of the Queen's family (the Wydevilles), to abandon those by whose help he had won and retained the throne, in favour of new friends. Like Warwick at this time, evidently Wenlock dissembled his feelings of opposition to the pronounced pro-Burgundian, anti-French trend of Edward IV's policy. And he continued to be employed in the conduct of foreign affairs. On 8 June 1468 he was paid £100 in advance as a member of the embassy which was to conduct the King's sister Margaret to Burgundy for her marriage with Charles the Bold. Another duty of this embassy was to treat at Bruges for the settlement of commercial differences, difficulties arising out of the policy of the Calais Staple and the embargo on English cloth in the Bur-

115. *C.P.R., 1461-7,* 450; T. Carte, op. cit., ii, 355.
116. T. Carte, op. cit., ii, 357-8.
117. Ramsay, op. cit., ii, 327.
118. *Wars of the English,* op. cit., ii, 790.

gundian lands.[119] And even a year later, when Wenlock had been relieved of his office of Chief Butler, he was commissioned, first on 6 May and then on 15 May 1469, to attend a diet at Bruges for the settlement of further trade disputes with Burgundy. (The same embassy was also appointed on 12 May to negotiate for peace with the Hanseatic League.)[120]

By this time, for over a year Warwick had been suspect to the Court, but he kept his plans well hidden : Lancastrian movements at his instigation in the autumn and winter of 1468 came to nothing but could not be laid at his door. And then, in the summer of 1469, after he had married his daughter Isabel to the Duke of Clarence, Edward IV's next younger brother, at Calais, and had incited his kinsmen and friends in Yorkshire to revolt, Warwick threw off the mask and returned to England, his intention being to bring the Wydevilles down and restore himself to power. Despite the rebel victory at Edgcote (26 July), the capture of the King, and the execution of the Earls of Pembroke, Rivers, and Devon, Warwick failed to re-establish himself in control. Consequently he continued to intrigue and, with Clarence, fomented the disturbances in Lincolnshire which Edward IV crushed near Stamford on 12 March 1470 in the "battle" of Lose-Coat Field.

V

Unable to arouse sufficient support, Warwick and his son-in-law fled the country about the middle of April 1470 and made for Calais. Here Lord Wenlock, apparently installed by Warwick himself as his deputy in command, refused him entry.[121] It is just possible that Wenlock so acted in order to ensure that Warwick would do just what in fact he did—throw himself into an alliance with the exiled Lancastrians, a drastic step which Wenlock himself was to take before so very long and may already have been seriously contemplating. At this juncture, however, it is more probable that Wenlock acted as he did towards Warwick because the garrison and the merchants of Calais were all on the King's side and pro-Burgundian, and because to have admitted Warwick would simply have been dangerous for himself. Wenlock was evidently taking no risks. His own immediate

119. P.S. warrants for issue, E 404/74/1, no. 35; *D.K.R.*, XLV, App. 1, p. 332; T. Carte, op. cit., ii, 359.
120. *D.K.R.*, XLV, loc. cit.; T. Carte, op. cit., ii, 360.
121. *D.N.B.*, XX, 1165.

safety and advantage were probably primary considerations. Certainly, we have to take into account the statements of the chronicler Commines, who says that the Duke of Burgundy now allowed Wenlock a pension of 1,000 *écus* and that Edward IV gave him full command of Calais. And the latter assertion, at least, is borne out by Wenlock's appointment on 26 May following as Lieutenant of Calais and the Marches.[122] Meanwhile, refused entry at Calais, Warwick landed at Honfleur on 5 May.

Within the next three months Wenlock's duplicity, the pressure of the diplomatic situation, and the near-hopelessness of the exiled Margaret of Anjou resulted in an alliance between Warwick and the Lancastrian Queen, Warwick undertaking to restore Henry VI on condition that the Lancastrian heir-apparent, Prince Edward, married his second daughter, Anne. This conclusion agreed, Warwick and his forces crossed the Channel and landed in Devon on 13 September 1470. Three weeks later Edward IV was in flight to the Netherlands. Already, at Calais, Wenlock had twisted round and declared for the new and ill-assorted Lancastrian coalition : Commines, at this time visiting the town as Burgundy's agent, found the badge of the ragged staff of Warwick being worn by all and the white roses of York discarded. In London, Henry VI was set free, and the Re-adeption began on 6 October. Summoned on 15 October, parliament met on 26 November to reverse the anti-Lancastrian Acts of Attainder and to re-establish the Lancastrian royal succession. Wenlock was not summoned. But it can only be because he was still out of the country.

It was not long before Edward IV was back in England. Landing in Yorkshire, he marched on London and got possession of King Henry. And on 14 April 1471 he won the battle of Barnet, where Warwick was killed. Wenlock had meanwhile joined up with his old mistress, Queen Margaret, and with her and Prince Edward had crossed from Honfleur.[123] They landed at Weymouth in Dorset on the very day of Barnet Field. Nevertheless, their force was soon swollen with levies from the West Country. So encouraged, and probably intending to join forces with Henry VI's half-brother, Jasper Tudor, as he moved out of Wales, they marched up through Exeter, Glastonbury (where

122. T. Carte, op. cit., ii, 361.
123. Waurin, *Chroniques, etc.*, VI, 656-7, 663; *The Arrivall of Edward IV, etc.* (Camden Society, O.S., vol. 1), *ed.* J. Bruce, p. 15. Polydore Vergil (*English History, ed.* Sir Henry Ellis [Camden Society, vol. 29, p. 148]) is clearly at fault in saying that Wenlock and others met the Queen at Beaulieu Abbey.

Wenlock deposited certain of his plate and jewels with the abbot),[124] Bath, and Bristol, to Gloucester. Arriving on 3 May, they found the gates of Gloucester locked against them. So they moved on to Tewkesbury. And here, on the following day, they faced Edward IV and his army. Wenlock was in charge of the Lancastrian centre-battle with Prince Edward and Sir John Langstrother, the Prior of the Hospital of St. John of Jerusalem in England. In the Lancastrian disaster which ensued, he fell in the fighting.[125]

Lord Wenlock was buried in Tewkesbury abbey, Doubtless his intention had been to be buried in the chapel that he had erected on the north side of the chancel of the parish church of St. Mary of Luton, where in the east window he was once depicted, wearing the Yorkist collar of livery of suns and roses, and mentioned as the founder of the chapel.[126] As recently as January 1466 he had petitioned Pope Paul II that all parishioners of Luton St. Mary's, for whom he had secured an indult enabling them to eat milk-foods in Lent and at other fasts, should pray for his good estate in life and after his death say for his soul, if clergy, the psalm *Miserere mei Deus*, or, if lay-men, a *Pater Noster* and *Ave*.[127]

Lord Wenlock's second wife, Agnes Danvers, survived him. And some time after September 1473 she married Sir John Say of Broxbourne (Herts.). A former member of the Lancas-trian Household and sometime Under-Treasurer of England, Chancellor of the Duchy of Lancaster under Edward IV, a mem-ber of his Council, and Speaker in the parliaments of 1449-50, 1463-5, and 1467-8, Say seems to have trimmed towards the Lancastrians in the crisis of the Re-adeption of 1470-71. But if this was so, it was in no decisive manner, and, unlike Wenlock, Say came safely through. Wenlock had had some private deal-ings with Say at the time of the latter's first marriage in 1446 and more recently in April 1466 (over land at Bedwell,

---

124. *Catalogue of Ancient Deeds*, iii, D 1278.
125. *The Arrivall* (Camden Society), op. cit., p. 30; Waurin, op. cit., VI, 671; *Paston Letters*, V, 104; C. L. Kingsford, *English Historical Literature in the Fifteenth Century*, App., p. 377. I know of no extant contemporary warrant for the late Tudor historian Holinshed's report that Wenlock was killed by the Duke of Somerset for attempting a final treachery to his own side on the battlefield itself. Such an act on Wenlock's part is not, however, unthinkable.
126. *The Topographer and Genealogist*, ed. J. G. Nichols, vol. 1 (1846), p. 77.
127. *Cal. of Papal Registers, Papal Letters*, XII, 492. As early as July 1455 Wenlock had himself procured an indult authorizing the confessor of his choice to license him to eat milk-foods in Lent and at other fasts and to commute his fastings into other works of piety (ibid., XI, 16).

Herts.).[128] But, these matters apart, the two men must have been
well acquainted : their careers had run along roughly parallel
lines, except that Say had never achieved the dignity of a peerage
in return for his support of Edward IV. Agnes, Wenlock's
widow, survived this third husband, too, but only by a couple of
months. She died in June 1478 and was buried with Sir John
Fray (her first husband) in the City church of St. Bartholomew
the Less. By her will she here caused to be established a chantry
for herself and each one of her three husbands, including Lord
Wenlock.[129] In this respect Wenlock was well provided for, even
apart from his own chantry at Luton : as far back as 1462 a
London clothier's widow had provided a chantry in St. Christopher's church in Breadstreet Ward, in which prayers were to
be said for Edward IV, for his father, Richard of York, and for
Lord Wenlock.[130] Incidentally, Wenlock had had relations with
a number of citizens of London : in 1463, for instance, he had
been feoffee to Geoffrey Boleyn, alderman of London, in four
Norfolk manors.[131]

By neither of his two wives, Elizabeth Drayton or Agnes
Danvers, did Wenlock have children, and at his death his heir
was Thomas, the son of his second cousin, William Lawley of
Much Wenlock, who, in 1477, surrendered to Bishop Rotherham of Lincoln whatever right he was deemed to hold in Lord
Wenlock's forfeited lands. The bishop had secured a grant of
them sometime between 1471 and 1475, when he was Chancellor
of England.[132]

128. *C.C.R., 1441-7, 441*; *Catalogue of Ancient Deeds*, i, B 412.
129. Somerset House, Register Wattys, fo. 34.
130. *C.P.R., 1461-7, 180*. Wenlock had close relations with the abbey of St.
Albans which was the patron of Luton parish church : in 1466-7, for instance,
two of his chaplains were given abbey livings at East Barnet and Letchworth
(*Registra Johannis Whethamstede, etc.* (RS), *ed.* T. H. Riley, vol. ii, p. 59).
131. *C.C.R., 1461-68*, 82, 144, 207 (Boleyn's feoffee), 457.
132. *V.C.H., Beds.*, ii, 305, 352, 358, 364; *C.C.R., 1476-85*, 65.

11

SIR THOMAS TRESHAM, KNIGHT
SPEAKER FOR THE COMMONS UNDER HENRY VI[1]

SIR THOMAS TRESHAM of Sywell and Rushton, was knight of the shire for Buckinghamshire in the Parliament of February 1447, for Huntingdonshire in the Parliaments of February and November 1449, for Northamptonshire in those of March 1453 and June 1467, and probably for Northamptonshire in the Coventry parliament of November 1459 when he was Speaker for the Commons.[2]

The Act of Attainder in the first Yorkist Parliament of 1461, by which Thomas Tresham incurred forfeiture of his estates, and the subsequent grants made of them to various supporters of Edward IV, furnish a fairly complete list of the landed properties of which he was possessed by that date. Those in Northamptonshire within easy reach of Northampton comprised the manors of Sywell, Hannington, Brampton, and Great Houghton, together with lands in Earls Barton, Ecton, Wellingborough, Hardwick, and Little Harrowden. In the east of the county and within easy reach of Higham Ferrers, he held the manors of Stanwick and Ringstead and lands in Knuston and Aldwincle. To the north of the main estates round Northampton was another group, including the manors of Rushton and Hazelbeech, with lands also at Rothwell and Hanging Houghton. In Northampton itself Tresham possessed burgages. In north-east Buckinghamshire he held the manors of Broughton Parva and Wavendon, and there was property at Stanton Barry and Bradwell, again in north Buckinghamshire. He also possessed some estates in Leicestershire, Rutland, Bedfordshire and Middlesex.[3]

Presumably some of these estates came into Thomas Tresham's possession as a result of his marriage with Margaret, daughter of the William, Lord Zouche of Harringworth who died in 1415, and sister of the William, Lord Zouche who was summoned to Parliament from 1426 to his death in 1463.[4] When Thomas Tresham married her, Margaret Zouche was the widow of Edmund Lenthall. The date of the marriage is not known, but Margaret was presumably still young at the time of her second marriage, and she was certainly the mother of Thomas Tresham's son and heir, John. She died at some time between December, 1483, and February, 1484.[5] Her niece, Margaret de la Zouche, was wife to William Catesby, Speaker in Richard III's only Parliament.

In the year following William Tresham's grant of the promise of the Chancellorship of the Duchy of Lancaster on the next vacancy, he and his son, Thomas, on 27 November, 1443, were appointed for life to share the stewardship of all the Duchy estates in the shires of Northampton, Huntingdon, Bedford and Buckingham, except the lands of the Honour of Leicester

[1] In this article the following abbreviations have been used in the footnotes:—
C.C.R. = Calendar of Close Rolls.
C.F.R. = Calendar of Fine Rolls.
C.P.R. = Calendar of Patent Rolls.
H.M.C. = Historical MSS. Commission.
P.R.O. = Public Record Office.
Rot. Parl. = Rotuli Parliamentorum.
An account of William Tresham of Sywell, Sir Thomas Tresham's father, was contributed by Professor Roskell to the 1957 issue of Northamptonshire Past & Present.
[2] Official Return of Members of Parliament, i. 335, 338, 342, 358, xxiv; Calendar of Fine Rolls, 1452-61, 44.

[3] C.P.R., 1461-7, 111, 153, 225, 369; ibid., 1467-77, 540; ibid., 1477-85, 194; G. Baker, History of Northants, i. 371; ibid., ii. 36, 69, 106, 373.
[4] G. Lipscomb, The History and Antiquities of the County of Buckingham, i. 176.
[5] Calendar of Ancient Deeds, vi. C5016; C.F.R., 1471-85, 260. There seems to be no basis for Wedgwood's assertion that c. 1450 Thomas Tresham married, as his second wife, Alice, daughter of Thomas Mulsho, knight of the shire for Northants in 1450, and niece of Sir Edmund Mulsho, a member of Duke Richard of York's council. (J. C. Wedgwood, History of Parliament, 1439-1509, Biographies, p. 870).

in Northants.[6] It was again doubtless the father's services and "pull" which enabled him on 12 February, 1445, to secure a royal patent associating his son with him in a grant for life in survivorship of an annuity of £40 (already enjoyed by William since May, 1440) charged on the royal manor of King's Cliffe (Northants).[7] A year later, on 17 March, 1446, the Treshams were given another joint grant for life in survivorship (as from Michaelmas 1445),—a further annuity of £40 but this time to be taken at the hands of the Receiver-General for the Duchy of Lancaster.[8] By the end of the year 1446 at latest, Thomas Tresham had joined the Royal Household, for on 16 November, 1446, he was one of the 240 odd *scutiferi aule et camere Regis* and entitled as such to a royal livery of robes worth £2 a year. He was still an esquire of the King's Hall and Chamber in September, 1452, and doubtless continuously served in the Household in this capacity until his promotion to be an usher of the King's Chamber sometime before 25 March, 1455.[9] It was, therefore, as a member of the Royal Household that he was for the first time elected as knight of the shire to the short Parliament which met at Bury St. Edmunds in February, 1447, when his father acted for the third time as Speaker for the Commons. William sat for Northants, Thomas for Bucks. Already by patent of 13 April, 1446, Thomas had been appointed with his father as a justice of the peace in Huntingdonshire, and it was as knight of the shire for this county that he was again returned to the next Parliament which met at Westminster in February, 1449, his father being re-elected for Northants. Thomas Tresham was to be a member of the commission of the peace in Huntingdonshire without intermission until July, 1459.[10]

When his second Parliament met, Thomas Tresham was the King's escheator for Northants and Rutland. His term of office ran from 6 November, 1448, to 11 December, 1449.[11] He was still escheator, therefore, when re-elected for Huntingdonshire to the Parliament of November, 1449—June, 1450, in which his father once again acted as Speaker, an office which occasioned his leading the impeachment for treason of the Duke of Suffolk. On 26 April, 1450, only three days before the third and last session of this Parliament began at Leicester, Thomas was included among a group of commissioners of oyer and terminer in Northants, authorized to investigate the treasons of John Harris, formerly a "shipman" of Terrington (near Malton, Yorkshire). As the King and his lords passed through Stony Stratford on their way to Leicester via Northampton, John Harris had used a threshing flail in front of them "to show that the Duke of York then in Yreland shuld in lyke manner fight with traytours at Leicester Parliament and so thrashe them downe as he had thrashed the clods of erthe in that towne;" he was arrested, imprisoned in Northampton castle, and then condemned, after Thomas Daniel, an Esquire of the Body and a member of this commission had "labored his deathe with yomen of the crowne."[12]

The parliamentary session which followed these incidents saw the passage of an Act of resumption on 6 May, 1450, and the Treshams lost their jointly held annuity of £40 charged on King's Cliffe, but no more than this apart from another annuity of £20, the one charged on the manor of Brigstock enjoyed by the father alone.[13] The Parliament broke up early in June on receipt of news of Jack Cade's rising in Kent and the attack on London.

The English hold on the lands won by Henry V in France was by this time restricted to a few important 'bridgehead' towns on the coast, and there was even great danger to Aquitaine. At home the government was feeble and only with great difficulty able to cope with a crisis. In the late summer of 1450 York returned from Ireland to impose his will on the Lancastrian government, and, despite his being treated as a traitor by the Court party who ordered his return to be opposed, the Treshams, father and son together, set out from Sywell on 23 September to meet the Duke as he moved down Watling Street towards London. They had not gone far before, at Thorplands near Moulton, they were set on in an ambush; the father was either killed outright

[6] R. Somerville, *History of the Duchy of Lancaster*, vol. i, 586.

[7] *C.P.R.*, *1441-6*, 331.

[8] Duchy of Lancaster, Accounts Various, D.L. 28/5/6.

[9] P.R.O., Household Account Books, E.101/409/16 (1446-7), E101/410/1, 6.9; E404/70(2)/48.

[10] *C.P.R.*, *1441-6*, 472; ibid., *1446-52*, 590; ibid., *1452-61*, 667.

[11] P.R.O., *List of Escheators*, 96.

[12] *C.P.R.*, *1446-52*, 383; C. L. Kingsford, *English Historical Literature in the Fifteenth Century*, Appendix xii, "John Piggot's Memoranda," p. 371.

[13] *C.C.R.*, *1447-54*, 391.

or soon died of his wounds, the son being merely injured.[14] Although both of the Treshams owed everything to their membership of the Court party, it is of course possible that they sought re-insurance for their political future by interviewing or joining Richard of York. Some support for such a view of the significance of their journey to see York might be discerned in the fact that the murder of the ex-Speaker was popularly attributed to the men of Lord Grey of Ruthin, a Lancastrian supporter at this time. But it should also be remembered that it was York, as Tresham's widow's petition to the King in the next Parliament makes clear, who had taken the initiative in writing to Tresham senior, presumably demanding his attendance; that the ex-Speaker's position as one of the Duke's feoffees might have prompted this demand and Tresham's concurrence; that Thomas Tresham's position in the Royal Household was neither then nor later in jeopardy nor his basic fidelity to the House of Lancaster ever in doubt; and that Tresham, senior, might very well have excited local hostility on the part of men who perhaps thought to use his meeting with York to justify their intended outrage.

Thomas Tresham was well enough recovered a month after the murder of his father and his own wounding to attend the Northamptonshire elections to the November, 1450, Parliament, but he was not elected to his father's seat, although his uncle, William Vaux, was sheriff; nor was he re-elected for Huntingdonshire. His father's influence is likely to have been behind his earlier elections, but in any case this was not a time when a young member of the King's Household could reasonably entertain great expectations of election to Parliament. In all probability Thomas Tresham was in attendance at the Court during the sessions of this mainly anti-curialist Parliament: his mother petitioned for her husband's slayers to be brought to justice in the Court of King's Bench and asked that, if she were unable to bring a criminal appeal, his next heir might have the benefit of the procedure for which she was petitioning; and this was allowed.[15] Thomas Tresham seems to have succeeded his father as Chancellor for the feoffees of those estates of the Duchy of Lancaster appropriated to the fulfilment of Henry VI's will.[16] But in 1451 he certainly had trouble with his mother, apparently over the execution of the terms of her late husband's will regarding his bequests of moveables to her, and on 22 October, 1451, her brother, William Vaux esquire, and Thomas Salisbury, Archdeacon of Bedford, as arbiters, made an award at Sywell between her and her son which required that she be satisfied of 1000 marks, this sum being made up from some of her husband's debts, including his 'knyghtes spençes' (his wages as knight of the shire) and what was due to him from the King.[17]

That Thomas Tresham was regarded as a safe Household supporter of the Lancastrian administration in this year of tension between the parties of York and Somerset, is clear from his appointment on 8 November, 1451, as sheriff of Cambridgeshire and Huntingdonshire,[18] and during his year of office he was for the first time appointed as a justice of the peace in his own county of Northampton (on 9 July 1452), a commission he continued to hold until September, 1460, when the Yorkists had secured control of the government.[19] He was elected as knight of the shire for Northants, for the first time, to the Parliament which met at Reading in March, 1453. At the beginning of the year he had served on a commission set up to raise Crown loans in the county, ostensibly to assist the Earl of Shrewsbury's vain efforts to stave off complete disaster in Aquitaine. During the second session of the Parliament, held at Westminster, (namely, on 8 June, 1453), Tresham was appointed *ex officio* as knight of the shire, to help his fellow knight, Sir William Catesby of the Royal Household, and Lord Rivers to apportion among the poorer vills of Northants that share of the reduction of the recently granted subsidy to which the county was entitled. On 12 July following, ten days after the session ended, he was made a commissioner of oyer and terminer in the North Riding of Yorkshire regarding felonies, trespasses, illegal assemblies and confederacies, and liveries of badges, gowns and caps, the reference here being

---

[14] *Rot. Parl.*, v. 212. See also *Northamptonshire Past and Present* (1957), vol. ii. no. 4, p. 201, for a detailed account of the murder. Thorplands is 4 miles from Sywell and 3 from Northampton on the main Northampton—Kettering road.

[15] *Rot. Parl.*, v. 212.

[16] R. Somerville, *op. cit.*, vol. i, p. 211, note 4; p. 586.

[17] *H.M.C. Report* (Clarke-Thornhill MSS.), vol. iii, p. 1.

[18] *P.R.O., Lists and Indexes*, no. ix (*List of Sheriffs*), p. 13.

[19] *C.P.R.*, *1446-52*, 592; *ibid.*, *1452-61*, 673.

almost certainly to the flaring-up of the feud between the younger members of the houses of Neville and Percy, which was threatening the peace of the whole North Country.[20]

It was shortly after this that Henry VI had his first attack of insanity, which lasted during the next eighteen months (until Christmas 1454). This illness quite incapacitated the King, so that some form of conciliar control of government or regency was required. The Queen, who in October, 1453, gave birth to a son, competed with the Duke of York for control of affairs. But on 27 March, 1454, during the third and last session of the 1453-4 Parliament, the Duke secured his own appointment as Protector, his most formidable opponent, Somerset, having been imprisoned in the Tower pending an inquiry into his responsibility for the loss of Normandy and Guienne. In the meantime, Parliament had met at Reading on 12 November, 1453, only to be prorogued to meet there again in three months' time. In January 1454, during the recess, Tresham is reported to have joined William Joseph, the King's Secretary, Thomas Daniel, Esquire of the Body, and John Trevelyan, usher of the King's Chamber and knight of the shire for Cornwall, in drawing up a bill for the Lords to consider, asking for a properly maintained garrison to be established at Windsor under their control, for the safeguarding of the imbecile King and the infant prince, Edward of Lancaster.[21] There is nothing to suggest that the bill prospered before the Parliament came to an end on 17 April. With the Duke of York and his friends in control of the Council, it was unlikely that it would. They cut down the establishment of the Royal Household and continued to exercise the royal authority until about Christmas, 1454, when Henry VI recovered.

Nothing more is known of Tresham's activities during 1454—presumably he was in attendance on the King—but on 30 December, he was entitled to share with Sir Richard Roos (a king's knight) and John Lovet the farming of the subsidy and alnage of cloth in Northants and Rutland for the next twenty years (as from Michaelmas 1454) for an annual payment of 11 marks. They lost the farm in February, 1456, when John Hampton and William Essex, however, undertook to pay 6s. 8d. less per annum.[22] On 25 March, 1455, Tresham was about to set out on royal business for Calais of which the captaincy had less than three weeks earlier been taken from the Duke of York and restored to the Duke of Somerset, recently set free from imprisonment since the King's recovery of health. A privy seal warrant dated at Greenwich provided that he and his companions in this enterprise—Thomas Lord Roos (a step-son of Somerset) and John Ormond (brother of the recently appointed Treasurer, the Earl of Wiltshire, and an Esquire for the Body)—were not to be delayed, and so their charges were to be met in advance. The warrant describes Tresham as 'squier and huissher of oure Chambre.' It is our first notice of his occupying this position. The Calais mission suggests a connection with Somerset. And on 14 May, 1455, Tresham was made a member of commissions for the raising of Crown loans for the defence of Calais in both Hunts and Northants.[23]

By this time there had been other changes in the controlling positions in the central administration, including the supersession of the Earl of Salisbury by Archbishop Bourchier in the custodianship of the Great Seal. So was York's Protectorship brought to an end. York and the Nevilles considered themselves personally threatened and determined to forestall any attempt by a *coup* of their own; marching on London, they explained their action in manifestos which never reached the King. The result was the first battle of St. Albans on 22 May, 1455. It is almost certain that Tresham was with the royal forces: in the July Parliament which followed the Yorkist victory he did not figure (in the bill in which the malcontents exculpated themselves) among those who, the Yorkists pretended, were responsible for the battle, but in a brief contemporary account he was listed among the 'solecytouriz and causerys [solicitors and causers] of the feld takying at Seynt Albonys.'[24] He was present at the elections for Northamptonshire to the July parliament, but not surprisingly was not himself re-elected. He was not removed from the Northants and Hunts commissions of the peace, but for almost the whole of the next two years he is otherwise lost to sight. However, he presumably remained a member of the Royal Household.

Four years of uneasy peace between the two main factions followed, although the government was not long in freeing itself from the effects of the Yorkist success at St. Albans and the

[20] *Ibid.*, *1452-61*, 53, 122-3; *C.F.R.*, *1454-61*, 44.
[21] *Paston Letters*, ii. 296.
[22] *C.F.R.*, *1454-61*, 103, 142.

[23] Privy Seal, Warrants for issue, E404/70(2)/48; *P.P.C.*, vi. 239, 242.
[24] *Paston Letters*, iii. 29.

second Protectorship of Richard of York in the winter of 1455-6. Thomas Tresham, after acting as a justice of gaol delivery at Oakham (Rutland) by patent of 20 May, 1457, and as a commissioner of array in Hunts and Northants by patent of 26 September following,[25] was appointed on 14 December, 1457, for the second time as sheriff of Cambridgeshire and Huntingdonshire.[26] Three days later he was made a commissioner for the apportionment among the hundreds and vills in Hunts and Northants of the quotas of archers and the assessment of liability to maintain them, in accordance with the provisions of a hitherto dormant Act of the Parliament of 1453.[27] His office as sheriff in the fenland counties did not prevent him from being appointed on 26 August, 1458, to membership of a commission set up to investigate and hear and determine cases of treason and risings in the lordship of Monmouth.[28]

Tresham's year of office as sheriff of Cambs and Hunts ended on 3 December, 1458. Already, on 7 November, contrary to the statutory usage that three years should elapse between tenures of the office of sheriff, he had been made sheriff of Surrey and Sussex.[29] He was still very likely in charge of this joint bailiwick late in 1459, and, if so, it was again contrary to Statute that he was elected as knight of the shire, probably for Northants (although the returns for this county are lost), to the Parliament which met at Coventry between 20 November and 20 December, 1459. The Commons had been openly packed: in some cases only writs of privy seal had been sent to the sheriffs, and the normal method of election was not always followed. The main business of the session was to register the recent Lancastrian victory, at the Rout of Ludford, near Ludlow, on 12 October, by attainting the Yorkist leaders (who had fled the country) and their foremost supporters, and to guarantee the Lancastrian succession. Thomas Tresham was elected by the Commons as their Speaker.[30] Whether he were already Controller of the Royal Household, which post he was certainly holding at the time of the battle of Towton (that is, in March, 1461),[31] is not known, although it is very likely that he was. During the session, and by parliamentary authority following the submission of a Commons' bill, the committee of feoffees in the Duchy of Lancaster estates set aside for the fulfilment of the King's will was re-modelled, and, like his father before him, Tresham was now included; it is possible that he was still the feoffees' Chancellor.[32] Again during the session, on 5 December, he was made a commissioner for the control of weirs on the river Ouse and its tributaries between Huntingdon and Holywell in Huntingdonshire, and on the day after the dissolution of the Parliament (on 21 December, 1459) he was put on a commission of array in Northants, part of a plan to resist any risings on behalf of the attainted Yorkist magnates.[33]

From the end of 1459 to the return of the Yorkist Earls of Salisbury and Warwick from Calais and their entry into London (2 July, 1460), the Court party busied itself with continuing the work of recrimination against the attainted rebels and the suppression of their adherents. On 5 February, 1460, at Northampton, expressly for his losses in the King's service and also for his services, presumably as Speaker, in the Coventry Parliament, Thomas Tresham was granted for life an annuity of £40 from lands and rents at Stamford and Grantham forfeited by the Duke of York, on the understanding that, if this source of income proved inadequate, he might have a new patent charging his annuity to another source.[34] On the previous day he had been included in commissions of oyer and terminer in Wales and the Marcher shires, and in the lordships of the Duke of York and the Earls of Salisbury and Warwick, touching all treasons, rebellions, and other offences, including breaches of the Statute of Liveries.[35] On 20 February he was authorized to act as a justice of gaol delivery at Northampton Castle with regard to a monk of Daventry.[36] On 4 June he was again made a commissioner of oyer and terminer in Oxon, Berks, Hants, and Wilts, and, by a different patent of the same date, was appointed one of a

[25] C.P.R., 1452-61, 369, 402-3.
[26] List of Sheriffs, loc. cit.
[27] C.P.R., 1452-61, 406, 408.
[28] Ibid., 444.
[29] List of Sheriffs, 136.
[30] Rot. Parl., v. 345.
[31] Ibid., v. 616b. When a successor as Controller of the Household to Sir Richard Haryngton, who held

office in 1455, was appointed, is not known.
[32] Ibid., v. 355.
[33] C.P.R., 1452-61, 556, 559.
[34] C.P.R., 1452-61, 577.
[35] Ibid., 564-5. A similar commission was again issued on 13 March, 1460, on which Tresham was appointed to serve, (see p. 562).
[36] Ibid., 563.

commission instructed to arrest and imprison all Yorkist supporters, with power to commandeer forces in these counties for the purpose. Tresham was one of a similarly constructed commission set up on 22 June to act in the same way in Herts, Middlesex, Kent, Surrey and Sussex.[37]

Less than three weeks later, as a result of the battle outside Tresham's own county town of Northampton on 10 July, 1460, the King was captured and the Lancastrians themselves were on the run. It is highly probable that Tresham fought there. Certainly, if this were so, he escaped being taken. In the Yorkist Parliament (summoned in Henry VI's name) to meet in October, 1460, the proscriptions of its predecessor at Coventry were undone, the reversion of the Crown settled on York and his male heirs, and York established as Protector. A new committee of feoffees in the Duchy of Lancaster was created to meet the changed political conditions, and Tresham was now excluded. He had already been dropped from the Northamptonshire commission of the peace when a fresh set of justices was appointed on 1 September, 1460. Seemingly, Tresham now lay low. According to a petition he made to Edward IV in 1467, he declined to join the Lancastrian army which defeated York's forces at Wakefield on 30 December, 1460, when York was killed and Salisbury executed.[38]

Soon after news of the success at Wakefield got through to her in Scotland, Queen Margaret of Anjou came south in January, 1461. And certainly by the time she reached Durham, Tresham had joined her, because, when she extorted a loan of 400 marks from the prior and convent there, it was he, along with Master John Morton (the Prince of Wales's Chancellor), William Grimsby (recently Under-Treasurer of England and Treasurer of the Chamber), and John Whelpdale, priest, who undertook to make repayment.[39] Margaret and her forces were at York by 20 January, and from here the Lancastrian army advanced towards London. Tresham fought in the second battle of St. Albans, where his side defeated Warwick's forces on 17 February and recovered possession of the person of Henry VI. After being knighted by his father, the young Prince Edward himself knighted about thirty men. Among these was Tresham.[40]

The Lancastrians' failure to reap the benefit of this victory by immediately attacking London, allowed Edward, York's heir, and Warwick to move into the City and the former to declare himself King on 4 March, 1461. Losing little time, Edward IV followed the Lancastrian army, which had retired northwards, to bring it to battle. On 6 March he had already ordered proclamation to be made in the north of England, promising a general pardon of life and estate to all those abandoning the Lancastrian cause within ten days, except for twenty-two named persons and all others worth over 100 marks a year in land, and the proclamation went on to put a price of £100 each on the heads of certain of the Lancastrian notables. These included Tresham.[41] On 29 March was fought the battle of Towton, just south of the crossing of the Wharfe at Tadcaster, in which the Lancastrians incurred a decisive defeat. Tresham, by this time Controller of Henry VI's Household, was taken prisoner.[42] Although his life was spared, in the Parliament of November, 1461, along with other Lancastrian adherents he was attainted of high treason as having "rered werre" and fought against Edward IV at Towton, and accordingly he incurred forfeiture of all his estates of inheritance as held on 4 March, including those held to his use.[43]

Already, on 14 May, 1461, the escheator in Northants and Rutland had been ordered to seize his possessions in these counties, and, on 8 July following, instructions were issued with the same intent to the escheator of Surrey and Sussex.[44] On 20 July special commissioners were authorized to take into the King's hands the lands in Northants and Bucks belonging to Tresham and Sir Thomas Thorpe of Barnwell, late Baron of the Exchequer and Keeper of the Privy Wardrobe to Henry VI, who had been beheaded by the Londoners in Harringay Park when attempting to escape to join Queen Margaret on the day of her victory at St. Albans on 17 February, 1461.[45] John Don, one of the ushers of Edward IV's Chamber, was evidently the key member of

[37] Ibid., 613-4.

[38] Rot. Parl., v. 616b.

[39] Surtees Society, vol. 44 (1863), Memorials of Hexham Priory, pp.cii, cvi. The priory of Durham was still seeking recovery of this debt in 1474, when the prior wrote to Morton about it.

[40] Camden Society (1876), Collections of a London Citizen, Gregory's Chronicle, p. 214.

[41] C.C.R., 1461-8, 56.

[42] Gregory's Chronicle, op. cit., p. 217.

[43] Rot. Parl., v. 477.

[44] C.P.R., 1461-7, 35-6.

[45] Ibid., 134.

this commission, his being the responsibility for accounting for the issues of the sequestrated property, and it was he who on 24 February, 1462, got a grant in tail-male of the bulk of Tresham's Northamptonshire manors and lands, including Rushton, on condition that he answered for all revenues in excess of £100 a year. Sywell manor and Broughton Parva (Bucks) and the reversion of Livedon went at about the same time to a new Yorkist peer, Walter Devereux, Lord Ferrers; on 1 August, 1462, the King's uncle, William Neville, Earl of Kent, came by a similar grant of Tresham's property in Northampton and the manor of Wavendon (Bucks), which in the following January were transferred to the Duke of Clarence; and as late as 12 December, 1464, certain small parcels of land and tenements went to Ralph Hastings, one of Edward IV's Esquires of the Body.[46]

As Tresham was to point out in the petition he made to Edward IV in 1467, he came to understand the King's "title roiall," never left the kingdom (as some hardened Lancastrians had done), and had been at no "journey or felde" against the King since the battle of Towton. He was, moreover, not entirely friendless at the Yorkist court. His wife, Margaret, was sister of Lord Zouche, and Sir William Peche of Lullingstone (Kent), his mother's second husband,[47] (to whom Tresham had been feoffee-to-uses in his manor of Ashways in Stepney (Middlesex) in February, 1459[48]), became King's Carver in October, 1461, was sheriff of Kent in 1461-2, and fought with the Yorkist forces in Northumberland in the winter of 1462-3.[49] But, despite these connections and the fact that on 26 March, 1464, Tresham received, by advice of the Council, a general pardon of all offences for which he had been attainted,[50] his estates were not yet restored to him.

Clearly, Tresham's rehabilitation was a slow process. He received no office at Court, but, nearly five years after Towton Field, on 25 January, 1466, he was once more re-included in the commission of the peace for his own county of Northampton.[51] Early in the following year (between 25 February and 5 April, 1467) he was appointed by royal writ one of a committee of arbitration between Robert Warner, a yeoman of Kentish Town, and a certain John Ive.[52] On 10 May following he was put on a commission of gaol delivery at Northampton Castle,[53] and he was elected for Northamptonshire to the next Parliament, which met at Westminster on 3 June, 1467. Tresham probably realised that, with the King requiring to strengthen his position in the country at large, in case the known discontents of the Nevilles assumed more serious shape, this was as good an opportunity as was likely to come his way to seek full re-instatement in his rights. As far back as March, 1450, he had been party as a feoffee to a settlement of the manor of Middleton Stoney (Oxon) on John Lord Lestrange and his wife Jacquetta,[54] who was sister to Edward IV's Queen, Elizabeth Woodville, herself a member of the Northamptonshire family of Woodville of Grafton, where in fact the King had secretly wooed and married her. It is just possible that help came from that quarter. His own family connection with Sir William Peche was possibly an asset, if his mother had forgiven the upset of 1451.

There is no knowing precisely, however, what personal influences favourable to his suit Tresham used when, in this Parliament of 1467-8, he petitioned the King to give a greater reality to his general pardon of over three years before. The petition recalled that by the patent of 26 March, 1464, he had been "abled unto youre Lawes" but not restored to his "lyvelode" [livelihood], and asked that consideration be given to the facts that he had been brought up in Henry VI's service since childhood; that at the time of the battle of Towton he was Henry's "menyall servant" and Controller of his Household and held other "notable offices"; that he had unavoidably been present at Towton Field as a "menyall servant of Household"; and that since then he had been loyal to Edward IV and had always "sued to stonde in the favour of your good grace." Tresham pointed out that by the King's licence he had "bargayned" with the grantees of his forfeited lands to the extent of 2,000 marks and more, and that as a result and because he could raise no loans (being unable to offer his estates as surety for repayment), he was in great debt; nor

[46] Ibid., 111, 153, 225-6, 369.
[47] G. Baker, op. cit., ii.36 (Isabel Vaux, Tresham's mother, had married Sir William Peche by February, 1455).
[48] Ancient Deeds, vi. C4128.
[49] J. C. Wedgwood, History of Parliament; Bio-

graphies, sub nomine.
[50] C.P.R., 1461-7, 321.
[51] Ibid., 569.
[52] C.C.R., 1461-8, 409.
[53] C.P.R., 1467-77, 30.
[54] Ibid., 1446-52, 311.

was he able, he said, to marry his son and heir unless by authority of Parliament he was restored to his estates. His petition concluded with the request that he might be so restored to all his possessions (except what he had been granted by Henry VI), and that his attainder and forfeiture be annulled, saving to the recipients of his lands surcease of any demand for waste or profits. The petition was granted.[55]

Tresham recovered sufficient influence in the Lower House during the course of this Parliament to be chosen by the Commons to be one of their eleven members of a commission of oyer and terminer, made up of lords, justices, knights of the shire and burgesses, entrusted on 20 May, 1468, with the investigation of accusations of coinage depreciation and over-charging for minting that had been laid against Hugh Brice, a London goldsmith, in his capacity as Keeper of the King's Exchange and one of the governors of the Tower Mint.[56] But his petition for re-instatement in his lands, although it was formally successful, did not in effect result in a complete restoration: in a patent of 9 November, 1467, John Don, by this time Esquire of the Body to Edward IV, was able to secure a grant to himself and his wife in tail-male of Tresham's forfeited manors of Rushton, Stanwick, Ringstead, Great Brampton, and Great Houghton.[57]

There can be little doubt of Tresham's financial embarrassment at this time: in May, 1466, he had felt impelled to mortgage for £400 his manor of Broughton near Aylesbury (Bucks) to William Stavely, and he had to confirm the conditional release in August, 1468.[58] Tresham's discontent with this situation seems to have soon resulted in his embroilment in certain movements of disaffection, of which Warwick, mainly on grounds of dissatisfaction with the King's pro-Burgundian and anti-French policy, became the centre. On 16 July, 1468, Tresham secured another royal pardon.[59] Nevertheless, following disclosures of treasonable activities on the part of Lancastrian sympathisers made by the Earl of Oxford after his own arrest and imprisonment in the Tower, Tresham was also arrested and imprisoned in the Tower on 29 November, 1468, and word was soon going round that "his livelihood . . . is given away by the King." Unlike the heir of the late Lord Hungerford and the heir to the Earldom of Devon, who were both condemned and executed at Salisbury on 17 January, 1469, Tresham seems, however, not to have been brought to trial. He very probably was kept in prison until released in October, 1470, by the Earl of Warwick, when the latter's coalition with the Lancastrians resulted in Edward IV's flight into exile and the restoration of Henry VI.[60] It is, however, important to notice that on 5 June, 1470, he figured among the feoffees of Edmund Grey, Earl of Kent, formerly Lord Grey of Ruthin, whose men were alleged to have been responsible for Tresham's father's murder in 1450, in a grant of the Norfolk manor of Saxthorp.[61]

Certainly, there is no doubt of Tresham's being at large in the autumn of 1470 and a supporter of the Lancastrian "Readeption." For on 5 November, 1470, he was granted, for seven years from the previous Michaelmas, the keeping of the honours of Peverell, Boulogne, and Haughley with their members in Bucks, Northants, and Leicestershire, and of the castle and honour of Huntingdon, on payment at the Exchequer of a yearly farm of £6.6s.8d. These honours had been held at his death in 1389 by John de Hastings, Earl of Pembroke, whose next heir had been Tresham's wife's grandfather, the William, Lord Zouche who had died in 1396.[62]

Summoned on 15 October, the single Parliament of the Readeption met at Westminster on 26 November, 1470. It is likely that Sir Thomas Tresham acted as Speaker for the Commons on this occasion.[63] The session saw the annulment of the attainders of Edward IV's time, and this meant the re-establishment of Tresham's legal rights in his own estates. What steps, if any, he took to secure re-instatement, we do not know. Whatever they were, they were not effectual for long.

In the middle of March, 1471, Edward IV landed in the Humber, and four weeks later was in London where Henry VI came into his hands. At Barnet Field on 14 April he disposed

[55] *Rot. Parl.*, v. 616b.
[56] *Ibid.*, 634a.
[57] *C.P.R.*, 1467-77, 60.
[58] *Ancient Deeds*, i. A684; iii. A5714.
[59] Wedgwood, *op. cit.*, *Biographies*.
[60] Camden Society (1839), *Plumpton Correspondence*, ed. T. Stapleton, p. 20; J. H. Ramsey, *Lancaster and York*, ii.335; C. L. Scofield, *The Life and Reign of Edward IV*, i. pp. 481-2.
[61] *H.M.C. Report, MSS. of Marquess of Lothian*, p. 55.
[62] *C.F.R.*, 1461-71, 279.
[63] J. C. Wedgwood, *History of Parliament, 1439-1509, Register*, p. 384.

of Warwick. Among those Lancastrians who joined Queen Margaret and her son after their landing at Weymouth was Sir Thomas Tresham, and when, on 27 April, proclamations were sent out in Edward IV's name, declaring Margaret, Prince Edward, and their adherents to be notorious traitors and rebels, and ordering no-one to assist them, he was among those individually named in the writs.[64] The Lancastrian force, moving up from Devon through Somerset into Gloucestershire, probably with the intention of joining Jasper Tudor in Wales, was met and cut to pieces at Tewkesbury on 4 May, 1471. Tresham was among those who fled the field and took sanctuary in the abbey church. Two days later the Duke of Somerset and a number of the Lancastrian notables, Tresham among them, were taken for trial before the Duke of Gloucester as Constable and the Duke of Norfolk as Marshal. They were condemned and immediately beheaded. Their bodies were not subjected to the usual indignities of "dismembringe or settynge up," and most were buried in the abbey church or precinct, Tresham's in the church "byfore a pilar betwyxt ye awtar of seint james and seint nicholas." His cousin, William Vaux, who had married in 1456 one of Queen Margaret's ladies (a Provençale), was also killed in the battle or executed afterwards, and buried in the parish church. A Sir Henry Tresham and his clerk, Thomas Tresham,—unless there is some confusion here—were also taken and beheaded.[65] What relationship, if any, these two bore to Sir Thomas is not known.

Sir Thomas's surviving son, John, afterwards secured a final restoration of his father's estates, but for the moment all was lost. Sir Thomas was posthumously attainted in the Parliament which met in October, 1472, and all his possessions were again forfeited. On 26 November, 1474, an inquiry into his lands in Northamptonshire and Huntingdonshire was ordered. When, on 8 December following, the Treasurer of the Royal Household was granted nearly £5,000 a year for ten years, the profits from the custody of the lands and person of Tresham's heir, including his marriage, were among the sources appropriated to this charge.[66] On 20 May, 1475, a further inquiry into the Tresham estate was ordered, and on 24 June Sir Thomas's lands were granted to the Queen, the Bishop of Salisbury and Master William Dudley, Dean of the Chapel of the Household.[67] This latter grant was probably made in connection with the appropriation Edward IV had provided in his will, drawn up at Sandwich on 20 June, 1475, by which all the issues of Tresham's forfeitures were to go to the building of the new chapel of the Order of the Garter in the College of St. George at Windsor.[68] A further inquiry into Sir Thomas's hereditaments was authorized on 18 February, 1477.[69] Not until Henry VII's first Parliament met in 1485 did John, Tresham's son and heir, secure the annulment of his father's attainder and recover seisin of the Tresham lands; his petition was granted by authority of Parliament.[70]

At some time after December, 1474, and presumably before 1485, Sir Thomas Tresham's heir had been married to Elizabeth,[71] daughter of Sir James Haryngton of Hornby (Lancs) and Brierley (Yorks), a firm Yorkist whose father and brother had lost their lives at Wakefield with Richard of York in 1460, and who himself, in 1465, had been largely responsible for the capture of Henry VI near Clitheroe in Lancashire. Sir James's second cousin, Sir William Haryngton, had lands at Wolfege in Brixworth, near some of the Tresham estates in Northants. This marriage may well have eased the situation of Sir Thomas's heir until the "Lancastrian" restoration of 1485 put the recovery of his hereditary estates beyond doubt. If it was intended to re-insure the Haryngtons, it failed. John Tresham's father-in-law was attainted as a Yorkist in the same Parliament which reversed the attainder of his father, Sir Thomas Tresham.

Sir Thomas Tresham's career provides something of an illustration of the heavy risks run by men who, in the second half of the fifteenth century, followed the path of self-aggrandisement offered by service at Court. Normally, membership of the Court circle was well worth while;

[64] C.C.R., 1468-76, 189.
[65] Camden Society, vol. 1, Historie of the Arrivall of Edward IV, ed. J. Bruce, p. 31; Recueil de Chroniques . . . par Jehan de Waurin (R.S.), ed. W. and E. L. C. P. Hardy, vol. v (1447-71), p. 671; Paston Letters, v. p. 105; C. L. Kingsford, English Historical Literature in the Fifteenth Century, App., p. 378.

[66] Rot. Parl., vi.145; C.P.R., 1467-77, 493; 478.
[67] Ibid., 570; 540.
[68] Excerpta Historica (1831, London), p. 372.
[69] C.P.R., 1477-85, 23.
[70] Rot. Parl., vi. 317b; the successful petition was exemplified on 5 February, 1488 (C.P.R., 1485-94, 207).
[71] G. Baker, Northants., ii., p. 69.

it conferred liveries and probably annuities and fees, and if the monetary rewards were frequently unreliable in times of royal financial stringency, they might be made up for by grants of wardships and Exchequer farms, that is, of Crown revenues procured at source, and by appointments to local or regional royal offices, that is, to the control of those agencies one of whose functions was to extract Crown revenues at source. All of such concessions could be made profitable in terms of both cash-income and social influence. By such a system, because of his position as an Esquire of Henry VI's Chamber and then as one of its more intimate staff, the Ushers, Thomas Tresham was able to profit. And if the royal government were in disrepute and its authority weak, for the conduct of its provincial concerns it would tend, whenever possible, to place reliance on such local men as were members of the King's Household, with the result that the opportunities for courtiers to "engross" offices in their own "country" were only enhanced. It was the exploitation of such opportunities which converted favoured courtiers into "caterpillars of the commonwealth," and so long as they could keep a right balance between their perquisites and the unavoidable "over-heads" of employment at Court, or in Crown service locally, (especially the expense involved in maintaining a necessarily increased staff of retainers and managerial assistants,) surely they could only continue to thrive. Where, then, were the risks ?

In a time of near financial bankruptcy, into which the Lancastrian state had fallen before the turn of the century, such a system of exploitation and perversion of the proper uses of royal administration almost logically necessitated (in order to keep it more productive for those who enjoyed its benefits) a restriction of the control of royal patronage, and, therefore, of the real management of government, to as small a coterie of the King's friends as was consonant with political safety. But there was the rub. As events under Edward II and Richard II had specially demonstrated, a restrictive monopoly of the control of royal government and, with it, of the dispensation of royal bounty could soon be turned, by any opposing aristocratic party excluded from its share of both, into a rather pious but (as propaganda) powerful complaint that the King was being alienated from his people and the Crown suffering dismemberment. During that part of Henry VI's reign for which he could be held in some sense personally responsible, first Cardinal Beaufort, then the Duke of Suffolk, and then (if on and off) the Cardinal's nephew, the Duke of Somerset, dominated the royal counsels, misusing their position for their own party and private ends and disposing a virtual monopoly of control of the royal patronage. That in itself was liable to cause the Lancastrian régime to forfeit respect and support in the country at large, or at least among the "outs" and "have-nots".

But the régime might have survived all this, had it not been held responsible for a complete and calamitous failure in France in both the military and diplomatic fields, at a time when the country was far from resigned to it, and also for a breakdown of orderly government at home. These important defects generated a profound lack of sympathy between Court and Country, and once the Yorkist aim to reform the Lancastrian administration by political pressure was thwarted, and so converted into a resolve to supersede the Lancastrian dynasty itself by military force, it was clear that, if this intention were successful, it would go ill with many of those who had enjoyed prestige and influence at Henry's Court,—men, in fact, like Sir Thomas Tresham, who had long been important there and by 1461 was well-placed in its official hierarchy as Controller of the Household. When in 1461 Henry VI gave way to Edward IV, individual survival with status and fortune intact could only be contrived by men of the old royal Household by an opportune but convincing transfer of allegiance and support, and provided that the new régime could maintain its own safety and continuance. This between 1461 and 1485 could not for long be taken for granted and unquestioned. It was this uncertainty which prevented men like Sir Thomas Tresham from coming to terms with themselves, and how much less on any comfortable basis with a hostile or indifferent government.

Some Lancastrian courtiers, like Sir John Wenlock of Someries, Queen Margaret's sometime Chamberlain, made the switch-over in good time; others, like Sir John Say of Broxbourne, before it was too late. Say had risen in Henry VI's Household to be an Esquire of the Body in the same period in which Sir Thomas Tresham and his father had come nearer to the front, but by 1461 had been Chancellor of the Duchy of Lancaster (in succession to William Tresham) for over ten years and had been Under-Treasurer of the Exchequer in 1455-6 and again in the last few months of Henry's reign. It was not so difficult for *this* type of royal retainer, with his professional and managerial capabilities, to survive the changes of 1461, as it was for the "simple courtier" type, even if he had not (as Say had) any connection with members of the aristocracy who had a foot in both the main parties. Such a member of the Court who was also a "civil servant" could be regarded as serving the Crown as much as the King, and he had therefore a better chance of pulling through a crisis like 1461. William Tresham, had he lived so long, would almost certainly have survived it intact and ready to turn it to advantage. Because he was a courtier and seemingly little more, Sir Thomas Tresham, as we have seen, could not extricate himself. And, although he did his best to temporize under Edward IV, he never succeeded in living down his Lancastrian past and, in the end, in 1471, perhaps in desperation, committed himself once more, and irrevocably (as it proved), to a cause whose defeat involved his own death.

12

SIR JAMES STRANGEWAYS OF WEST HARLSEY AND WHORLTON.

SPEAKER IN THE PARLIAMENT OF 1461.[1]

The history of the early Speakers and their office (which dates from 1376) has some bearing on the problem of the political significance of the Commons in the parliaments of the later medieval period. The Speaker's frequent connection with some organ of royal government or attachment to a powerful faction or interest suggests that his election was often the object of political manoeuvre. This was because his official capacity for managing the Commons is likely to have been considerable. That the Speaker's services in this regard were coming to be more and more valued is clear from the fact that under Henry VI and afterwards the government of the day was often prepared to reward him quite handsomely for them. Such a practice also betokens a great measure of official interest in the Commons' doings and a realization in high places that the lower house of parliament required careful handling. Undoubtedly, the personal history of the early Speakers is worth scrutiny in any detailed inquiry into later medieval parliamentary history. The career of Sir James Strangeways of West Harlsey and Whorlton and his Speakership in Edward IV's first parliament, which met in November 1461, have their place in such an investigation.

Although in the whole history of the Speakership there have been very few elected to the office who represented a north country shire or borough, Strangeways was not the first knight of the shire representing Yorkshire to be made Speaker. Sir James de Pickering and Sir Richard Redmayne of Harewood when so acting had been Speaker in 1383 and 1415 respectively. But nearly a century passed by after Strangeways before another Yorkshire knight of the shire was elected to the chair in the person of Sir Thomas Gargrave, who functioned in the first parliament of Elizabeth I.

The rarity of a Speaker of northern provenance naturally draws attention to Strangeways' career. But that career has certainly an intrinsic interest. He was sheriff of Yorkshire three times in all, in 1445-6, 1452-3, and 1468-9. At one time or another he was a J.P. in each of the three Ridings. And he is known to have represented the county in the parliaments of February 1449, October 1460, and November 1461.[2] The son of one of Henry VI's judges, he became connected with several important northern

---

[1] For list of abbreviations see footnote at end of the article.
[2] *Official Return of Members of Parliament*, i, 340, 356, App. XXIV.

baronial families by his own marriage and through the marriages of some of his children and kinsfolk. But his own most crucial link in this age of "bastard feudalism" was with the Nevilles, especially with Richard, earl of Salisbury, and his son, Richard, earl of Warwick, the "Kingmaker", who, in the civil commotion and strife between the Lancastrians and the Yorkists, were themselves partizans, with greater or lesser enthusiasm, of Richard, duke of York, and his family. For the most part, Strangeways' career is something of a commentary, now clear, now hazy or distorted, on Neville and Yorkist politics.

The Strangeways family was seemingly of no importance, probably not even armigerous in rank, until the turn of the fourteenth century. At the head of its accepted pedigree stands Henry Strangeways, very probably the same who (described as 'of Manchester') was paid in February 1402 at the Lower Exchequer 40 marks (by assignment) 'per manus Jacobi Strangways', for wines which Richard II's Chief Butler had sometime taken for the royal use at Chester, who between 1399 and 1401 held the office of clerk and keeper of the King's mills on the Dee at Chester and the fishery there, and who, appointed in June 1404 as chief chamberlain of the Exchequer of Ireland, was granted this office for life in the following January and confirmed in possession by Henry V in May 1414.[1] This Henry Strangeways was seemingly the Speaker's grandfather. One of his sons, Thomas, eventually married into the great northern clan of Neville, being the second husband of Katherine, daughter of Ralph Neville, first earl of Westmorland, by his second wife, Joan, the legitimated daughter of John of Gaunt and Katherine Swynford. (Katherine Neville's first husband was John Mowbray, duke of Norfolk, who died in October 1432.)[2] Henry Strangeways' other children seem all to have married into families of Lancashire and Cheshire, including the families of Orell, Worsley, Bulkeley, and Wooton. His son James married Joan, daughter of Nicholas Orell, and James the Speaker was one of the children of this union. James senior's earliest connections appear to have been with Lancashire[3] and two of his daughters were married into Lancashire families,[4] but an expanding legal career presumably enabled him to make purchases of property in the North Riding of Yorkshire and certainly by 1423 (if no earlier) he was established in the manor of West Harlsey near Northallerton, under the western edges of the North York Moors, where his superior feudal lord was the

---

[1] Issue Roll, E403/571, mem. 23; *CPR*, 1399-1401, 11; *ibid.*, 1401-5, 403; *ibid.*, 1408-13; 191; *ibid.*, 1413-16, 73. For the Strangeways pedigree, see Surtees Society, vol. CXLIV, *Visitations of the North*, p. 106; *Pedigrees of the County Families of Yorkshire*, Joseph Foster, vol. iii; *The Genealogist* (N.S.), *Dugdale's Visitation of Yorkshire*, p. 181.

[2] *The Complete Peerage*, VI, 42.

[3] *CPR*, 1405-8, 53, 479.

[4] Isabel married Sir Peter Gerard, knight of the shire for Lancashire in 1445, and Maud married a Ralph Staveley (*The Genealogist, loc. cit.*).

bishop of Durham.[1] Two other of his daughters married into the families of Surtees of Dinsdale (Durham) and Montfort of Hack-forth (N. Riding).

Called to be serjeant-at-law in 1411 and in 1415 appointed king's serjeant-at-law, the Speaker's father served as justice of the peace in the North Riding from 1412 to his death in 1442, but his chief legal occupation was in the central courts at Westminster, as a justice of assize in the Midlands from 1416 onwards, and then from 1426 until his death as a puisne justice in the Court of Common Pleas with an annual fee of 110 marks; in the mean-time, in 1427, he had been made Justice of North Wales with additional fees of 20 marks per session.[2] Cardinal Thomas Langley, bishop of Durham from 1406 to 1437, Chancellor of England from 1405 to 1407 and from 1417 to 1424, himself in origin a native of Middleton (Lancs.) and a near neighbour of the Manchester Strangeways, may very well have had much to do with the settlement of the Speaker's father as an episcopal tenant at West Harlsey; certainly Justice Strangeways was one of the Cardinal's executors, and he appears to have acted as a senior justice in the courts of the Durham palatinate in Langley's as well as in his successor Neville's tenure of the see. The legal and professional colouring of the background of the Speaker's family was enriched by the appointment of one of his uncles, Roger Strangeways, in July 1439 as king's attorney-at-law in North Wales, and of another, Nicholas Strangeways, as the Speaker's grandfather's successor in October 1430 as chief chamberlain of the Exchequer of Ireland.[3]

Justice Strangeways' son and heir, James (the Speaker), married Elizabeth, the elder daughter and coheir (born in the spring of 1417) of Philip Darcy, the son and heir of John Lord Darcy of Knaith (Lincs.), who died (while himself still under age and a royal ward) in August 1418, and of his wife, Eleanor, daughter of Henry Lord FitzHugh of Ravensworth. Elizabeth's younger sister and coheir, Margaret (born in September 1418), married Sir John Conyers of Hornby (N. Riding). Both marriages had taken place by November 1431.

The Darcies, who had been peers of parliament since about the beginning of Edward III's reign, already had a family con-nection with many baronial and other substantial families of the north-east and elsewhere, including the families of Roos of Helmsley, Grey of Wilton, and Gray of Heton. The grandmother of the Darcy heiresses, on the death (in 1411) of her husband, John Lord Darcy, had married Sir Thomas Swynford of Kettle-thorpe (Lincs.), son of Katherine Swynford, John of Gaunt's mistress, by her first husband, and uterine brother of the Beaufort

[1] VCH, N. Riding of Yorkshire, vol. I, p. 437.
[2] E. Foss, Judges of England, IV 361; CPR, passim.
[3] CPR, 1436-41, 171; 288; 132.

progeny, John, earl of Somerset, Thomas, duke of Exeter, Cardinal Henry Beaufort, bishop of Winchester, and Joan, the second wife of Ralph Neville, earl of Westmorland. The mother of the Darcy heiresses, Eleanor FitzHugh, after the death of their father, married as her second husband Sir Thomas Tunstall of Thurland (in Lonsdale, Lancs.). This marriage brought her contacts with the northern families of Haryngton, Parr, Pudsey, and Pennington. The most important of her children by this alliance was her son, Sir Richard Tunstall of Bentham (Yorks.) and Thurland (Lancs.), a Lancastrian courtier who was esquire of the body to Henry VI from 1452 to 1455, king's carver from 1450 to 1460, chamberlain of Chester from 1457 to 1460, and chamberlain of the Exchequer from late in 1459 until Edward IV's accession in 1461; he fought as a Lancastrian at Wakefield and Towton, escaped to Scotland, was attainted in 1461, went off to join the small band of Lancastrian devotees after the fall of Dunstanborough, and was still with Henry VI at the time of his capture in 1465; not until 1468 did he surrender at Harlech in return for a pardon. Eleanor FitzHugh by March 1453 had married, as her third husband, Henry Bromflete, Lord Vessy, who was summoned to parliament as a baron between 1449 and his death in 1469; her daughter by this marriage, Strangeways' wife's young half-sister, married the Lancastrian, Lord ("Butcher") Clifford.[1]

The Baroness Vessy survived until September 1457, and not until then did Strangeways and his wife come to share her dower estates. The dower estates of Margaret Baroness Darcy, Strangeways' wife's grandmother, had only been divided early in 1455, following her death in June 1454.[2] But already, since November 1431, when Strangeways' wife had proved her age, she and he had been in possession of her purparty of the Darcy estates in Yorkshire, Northumberland, Nottinghamshire, Derbyshire, and Leicestershire, and at Calais, and also of her share of the family's Irish properties.[3] His marriage had also brought Strangeways a part interest in the royal annuity of £40 granted by Edward III in 1341 to his wife's great-great-grandfather, John Darcy le Fitz, and his heirs; and Exchequer assignments of very dubious value occasionally came their way as payment of what was owing under this head.[4] The Darcy estates in Ireland which came into Strange-

---

[1] CCR, 1429-35, 143; Complete Peerage, IV, 65-6; The Genealogical Magazine, vol. V, p. 367; Yorkshire Archaeological Society. Record Series, vol. LXXXIII, Yorkshire Deeds, vol. VII, pp. 141-2. J. C. Wedgwood, History of Parliament, Biographies, sub Sir Richard Tunstall. Elizabeth and Margaret Darcy's uncle, their father's younger brother, Richard Darcy, married Eleanor, daughter of John Lord Scrope of Masham, and their son and heir eventually did something to recover many of the lands of that family which had been forfeited by the treason of Henry Lord Scrope of Masham in 1415.

[2] CCR 1461-8, 45; Complete Peerage, loc. cit.

[3] CCR 1429-35, 143.

[4] Issue Roll, E 403/719, mem. 4.

ways' control were a moiety of the manors of Garristown (Co. Dublin), Assey and Dunmoe (Co. Meath), Castlerahan (Co. Cavan), and Louth (the chief town in Co. Louth). On 15 May 1447 Strangeways and his brother-in-law, Sir John Conyers, jointly took out a royal licence in survivorship permitting their absence from Ireland and the right to take out of the country the revenue from their estates there, and relieving them of services, including scutages, arising out of their tenure. Eventually, before his wife's death but after 1447, Sir James and Elizabeth leased their share of the Irish lands of the Darcies for £40 a year, and Elizabeth's sister and her husband (Sir John Conyers) did the same; the coheirs were certainly, however, back in possession of Garristown and Louth by August 1465, when they regularized an enfeoffment by royal licence.[1] On 13 March 1456 Sir James and his wife also secured a royal patent licensing their alienation in mortmain of the advowson of the church of Beighton (Derbyshire), which had formerly belonged to the FitzHughs, to the Carthusian priory of Mountgrace in the parish of East Harlsey.[2] In Northumberland, the Darcy coheirs held the great waste of the forest of Cheviot, the advowson of the hospital of Wooler, and the manors of Wooler, Hethpool, Hetherslaw, Belford, Easington, Lowick, and Hadstone.[3]

It was, however, clearly in the North Riding of Yorkshire that Strangeways and his wife's main territorial interests lay and where they resided. Here the stock of land added by his marriage to his father's holding at West Harlsey and thereabouts was considerable, and eventually he had a chain of manors (some in his own, some in his wife's right) reaching from the neighbourhood of Northallerton towards the mouth of the Tees, including Warlaby (a moiety), Hallikeld,[4] West Harlsey, Whorlton (the old home of the Menille family),[5] Potto, Seamer,[6] Upsall,[7] Greenhow (on lease from his mother-in-law),[8] and Acklam.[9] Other Yorkshire manors which Sir James Strangeways held were those of Aislaby (near Whitby),[10] Boynton (near Flamborough Head),[11] and Notton (near Wakefield).[12] He and his wife shared with the other coheir, her sister, the patronage of the priory of Austin canons at Guisborough, just north of the Cleveland Hills, a place which, at the time of the Dissolution in the next century, was the fourth richest of the Yorkshire monasteries.[13] West Harlsey, the property first of Justice Strangeways, the Speaker's father, was held, as has been said, of the bishopric of Durham. The

---

[1] *Rot. Parl.* V. 485; *CPR* 1446-52, 66; *ibid.*, 1461-7, 466.
[2] *CPR* 1452-61, 277.
[3] *CCR*, 1454-61, 126, 238.
[4] *V.C.H., N. Riding Yorks.*, i, 147, 408. [5] *ibid.*, ii, 312.
[6] *ibid.*, 291. [7] *ibid.*, 281.
[8] Yorks. Arch. Soc., Record Series, vol. LXXXIII, *Yorkshire Deeds*, vol. VII, pp. 141-2.
[9] *V.C.H., N. Riding*, ii, 221. [10] *ibid.*, 518.
[11] *The Genealogist*, N.S., XVIII, 103.
[12] *Yorkshire Deeds, loc. cit.*
[13] *Yorkshire Archaeological Journal* XXXI, 34.

Speaker's other home, some five miles or so to the east, at Whorlton, was held of the archbishop of Canterbury in return for serving him with the cup out of which he should drink on the day of his consecration.[1] Here, Strangeways and his wife (in her right) had the patronage of the free chapel.[2]

James Strangeways junior, as he was called then and during the time of his father, Justice Strangeways, makes his first recorded appearance on the last day of 1430 when, with his father and his uncle, Roger Strangeways, and others, he witnessed a ratification of an estate in the manor and vill of Auckland St. Helens.[3]   Certainly before another year had elapsed he had married one of the Darcy coheirs, a match which, when his wife Elizabeth proved her age in the autumn of 1431, immediately assured him of more than a competence from lands in the North Riding of Yorkshire alone, with the prospect of his own patrimony still to materialize: on 20 November 1431 the escheators of York-shire, Northumberland, Notts, Derbyshire, Lincolnshire, and Middlesex were ordered to partition the Darcy lands between James and Elizabeth and her younger sister and her husband, John Conyers, and on 24 November a similar writ was issued to the chancellor of Ireland.   James and Elizabeth were to enter into possession of their purparty (dower estates excepted) forth-with; the other couple only took seisin in the spring of 1433.[4] On 5 February 1432 the Strangeways pair took out letters patent from the English Chancery nominating two of James's kinsmen, Hugh Orell and Nicholas Strangeways, the chief chamberlain of the Exchequer of Ireland, as their attorneys in Ireland for one year; and they reappointed them on 24 November following.[5] On 1 June 1435 they were paid at the Lower Exchequer at West-minster (by assignment) Elizabeth's share of an accumulation of instalments of the nearly century-old annuity of £40 granted to her ancestor by Edward III: £29. 16s.   Four years (to the day) were to elapse before they received their next assignment.[6]

Considering the position of his father as a Justice of the Common Bench, James Strangeways junior was called upon in these years to serve on surprisingly few royal commissions of even local importance.   Before his father's death in 1442 the only commissions of which he was appointed a member were two commissions of array in the North Riding, set up respectively on 10 July 1434 (when his patron, the earl of Salisbury, was warden of both Marches towards Scotland) and on 18 January 1436.[7] On 1 February 1439 Strangeways junior and William Orell, clerk, (presumably a kinsman of Strangeways' mother) entered into a

[1] Surtees Society, *Testamenta Eboracensia*, ii, 109n.
[2] *Yorks. Arch. Journal*, XXII, 211n.
[3] *Archaeologia Aeliana*, 3rd Series, vol. 14, p. 163.
[4] *CCR*, 1429-35, 143, 207.   [5] *CPR*, 1429-36, 183, 248.
[6] Issue Roll, E 403/719, mem. 4; E 403/735.
[7] *CPR*, 1429-36, 360, 521.

recognizance in 200 marks payable to the executors of the King's late mother, Queen Katherine, undertaking that if Strangeways' uncle, Roger Strangeways esquire, the late Queen's receiver in Anglesey, should be set free from his imprisonment at Beaumaris within the next month he would render his account of receipts before the executors or their auditors in London. Clearly all went well with Roger, for in July following he was made king's attorney-at-law in North Wales, an Exchequer appointment.[1]

In the following year, 1440, we find for the first time clear evidence of the existence of the most important single *motif* in the pattern of Strangeways' political career : his connection with the Nevilles, and especially with Richard Neville, earl of Salisbury, the eldest son of Ralph, earl of Westmorland, by his second wife, Joan Beaufort, and, therefore, head of the younger branch of the house of Neville. The connection need come as no surprise. It had already to a certain extent been prepared for by the links between Richard Neville and Strangeways' father: as far back as October 1423 Justice Strangeways had acted as a feoffee in the leasing for 15 years by Richard Lord Scrope of Bolton to Sir Richard Neville (as the earl of Salisbury then was) of the manor of Langley-by-Durham, and four years later (in November 1427) he had been Neville's co-grantee at the Exchequer of the custody of the castle and manor of Ludlow and other Mortimer estates of the late earl of March.[2] Now, on 29 November 1440, Strangeways junior was one of a group of north countrymen (headed by Lords Graystoke and FitzHugh) who were granted by Henry VI all the lands and rents (with certain specified exceptions) of Salisbury's mother, the late countess of Westmorland, from the time of her death on 13 November last, for as long as they were technically in the King's hands; they were expressly to hold them to the use of Salisbury who was her heir. The custody of the late countess's Cumberland estates called 'the FitzWalter lands' passed two months later on from this group of grantees to Sir Henry Fenwick, and the rest of the property in their temporary holding went direct to Salisbury himself, in a fresh royal grant, on 22 February 1441. A year later Strangeways and his fellow-custodians to the earl's use secured a royal pardon of all accounts.[3] Of these lands the most important were the Neville estates in Yorkshire centred in Middleham in Wensleydale and Sheriff-Hutton, which Richard Neville's mother had held in jointure since the late earl of West-morland's death in 1425. The younger Neville branch, with the earl of Salisbury at its head, withstood all efforts of the members of the senior line to dispossess them. Force proved necessary, but Salisbury was "well in" at Court, being at this time related to the duke of York, who was his brother-in-law, and to the Beauforts, directly through his mother and indirectly through his wife.

[1] *CCR*, 1435-41, 247; *CPR*, 1436-41, 288.
[2] *Catalogue of Ancient Deeds*, ii, B 1860; *CFR*, 1422-30, 202.
[3] *CFR*, 1437-45, 185, 187; *CPR*, 1441-46, 44.

Properly to appreciate the strength of these ties of Strangeways with the earl of Salisbury and others of the Nevilles, we need to look ahead for further evidence. On 20 March 1442 it was doubtless in Salisbury's interest that Strangeways was associated with him, his brother George (Lord Latimer), and Lord FitzHugh, in a recognisance for 2000 marks, undertaking to pay the bishop of Salisbury, the earl of Suffolk and others £1000 by 29 October following.[1] It was again almost certainly in the earl's interest that on 11 March 1454 to Strangeways and others were released the castle, lordship and manor of Mold and Moldsdale in Flintshire by the heir of one of the feoffees of the countess of Salisbury's grandfather, John Montagu, earl of Salisbury, who had incurred forfeiture for treason in 1400;[2] and, in the next year, Strangeways and the same feoffees acted in a fine relating to the Flintshire manor and lordship of Hawarden when the Countess Alice entailed the manor on Sir Thomas Stanley, Controller of the royal Household, and his male heirs.[3] Furthermore, on 10 May 1459 the earl made Strangeways one of his executors, an appointment likely only to have resulted from an important measure of intimacy and identity of interest between them, and in his will the earl left him a covered silver cup.[4] At the end of the following year Salisbury was killed at the battle of Wakefield along with Richard, duke of York, his brother-in-law, whose policies he had generally favoured. Strangeways fought there too, but escaped with his life. He was afterwards, as we shall see, feoffee to Salisbury's son, Warwick (in estates worth £1000 a year, to fulfil the latter's will). He was also a feoffee of Ralph Neville, second earl of Westmorland, Warwick's cousin.[5] His son and heir he first contracted in marriage with the daughter of William Neville (who became earl of Kent at the accession of Edward IV), his old master Salisbury's younger brother.[6] One of his daughters (Elizabeth) married a kinsman of the Nevilles, Marmaduke, son of Sir Richard Clervaulx and great-great-grandson of John Lord Neville of Raby.[7] Sir James was also a feoffee to George Neville, Lord Latimer, another younger brother of Salisbury's.[8] It is not too much to assume that Strangeways' ties with the Neville family were generally and continuously close, that from the beginning of his career he was in all probability a member of the household of

[1] CCR, 1441-7, 59.

[2] ibid., 1447-54, 494; CPR, 1446-52, 538.

[3] D.K.R., XXXVII, App. ii (Recognisance Rolls of Chester), p. 355. Stanley as long ago as 1443 had got a royal grant of the entail of Mold as well. He had connections with the Montagus, his mother's first husband having been cousin of the grandfather of the Countess Alice, and his own son and heir married a younger daughter of the earl and countess, Eleanor Neville.

[4] N. H. Nicolas, Testamenta Vetusta, i, 288; Surtees Society, Testamenta Eboracensia, ii, 244.

[5] CPR, 1461-7, 270; ibid., 538.

[6] For Strangeways pedigrees, see above, note 2.

[7] Collectanea Topographica et Genealogica, i, 305.

[8] British Museum, Harleian Ms., no. 433, fo. 176v.

Richard, earl of Salisbury, and perhaps one of his officials, and that this intimate connection conditioned Strangeways' later service to Salisbury's heir, the earl of Warwick.

Strangeways served on local commissions of royal appointment on hardly more occasions in the 1440's than during the preceding decade, although he had succeeded in 1442 to the estates of his father, Justice Strangeways. He was, of course, so well connected in Yorkshire, his Neville affiliations apart, that it is rather surprising that his first tenure of the shrievalty of Yorkshire came no earlier than on 4 November 1445;[1] he held office for the usual term of a year. By the time of his appointment Strangeways had been knighted. On 28 January 1448 he received at the Exchequer a grant of the right to farm a toft and a bovate of land at Boltby in the Hambleton Hills near Thirsk (Yorks.) for 40 years (as from the previous Michaelmas) at a rent of 8/- a year. On 7 November 1448 he was again made a commissioner of array in the North Riding (commissions being also then set up in the other Yorkshire Ridings and in Cumberland and Westmorland as well) to resist the Scots, following war on the borders which had taken even Henry VI as far north as Durham in the previous month.[2]

At a time when the nation's interest was being concentrated on the threatening situation in France and the failure of Suffolk's foreign policy, Sir James Strangeways was for the first time elected as knight of the shire for Yorkshire to the parliament of February 1449, along with Sir William Eure, a middle-aged knight of Witton-le-Wear (Durham) and Old Malton (Yorks.) who was Strangeways' wife's uncle by marriage. Their election was held on 13 January 1449 by Strangeways' brother-in-law, Sir John Conyers, then sheriff of Yorkshire. The sessions of the parliament were held at Westminster from 12 February to 4 April and from 7 to 30 May, and at Winchester from 16 June to 16 July 1449, when the parliament was dissolved. It was during the second Westminster session that on 15 May 1449 Strangeways secured at the Lower Exchequer for himself and his wife a grant of two tallies of assignment together nominally worth £80. 3s., presumably representing payments of arrears of the Darcy royal annuity of which she was entitled to a share; two and a half years later they were to bring them back for cancellation as unrealizable, in order to secure a fresh assignment.[3] After the parliament, by patent of 1 August 1449, he and his fellow shire-knight were put on commissions for each of the Yorkshire Ridings to apportion among their poorer vills the county's share of the general rebate attached to the recently granted parliamentary subsidy of two moieties of a tenth and fifteenth.[4] This was become a stock duty of ex-knights of the shire after every act of taxation of the regular sort.

---

[1] P.R.O. Lists and Indexes, no. IX (Lists of Sheriffs), 162.
[2] CFR, 1445-54, 85; CPR, 1446-52, 238.
[3] Issue Roll, P.R.O., E 403/791, mem. 4.
[4] CFR, 1445-54, 122.

On 27 August he was included with Viscount Beaumont, Lord Graystoke, Sir Thomas Stanley (the Controller of the royal Household), and Dr. Richard Andrew (the King's Secretary) in a commission to treat for a truce with Scotland, and this they achieved on 23 October for an indefinite period, Strangeways being subsequently appointed one of the *conservatores* of the truce.[1]

Himself present at the Yorkshire elections, Strangeways was not re-elected to the next parliament of November 1449 to June 1450, which saw the elimination of some of the duke of Suffolk's allies in the government and then his own impeachment and fall. The parliament was brought to a hasty end by news of the outbreak of Cade's revolt in Kent and neighbouring counties. It was at this point that the duke of York first came properly into the political limelight. The Kentish rebels had shown themselves his friends, and even in parliament there were some who, in these circumstances of governmental debility, were already prepared to point the way towards a recognition of his hereditary title to the throne as superior to that of the Lancastrians, a claim that was to be eventually admitted in the compromise settlement of 1460. At the end of the summer of 1450 York returned from his exilic lieutenancy in Ireland and demanded a newly constituted royal Council and a meeting of parliament. It is doubtful whether, at this stage, his brother-in-law, Salisbury, was disposed to be so energetic a Yorkist partizan as eventually he became.

Before York's return, Strangeways was appointed by the royal Council on 8 August 1450 to be a member of a committee of four commoners entrusted with the job of acting as receivers and treasurers of the graduated income-tax recently voted at Leicester and of loans to the Crown, all of the proceeds from which they were to spend on the wages of retinues engaged in defence; the receivers were each to receive 4s. a day for their own wages.[2] Strangeways on the same day was also included among the N. Riding commissioners charged with the local assessment of the tax; eight months later there were still certain Yorkshire lords and ladies still unexamined about their income.[3] In the meantime, early in the second stormy session of the 1450-51 parliament, Strangeways and one Robert Kelsey, who had been parliamentary burgess for Appleby at Bury St. Edmunds four years before, were able to profit by the Act of Resumption passed at Leicester in the spring of 1450, to the extent of receiving on 27 January 1451 a grant of the right to farm the manor of Laverton (in Kirkby Malzeard, near Ripon) for 10 years (as from November 1449) at a farm to be agreed at the Exchequer.[4] Some three weeks later, by a patent of 18 February 1451, Strangeways was included with the earl of Salisbury and Lord Graystoke in a commission to arrest a Scarborough ship-owner and bring him before the Council

[1] *Rot. Scot.*, ii, 335a, 340b.
[2] *CPR*, 1446-52, 377; *Rot. Parl.*, V 173.
[3] *CFR*, 1445-54, 169, 207.   [4] *ibid.*, 188.

on a charge of capturing a vessel of Dordrecht and so breaking the Statute of Truces of 1414.[1] On April 28 following, he was again appointed a commissary with authority to help define the duration of the existing truce with Scotland and also to correct infringements, and at the same time he was made one of a commission given power to punish negligence on the part of his fellow conservators of the truces. On 22 July he was also appointed to treat at Newcastle-on-Tyne with a Scottish embassy for the renewal of the truce. By the middle of August (1451) they were meeting and within a month had negotiated a truce to last until August 1454.[2]

Domestically, the Lancastrian government was now recovering something of its poise. On 28 July 1451 Strangeways had been for the first time made a justice of the peace in the North Riding, an appointment which suggests that neither he nor perhaps his friends the Nevilles were regarded as anything but friendly disposed to the Court party; he was to retain his place on the commission without a break until June 1460.[3] Early in 1452, when York attempted his *putsch* at Dartford, the earl of Salisbury (at this time co-warden of the western march towards Scotland with his son, Warwick) did his best to bring about a settlement between his brother-in-law of York and the Court, although the resulting reinforcement of Somerset's authority can hardly have been entirely satisfactory to him, kinsman of Somerset's though he was. On 19 March 1452 Strangeways was put on a commission with Lord Clifford for the requisitioning of shipping and crews at Newcastle-on-Tyne, presumably for service against France,[4] and on 3 June following was made one of the commissaries instructed to treat with James, the new earl of Douglas, and admit him to do homage to Henry VI.[5]

There was at this time civil war in the northern kingdom between King James II and the Douglases, following on the murder of the new earl's elder brother and predecessor in the title at Stirling in the previous February; the summer saw an accommodation made between the Douglas clan and James II, but the feud was only thinly overlaid and open conflict was to flare up early in 1455. At the end of May 1453 Strangeways had again been made one of the conservators of the Anglo-Scottish truce, which by this time had been extended until May 1457.[6]

In the meantime, on 23 November 1452 Strangeways had been granted at the Lower Exchequer 100 marks (by assignment only) for former ambassadorial work at Durham and Newcastle about the truce with the Scots, presumably during the negotiations of the late summer of 1451. It was on the same day that he had

[1] *CPR*, 1446-52, 438.
[2] *Rot. Scot.*, ii, 345a, 345b, 347b, 349b, 354b.
[3] *CPR*, 1446-52, 598; *ibid.*, 1452-61, 683.
[4] *ibid.*, 1446-52, 540.　　　　　　　　[5] *Rot. Scot.*, ii, 358a.
[6] *ibid.*, ii, 366b.

been appointed (for the second time) sheriff of Yorkshire, and only the day before he and his wife had received fresh Exchequer tallies of assignment for £80 odd, following their restitution of the "dud" tallies for this amount given them in May 1449, plus another additional tally of assignment for £40. 4s., which was to prove equally worthless.[1]

It was early in his year of office as sheriff, which lasted from 23 November 1452 to 5 November 1453, that Strangeways was understandably made a member of the Yorkshire commission set up in January 1453 for the raising of loans to the Crown for the financial relief of the earl of Shrewsbury, then engaged in Aquitaine and with apparently great (if what was to prove only transitory) success.[2] On 5 March, as sheriff, he held the elections to the Reading parliament which met on the following day. In May he was appointed, as we have seen, to act as a conservator of the truce with Scotland, in July as one of a committee of inquiry at Newcastle regarding the negligence of its port-officials for the past three years, and just two months later (on 26 September 1453) to membership of a royal commission ordered to arrest a Newcastle ship-master for seizing a Danzig vessel off the Humber and so contravening both the Statute of Truces of 1414 and the Anglo-Prussian trade *entente*.[3]

The period of Strangeways' shrievalty had held for him some compensations of a private nature: in the course of the year John Greenwell, abbot of Fountains, had visited him at Harlsey Castle to christen a son of his,[4] and early in March Strangeways had come to an agreement with his mother-in-law and her third husband, Lord Vessy, to pay them a rent for certain of her dower lands in order to have possession.[5]

Strangeways can hardly have had a very comfortable term of office as sheriff. The North was generally disturbed by a renewal of the old rivalry between the Nevilles and the Percies. This took the form of open hostilities between the younger sons of the earls of Salisbury and Northumberland. The Percies were safe supporters of the Queen and her party at Court (a party which, with the onset of the King's first bout of insanity in August 1453 and the birth of her son in October following, became the core of the royalist cause), and the quarrel between these two great northern families helped to move the Nevilles to give firm support to York in his bid for a Protectorship. York was given this office in parliament on 27 March 1454, and on 1 April his brother-in-law, Salisbury, succeeded to the custody of the great seal. With his eldest son, Richard of Warwick, and his two

---

[1] P.R.O., E 403/791, mem. 4; E 403/817. (this tally for £40 odd they returned to the Exchequer in December 1458 as unpaid); *List of Sheriffs*, loc. cit.

[2] *CPR*, 1452-61, 53. [3] *ibid.*, 123, 174.

[4] Surtees Society, vol. 67, *Memorials of Fountains Abbey*, vol. II, part I, p. 105.

[5] *ibid.*, vol. 83 *Yorkshire Deeds*, vol. VII, p. 141-2.

younger brothers, Lord Fauconberg and Lord Abergavenny, being regular members of the royal Council, and with another brother (Robert) established as bishop of Durham and his own son George promised the next episcopal vacancy, Salisbury was in a strong political position. It was only a few weeks before Salisbury became Chancellor that Strangeways had been involved in a settlement of the lordship of Mold (Flintshire), in which Salisbury was interested.[1]

Sometime between 15 March 1454 and the dissolution of parliament on 17 April following, Strangeways was caught up in the negotiations for the commitment of the administration of Calais and the March to the duke of York. Evidently, Strangeways was up in London at the time, probably attached to Salisbury's company. As conditions of his appointment, York demanded guarantees from the merchant-staplers of Calais, and adequate provision for control of the Dover Straits to enable the passage of any relief force that might be needed in answer to French threats. Various alternative suggestions were considered, among them being one that Sir James Strangeways and Master Robert Beaumond should make contact with the merchants 'to fele thcim if they wull take uppon theim the . . . charge' of safe-keeping the sea,[2] for which parliament had already voted tunnage and poundage. Eventually, it was Salisbury and four other peers who undertook the charge for the next three years.

Salisbury was almost certainly at this time considerably distracted by events in the north, where the Neville feud with the Percies was now so serious that the Protector (York) himself went up to Yorkshire in May 1454 to repress risings led by Thomas Lord Egremont, son of the earl of Northumberland, and his friend, Henry Holland, duke of Exeter. The latter fled to sanctuary at Westminster, but York 'fet hym owte' and on 24 July he was sent to the duchy of Lancaster castle of Pontefract, of which Salisbury had been constable for nearly thirty years. It was from Pontefract that, as Chancellor but in the interest of his family, Salisbury issued royal letters patent under the great seal at Michaelmas 1454 appointing commissioners to muster the defensibles of Yorkshire in each of its three ridings for the purpose of resisting those who had risen in Lancashire and elsewhere to spoil and plunder and generally upset the countryside. Strangeways figured in the North Riding one of these commissions.[3]

In 1455 civil war was precipitated by the consequences of Henry VI's recovery of health: the end of York's Protectorship, Salisbury's dismissal from the Chancellorship on 7 March, and the summoning of a Great Council to Leicester to provide for the king's 'surety'. York and the Nevilles, considering themselves threatened, took up arms in self-defence and defeated the royalist forces in the first battle of St. Albans on 22 May 1455.

[1] *CCR*, 1447-54, 494.
[2] *Rot. Parl.*, V, 255a.
[3] *CPR*, 1452-61, 219.

Whether Strangeways was implicated in this Yorkist revolt is not known. He had, of course, his connections with influential men on the Lancastrian side: sometime in this year he was feoffee to Sir Thomas Stanley, the Controller of the royal Household, in a conveyance to him by the earl and countess of Salisbury of the lordship of Hawarden (Flintshire); his wife's half-brother, Sir Richard Tunstall, was one of Henry VI's immediate Household entourage, and her half-sister was wife to the Lancastrian Lord Clifford. We need hardly remind ourselves that these family relationships did not necessarily imply even personal friendship, much less any identity of political outlook. Strangeways' Neville connections were strong, admittedly, but his presence at the Yorkshire elections to the parliament now summoned to meet early in July 1455—two supporters of the earl of Salisbury were in fact returned—suggests that he had kept out of the recent Yorkist "show-down" and stayed up in the north.[1] Had he been a member of Salisbury's retinue at St. Albans, it is more likely that he would have gone on with him to London.

Nothing further is known of Sir James Strangeways over the whole uneasy course of the next two years, except for one or two items of information of a private character. On 3 March 1456 he and his wife secured a royal licence to endow the York-shire Carthusian priory of Mountgrace, nearby their castle at Harlsey, with the advowson of the church at Beighton (Derby-shire).[2] Along with William Orell, doubtless one of his mother's kinsmen, Sir James was party to a recognisance for £100, under-taking to pay the Master of the Rolls, Thomas Kirkby, an annual rent of nearly £4 at his place at the *Domus Conversorum* in London.[3] Sometime during the year 1455-6 he was again visited at Harlsey by the abbot of Fountains; this was probably in connection with some business of the monastery, because in the abbey-bursars' books for the next year (and also for 1457-8) Strangeways is noted as being paid an annual fee of 2 marks, presumably for his services as a feodary of the abbey or as its legal counsel.[4]

In July 1457, after troubles on the Border in 1455 and 1456, a renewal of the truce with Scotland for two years was made at Coventry, and Strangeways was appointed once more as a *con-servator*.[5] This, his first royal commission for almost three years, was followed on 17 December 1457 by his inclusion in a com-mission to apportion the liability for maintaining a force of over 700 archers which was to be raised in Yorkshire as the county's contribution to a national force of archers. The scheme, originally granted for defence in the parliament of 1453-4, had since then

[1] Wedgwood, *History of Parliament, Biographies*, p. 820.
[2] *CPR*, 1452-61, 277.   [3] *CCR*, 1454-61, 130.
[4] Surtees Society, vol. 130, *Memorials of Fountains Abbey*, vol. III, pp. 25, 31, 73.
[5] *Rot. Scot.*, ii, 383a.

not been followed up.[1]   Its present resurrection boded no good
for the peace of the realm, which had again recently been ex-
cessively disturbed, at any rate in the North and particularly in
North Yorkshire, by open conflict between Nevilles and Percies,
whose feud had been made all the keener by the killing of the
earl of Northumberland at the battle of St. Albans.   A Great
Council met early in 1458 especially to deal with the problem, and
the Lancastrian and Yorkist leaders reached a hollow reconciliation
in a 'love-day' on 25 March 1458.   In the "deceitful lull" in the
struggle between the two main political parties that followed,
Strangeways was appointed on 24 November 1458 as a justice of
the peace in the East Riding of Yorkshire as well as in the North
Riding.[2]   On 5 December following, by the hands of his wife's
half-brother, Sir Richard Tunstall, (now chamberlain of Chester
as well as the King's carver), he and she were given at the Lower
Exchequer a fresh tally of assignment for £40, in place of the one
of November 1452 which evidently they had failed to turn to
account.   This tally, too, they were unable to cash and on 22
June 1459 received another for only 50 marks instead.[3]

By this time Lancastrians and Yorkists were both openly
preparing to settle their dispute by war.   On 10 May 1459 Salisbury
had made his will and appointed Strangeways as one of his
executors.[4]   The latter was not apparently open to suspicion at
Court, if one may conjecture this from his being appointed at
Coventry on 25 July to a commission to treat with the Scots for
a further truce and to deal with cases of breach of the existing
one.   He was not, however, among those members of this commission authorized to deal with the Scots *de certis secretis materiis*.
Nor was he appointed to treat in the next embassy, whose formation (at the end of October 1459) followed both Salisbury's victory
over a Lancastrian force at Bloreheath (Staffs.) on 22 September,
when the earl was on his way to join York at Ludlow, and the
bloodless dispersal of the Yorkist army and its leaders at the
Rout of Ludford on 12 October.   By this time, and in the circumstances, Strangeways' connections with the Nevilles might have
created some doubt of his political reliability.   Nevertheless, the
absence of his name from the list of those attainted in the Coventry
parliament of November 1459 for taking part in the recent rising,
is tangible proof that he had steered clear of active treason.   In
June 1459 he had been dropped from the commission of the peace
in the East Riding after serving for no longer than half a year,
but on 7 March 1460 he was confirmed in his commission as J.P.
for the North Riding.   It was his known Neville connections,
however, which resulted in his not being included in the re-formed
commission of the peace issued from Coventry on 25 June 1460,
a commission of which he had been continuously a member for

[1] *CPR*, 1452-61, 408.   [2] *ibid.*, 682.
[3] P.R.O., E 403/817; E 403/819, mem. 4.
[4] *Testamenta Eboracensia* (Surtees Society), ii, 246.

the past nine years.[1] The date of his dismissal is of some signifi-
cance—the very day before the threat of Yorkist invasion from
Calais actually materialized with the crossing (to Sandwich) of
York's eldest son and the earls of Salisbury and Warwick.

Within a week of their landing, such was the support they
gathered in Kent, these Yorkist forces were in a position to enter
London on 2 July 1460. Eight days later the Lancastrian army
in the Midlands was heavily defeated at Northampton and Henry
VI was brought back, a virtual prisoner, to the capital. On 30
July, by which time Salisbury's son, George, bishop of Exeter,
had been made Chancellor and other changes had been effected
in the key royal administrative offices, parliament was summoned
to meet on 7 October. Sir James Strangeways and his brother-
in-law (his sister Elizabeth's husband),[2] Sir Thomas Montford of
Hackford, were elected on 25 August as knights of the shire for
Yorkshire, Strangeways as senior knight. Only two days before,
Sir James had been once more included in the commission of the
peace for the North Riding, and on the eve of the shire elections
had been associated with the duke of York and his Neville supporters in a royal commission to arrest and imprison their
opponents or, to use the more technical language of the patent,
certain gentry of south Yorkshire and certain artizans of York
and all others in the city and county who uttered falsehoods and
so, by promoting discord among the magnates, contravened the
Statute of *Scandalum Magnatum* of 1378. And on 8 December
following, a week after the close of the first session of the parliament, which had seen the acceptance of the duke of York as heir
to the throne, Strangeways, along with York and his friends, including the Nevilles, was put on a commission of *oyer and terminer*
touching treasons, insurrections, riots, etc., in ten counties of the
north and the northern midlands.[3] On the next day York left
London with the earl of Salisbury for the purpose of suppressing
the activities of the Lancastrian lords of the north. On 30 December with many of their supporters York met his death in
battle at Wakefield and Salisbury, by execution, on the next day
at Pontefract. Strangeways was in the thick of it at Wakefield,
and when, on 23 January 1461, Clement Paston wrote to his
brother John, at a time when Queen Margaret was moving her
army southwards to the capital, rumour had it that Sir James
was 'taken or ellys dede', but more likely killed.[4] That he was
captured is very doubtful. Killed, he certainly was not.

The earl of Warwick now became head of his branch of the
Neville family, adding his father's earldom of Salisbury and its
lands, as well as the Neville property in the north centred on

[1] *Rot. Scot.*, ii, 390b, 397b; *CPR*, 1452-61, 682-3.
[2] Joseph Foster, *Pedigrees of the County Families of Yorkshire*, vol. iii,
pedigree of Strangeways of Harlsey castle; *The Genealogist*, N.S. 181.
[3] *CPR*, 1452-61, 683; 608, 653.
[4] *The Paston Letters*, ed. Jas. Gairdner (1910), i, 540.

Middleham and Sheriff Hutton, to the estates of the Beauchamp inheritance which he held in right of his wife. With his brother John (Lord Montagu) being Chamberlain of the royal Household, and his other brother George being Chancellor of England, Warwick, himself Great Chamberlain of England, would probably have been fain to continue with Henry of Windsor as titular king. His own defeat at St. Albans by Queen Margaret's forces on 17 February 1461 and the victory of Edward, the new duke of York, at Mortimer's Cross against the western loyalists forced Warwick, however, to commit himself entirely to the Yorkist cause. On 3 March 1461 Edward got himself declared King in London, and the battle of Towton on 29 March enveloped the only Lancastrian army now in the field in utter disaster. What part Strangeways played in this rapidly changing pattern of events is not known. It is probable that both he and his eldest son, Richard, gave their personal support to the Yorkist campaign and that they went further northwards with Edward IV to Durham and New-castle. It is almost certain that they were with the King at York on 10 May when both were made justices of the peace in the North Riding, and when Sir James was also put (for the first time) on the commission of the peace for the West Riding. Sir James was then also included in a commission of *oyer and terminer* touching the treasons committed at York by Dr. John Morton, the recently captured ex-chancellor of the duchy of Cornwall, who was later to go into exile with other Lancastrian die-hards; and three days later (on 13 May) he, his son Richard, and his brother-in-law, Sir John Conyers of Hornby, were put on a com-mission for imprisoning Lancastrian rebels in the North Riding, as fellow-commissioners with Warwick, his brother, Lord Montagu, and his uncle, Lord Fauconberg.[1] Sir James's son, Richard, had already married Elizabeth, daughter of the last-named, who was now to be created earl of Kent.[2]

Edward IV's first parliament was summoned on 23 May 1461 to meet in July, but, although it was possible for the coronation to take place on 28 June, already (on 13 June) writs had gone out postponing the meeting of parliament to 4 November in view of the disordered state of the country. No electoral returns for Yorkshire have survived, but Strangeways was certainly re-elected as knight of the shire, for he was chosen by the Commons as their Speaker. They presented him to the King for acceptance on 6 November, and he made at the same time the customary Speaker's 'protestation' and claim of privilege.[3] Six days later, on the Common's behalf and at their head, Strangeways expressed their joy at the King's victories and at his courage in asserting his royal rights, and successfully petitioned for the acceptance of

[1] *CPR*, 1461-7, 576; 30.
[2] *V.C.H., Yorkshire, North Riding*, ii, 408 (Richard's eldest son, James, was 28 years old at the time of his father's death in 1488).
[3] *Rot. Parl.*, v, 462.

Edward's title to the throne as justified by his lineage. Strangeways stated that the Commons were well aware that Edward was
King by divine, human, and natural law, and further asked that
the Lancastrian régime should be stigmatized as usurpative, and
that the recent compromise, under which Henry VI was to enjoy
the throne for life, should be annulled, since he had broken its
terms. The session ended on 21 December. By this time the
official bills for the attainder of the Lancastrians and for the
reversal of the attainders enacted by them at Coventry had passed
both Houses, and the bills were delivered by Strangeways as
having received the Commons' assent on what proved to be the
last day of the parliament for purposes of business. The King
himself was pleased graciously to thank the Commons and their
Speaker—'James Strangeways and ye that be commyn for the
Common of this my Londe'—for their loyal support, promising to
be their just and loving liege lord.

The session had proved personally satisfactory to Strangeways himself in other ways. The Commons adopted as their own
a petition to the King made by Strangeways, his son Richard
(as heir of his mother, Elizabeth Darcy), and Sir John Conyers
and his wife Margaret (Elizabeth's sister and coheir), referring to
a former lease of certain of their respective moieties of the Darcy
Irish estates to one Sir Thomas Bathe, who had incurred forfeiture
by a judgement made by the duke of York in a parliament held
at Drogheda in February 1460. The estates ought to have reverted
to the lessors, because the rents were in arrears and the lease had
provided for their re-entry in such a circumstance. The petition
went on to represent how at that time Strangeways senior and
his brother-in-law (Conyers) were 'driven to such streitnesse',
because of their service to the present King and his father and
other 'true Lordes of his blode', that they were not able to take
proper action in Ireland. The petitioners now requested that
parliamentary authority be given for their re-entry, and for their
recovery of the mesne issues, and for Strangeways senior to enter
his share of the estates 'by the curtesie'; the petition was successful.[1] And three days before the parliamentary session was
adjourned, namely on 18 December, the Lower Exchequer was
ordered to pay the Speaker arrears of his late wife's share of her
grandmother's and mother's interest by dower in her ancestor's
royal annuity of £40 (granted in 1341), which now amounted in
all to over £75.[2] Only a week after his official acceptance as
Speaker, Strangeways had been appointed on 13 November,
along with his two sons (Richard and James), to membership of a
commission of array in Yorkshire for defence against the Lancastrians and their Scottish allies. On 4 February 1462, during

---

[1] *Rot. Parl.*, v, 485; Sir James Strangeways' first wife, Elizabeth Darcy,
had died sometime between June 1459 and the beginning of this parliament of 1461.
[2] *CCR*, 1461-8, 45.

the parliamentary recess, Sir James Strangeways was also put on the Yorkshire commission—others were authorised to act in Nottinghamshire and Derbyshire—for the arrest of a Lancastrian agent, a Retford man, who was inciting men to rebel.[1]

The parliament of which Strangeways was still Speaker came together again on 6 May 1462, only to be instantly dissolved by Archbishop Bourchier in the absence of the King and of many of the Yorkist lords, including Warwick himself. Of the royal satisfaction with Strangeways' conduct as Speaker signal proof was soon to be forthcoming: despite the fact that the Commons had not voted any taxation—perhaps none was asked for, although the southern Convocation had made a grant in July 1461—three weeks after the dissolution, on 27 May, at Leicester, where the King had spent Easter and was still staying, the late Speaker was granted 200 marks (£133. 6s. 8d.) 'quas dominus Rex, de gratia sua speciali, eidem Jacobo liberari mandavit, consideracione boni veri ac fidelis servicii necnon diligenciae eidem domino Regi per dictum Jacobum in parliamento suo ut prolocutor eiusdem impensi, habendas de regardo'.[2] Not until over a year later, on 18 June 1463, did the Exchequer make payment and then in the somewhat unsatisfactory form of a grant by assignment, at the same time, however, making an additional assignment for £195. 10s. 5d. for the arrears of the Darcy annuity to which Strangeways was entitled in right of his late wife.[3] That date, 18 June 1463, was the date of the last day of the first session of the next parliament, which, summoned first of all to meet at York in the previous February and then adjourned to Leicester, had finally met at Westminster on 29 April. The names of the Yorkshire knights of the shire in this parliament are not known: but it is not improbable that the ex-Speaker was one of them.

In the meantime, the main focus of interest in 1462 had been in the north of England, where the Lancastrian alliance with Scotland had at first given, and the Lancastrians' retention of certain of the Northumbrian strongpoints had continued to cause, considerable trouble to the Yorkist régime. Warwick had been much preoccupied with these problems. In the autumn Warwick moved forward into Northumberland to counter a force brought from France by Queen Margaret. He was followed by Edward IV himself. Strangeways was evidently himself in the north at this time, being appointed on 21 November 1462 to a commission of *oyer and terminer*, headed by Warwick, his uncle (the earl of Kent) and his brother (Lord Montagu), instructed to deal with treasons and acts of rebellion in Northumberland and Newcastle.[4] Early

---

[1] *CPR*, 1461-7, 66, 102.
[2] Not as in Wedgwood, *Biographies*, £88. 6s. 8d.
[3] Issue Roll, P.R.O., E 403/829, mem. 5; C. L. Scofield, *The Life and Reign of Edward IV*, i, 246.
[4] *CPR*, 1461-7, 233.

298

in January 1463 effective resistance in this region seemed at an end, Bamborough, Dunstanborough, and Alnwick having all been taken.

It was at this time, on 9 January 1463, that William Neville, earl of Kent, Warwick's uncle, died. His heirs were his three daughters, of whom the second, Elizabeth, now aged 28 years, was wife to Sir James Strangeways' eldest son Richard, and the third (Alice) was wife of the heir of Sir James's brother-in-law, Sir John Conyers of Hornby. Their mother, Joan de Fauconberg, was reputed to be an idiot and incapable of governing her possessions, and it was to inquire into this in Yorkshire that Strangeways senior and others, including the chancellor of the Exchequer (Thomas Colt) and Strangeways' sister's son (Thomas Montford esquire), were deputed by royal commission of 12 March 1463.[1] His son and young Conyers, another member of the Strangeways family group, clearly had much to gain if the countess's sanity were impugned and her inability to administer her dower substantiated. Presumably they did not succeed, because Joan married again (and survived until 1490).

When these private developments were going forward, in spite of Burgundy being friendly to the Yorkists, Louis XI wavering in his support for his Lancastrian cousins, and the pro-Lancastrian party in a disunited Scotland cooling off from its early concern for the Lancastrian cause, Bamborough and Alnwick were retaken in its interest. On 3 June 1463 Warwick was required to leave parliament and follow his brother Montagu northwards, and, when parliament could conveniently be adjourned, Edward IV himself again set off to join them. It was at this juncture that, on 14 June, royal licence was obtained by Warwick to settle estates held in chief worth £1,000 a year (for the payment of his debts and the fulfilment of his will) on a committee of feoffees, including his brother George, bishop of Exeter, the earl of Worcester (then Treasurer of England and Steward of the Household), the two Chief Justices, and (among others) Sir James Strangeways.[2]

Part of the trouble in the north was undoubtedly due to the restiveness of the younger members of the senior branch of the Neville family (which had its origin in the first marriage of Ralph, the first earl of Westmorland) who, unlike their kinsmen of the half-blood, tended to support the Lancastrian cause. One of them was Humphrey Neville, a nephew of Ralph the second earl of Westmorland, who had been attainted in Edward IV's first parliament and imprisoned in the Tower. He had, however, escaped and got away to Northumberland where he had 'made commotion of people against our sovereign lord the king'. And on 7 April 1463, along with the mayor of York and others, Strange-

[1] *CPR*, 1461-7, 277.
[2] *ibid.*, 270.

ways was ordered to arrest and bring him before the Council.
This was before parliament met. Eight weeks later, on 3 June,
during the parliament Strangeways and Lord Montagu were
instructed to decide for themselves whether to take him into the
King's grace and promise him letters of pardon.[1] Evidently
Strangeways was to be engaged in anti-Lancastrian activities in
the north. Here the Yorkist Nevilles eventually won back the
lost Northumbrian castles, after Montagu had virtually applied
the quietus to the northern Lancastrians in April and May 1464
at the battles of Hedgeley Moor and Hexham.

These events constituted merely the final strangling of the
Lancastrian die-hard remnant, caught in the toils of Warwick's
diplomacy. Particularly successful had the Nevilles been *vis-à-vis*
Scotland, and the success of the Yorkist military activity in this
spring of 1464 was largely conditioned by the fact that negotiations
were all the time going forward for a peace and close alliance
with Scotland: on 5 April and again on 25 May 1464, when
Edward IV was himself at York, Strangeways was among those
appointed with Warwick, Montagu, and their brother, the
Chancellor, to meet the Scottish commissaries to this end.[2] Only
six days before his appointment to this second embassy, that is,
in the evening of 19 May, Strangeways had been present with
Warwick, Montagu and others in the hospital of St. Leonard's at
York when two chancery clerks returned to the Chancellor the
great seal which had been given to the Master of the Rolls to keep,
presumably during the bishop of Exeter's occupation with the
Scottish business.[3] In June Montagu was invested with the
vacant earldom of Northumberland as his reward, and the death
of Archbishop William Bothe in the following September permitted the translation of Warwick's other influential brother,
George, bishop of Exeter and Chancellor of England, to the
primacy of the northern province.

This preferment of George Neville to the see of York was
perhaps more a sign of the (temporarily) quite unshakeable
strength of the Nevilles than one of the King's continuing intention
to rely on them. Edward IV's marriage to Elizabeth Wydeville,
which entirely confused Warwick's foreign policies, and the rapid
promotion of members of her hitherto pro-Lancastrian family
seriously irritated the Neville *bloc*, and a breach between them and
the King steadily widened from this time on. As Edward IV began
to build up a Court party of his own, there can be no doubt of
which camp Strangeways considered himself to be a follower:
his relations with the Nevilles remained as close as ever. On 23
February 1465 he was appointed by Warwick to be his deputy
in the stewardship of the duchy of Lancaster lordship of Pickering

[1] *CPR*, 1461-7, 279; 267.
[2] *Rot. Scot.*, ii, 410b, 411a.
[3] *CCR*, 1461-8, 261.

(an office which Warwick had taken up in December 1461).[1]
After having been exempted from the Act of Resumption passed in
the second and final session of the 1463-5 parliament (which lasted
from 21 January to 28 March 1465),[2] on 20 June 1465 Strangeways
was made a member of the commission, with John Neville, the
new earl of Northumberland and warden of the East March, at
its head, empowered to contract marriages between English and
Scottish subjects, including a possible marriage between the
young James III of Scotland and an Englishwoman, and to treat
for a perpetual peace.[3] Strangeways was with John Neville at
Alnwick Castle engaged in this business with the Scottish embassy
on 17 July (when the new prior of Holy Island, a cell of the priory
of Durham, reported his election to both parties).[4] In the following
September he was doubtless present at the splendid feast provided
by George Neville, the new northern primate, for his installation
at York, which was made the occasion for a "great family gathering"
of the Nevilles, the King and Queen however being absent; certainly his son, Sir Richard Strangeways, was one of the officers
of the feast in the capacity of sewer.[5]

Sir James was again appointed, on 20 November 1465,
along with Warwick, Northumberland, and their brother, the
archbishop, to treat for a truce with commissaries from Scotland
who were to meet them at Newcastle a fortnight later,[6] a royal
privy seal warrant to the Lower Exchequer authorizing him (two
days after the issue of the commission) to be paid 40 marks as
recompense for his 'service and costs' done and incurred 'by
virtue of oure [the King's] commandement and oure commission
to hym directed in the north parties and elleswhere'.[7] On 1 June
1466 was ratified the truce with Scotland from 1464 to 1479 but
now extended to 1519, an arrangement to which, again as a
commissary with Warwick and his brothers, Strangeways had
recently been party.[8] Together with Warwick and Northumberland and others, he was appointed on 10 October 1466 to treat
at Newcastle in December for the keeping of the truce.[9]

Despite the growing breach between the Nevilles and
Edward IV, in which an important stage was reached when the
archbishop of York was deprived of the great seal on 8 June 1467
and Warwick's proposals for a French as against a Burgundian
alliance were shortly afterwards rejected, Strangeways was able
to secure an exemption from the Act of Resumption passed in the

[1] R. Somerville, *History of the Duchy of Lancaster*, i, p. 534.
[2] *Rot. Parl.*, V, 530b.   [3] *Rot. Scot.*, ii, 417a.
[4] Surtees Soc., (1841), *The Priory of Coldingham*, 198.
[5] W. Somner, *The Antiquities of Canterbury*, (2nd ed., London 1703,
by N. Battely), Part II, App. to Supplement, p. 29.
[6] *Rot. Scot.*, ii, 418b.
[7] P.S. warrants for issue, P.R.O., E 404/73/1, no. 103.
[8] *Rot. Scot.*, ii, 419b.   [9] *ibid.*, 420b.

short parliamentary session of 3 June-1 July 1467.[1]   It is, however, perhaps an indication of the new weakness of the Neville
interest that for nearly a year and a half after his appointment
on 20 February 1467 to serve on a commission of *oyer and terminer*
at York and in the county,[2] Strangeways was appointed to no
other royal commission, save the commissions of the peace for the
North and West Ridings of Yorkshire, from which he was locally
perhaps too influential to be removed.

There was a reconciliation at Coventry between the Nevilles
and the Wydevilles and the Court party early in 1468, but it
proved empty of all but formality, and Warwick now began to
stoop to intriguing with the Lancastrians and plotting for a
northern rising under cover of secrecy.   It was not until the
summer of 1469 that Edward IV realized the extent of the earl's
treachery and the wide range of disaffection of which he was the
centre.

In the meantime, on 6 June 1468 Sir James Strangeways
had been appointed as one of a commission to investigate the
circumstances behind a petition presented to the King by Sir
John Salvan; the latter denied that he had been enfeoffed in the
manor of Doncaster by Henry Percy, earl of Northumberland,
whose son and heir had been attainted in 1461 and had incurred
forfeiture.   And at the end of the same month Strangeways had
been appointed (with others) to hold inquisitions *post mortem*
regarding the estates of Sir Thomas Haryngton of Hornby (Lancs.)
and his son Sir John, both of them killed at the battle of Wakefield in 1460.[3]   On 10 August following (1468) Archbishop Neville
gave permission for Strangeways' daughter Margaret, widow of
John Ingleby, to be married (after publication of banns) in the
chapel of her father's manor-house at Harlsey to Richard Lord
Welles and Willoughby.[4]

Presumably not long after this marriage took place, Sir
James was appointed sheriff of Yorkshire on 5 November 1468 in
succession to his kinsman by marriage, Sir John Conyers.[5]   The
appointment may perhaps be regarded as a tribute to the capacity
of the Nevilles to dissemble their disaffection.   Six days later
Strangeways received an indemnity in advance for the great costs
he was bound to incur in discharging his office, in the form of an
assignment at the Exchequer for £340 which the King, 'certis de
causis et grandis consideracionibus ipsum specialiter moventibus',
granted him as a 'reward'. On 15 November, by privy seal warrant,
Strangeways was allowed to charge the issues of his office with
this allowance.[6]   This was a very material concession.

[1] *Rot. Parl.*, V 598b.   [2] *CPR*, 1461-7, 530.
[3] *ibid.*, 102, 103.
[4] Surtees Society, *Testamenta Eboracensia*, iii, 339; *Complete Peerage*,
VIII, 143.
[5] *List of Sheriffs*, 162.
[6] Issue Roll, P.R.O. E 403/841, mem. 4; P.S. warrants for issue,
E 404/74/1, no. 122.

As at the time of his previous occupation of the shrievalty of Yorkshire in 1452-3, Strangeways' present tenure of the office was one of great difficulty. There was a local revolt in the late spring of 1469, headed by 'Robin of Holderness' in favour of the Percies and suppressed by the Nevilles. Another rising, under the standard of 'Robin of Redesdale' and led by Sir John Conyers (Strangeways' nephew, by marriage), a rising with which the Nevilles and their friends were directly connected, was much more serious. It was fomented from Calais by Warwick and his new ally, Edward IV's brother George, duke of Clarence (who had recently married Warwick's daughter, Isabel), and was aimed at the King and the Wydevilles. These Yorkshire insurgents moved south in July, intending to join forces with Warwick. The great earl, crossing from Calais and raising the men of Kent, moved through London up into the Midlands to meet them. Before he could do so, the northern rebels defeated a force of Welsh and other loyalists under the earl of Pembroke at Edgecote Field on 26 July. Within a few days Pembroke and the earl of Rivers and his son had been executed by Warwick, and Edward IV himself was taken prisoner and a few weeks later carried off to Wensleydale to the Neville stronghold at Middleham. Public opinion, apparently even in Yorkshire, was too much for this, and the King soon regained his freedom of movement and was able to return to London. But temporarily the Nevilles were in the ascendancy, and that Sir James Strangeways was on 25 October following pardoned of all offences committed by him, and of all debts and accounts due by him as sheriff to the Crown,[1] suggests that his part in recent events, whether active or passive, had been satisfactory from the Neville point of view. There is no clear evidence that he had been directly implicated in the 1469 revolt, but it is difficult to believe, in face of the circumstantial evidence, that his conduct had not been, to say the least of it, equivocal from the King's point of view.

That Warwick and Clarence his son-in-law soon felt their position to be precarious is amply illustrated by their close connection with the Lincolnshire rising which broke out in February 1470. At this time the King did not know who were his friends and who his enemies in the north, and on 2 March Strangeways was appointed to serve under John Neville, earl of Northumberland, as a commissioner of array in the North Riding and in other parts of the county.[2] Two days later Edward IV left London for the new centre of disturbance; Strangeways' son-in-law, Richard Lord Welles and Willoughby (the father of Sir Robert Welles, the leader of the Lincolnshire rising), who had recently answered a royal summons to appear at Court, was ordered to be brought up in the King's rear. At Huntingdon he was ordered by Edward to have the rebellion put down on peril of his life. In the hope of

---

[1] *CPR*, 1467-77, 177.　　　　　　　　　　[2] *ibid.*, 200.

saving his father's life, the son decided to give battle instead of joining Warwick at Leicester. The King immediately (on 12 March) ordered Lord Welles's execution, and went on to win the rout of Lose-coat Field, young Welles being turned in a prisoner within a day or two of the engagement and shortly afterwards executed. Warwick and Clarence were now hopelessly compromised. When faced at Chesterfield with the prospect of a pitched battle with the royal army, they fled westwards and, disappointed of support there, left the country for Warwick's old refuge at Calais. Via Pontefract Edward moved to York on 22 March, 'and ther camme in to hym all the gentilmen of the shire', including, for sure, Strangeways' nephew by marriage (and his own eldest son's brother-in-law), Sir John Conyers of Hornby.[1] Sir James's younger son Robert, however, had been directly caught up in the recent commotions, and when, on 25 April following, commissions were issued ordering the seizure of the estates of Clarence and Warwick and other rebels, this son's lands (and those of his cousin, Conyers) were amongst those to be sequestered.[2] By this time the ex-Speaker must have been at least sixty years old, and in all probability had managed to keep clear of open complicity in treason. It was perhaps sound family policy, however, to show sympathy by allowing one's sons to serve as rebels: any resultant forfeiture of property for treason was unlikely to be expensive, if a revolt went wrong; if rebellion was successful, then the family would have done its part.

Just about the time when Warwick and Louis XI of France were busy at Angers persuading Queen Margaret to accept Warwick's offer to effect a Lancastrian restoration in return for the marriage of Prince Edward of Lancaster to his daughter, Strangeways was appointed (on 18 July 1470) a member of an English embassy to treat with the Scots early in August for proper adherence to the truce.[3] Within two months' time Warwick and Clarence had landed in England, Edward IV had fled to Flanders, and Henry VI's "readeption" government was in being. It would appear that in this present highly inflammable situation Strangeways was regarded as not now so positive a supporter of Warwick, or as too good a Yorkist to stomach the earl's recent *volte-face* or seek favour with his Lancastrian allies: certainly on 19 November, about when the government of the Readeption re-formed the commissions of the peace, Sir James was dropped from the West Riding commission and, on the next day, even from that of the North Riding.[4]

Failed by his brother, Montagu, in the North, and betrayed by Clarence, Warwick met his end at Edward's hands at Barnet on 14 April 1471. Landing on the same day at Weymouth, Queen

[1] J. H. Ramsay, *Lancaster and York*, ii, 351.
[2] *CPR*, 1467-77, 218.
[3] *Rot. Scot.*, ii, 423a.
[4] *CPR*, 1467-77, 637-8.

Margaret spent some time in the south-west raising forces that were crushed at the battle of Tewkesbury on 4 May. The leading Lancastrians in her army were either killed or afterwards executed, including Prince Edward. Less than three weeks later, when Edward IV entered London, Henry VI himself met his death in the Tower.

Discord within the royal family was soon to create fresh trouble, especially the rivalry of Clarence and Gloucester. But, in the meantime, there was need to tie up the diplomatic threads between England and other powers that had been either snapped or frayed in the recent upsets. One of the present needs was to re-confirm the truce with Scotland and suggest a marriage-alliance, and it was arranged on 26 August 1471 that the negotiation should take place at Alnwick four weeks later. Sir James Strangeways was one of the commissaries appointed. On 6 February 1472 a new commission, of which he was again a member, was set up to meet at Newcastle on 25 April to correct violations of the truce, and he was also, before this meeting could take place, one of those instructed on 16 March to treat for a perpetual peace between the two kingdoms.[1] In the interim, on 25 February (1472) Strangeways had been re-appointed J.P. in the North Riding, and on 7 March he was made a commissioner of array there. He continued to act as a J.P. in this his own Riding until his death in 1480, being re-appointed in November 1475, February 1476, and February 1477.[2] And he continued to be called upon to act in negotiations with Scotland, being appointed as a commissary to assist the examination of cases of breach of truce in May and August 1473 and, in February 1474, to confer about fishing rights in the River Esk, about which there was some doubt as to title.[3]

Otherwise, there is not much to record of Strangeways' latest years. In September 1472 his grandson James, then a boy of perhaps twelve years of age, was contracted in marriage with Alice, daughter of Thomas Lord Scrope of Masham who died in 1475. On 18 August 1473 Sir James had been put on the North Riding commission in a general inquiry about payments due to the royal Exchequer that had fallen into abeyance.[4] This was his last casual commission, excluding his Scottish mission of February 1474. When during the third session of the parliament of 1472-5, which lasted from October to December 1473, another Act of Resumption was passed, one of the exemption clauses (not provided for in the body of the bill but tacked on by the King) excluded from the effects of the act any lease or demise for term of years under the seal of the duchy of Lancaster made to Sir James Strangeways of any parcel of the duchy honour of Pickering and Pickeringlythe.[5] Of the last five years of his life nothing at all is known beyond the fact that on 1 October 1476 the feoffees of

[1] *Rot. Scot.*, ii, 430a, 430b, 433b, 434a.
[2] *CPR*, 1467-77, 349, 637.
[3] *Rot. Scot.*, ii, 437a, 438b, 451a.
[4] *CPR*, 1467-77, 408.   [5] *Rot. Parl.*, VI, 96.

a draper of mark in Northallerton, Richard Moore, conveyed property there to Sir James and his son Richard, on the understanding that they assumed patronage of a Maison-Dieu for a chaplain and thirteen poor people which Moore had founded in a chantry established in Northallerton parish church.[1]

Strangeways' interest in religion seems to have followed very orthodox lines. His and his wife's endowment of the Carthusian priory of Mountgrace with the advowson of the church of Beighton (Derbyshire) in 1456, has already been noticed. And so have his relations with the great Cistercian abbey of Fountains. Besides these connections, sometime in 1470 he and his second wife Elizabeth, daughter of Henry Eure esquire of Bradley (Durham), great-granddaughter of Henry Lord FitzHugh and widow of Sir William Bulmer of Wilton (near Redcar, Yorkshire) whom Sir James had married sometime between 1463 and 1468, were admitted to the Gild of Corpus Christi at York along with his daughter, Margaret Baroness Welles, and his younger son, James, and *his* wife.[2] Another younger son, George, rector of Bulmer and chaplain at Whorlton Castle by his father's gift, became Rector of Lincoln College, Oxford, in the year before his father's death.[3]

Sir James died shortly before 20 August 1480, when writs were issued from the royal Chancery authorizing inquiries on behalf of the Crown into his lands in Yorkshire, Lincolnshire, Derbyshire, Lancashire, Northumberland, and Middlesex. Sir Richard, his son and heir, was of considerably more than full age and, on 13 November following, for a fee of £20 to the King, received licence from the Chancery freely to enter his inheritance, saving homage, fealty, and relief.[4] Sir James's widow did not long survive him, dying on 13 (or 14) March 1482. Nor did his heir, for Sir Richard died on 13 April 1488, leaving as his widow his second wife Jane, daughter of Sir John de Assheton of Ashton-under-Lyne (Lancs.) and once widow of Roger Dutton esquire of Cheshire.[5] Sir Richard's son and heir, the Speaker's grandson, another James, then aged 28 years, had been knight of the body to Richard III, who had granted him 100 marks a year in the manor of Deighton and from the lordship of Middleham.[6] This James had been knighted by Richard III when as duke of Gloucester he had led the Scottish expedition of 1480.[7] He had come through the crisis of 1485 without much trouble, in spite of the fact that his brother-in-law, Thomas Lord Scrope of Masham, to

---

[1] V.C.H., Yorkshire, iii, 318; V.C.H., Yorkshire, N. Riding, i, 432.

[2] Complete Peerage, IV 66n; Surtees Society, vol. LVII, The Register of the Gild of the Corpus Christi, York, p. 75.

[3] Sir James's son, James of Ormesby and Sneaton, died in 1507-8. Testamenta Eboracensia, IV 39n; Notes and Queries, vol. 191 (1946), p. 72.

[4] CFR, 1471-83, 196; CPR, 1477-85, 225.

[5] Testamenta Eboracensia, IV, p. 186.

[6] ibid., 435.

[7] British Museum, Harleian MS. no. 293, fo. 208.

whom this Sir James was feoffee for the execution of his will, had certainly not found the transition from Yorkist to Tudor rule a comfortable one, and he was sheriff of Yorkshire in 1492-3 and 1508-9. This Sir James, who has been sometimes confused with his grandfather,[1] died on 16 December 1521.

[1] e.g. in the *D.N.B.* article on the Speaker, and by R. Somerville, *Duchy of Lancaster, op. cit.* For Lord Scrope of Masham's will, v. *Test. Ebor.*, IV, 72. Lord Scrope was a supporter of Lambert Simnel in 1487.

The following abbreviations have been used in the footnotes :—DNB= *Dictionary of National Biography;* CPR=*Calendar of Patent Rolls;* CCR= *Calendar of Close Rolls;* CFR=*Calendar of Fine Rolls;* Rot. Parl.= *Rotuli Parliamentorum;* DKR=*Deputy Keeper's Reports;* VCH=*Victoria County History;* Rot. Scot.=*Rotuli Scotiae;* PRO=*Public Record Office.*

13

WILLIAM CATESBY, COUNSELLOR TO RICHARD III

THE writer's interest in William Catesby arose in the first place mainly on account of Catesby's election as Speaker for the Commons in the short parliament of January-February 1484,[1] the only parliament held by Richard III during his brief reign of little more than two years. It had been the case that in more than half of the forty parliaments which had met since the accession of Henry V in 1413 the Speaker was a trained lawyer who more likely than not filled an administrative or legal office in the royal civil service in one or other of its branches. Some Speakers of this type had been caught up in high-level politics during the struggle for power which had led to the displacement of the Lancastrian by the Yorkist dynasty in 1461. Catesby belonged to this kind of professional administrative expert who, in a determined and even ruthless pursuit of private interest and self-aggrandisement, was prepared to run the risks of involvement in political intrigue. But it was only in the sharp hectic crisis of 1483, in which Richard, Duke of Gloucester, converted his Protectorship for the minority of his twelve-years-old nephew, Edward V, into an usurpation of the throne itself, that Catesby came into prominence as one of the assistant-engineers of this palace revolution.

Catesby was a member of a family whose social status was not particularly outstanding. As gentry they were well found. But as the son and heir of a former retainer in the Household of Henry VI whose real sympathies had remained Lancastrian, his way in politics was very much his own to make. An apprentice-at-law, before the end of Edward IV's reign he was acting as legal counsel to those who controlled that peculiar complex of royal estates, the Duchy of Lancaster, and also putting his talents as an estate-agent at the disposal of a number

[1] Rot[uli] Parl[iamentorum], vi. 238.

of aristocratic families which had property in the area of his own family's possessions in Warwickshire, Northamptonshire, and thereabouts. Members of these peerage families who used Catesby's managerial services included some of his wife's family—the Zouches of Harringworth—and influential relatives of theirs like Lord Scrope of Bolton. They also included a new Yorkist peer, William Lord Hastings of Kirby Muxloe and Ashby-de-la Zouche, Edward IV's Chamberlain and his close and steadfast personal friend, whose territorial interests and amassment of local royal offices in the central and northern mid-lands allowed him a remarkable domination of those areas.

Edward IV's early death in 1483 seriously endangered such internal stability as England had managed to acquire under his rule. There was need for peace, established government, and competent administration : instead, there was the prospect of minority rule under Edward V and (as if that were not in itself depressing enough) of a more fundamental breach in the soli-darity of the royal family than had even been the case sixty years before, when the infant Henry of Windsor had followed Henry V. Competing for the control of the person and authority of the young king were his mother, Queen Elizabeth, and members of her formerly pro-Lancastrian family, the Wydevilles, who hitherto had had much to do with his upbringing, and Richard of Gloucester, the sole surviving brother of the late king who, in his will, had appointed him to be Protector. Neither party felt itself safe from the other. Lord Hastings was no friend of the queen or of her family and on Edward IV's death, therefore, approved of Gloucester's Protectorship. But further than this Hastings was not prepared to go. And when Gloucester, whether moved by the stern necessities of the situation or deluded by crude ambition, resolved to be king himself and sought Hastings's support, the latter refused and paid with his life the price of fidelity to Edward IV and his issue.

In his recent book, *Lord Hastings' Indentured Retainers, 1461-1483*, W. H. Dunham Jr. prefers to regard the practice of engaging retainers as " a refinement, and not a degeneration, of an earlier feudal custom ", as legally founded upon contract, and as socially conditioned by an unstrained acceptance on the part of both lord and retainer of their mutual fidelity : "the values which governed this politico-military system were", insists Mr. Dunham, "honor and integrity, good faith and the keeping of contracts" (p. 13). This hypothetically rosy view of bastard feudalism noted, it is not surprising to find in his book only the barest allusion to the part played in Hastings's betrayal by William Catesby, who appears in Mr. Dunham's narrative simply as "common friend" of Hastings and the Protector (p. 15). Now, as is made clear in Sir Thomas More's story of Richard III's usurpation—and there is no special reason why More's details about minor personages involved in its consummation should be open to suspicion—Catesby was an intimate enough member of Hastings's affinity to be one of his private council. His appointment as Chancellor of the Earldom of March during the brief reign of Edward V may be regarded, in fact, as a move on Gloucester's part to maintain Hastings's support for his Protectorship. Then, with Hastings done to death—and Catesby was privy to the exchanges, the effect of which precipitated Hastings's fall and resulted in his execution— Catesby climbed over the body of his patron into possession of certain of his posts : Richard III, soon after his accession, granted him the office of Chamberlain of the Exchequer and (with Viscount Lovell, who followed Hastings as King's Chamberlain) the Constableship of the castle and the master-forestership of the forest of Rockingham, together with the Stewardship of certain Northamptonshire crown-lands, all of which offices Hastings had held. Also granted by Richard III the Chancellorship of the Exchequer and made an Esquire of the Body and a member of his Council, Catesby rose rapidly higher in the usurper's favour. Whatever contract had subsisted between Catesby and Hastings, it had clearly waited upon expediency.

Partly constructed on the basis of the adherence of such men as Catesby, and troubled by rebellion and rumours of foul deeds, Richard III's rule never inspired confidence. Catesby held by him to the end, much as a previous Speaker and "caterpillar of the commonwealth", Sir John Bussy, had done by Richard II, nearly a century before. But, as perhaps in this earlier instance, it may have been because he had committed himself too far to be other than dependable. Certainly, Catesby's will, with its revelations of his disappointment at not escaping the effects of his fidelity to Richard III at Bosworth Field, suggests that he would have followed a policy of re-insurance *vis-à-vis* Henry Tudor, had it been open to him to adopt it. He was seemingly sanguine in temperament, a born gambler. And had it not been for the circumspection of those who finally threw in their lot with Henry at Bosworth, Catesby's speculations would doubtless have paid richer dividends than even hitherto had been the case. He had been unable to extricate himself from the consequences of his heavy investment in Richard III's stocks, which now were proved to have been far from gilt-edged, and his personal liability stood no chance, in the circumstances, of being regarded as a limited one.

By a succession of profitable marriages with local heiresses, that branch of the Catesby family to which William Catesby belonged had built up for itself in the course of the fourteenth and fifteenth centuries a very substantial collection of manors and lands in the adjacent counties of Warwickshire and Northamptonshire.[1] The bulk of them straddled the boundary between the two shires, being contained in the wide angle to the south of the crossing of the Fosse Way and Watling Street. The manor of Ladbrooke (Warwicks.) had come into the family by marriage early in the fourteenth century. Nearby Radbourne came in the next generation with the marriage of the Speaker's great-great-grandfather, who had been connected with the household of Edward III, the same William Catesby who had represented Warwickshire in seven parliaments between 1339 and 1365 and had been the royal escheator in 1340-1 in Warwickshire, Leicestershire, Nottinghamshire, Derbyshire, and Lancashire, and in 1368-70 in Warwickshire and Leicestershire.[2] The marriage of this William's son, John, who was knight of the shire for Warwickshire in 1372 and 1393, king's steward of Coventry in 1383, and later in Richard II's reign steward of the Earl of Warwick's courts in Northamptonshire, brought Ashby St. Legers (Northants.), a Duchy of Lancaster tenancy, into the

[1] G. Baker, *History and Antiquities of Northamptonshire*, i. 244-5.
[2] *Cal. Charter Rolls*, v. 447 ; C[alendar of] P[atent] R[olls], *1485-1494*, p. 209.

family collection.[1] This John Catesby's younger son but eventual heir, John Catesby of Althorpe, the Speaker's grandfather, by his marriage secured possession of the manors of Lapworth (Warwicks.),[2] and Braunston (Northants.)[3]. Between his occupation of the office of escheator for Northamptonshire and Rutland in 1423-4 and of the shrievalty of Northamptonshire in 1425-6, he sat in parliament for the latter county in the spring of 1425 and was again knight of the shire in 1429-30. *His* son, the Speaker's father, Sir William Catesby of Ashby St. Legers, wedded, as his first wife, Philippa, daughter and coheir of Sir William Bishopston of Castleton (knight of the shire for Warwickshire in 1426), and this marriage eventually brought her son, the Speaker, possession of the manor of Bishopston in south-west Warwickshire.[4]

The Speaker's inheritance and his own purchases altogether comprised more than a dozen manors, roughly divided equally between Warwickshire and Northamptonshire, as well as other properties : in the former county were the manors of Ladbrooke, Radbourne, Lapworth, Bishopston, Oxhill (secured in 1482),[5] and Grandborough,[6] estates in Gaydon, Hodnell, Hardwick Priors, Napton, Corley, and property in the town of Coventry ; in Northamptonshire, the manors of Ashby St. Legers, Long Buckby, Watford, Welton, Great Creaton, and Braunston, and lands at Yelvertoft, Silsworth (in Haddon), Snorscombe, Everdon, and Hellidon.[7] Over in Leicestershire he held the manor of Kirby Bellars and property at Husband's Bosworth and Dunton Bassett ; in Huntingdonshire, the manor of Tilbrook; and, far away in Norfolk, the manor of Redenhall.[8] The Speaker's close connection with Richard III enabled him to

[1] *Feudal Aids*, iv. 35 ; *Cal. Charter Rolls*, loc. cit.
[2] Sir William Dugdale, *The Antiquities of Warwickshire*, p. 585a ; *VCH, Warwickshire*, v. 111.
[3] *C.P.R., 1485-1494*, p. 96.
[4] Ibid. p. 209 ; Dugdale, op. cit. p. 526b.
[5] *C.P.R., 1485-1494*, p. 275 ; *Cat. of Ancient Deeds*, iii. A 4575.
[6] *Ancient Deeds*, iv. A 10387.
[7] *C.P.R., 1485-1494*, pp. 209, 275, 340.
[8] Ibid. pp. 275 ; 100 ; 129 ; *Ancient Deeds*, iv. A 8481 ; *VCH, Bedfordshire*, iii. 173 ; F. Blomefield, *An Essay Towards a Topographical History of the County Norfolk*, v. 368.

secure great advantage from the forfeiture of estates which followed the rebellion of Henry Stafford, Duke of Buckingham, in
the autumn of 1483, including some of the escheats of the duke
himself and of the Marquis of Dorset. In Surrey Catesby got
the duke's lordships of Camberwell and Peckham, but he mainly
had his pick of places in his own region where he took the
opportunity to strengthen his hold. In Warwickshire, he
secured in tail-male the manors of Wootton Wawen, Little
Halford, Great and Little Wolford, and Ascott; in Northamptonshire, the manors of Brington, Crick, Lilbourne, Clay-
coton, Rothwell, and Glapthorn, and, over in south Leicestershire, the manor of Broughton Astley. When this transfer was
complete, he had an interest in some two score places in this
region of the central Midlands. What was the annual value of
all Catesby's estates is not known, but those he received from the
forfeitures of the rebels of 1483 were alone worth £273 11s. 8d.,
from which he paid to the king no more than £20 12s. 9d. a
year.[1]

The family had come some way towards a position of more
than merely local influence under the Speaker's father, Sir
William Catesby. When his first wife, Philippa Bishopston
(the Speaker's mother), died in 1446, he was a member of the
household of Henry VI merely as an Esquire of the King's
Hall and Chamber.[2] By May 1453, however, he was an Esquire
of the Body to Henry VI and was probably soon afterwards
knighted.[3] He had already been sheriff of Northamptonshire
in 1442-3 and 1451-2, knight of the shire first for Northamptonshire and then for Warwickshire in the two parliaments of 1449,
and he sat again for Northamptonshire in the parliament of
1453-4. He was once more sheriff of Northamptonshire in
1455-6. In February 1458 he was made constable of Northampton castle for life, and at the end of this year, as one of the King's
carvers, he was granted an annuity of £40. Half of this sum
was to be charged on the issues of Herefordshire where, at
this time (November 1458-9), he was occupying the shrievalty.

[1] British Museum, Harleian MS. 433, fol. 286ᵛ.
[2] Exchequer, P.R.O., E. 101/409-10.
[3] J. C. Wedgwood, *History of Parliament, Biographies*, pp. 163-4.

His rising fortune had already been signalled (and doubtless assisted) by his second marriage :[1] with Joan, daughter of Sir Thomas Barre and widow of a Herefordshire knight, Sir Kynard de la Bere of Kynnersley. She was very well connected, being on her mother's side a niece of John Talbot, first Earl of Shrewbury, who had appointed the Speaker's father as one of his executors just before he went to fight for what little was left to the English in Aquitaine (where, in July 1453, he was killed).[2] In the last two years of Henry VI's reign, 1459-61, Sir William was a firm supporter of the Lancastrian party against the Yorkists : he was one of a committee of loyalists to whom some of the estates forfeited by the Duke of York—a large group of forty-five manors—were granted (to administer) at Coventry in December 1459 ; on 15 March 1460 he was given for life the stewardship of all York's sequestered estates in Northampton-shire, Buckinghamshire, and Herefordshire, together with the constableship of the old Mortimer stronghold of Wigmore ; and only a few days later he was granted the custody of the attainted Earl of Warwick's lordship of Fownhope (Herefords.), upon which, moreover, his annuity of £40 as King's carver was now charged.[3] It is very likely that Sir William fought with the Lancastrian forces defeated at Northampton in July 1460, and almost certain that he did so in the disaster which befell them at the battle of Towton Field in March 1461, for on 14 May 1461 his estates in Northamptonshire and Rutland were ordered by Edward IV to be seized, and it was not until the following December that he was able to make fine and secure a royal pardon.[4] There was a rumour current in the following year that he was with the Lancastrian exiles in Scotland,[5] but in view of his pardon this is most unlikely. Certainly, Sir William

[1] Baker, *loc. cit.* (Wedgwood [*loc. cit.*] is in error in making Sir William Catesby's marriage with Joan Barre his first one, and his marriage with Philippa Bishopston his second. Philippa died on 20 December 1446, Joan on 11 August 1471.)

[2] Lambeth Palace Library, Kemp Register, fol. 311b.

[3] *C.P.R.*, *1452-1461*, pp. 542, 550 ; 581(461).

[4] Ibid. *1461-1467*, pp. 35, 120.

[5] *Three Fifteenth Century Chronicles*, ed. J. Gairdner (Camden Society, 1880), p. 158.

was put back on the commissions of the peace in both Northamptonshire and Warwickshire in 1465. In spite of this, he clearly supported the Lancastrian restoration in 1470, being once again made sheriff of Northamptonshire by the "Readeption" government in November 1470, an office in which he was superseded by Lord Hastings's younger brother as soon as Edward IV re-established himself in April 1471. Sir William was not re-included in the Northamptonshire commission of the peace until November 1475, an appointment which he may have owed to the influence of George, Duke of Clarence, for whom he acted as a feoffee.[1] It was, however, after Clarence's execution (in November 1478) that he was made sheriff of Northamptonshire once more. He was still holding this office when he died.[2]

It is not very likely that the later Speaker, then a rising young apprentice-at-law, had hitherto found his father's antecedents and connections to be of much advantage to his own career. Nothing of William Catesby esquire is known until after the Yorkist restoration of 1471, apart from the fact that on 20 March 1460, shortly before the Lancastrian *débâcle*, his father and he secured a royal licence to establish a family chantry in the church of Ashby St. Legers.[3] Very probably by this time the younger William was already married to Margaret, daughter of William, the sixth Lord Zouche of Harringworth who died in January 1468. The marriage had certainly taken place by December 1471 when young Catesby's wife's mother (Elizabeth) and her second husband, John Lord Scrope of Bolton, granted him for her lifetime all their lands in Houghton-on-the-Hill (Leics.).[4] The Zouches were themselves of the parliamentary peerage and in the top flight of the landowning society of the East Midlands. Lord Scrope of Bolton, Catesby's wife's stepfather, was a prominent northern Yorkist whose adherence to the Earl of Warwick during the Lancastrian Re-adeption Edward IV thought it prudent to overlook, especially perhaps as Scrope's

[1] *C.P.R., 1467-1477*, pp. 530, 597.

[2] P.R.O., *Lists and Indexes*, no. IX (*List of Sheriffs*), p. 93.

[3] Ibid. *1452-1461*, p. 551. The Speaker's father simultaneously secured a licence to impark 300 acres of land at Ashby St. Legers and 1,000 acres at Lapworth (Warwicks.).

[4] *Ancient Deeds*, iv. A 6808.

wife, Catesby's mother-in-law, was a friend of the queen. (Lady Scrope was with the queen in the Westminster sanctuary when her first son, Edward, was born during his father's exile, and had stood godmother to the child at its rather unceremonious christening.) Had Catesby later on not so hopelessly compromised himself as a supporter of Richard III, his marriage might conceivably have proved of great assistance to him in other directions : Catesby's wife's mother was half-sister to Lady Margaret Beaufort, mother of Henry VII ; Catesby's wife and Richard III's supplanter were cousins.[1]

Little of immediate moment seems to have come the younger Catesby's way in the 1470s. In fact, surprisingly little information about him of any sort is forthcoming before the last two or three years of Edward IV's reign. It was not until 18 May 1473 that he was put on his first commission by royal appointment: an inquiry into the estates of the late Ralph Lord Sudeley in Warwickshire.[2] On 5 July following, he and his wife, his father, his two younger brothers, and others of their kinsfolk were admitted to the confraternity of the priory of Christchurch, Canterbury.[3] On 5 October 1474 he sold to Sir William Stock (for £42) all the wood and underwood (except crab trees) in a coppice in Grettonwood in the forest of Rockingham, for three years.[4] Here he was very likely acting for the man who was certainly later on his master : William Lord Hastings, the King's Chamberlain, who since 1461 had shared with his younger brother the master-forestership of the royal forest of Rockingham. In June 1475 Catesby and his father were acting as feoffees-to-uses to Richard, son and heir of the Richard Knightley of Fawsley (Northants.) who had been a teller of the Exchequer between

[1] *The Complete Peerage*, ed. G. H. White, xi. 545 ; Dugdale, *The Baronage of England*, i. 692 ; *VCH, Beds.* iii. 41. Catesby's wife's mother, Elizabeth, was daughter of Sir Oliver St. John by Margaret, daughter and eventual heir of Sir John de Beauchamp of Bletsoe (Beds.), which Margaret after Sir Oliver's death married John Beaufort, Duke of Somerset, by whom she became mother of Lady Margaret Beaufort, whose son by Edmund Tudor became Henry VII. Margaret de Beauchamp died in 1482-3 when her heir was John St. John, her son by her first husband.

[2] *C.P.R., 1467-1477*, p. 403.
[3] B. M., Arundel MS. 68, fol. 3b.
[4] *Ancient Deeds*, iv. A 6499.

1422 and 1438.[1]   Nearly two years later he was one of a small
group, including Chief Justice Billing, Sir Richard Tunstall
(a sometime Lancastrian diehard), Catesby's uncle, John
Catesby, a royal serjeant-at-law, Robert Whittlebury, his
brother-in-law, and Oliver Sutton, who were granted by a royal
patent of 1 March 1477 the custody of the castles and lands of
John Stafford, late Earl of Wiltshire, and his countess (Constance,
daughter of Sir Henry Green of Drayton, Northants), during the
minority of Edward, their son and heir.[2]   The latter, who on the
death of his father nearly four years before was aged only three
years, was a first cousin to Henry Stafford, Duke of Buckingham.
Shortly before Richard III's accession these same associates
(except that Chief Justice Husee had been substituted for his
predecessor at the King's Bench) were given the heir's wardship
and marriage ; confirmed in it a year later, they were still enjoying the wardship in December 1484 when they had an acquittance for a payment of £1,000.[3]

In the 'seventies, meanwhile, Catesby was beginning to be
active as an agent for some of the more considerable landowners
of his own region.   On 1 October 1477, for example, Elizabeth,
daughter and coheir of Richard Beauchamp, Earl of Warwick,
and widow of George Neville (Lord Latimer) and more recently
(in 1476) of Thomas Wake esquire of Blisworth, granted for
life to Catesby and his son and heir, George, rents of £10 and
10 marks respectively from the manors of Kislingbury (Northants)
and Bewdley (Worcs.) for William's services on her behalf.[4]
William Catesby, as a member of her council, was still in receipt
of her annuity when she made her will on 28 September 1480 :[5]
she appointed him one of her executors, along with John Sapcote,
Esquire for the Body to Edward IV, and William Lord Hastings,
the King's Chamberlain, who was also appointed an overseer
of the will together with the Duke of Gloucester and Bishop
Morton of Ely ; Catesby was appointed one of a small group of
three of the executors who were to have the receipts of all her

[1] C.P.R., 1467-1477, p. 531.
[2] Ibid. 1477-1485, p. 19.
[3] B.M., Harleian MS. 433., fol. 69ᵛ, fol. 197.
[4] Ancient Deeds, iv. A 7459.
[5] N. H. Nicolas, Testamenta Vetusta, i. 360.

enfeoffed lands (in Northamptonshire, Buckinghamshire, Worcestershire, Gloucestershire, Devon and Somerset) and make annual account before the overseers. (His fellows in this business were John Wake, who became usher of the Chamber to Richard III, and Thomas Limerick, steward of the Latimer lands.) The Baroness Latimer died within the next few days. Two months later, the feoffees procured a royal pardon for the conveyances and a licence to enter, and at the end of December 1480 Catesby and the other operative executors began to farm (as responsible to the Exchequer) some of the Latimer estates in Worcestershire during the minority of the Baroness Latimer's grandson and heir, Sir Richard Latimer, who was then in the wardship of his mother's kinsman, Cardinal Bourchier. The Latimer feoffees were still involved in the trust in November 1483.[1] In the meantime, on 3 July 1482, Sir Thomas Vaughan (Treasurer of the King's Chamber) and John Wood (Under-Treasurer of England) had made Catesby steward of the Latimer manors of Corby and Burton Latimer (Northants.), with an annual fee of two marks and for the duration of the heir's minority.[2] He was already associated with Lord Hastings in other ways than as co-executor to Dame Latimer : on 1 October 1478, for instance, the two men were involved (with others) in leasing a place called "Over Court" in Farthingstone (Northants.).[3]

It was shortly after this that Catesby's father, Sir William, was for the last time appointed sheriff of Northamptonshire. At the previous midsummer (1478) Catesby himself had been put on a royal commission to hold an inquest post mortem regarding the lands of a Northamptonshire widow,[4] and, more recently, on 30 July 1478, father and son had together been made commissioners of inquiry into cases of forestalling and regrating of grain and malt in Northamptonshire.[5] Early in his father's year of office as sheriff, William Catesby esquire was also put on a commission of gaol delivery at Northampton (by patent of 8 February 1479).[6]

[1] C.P.R., 1477-1485, pp. 233, 241 ; B.M., Harleian MS. 433, fol. 124ᵛ.
[2] Ancient Deeds, iv. A 8428.   [3] Ibid. A 6469.
[4] C.P.R., 1477-1485, p. 111.   [5] Ibid. p. 144.   [6] Ibid. p. 146.

Before his year of office as sheriff was ended, Catesby's father died. This was probably not long before 22 October 1479, when writs of *diem clausit extremum* were sent by the Chancery to the escheators in Northamptonshire and War-wickshire.[1] It can only have been shortly after this that Catesby came into possession of his own family-estates.

This accession of sources of income in land was quickly followed, as it happened, by a burgeoning of Catesby's managerial interests in a number of directions. On 12 January 1480 he was involved in a purchase of the manor belonging to the Staffords at Tilbrook (Huntingdonshire), a former De Bohun manor.[2] Sometime between then and the Duke of Buckingham's execution for treason in the autumn of 1483, Catesby became his steward and surveyor in the manor of Rothwell (Northants.), a property which Catesby then secured for himself along with other of the Duke's forfeitures;[3] on 11 March 1481 he was already included among the Duke's feoffees in Rothwell, some Stafford family estates in Essex, and the lordship of Thornbury (Glos.).[4] In the spring of 1484 he was still interested in Buckingham's affairs, being a member of a small group of Richard III's advisers charged with meeting the Duke's debts out of some of his es-cheated property.[5] Meanwhile, on 10 January 1481, his mother-in-law and her second husband, John Lord Scrope of Bolton, appointed Catesby (" their son ") to be steward and surveyor of all the lands held in Northamptonshire by Lord Scrope in right of his wife; the office was to last for the lady's lifetime and carry with it a £4 fee from the issues of the lordship of Brayfield.[6] Some of these estates, the Zouche manors of Barby, Onley, and Gretton (Northants.), they demised to him for the same term on 16 February 1484.[7] Within half a year of this stewardship coming his way, Catesby was also appointed by his brother-in-law, John Lord Zouche (who had just come

[1] *C.P.R., 1471-1485,* p. 175.
[2] *Ancient Deeds,* iv. A. 8481.
[3] *C.P.R., 1485-1494,* pp. 232-3.
[4] Ibid. *1477-1485,* p. 257.
[5] Ibid. p. 498 ; B.M., Harleian MS. 433, fol. 176^v.
[6] *Ancient Deeds,* iv. A 8336.
[7] Ibid. iii. A 4786.

of age) as steward and surveyor for life of all his manors and lands in Bedfordshire, Buckinghamshire, Hertfordshire and Warwickshire, and as surveyor of all his estates in Northampton-shire and Leicestershire : part of Catesby's reward was a grant to him (also for life) of all Lord Zouche's lands in Yelvertoft (Northants.).[1]   Already, in February 1481, he had been retained as one of the apprentices-at-law engaged as counsel by the administration of the Duchy of Lancaster, with a fee of 13s. 4d. per annum ; and Catesby was to retain this office under Richard III.[2]

In the last year or so of Edward IV's reign, Catesby continued to engross local administrative offices and occasionally to act simply as a fee-ed counsellor. On 8 March 1482 the Augus-tinian priory of Laund (Leics.) made him a grant for life of an annuity of 2 marks (26s. 8d.) for his good counsel past and to come.[3]   A yearly rent of £2 charged on the manor of Farndon-in-Woodford (Northants.) was granted him for life on 16 May following, for counsel given by him to Edward (Grey) Lord Lisle, the second son of Edward Lord Ferrers of Groby and brother to the queen's first husband (John Grey), who had married a grand-daughter of the first Earl of Shrewsbury and was to be created Viscount Lisle by Richard III in the first week of his reign.[4]   Only a fortnight or so later and, on 1 June 1482, Lord Hastings's younger brother, Sir Ralph Hastings of Harrow-den, Knight of the Body to Edward IV, made Catesby steward of his manor of Harpole for life and also steward of the manor of Harleston during the minority of the son and heir of John Dive, Attorney-General to Edward IV's queen from 1465 to 1474 ; Catesby was to take a fee of £1 a year in each case.[5] It was a month after this (3 July 1482) that he became steward of two of the Northamptonshire manors of Lord Latimer (then still in his nonage) at 2 marks a year. And Richard III had been reigning for little more than a year when, on 1 August 1484,

[1] *Ancient Deeds*, iv. A 9650.

[2] Duchy of Lancaster, Accounts Various, P.R.O., D.L. 28/5/11 ; R. Somerville, *History of the Duchy of Lancaster*, i. 454.

[3] *Ancient Deeds*, iv. A 13424.

[4] Ibid. A 6600.

[5] Ibid. A 9178.

describing Catesby as his kinsman, John Lord Dudley appointed him steward for life of the lordship of Rugby (Warwicks.) with a fee of 10 marks a year, when the life-tenant (Lord Stanley) should die, and also made him steward for life of the manors of Aston-le-Walls and nearby Appletree (Northants.) with a yearly fee of £2.[1]

It is probable that William Catesby sat as knight of the shire in Edward IV's last short parliament which came together on 20 January and was dissolved on 18 February 1483. If so, it may well have been that he represented Northamptonshire, because—although the returns of elections to this parliament for Warwickshire as well as for Northamptonshire have been lost— the sheriff of Northamptonshire at the time of the election was Catesby's brother-in-law, Robert Whittlebury, whose influence on the election was more likely than not to have assisted his chances. Incidentally, the family's prestige certainly received something of a fillip when, at the end of this 1483 parliament, the king knighted Catesby's uncle, John Catesby of Whiston (Northants.) (a Justice of the Court of Common Pleas since November 1481).[2] Within two months of the dissolution Edward IV died (on 9 April 1483). Eleven weeks later, on 26 June, the Protector, Richard, Duke of Gloucester, usurped the throne of his nephew, Edward V. The *interim* had been full of momentous activity for Catesby.

So far in Catesby's career there is no evidence to connect him with the royal household or administration, although his legal services presumably had been used by the Duchy of Lancaster. His father, not long deceased, had been a Lancastrian in sympathy (even as late as 1470) and after the extinction of the Lancastrian dynasty of the direct line in 1471 had had no better fortune than to be linked with the unhappy Clarence ; he had, however, escaped damning or serious entanglement at all stages of his career. His son at Edward IV's death held no proper office by Crown appointment : well-connected by the marriages of his forbears and his own, he was a considerable landowner in the central Midlands, but it was as a lawyer, ready with his

[1] *Ancient Deeds*, A 8428 ; A 7654.
[2] W. C. Metcalfe, *A Book of Knights Banneret, etc.*, p. 6.

advice to local aristocratic and other families and as a professional land-agent to such like, that he was making his way. Thanks to a later Speaker's *History of Richard III* (Sir Thomas More's) we are enabled to see something of the quick steps that Catesby was enabled to make, taking him from a relative obscurity, where his political place is very likely to have been chiefly derived from his membership of Lord Hastings's personal council and of the committee of the Duke of Buckingham's feoffees, into the relative glare of his position as one of the foremost counsellors to Richard III.

Much of More's information was doubtless derived from the memory of Cardinal Morton, with whom he took service as a page some four or five years after the crowning mercy of Bosworth Field. But whatever may be thought of the outcome of this relationship, in terms of the author's partisan approach or of his tendency to dip into the " inward disposition of the mind " of his *dramatis personae*, the relation of his facts about the minor characters in his story is very credible.

The death of Edward IV " at once broke up the unity of the court " (Stubbs). The Duke of Gloucester got possession of the person of the young king, imprisoned in the north such of the queen's kinsmen (the Wydevilles) as could be seized (chief of them Earl Rivers), and got himself accepted as Protector by the royal Council, mainly through the agreement of Lord Hastings, the Chamberlain. Edward V's coronation had already been put off from 4 May to 22 June 1483. It was on this day that Richard of Gloucester's right to the crown was publicly referred to in a sermon at Paul's Cross, the " Broadcasting House of the day " (as Professor Knowles has happily termed it). Three days later he was " persuaded " to accept the crown, mainly on the grounds of his royal nephew's supposititious illegitimacy, and on 26 June he began his reign. To bring this about, Lord Hastings's removal had proved necessary.

Opposed to the Wydevilles, Hastings had supported Glouces-ter's Protectorship but could not be won over to the scheme which would realize the duke's greater ambition. It was Catesby, Hastings's own retainer, who was given the chance to secure his lord's support for Gloucester's usurpation of the throne, and who (if we may believe More's account) failed of a purpose, so that on 13 June Hastings was arrested at the Tower for treason against the Protector and immediately executed. Hastings, Lord Stanley, and other lords had deliberated measures for Edward V's coronation in the Tower where the king was, while at the Protector's house in the city another part of the Council plotted to make him king in his nephew's place. Hastings was easy on the point of the Council's division and told Stanley so and why: " for while one man is there, which is never thence, never can there be thing once minded that should sound amiss towards me but it should be in mine ears ere it were well out of their mouths ". And More went on: " this meant he by Catesby, which was of his near secret counsel, and whom he very familiarly used, and in his most weighty matters put no man in so special trust, reckoning himself to no man so lief, since he well wist there was no man to him so much beholden as was this Catesby, which was a man well learned in the laws of this land, and by the special favour of the Lord Chamberlain [Hastings himself] in good authority, and much rule bore in all the county of Leicester, where the Lord Chamberlain's power chiefly lay . . . surely thought he that there could be none harm towards him in that Council intended where Catesby was ". Richard of Gloucester used Catesby to try to win Hastings over to his plan. And then More's relation continues: " But Catesby, whether he essayed him or essayed him not, reported unto them that he found him so fast, and heard him speak so terrible words, that he durst no further break. And of truth, the Lord Chamberlain of very trust showed unto Catesby the mistrust that others began to have in the matter. And therefore he, fearing lest their motions might with the Lord Hastings diminish his credence, whereunto only all the matter leaned, procured the Protector hastily to rid him. And much the rather for that he trusted by his death to obtain much of the rule that the Lord Hastings bore in his country, the only desire whereof was the allective that induced him to be partner and one special contriver of all this horrible treason."[1]

If all this was so, Catesby's was a double treason. And

[1] *The English Works of Sir Thomas More*, ed. W. E. Campbell (1931), p. 53.

certainly he directly profited by his former patron's death even before Richard of Gloucester took the crown. Already, however, a month before Hastings's execution, Catesby was clearly in favour with the then newly-recognized Protector, on 14 May 1483 being granted for life the office of Chancellor of the peculiarly Yorkist Earldom of March with an annual fee of £40. This was doubtless part of a move on Gloucester's part to put into his friends' hands that administrative machine which Edward IV had devised for the government of the unruly March of Wales, a plan recently under the nominal control of his son who was now the nominal king but under the actual control of a group of men among whom Edward V's maternal uncle and governor, Earl Rivers, had been pre-eminent. In this office Catesby was to be under the orders of the Duke of Buckingham.[1] And on the day after this appointment—15 May—Catesby was for the first time made a J.P. in his own county of Northampton-shire.[2]

Catesby's advancement opened up the way to private as well as public preferment. For twelve years a Hertfordshire lawyer, John Forster esquire, a member of Edward IV's house-hold and a close connection of Lord Hastings, had been steward over all the manors and franchises of the great Benedictine abbey of St. Albans, and more recently Hastings had been associated with Forster in this office by a grant of it to them both for life (in survivorship). Hastings's " treason " involved Forster in immediate arrest and imprisonment in the Tower, where he remained in custody for nearly nine months ; within two days of his arrest he was compelled to make over his office of steward to Catesby ; and the appointment was ratified, presumably without any option in the matter, by Abbot Wallingford and his monastic chapter on 1 August following.[3]

Twelve days after Hastings's death, Edward V was deposed. On the same day, 25 June, Earl Rivers was put to death without proper trial at Pontefract, along with two other members of

[1] B.M., Harleian MS. 433, fols. 6, 12b.
[2] C.P.R., 1477-1485, p. 587.
[3] Registra Abbatum monasterii Sancti Albani, ed. H. T. Riley (Rolls Series, 1873), ii. 113, 200, 266.

Edward's former council, Sir Thomas Vaughan (his chamber-lain) and Sir Richard Hawte (a cousin of Queen Elizabeth). In charge of their execution was Sir Richard Radcliffe, a Yorkshire knight, who was hurrying south from the dales with forces to put at Gloucester's disposal, there soon to become, like Catesby, one of the usurper's right-hand men. Radcliffe and Catesby were already related : they shared Lord Scrope as father-in-law. Only two days before the butchery at Pontefract, in the Protector's own castle at Sheriff Hutton, with full knowledge of his impending fate, Rivers had drawn up his will : Catesby was among the executors recommended, Gloucester himself being written down as overseer, if he would act.[1] Hawte, whom Rivers obviously did not expect to die and appointed as another of his executors, before his own execution left the Bishops of Worcester and Durham bound (as his sureties) to Catesby in an obligation of 700 marks ; and in December 1483 they were granted Hawte's land-rents to enable them to meet the charge.[2]

On the fifth day of Richard III's reign (30 June 1483) Catesby was by royal patent confirmed for life in his new office of Chancellor of the Earldom of March and, by separate patents of the same date, grants for life were also made to him of the Upper Exchequer office of Chancellor of the Exchequer and of the Lower Exchequer office of Chamberlain of the Receipt which his late master, Hastings, had held at his death.[3] He was admitted to the Chamberlainship ten days later (on 10 July).[4]

Catesby's engrossing of local offices continued with an appetite further sharpened by his membership of Richard III's Council and by a proximity to the king's person that was even further assured by his new office in the royal Household of Esquire for the Body. He and Francis Viscount Lovell, Richard III's Grand Chamberlain, together got a grant of the constable-ship of Rockingham castle (Northants.), an office given by Edward IV in 1461 to Lord Hastings and his younger brother Ralph ;

[1] *Excerpta Historica* (London, 1831), p. 248. (The will was never proved.)
[2] B.M., Harleian MS. 433, fol. 129v.
[3] *C.P.R., 1477-1485*, pp. 360-1. There were, of course, two Chamberlains of the Receipt. Catesby enjoyed the right to appoint one of the ushers of the place.
[4] P.R.O., typescript *List of Officials*, p. 9.

and they also followed Catesby's former patron in the connected offices of master-forester of the forest of Rockingham, steward of the manors of Rockingham, Brigstock, and Cliffe, parker of Brigstock, and overseer of the herbage, pannage, and foreign wood of these manors for the term of Catesby's life.[1] Catesby was also, early in 1484, occupying the office of justice of the forest of Whittlewood, out of which he was instructed to make large grants to Lord Lovell.[2] He held on to this latter office, but the Rockingham offices were early in 1485 restored to Sir Ralph Hastings who had received a royal pardon since his brother's death and was now a Knight of the Body to Richard III. The act of restitution was apparently made with Catesby's agreement, for the exemplification of the patent embodying the original grant of 1461 was conceded on 20 February 1485 expressly at his request.[3] Meanwhile, on 16 August 1483, Lord Lovell, Chief Butler of England as well as Lord Chamberlain, had appointed Catesby as one of his two deputy-butlers in the ports of Bristol, Exeter, and Dartmouth.[4] And on 25 September following, Catesby, now for nearly three years one of the legal experts in the service of the duchy of Lancaster, was appointed for life as steward of the duchy lordships of Higham Ferrers and Daventry, Peverell's fee, and other duchy estates in Northamptonshire.[5] (Catesby's step-father-in-law, Lord Scrope, was Chamberlain of the Duchy and therefore nominal head of its council.) His links with Viscount Lovell quickly multiplied: it was at the King's instance that, on 5 October 1483, the abbot of the south Yorkshire Benedictine house of Selby gave Lovell and Catesby a grant for their lives (in survivorship) of the office of steward of the manor of Stanford (Northants.), near where Catesby's own estates were thick upon the ground.[6] Later in the year, on 17 December 1483, Lord Stanley, who more by good luck than good management had survived the usurpation-crisis of the summer and who, now that the sons of Edward IV and the

[1] B.M., Harleian MS. 433, fols. 104, 286^V.
[2] Ibid. fols. 153, 195^V.
[3] *C.P.R., 1477-1485*, p. 536.
[4] Ibid. p. 465.
[5] B.M., Harleian MS. 433, fol. 29 ; R. Somerville, op. cit. i. 586.
[6] *Ancient Deeds*, iv. A. 11064.

Duke of Buckingham had been done to death, was in an especially difficult position because his stepson, Henry of Richmond, was Richard III's only potentially serious challenger for the throne, saw fit to bestow for life on Catesby an annuity of five marks for his goodwill and counsel ; the sum was to be charged on the manor of Kimbolton (Huntingdonshire), an estate granted to Stanley out of Buckingham's forfeited property.[1]

Esquire of the Body to the King and a member of his Council, holding the two Exchequer offices of Chancellor and Chamberlain and the Chancellorship of the Earldom of March, Catesby was entirely committed to stand or fall with the new régime. That there was a persistently serious possibility of its collapse is evident from the fact that within four months of Richard's accession the chief supporter of his usurpation, the Duke of Buckingham, was plotting his overthrowal in concert with Lancastrian sympathizers and other hostile elements. Buckingham's rising failed, and he was executed on 2 November at Salisbury. The king, who had refused him an interview, then moved to deal with the other rebel sectors in the south-west, Catesby almost certainly in attendance. It was as an Esquire of the Body that, at Exeter on 13 November (the day after the king's arrival there), Catesby was appointed to serve on a royal commission to arrest and imprison rebels in Oxfordshire and Berkshire. He was back at Westminster with the king on 26 November when he was present at the ceremony in which Richard gave the great seal back into the keeping of the Chancellor, Bishop Russell of Lincoln ; the king had had it with him since 19 October.[2] Already, since the early part of August, a justice of the peace in Leicestershire, Warwickshire, Worcestershire, and Gloucestershire [3] (as well as in Northamptonshire), Catesby was also put on the commission of the peace in Oxfordshire and Berkshire on 5 December 1483 and in Hertfordshire too (here, perhaps because he was steward of the lands of the abbey of St. Albans).[4] A few days later (on 10 December) he was made a

---

[1] *Ancient Deeds*, A 10182.
[2] *C.P.R., 1477-1485*, p. 371 ; T. Rymer, *Foedera*, xii. 203.
[3] *C.P.R., 1477-1485*, pp. 561, 564, 576, 578.
[4] Ibid. pp. 554, 562, 569.

member of royal commissions of inquiry into treasons and acts of rebellion in his own territory of Northamptonshire, Warwickshire and Leicestershire, with authority to seize the estates of delinquents.[1]

Catesby's appointment to this commission followed by one day the issue of writs re-summoning Richard III's first parliament. Its earlier assembly, fixed for 6 November 1483, had been postponed on account of the Duke of Buckingham's revolt. Now parliament was called for after Christmas. Catesby was elected, but whether for Warwickshire or Northamptonshire is not known. Northamptonshire is the more likely alternative, if only because in the shrievalty of this county one brother-in-law of Catesby's, Robert Whittlebury, had just been succeeded by another, Roger Wake esquire. The parliament began, as summoned, at Westminster on 23 January 1484 and the Common's choice for their Speaker fell on Catesby, whom they presented for his royal master's formal acceptance on 26 January. This parliament was to have a short session of barely four weeks, ending on 22 February, but some of the business transacted was of great importance. One of the first matters to come up was the ratification by parliamentary authority of the proceedings by which Richard III had obtained the crown. A bill to this effect was introduced in the Lords and came down to the Commons for their approval. Then came the attainders of those who had committed treason in the late rebellion. Another act invalidated the letters patent made to Edward IV's queen, Elizabeth Wydeville. The king's need for popularity inhibited the expression of any royal desire for direct taxation, and no vote was volunteered, but the Commons under Catesby took an unprecedented step in granting to the king, in his first parliament and in the first year of his reign, tonnage and poundage and the wool subsidies for life. (Edward IV had been voted such a grant only in his second parliament and after four years of his reign had elapsed.)

Contrary to what was becoming the usual practice, Catesby does not seem to have received a money reward, charged on the Exchequer, in return for his prolocutorial services. But

[1] *C.P.R., 1477-1485*, p. 393.

he certainly did well out of grants of recently forfeited estates :
property worth some £273 odd a year, in Warwickshire,
Northamptonshire, Leicestershire, Surrey, and in London,
fallen into the king's hand by the attainders of the Duke of
Buckingham, the Marquess of Dorset, and Sir George Browne,
was bestowed on him and his heirs-male, at a mere rent of £20
odd.[1] What he picked up " on the side " from his Speaker's office,
there is no means of knowing. During the session, however,
another fresh if small item of income came his way in the grant
(on 3 February) of a yearly fee of 2 marks for life from the abbot
and convent of the little Cistertian house at Combe near Coventry,
with licence to enter its lands in Harbury (Warwicks.), a mile or
two away from his own manor of Ladbrooke, in case of non-payment.[2] And when the parliamentary session had still a week to
run, on 16 February, his wife's step-father and her mother
(Lord Scrope and his lady) granted him three Northamptonshire
manors for the duration of her lifetime.[3] A fortnight after the
session was done, a further piece of royal bounty came to Catesby
in the form of a grant of the wardship of the lands and the
advowson of the church of Braunston (near Ashby St. Legers)
during the minority of the son of a former usher of the Chamber
to Edward IV, John Acton esquire.[4] The seven years' occupation
of Stafford lands in nine counties which Catesby, along with
Chief Justice Hussey, William Beverley (Dean of the King's
Chapel), and Edmund Chadderton (Treasurer of the King's
Chamber and receiver and surveyor of Buckingham's forfeitures)
was granted on 23 May 1484, was, of course, for the payment
of the late Duke's debts.[5] But the grant for a term of years to
Catesby, referred to in a warrant dated at Pontefract a week
later (on 30 May) and ordering the tenants of a number of
forfeited Wiltshire manors to pay him their dues and give him
obedience, was one made by the king " for the contentacion
of certain dettes by us to hym appointed to be satisfied ".[6]

[1] B.M., Harleian MS. 433, fols. 45^V, 286^V.
[2] *Ancient Deeds*, iii. A 4306.
[3] Ibid. A 4786.
[4] *C.P.R., 1477-1485*, p. 419.
[5] Ibid. p. 498.
[6] B.M., Harleian MS. 433, fol. 174^V.

In this year of his Speakership, Catesby inevitably served on a number of casual royal commissions in addition to discharging the duties of his offices and more permanent commissions. The first of these occasional commissions passed the great seal on 1 March 1484 : a commission to the Duke of Norfolk and others, including Catesby and his kinsman, Justice Catesby, to deliver Newgate gaol of Sir John Guildford of Rolvenden, who had led the rising of the men of Kent in the previous autumn and had suffered attainder in the recent parliament.[1] Thwarted in the autumn of 1483, Henry Tudor was still in exile. But he was supported at the Court of Brittany where at Christmas he had actually been proclaimed King of England, and there was a constant anticipation of landings on the south coast of England in the spring of 1484. On 1 May 1484 Catesby himself was made a member of commissions of array in Berkshire, Oxfordshire and Northamptonshire.[2] A truce with Brittany, made early in the following month, profited Richard III little if at all, for Henry Tudor moved into an even more cordial atmosphere at the court of the young Charles VIII of France. On 26 June Catesby was included in a commission authorized to take (at Southampton) the muster of a retinue of 1,000 archers which Lord Powis was supposed to be taking to Brittany, presumably as a consideration for the truce and perhaps for the seizure of the English exiles ; but the force seems never to have gone overseas. On 20 February 1485 Catesby was one of those appointed to negotiate for an extension of the Anglo-Breton truce ; this they secured, the existing truce from 1 July 1484 to 24 April 1485 being continued to Michaelmas 1492.[3] In the meantime Richard III's efforts to gain credit by invading Scotland had come to nothing, so that, and in face of the threat of attack from across the Channel, by the end of the summer of 1484 he had to reconcile himself to an Anglo-Scottish peace, and on 11 September an embassy from James III arrived in Nottingham with full powers to negotiate. On 20 September fifteen of Richard's counsellors, headed by the Chancellor and including Catesby, were authorized

[1] *C.P.R., 1477-1485*, p. 465.
[2] Ibid. p. 400.
[3] Ibid. p. 547 ; Rymer, *Foedera*, xii. 261.

to treat with the Scottish emissaries for a peace ; only four of these English commissaries—the Chancellor, the Duke of Norfolk, Radcliffe and Catesby—made up the select group separately entrusted with the negotiation of a marriage between James III's heir and Anne, the daughter of the Duke of Suffolk and Richard III's niece.[1]   Both objects were guardedly conceded by the Scots whose faith in Richard's political stock was presumably not boundless.

The king's difficulties, given the best will in the world to pacify the country and appease the many malcontents that his usurpation and the manner of it had raised up, did not diminish as time went on.   Rather, they grew.   The structure of his government was narrowly based.   Catesby was one of the few who enjoyed his real confidence.   Sometime in the second half of this year, 1484, one William Collingbourne was lampooning the triumvirate of chief counsellors in the well-known couplet :

> The catte, the ratte, and Lovell our dogge
> Rulyth all Englande under a hogge.

Which meant, as Fabyan was to put it, that " Catesby, Ratcliffe, and the lorde Lovell ruled the lande under the Kynge, which bare the whyte bore for his conysaunce ".   This critic of the Ricardian régime, a Yorkist agent of the king's mother deprived of his job in favour of Viscount Lovell, was too dangerous to live (it was felt), and he was condemned for treason before the end of 1484.[2]   But there was no stopping the rot.   Fresh commissions of array were issued on 8 December 1484, Catesby serving on those for Northamptonshire, Buckinghamshire, Oxfordshire, Berkshire, and Hertfordshire.[3]   He continued to profit by his close contacts with the king.   On 15 February 1485, as one of the royal Esquires of the Body, he was granted in tail-male the hundred of Guilsborough (Northants.) with fines and franchises, at a rent of 4 marks a year to the king.   At his death—although for how long is not known—he also occupied

[1] *Rotuli Scotiae*, ii. 465-6.
[2] J. H. Ramsay, *Lancaster and York, 1399-1485*, ii. 528-9.
[3] *C.P.R., 1477-1485*, pp. 488-9, 491.

the offices of constable of the castle and parker at More End in south Northamptonshire.[1]

Catesby's authority as a member of the royal Council (or his reputation for great influence with the king) was particularly exemplified shortly after the death of Richard's Queen, Anne Neville, on 16 March 1485. Following the death of their son nearly a year before, Richard had recognized his nephew, the Earl of Lincoln, as his heir-presumptive, but it appears that even before his Queen died he was worried over the need for a direct heir and perhaps contemplated a divorce. A report was even going about that the king intended to marry his niece, Elizabeth, Edward IV's eldest daughter, whom there had already been plans to marry to Henry Tudor, and within three weeks of Queen Anne's death the king himself had to deny the truth of the slander to the chief citizens of London. Clearly, as a possible plan it was in shape. If we may believe the Croyland Chronicle, those in the royal Council most opposed to this choice of a second queen were Radcliffe and Catesby, *quorum sententiis vix unquam Rex ipse ausus fuit resistere.* This source relates that they told Richard to his face that even the northerners (among whom he enjoyed love and respect) would charge him with procuring the death of his queen, a daughter and heir of Warwick the Kingmaker, in order to enter an incestuous relationship, and that he must deny any such scheme. The chronicle further alleges that Catesby and his colleague (and kinsman) were afraid of the vengeance that Elizabeth of York would take on them, should she be made queen, for the death of those members of her mother's family (her uncle, Earl Rivers, and her step-brother, Sir Richard Grey) executed nearly two years before.[2]

In the uneasy months that lay between Easter 1485 and the final ruin of Catesby's lord and his own, but little is known of his activities. On 6 May his uncle, Sir John Catesby, Justice of Common Pleas, appointed him one of the executors of his will, which made provision for the disposal of nearly £800 between the testator's wife, two daughters, and eight sons, and for the

---

[1] *C.P.R., 1477-1485*, p. 497 ; ibid. *1485-1494*, p. 60.
[2] *Rerum Anglicarum Scriptorum Veterum* (Oxford, 1684), i. 572.

entailing of most of his real estate on his eldest son, Humphrey : the money to be taken to the chamber of the Guildhall in London, there to be kept *secundum consuetudinem civitatis*.[1] On 25 May, both William and Justice Catesby were appointed members of a royal commission of oyer and terminer regarding counterfeiting and other coinage offences in the midland shires and especially in Coventry.[2] On 10 June, Francis Viscount Lovell, the King's Chamberlain, arranged for the feoffees of five of his Northampton-shire manors, among whom were his colleagues in the King's Council, Radcliffe and Catesby, to convey these estates to his wife for life, should he have died before her, on the understanding that, if they did so, she should find two priests to celebrate mass for his soul for thirty years in the University of either Oxford or Cambridge.[3]

At this time Richard III was standing by at Nottingham to meet alarms as they arose. On 7 August Henry Tudor, Earl of Richmond, landed at Milford Haven in Pembrokeshire. Eight days or so later he was at Shrewsbury. Another week later still, and the forces of the two contestants for the throne faced one another at Bosworth Field. Viscount Lovell, Lord Zouche (Catesby's brother-in-law), Sir Richard Radcliffe (his wife's kinsman by marriage), and Catesby himself were with the royal army. On 22 August 1485 the issue was decided, Richard III being killed in the battle, and in the evening of the day of his victory Richmond entered Leicester in triumph. Radcliffe had been killed. Lovell escaped to sanctuary at Colchester. Zouche, too, got away. But Catesby had been taken prisoner, and he alone of men of importance in the royal army who were so captured was executed after the battle. An exception to Henry VII's otherwise remarkable clemency, he went to the block at Leicester, possibly a sacrifice to local resentments generated in this, his own, region. This was presumably three days after the battle.[4] The Croyland Chronicle merely notices his capture

[1] Somerset House, Register Milles, fol. 1. (The will was re-made on the day after Bosworth Field).

[2] *C.P.R., 1477-1485*, p. 544.

[3] *Ancient Deeds*, iii. A 4790.

[4] *The Three Books of Polydore Vergil's English History* (Camden Society, 1844, vol. 29), ed. Sir Henry Ellis, p. 224. Polydore says that Catesby was

and death without giving a date : *qui inter omnes consiliarios defuncti jam Regis preeminebat, cujus caput apud Leicestriam pro ultima remuneratione tam excellentis officii sui abscisum est.*[1] It was at any rate on 25 August that Catesby made his will.[2]

This last deed of Catesby is a remarkable document in many ways, its terms emotionally instinct with their author's knowledge of his coming end. His wife Margaret was to be sole executrix, his " dere and welbeloved wife to whom I have ever be trew of my body ". Requesting her forgiveness for any uncourteous dealings with her, he asked her not to re-marry but for all her days " to do for my soule ". Not until the last apparently had he given up the hope that some of his earlier connections might yet bring him through, especially his wife's uncle by marriage, Lord Stanley, and his family : " my lordis Stanley, Strange [Lord Stanley's son], and all that blod, help and pray for my soule, for ye have not for my body, as I trusted in you ". His previous relations with Lord Lovell had clearly been on an intimately friendly basis : " and [if] my lord Lovell come to grace than [then], that ye shew to hym that he pray for me." No reproach there. But even in his own family there were those who thought of him less, in his view, than they might have done : " and Uncle John [Justice Catesby], remembre my soule as ye have done my body, and better ". His reference to the new king, his wife's own kinsman, was perhaps abject, but he was thinking of his children's rights in lands that now would likely go to some of Henry's supporters, following his own attainder : " I doute not the king wilbe good and gracious lord to them [his children], for he is callid a full gracious prince, and I never offended hym by my good and free will, for, God I take to my juge, I have ever lovid hym ". There was some provision made for transactions in landed estate, " truly bought ", that had not been entirely completed, at Buckby and Redenhall (in Norfolk), and any wrongfully purchased property was to be

executed two days after Bosworth Field, that is, on 24 August. The inscription on the brass over Catesby and his wife's tomb at Ashby St Legers gives the date of Catesby's death as 20 August. But this antedates the battle of Bosworth by two days, and, in any case, Catesby's will is clearly dated 25 August.

[1] *Rerum Anglicarum*, op. cit. i. 575.

[2] Somerset House, Register Logge, fol. 15.

restored. Catesby made reference to some of his debts, including the one outstanding to his saddler. His father's debts, especially what he had given to the house of Austin canons at Catesby, were also to be discharged. There were a few individual bequests : his wife's aunt, Margaret St. John, Abbess of Shaftesbury, was to receive 40 marks, and " my lady of Buckingham " (Katherine, Duchess of Buckingham and sister of Edward IV's queen) was to have £100 to help her children and to see the debts of the late duke paid and his will executed, especially regarding a grant of land in mortmain to the college of secular priests at Pleshey (Essex). The Bishops of Winchester, Worcester, and London were asked to help Catesby's wife to execute the will " and [if] they will do sume what for me ".

The will was proved by Cardinal Bourchier (exercising his archiepiscopal prerogative) at Knole on 31 January 1486, Catesby's widow acting as executrix by proxy. Henry VII's first parliament had met at Westminster on 7 November 1485, and by this time its second and final session was a week old. The Speaker was Catesby's successor also in his office of Chancellor of the Exchequer, Thomas Lovell. The first session had seen the passage of an Act of Attainder against the most important of those who had taken up arms against the present king and levied war at Bosworth Field. They included William Catesby, who was condemned for treason to forfeit his estates whether held in fee-simple, fee-tail, or for term of life or lives.[1] There was some opposition among the Commons to the Act as a whole, but Henry VII was adamant : a correspondent of Sir Robert Plumpton wrote that " ther was many gentlemen agaynst it, but it wold not be, for yt was the Kings pleasure ".[2]

Catesby's rôle in 1483 (after Buckingham's rebellion) was now assumed by others at his own family's expense, and for the next nine years royal grants parcelled out what of his forfeitures had at first come into immediate royal control. The work of a

[1] *Rot. Parl.* vi. 276a.
[2] *Plumpton Correspondence* (Camden Society, 1839), ed. Thomas Stapleton, p. 48.

century-and-a-half of steady, quiet accumulation of estate, mainly by marriage alliances, was soon at least partially undone. By the time that Catesby's " anniversary " came round, Kirby Bellars, Tilbrook, Braunston, Redenhall, and Botesworth had all been the subject of royal grants in tail-male, and more grants and re-grants followed, members of the new Tudor royal household being the chief recipients.[1] It is possible that the 1,000 marks-worth of goods belonging to Catesby, which the Chancellor (Bishop Alcock of Worcester) was granted by Henry VII on 5 April 1486, was used by him to assist the administration of Catesby's estate as the latter's testament had suggested. It is possible, but doubtful. There was really little room for clem-ency, accepted the thesis of Henry of Richmond's dynastic rights. Catesby's widow was related by blood with the new royal family, but both her husband and brother had fought for Richard Crookback. Her husband's fellow-counsellor, Sir Richard Radcliffe, killed at Bosworth, was husband to her step-sister. And in spite of the marriage of Catesby's son and heir, George, with Elizabeth, daughter of the Sir Richard Empson of Easton Neston (Northants.) who with Henry VII's accession resumed his former office of Attorney-General for the Duchy of Lancaster and became one of the " great projectors " of this reign,[2] it was not until after the passage of some ten years that Catesby's attainder was reversed, in the parliament of Octo-ber 1495. Even then, the petition for the heir's rehabilitation, preferred by the Commons as one of their own bills, itself contained a proviso that restitution was not to apply to such grants of Catesby property as were then in force, and that the King's Chamber should be paid £100 a year for seven years by Bishop Alcock (now of Ely), Sir Richard Empson, and John Spenser (a creditor of William Catesby), who were to occupy those Catesby estates which were still in royal custody, merely as tenants, presumably on the heir's behalf.[3] William Catesby's widow, Margaret, did not live to see this " act of adnullacion

---

[1] C.P.R., *1485-1494*, pp. 78, 96, 100, 121, 129, 209, 231, 275, 340, 404 ; ibid. *1494-1509*, p. 11.

[2] Dugdale, *Warwickshire*, op. cit. p. 399a.

[3] *Rot. Parl.* vi. 490b ; C.P.R., *1494-1509*, p. 40.

and restitucion " in her son's favour: she had died on 8 October 1494.[1]

[1] Baker, op. cit. i. 244-5. William Catesby's family continued to hold the estates which had been restored and materially added to them during the sixteenth century. William's grandson, Sir Richard, was twice sheriff of Warwickshire and Leicestershire (in 1540-1 and 1545-6) and twice of Northamptonshire (in 1542-3 and 1549-50), and he was knight of the shire for Warwickshire in Edwards VI's last parliament in 1553, before the dissolution of which he died. But later came setbacks culminating in disaster. Sir Richard's grandson and heir, William, was a staunch adherent of the old faith and suffered as a recusant, and *his* son Robert was so fanatical a Roman Catholic as to be involved in treason in Essex's Rebellion and again in the Gunpowder Plot, immediately after the discovery of which he was rooted out and killed. And, of course, he was attainted and incurred forfeiture. Both his two sons died without issue.

INDEX TO VOLUME II

[Contractions: archbp. for archbishop; bp. for bishop; kg. for king; qn. for queen; † for died]

354

356